Corydon Charles Merriman

Lectures, essays and published articles on scientific and literary subjects and on foreign travel

Corydon Charles Merriman

Lectures, essays and published articles on scientific and literary subjects and on foreign travel

ISBN/EAN: 9783337204488

Printed in Europe, USA, Canada, Australia, Japan

Cover: Foto ©Andreas Hilbeck / pixelio.de

More available books at **www.hansebooks.com**

AND

PUBLISHED ARTICLES

ON

SCIENTIFIC AND LITERARY SUBJECTS

AND ON

FOREIGN TRAVEL,

BY

C. C. MERRIMAN,

ROCHESTER, N. Y.

1885.

ROCHESTER, N. Y.:
JUDSON J. WITHALL, BOOK AND JOB PRINTER, UNION STREET.

THIS COLLECTION OF MY VARIOUS WRITINGS,

PROBABLY THE ONLY BOOK I SHALL EVER PUBLISH,

I TAKE GREAT PLEASURE IN DEDICATING TO ONE WHOSE

CONSTANT FAITH IN MY SUCCESS,

AND GRATIFICATION IN THE RESULTS, HAVE BEEN THE

CHIEF INCENTIVES OF MY LITERARY EFFORTS,

TO MY DEAR AND LOVING WIFE.

CONTENTS.

BEYOND THE LIMITS OF VISION;

Or, The World Below the Microscope. — The infinitude of the stellar universe. — Contrast of natural with magnified vision. — The limit of microscopic vision. — The evidences of germ life below the reach of the microscope. — How scientists have got at the size and the numbering of the atoms. — The thousands of millions of molecules that are still in the smallest object that has ever been seen under the microscope. — The recent theory of the scientists that each atom is constituted like smoke rings, that is of the vortical whirl of innumerable particles of ether immeasurably smaller than the atom. — The world of small things as well as of great merges into the infinite. - - - - - 5

THE POLAR GLACIERS. Part I.

There must be elevations above the ocean in the southern hemisphere sufficient to balance the great excess of land in the northern. — Other evidences of an enormous ice-cap at the South Pole. — Astronomical causes for the alternate glaciation of the two polar regions. — The period is 21,000 years. — The northern hemisphere is now in the midst of its great secular summer. — In 10,500 years it will be as much covered with water and ice as the southern is now. — Former periods have been of far greater severity than the present. — Evidences of the great ice-cap all over the State of New York. — About 70,000 years ago it retreated for the last time, and man appeared on the stage of life. - - - 21

THE POLAR GLACIERS. Part II.

The causes of the prevailing winds, especially the trade winds. — Their effect on ocean currents. — These always flow into, and warm most, the hemisphere that is in its secular summer. — Particular description and geographical effects of the four seasons of one of the most glacial of the great secular years. — Evidences in the earth's strata of previous glacial periods; and the help which they give towards estimating the age of geological epochs and of the world. - - - - - - - 31

UNIVERSITIES VS. SCIENCE.

An attempt to represent the arguments and convictions of the good Methodist curators of the Vanderbilt University, of Nashville, Tenn., when they removed Prof. Alex. Winchell from his Lectureship in Geology on account of scientific heterodox opinions. — Showing the unfavorable influence on religious tenets, and the logical materialistic conclusions, that must follow from modern scientific teachings, and particularly from the Darwinian theories. - - - - - - - 43

WHAT THE CHEMISTRY OF THE ROCKS TEACHES.

The nebular theory of the origin of the earth proved from the chemical condition and composition of the rocks. — The order of position of the gases and vapors of minerals in the atmosphere, according to their specific gravities. — The oxidation of silicon and formation of the granites would be the first result of consolidation. — Then followed the great storms and down-pourings of the metals in their order, the most infusible first. — Then the formation of water, bringing down sulphuric and carbonic acid in solution. — The succession of the strata in the earth corresponds to what would be the order of combination and condensation in the atmospheric strata. — The constitution of the other planets as judged of by chemical laws. - - - - - - - - 53

THE GENESIS OF WORLDS.

Outlines of the "Nebular hypothesis." — Action and transmutation of the forces engaged in the consolidation of worlds from the gaseous state. — First effect of the condensation of gases is heat. — To a certain extent this heat is transformed into the motion of the masses, that is planetary revolutions; the remainder is radiated

CONTENTS. vii

PAGE

into space. — All worlds must eventually become cold and solid. — Then, from the arrest of motion by friction in space, they must fall into each other. — Motion stopped is again transformed into heat, and all matter is again expanded into gases with its original endowment of heat. — Thus the never ending succession of world formation and world destruction. - - - - - 69

ON THE STRUCTURE OF ATOMS.

Atoms in uniting to form compounds divide themselves into various fractions, at least up to twelfths. — Instances and a table given. — The composite structure of atoms inferred from each separate kind producing its own characteristic bands in the spectrum. — Also inferred from the remarkable property of "specific heat," and from other peculiar chemical principles. — A mixture of gases of all weights is found in each of the planets. — The existence of hydrogen, the lightest of all the elements, in the inner planets and notably in the sun, can only be accounted for on the supposition that it has been newly created in those bodies. - - - - - 79

EVOLUTION THE RESULT OF CHEMICAL FORCES;

OR, "EVIDENCES OF DESIGN IN EVOLUTION." — The quantities and affinities of the elements that compose the earth might just as well, on the doctrine of chances, have varied in any number of ways that would have failed to produce a habitable world. — The exceptional properties of water alone prove adaptation in the formation of the elements. — The power of the atoms of carbon to unite in hundreds and to hold together hundreds of other atoms in one molecule of protoplasm is both the condition and cause of organic life. — Wherein the Darwinian theory fails to account for the facts of organic development. — It acts and can act only within very narrow limits. — The great advances from one order to another were always sudden, with no intermediate links. — Examples from the quadruped orders. — Marsupials particularly described. — The lowest races of mankind do not approach the ape species in brain size or in any physical peculiarity. — How and to what extent the increasing complexity of carbon compounds explains the progress of evolution. - - - - 91

THE MICROSCOPIST IN BERMUDA.

The situation, description and history of these small islands. — The formation is "Æolian," and dependent on coral reefs. — It is entirely organic. — The life history of the Foraminifera, the most numerous of the shells in the sand. — Life history of the Echinus, or sea-urchin. — Wonders and beauty of its structure as revealed by the microscope. — The bird's-head Polyzoa. — The Hydrozoa, and their intermediate generation, the jelly-fishes. — The great interest there is in the Invertebrate kingdom. - - - - - - - - - 115

MICROSCOPICAL COLLECTIONS IN FLORIDA.

Florida peculiarly adapted to the development of air-plants and of organs for the absorption of aerial nutrition. — Glandular cells, like inlaid pearls, on leaves of Onosmodium. — Stellate scales on leaves of Croton plants. — Beauty and object of the scales on Florida moss. — Resin dots on leaves of Calicarpa and sweet myrtle. — Insectivorous plants. — Drosera, or sun-dew. — A new, floating, variety. — Utricularia, or bladder-wort. — Pitcher plant, the most wonderful instance of adaptation to special purposes. — Its development cannot be explained under the Darwinian theory. - - - - - 131

ON THE PREPARATION OF OBJECTS FOR THE MICROSCOPE.

Spiral tissue in leaf stem of castor-oil plant. — Methods of staining vegetable tissues of all kinds. — Methods of mounting in cells, both with fluids and as dry mounts. — The author's views on the various cements used in mounting. - - - - - - - - - 145

PREPARATION AND MOUNTING OF DOUBLE STAININGS.

A paper read before the American Microscopical Association, giving a full account of the author's methods of multiple staining, and of mounting the specimens both in Canada balsam and in aqueous fluids. - - - - 155

CONTENTS. ix

SOME NEW FORMS OF MOUNTING.

A paper read before the American Microscopical Association. — Method of making the transparent shellac cells. — Curtain ring cells. — A cement cell that will withstand the action of Canada balsam or turpentine. — Method of mounting certain opaque objects in Canada balsam, for the Lieberkühn. - - - - - - - 159

THE MICROSCOPE AND ITS PREPARATIONS.

Objects that are beautiful to natural vision are not so under the microscope. — The two worlds seem to be entirely distinct. — The fineness of the markings on Podura scales and on diatoms. — Woodward's photograph of lines so fine that 400 would be covered by the ordinary ruling mark on writing paper. — Remarkable structure and contrivances of the fly-catching Pitcher plant. — Also of the bladders of the Utricularia, catching insects in water. — The beautiful spores of a Mexican fern. — Peculiar method of reproduction among ferns. - - 163

DIVERSITY OF RACES.

Written for a Yale College Senior Prize; but denied the prize, by the acknowledgment of the Faculty, solely on account of its unorthodox sentiments. — It is an attempt to show the impossibility of the descent of all the races of mankind from one human pair, and within the Biblical chronology. — Of interest chiefly as an example of the earliest writings on this subject, (the first the writer has any knowledge of), and as showing that 36 years ago subjects were tabooed that are now preached about in every pulpit. - - - - - - - 171

CHILDHOOD OF SCIENCE.

Intellectual gloom of the dark ages. — The rise of the arts, discoveries, and literature, three to four hundred years ago. — Errors of the middle ages, astrology and alchemy. — Roger Bacon, Basil Valentine, and Paracelsus. — The inductive method of reasoning. — Francis Bacon. — The discoveries of Copernicus. — Sketches of the life and work of Kepler. — Galileo the first true scientist. — His contests with the church, the schools, and every form of error. - - - - - - - 187

THE HUNS OF ATTILA.

Their origin on the steppes of Tartary in central Asia. — These Highlands the prolific source from which have sprung all the dominant races. — The migration of the Huns into Europe. — Their progress set in westward motion all the intervening tribes of barbarians, causing all the successive nomadic irruptions into the Roman territory. — Sketches of these irruptions. — The Huns under Attila were the last. — Their meeting with the Roman armies in the heart of France. — The bloody and eventful battle of Chalons. — One of the great decisive battles of the world. — Final triumph of Christianity over barbarism. - - - - - 207

ANCIENT PAINTING AS AMONG THE LOST ARTS. Preface.

American travelers as a class do not take interest in the ruins and relics of ancient structures and art that abound in Italy. — There is however great value and absorbing interest in old things that are "good for nothing," as the following discourse will attempt to show. - - 225

ANCIENT PAINTING AS AMONG THE LOST ARTS. Lecture.

The rare and uncertain visits of the genius of culture to mankind. — What we know of Grecian painting from the classical writers. — Its processes are Lost Arts. — Sketches and noted productions of some of the Greek painters. — Story in regard to Benj. West as illustrating the cause of the great superiority of the Grecian artists. — Farnese Bull and Laocoon described. — The abounding wealth of ancient sculpture. — Art remains found in Pompeii. — The causes that brought about the extinction of all art knowledge and the destruction of all art remains. — The decay of Roman culture and empire, along with the gradual demolition of the great city of Rome. - - - - - - - - - - 227

CONTENTS. xi

SKETCHES OF THE "OLD MASTERS" IN PAINTING.

PAGE

Giving a brief account of what is most noteworthy in the lives and character, the work and master-pieces of the early Italian painters; forming a kind of introduction to the following more extended description of their works. - - - - - - - - - - 245

STORIES OF NOTED PAINTINGS.

Descriptions and narratives explaining the most noted works of the "Old Masters," as well as of many of the celebrated paintings of modern artists. — The author has endeavored to make them models of concise story-telling, such as in his judgment should characterize descriptive catalogues. - - - - - - - 257

A TRIP TO MEXICO.

A visit to "old Mexico" in the winter of 1875-6. — Vera Cruz railway. — 9,000 feet up the mountains. — The extensive fields of the "century plant" that produce the notorious Mexican drink "pulque" (*pool-kay*). — The valley of the city of Mexico an undrained basin, with the salt lake Tezcuco in the lowest part. — The City of Mexico. — Its conquest by Cortez. — The Diaz-Lerdo revolution, in progress at the time of this visit. — Poverty of Mexico and its causes. — The fallacy and folly of the modern disbelievers in the Spanish accounts of Aztec civilization and the "Conquest of Mexico." — The beauty and variety of Mexican scenery. - - 283

SIGHT-SEEING IN NEW ZEALAND.

Its native animals and plants represent a geological age nearly back to the Carboniferous. — The Maoris (native races) are a quite recent imigration. — How New Zealand got its inappropriate name. — Description of Auckland. — Visit to the hot springs and lakes. — Accounts of Maoris. — New Zealand "bush." — The remarkable Terraces. — Lake Rotomahana. — Hot water bathing. — The sheep-killing parrot. — Ravages of im-

xii   CONTENTS.

                                                                                                         PAGE

ported weeds. — The rabbit plague. — The Albatross. — Its soaring with motionless wings explained. — The Moa skeletons. — Maori "carved houses."— The sounds or fiords on the southern coast. — The southern constellations. — Unfavorable conclusions in regard to New Zealand, agriculturally and financially.   -   -   - 297

THE SCIENCE OF RELIGION.

A plea for a broader liberalism in Christian theology.— The critical comparison and contrast of the Christian with the older religions of the world show it to be derivative and not original. — Consequently it has no right to exclusiveness. — The Greek philosophy of Socrates and Plato taught the Trinity of Gods, the immortality of the soul and the doctrine of future rewards and punishments. — The Vedas of the Brahmans were written a thousand years before the Flood. — Yet they tell the stories of Adima and Heva, the first parents, and of Chrishna the Redeemer of mankind, almost word for word as they are related in the Bible. — There were religious sects in Egypt shortly before the Christian era so closely resembling the Church of the New Testament that they could not be distinguished from it. — From all this it is argued that in all ages and nations the man who has lived an upright and God-fearing life according to the light that has been given him, is entitled to all the rewards that are promised to the faithful. - - - - - - - - - - 321

SKETCHES OF SEA-LIFE.

The story of the author's first voyage "before the mast," in the year 1847. — It was in the new packet ship, St. Denis, from New York to Havre in France.— The trip forth and back occupied about four months.— It occurred in the writer's sophomore year at Yale College; but all examinations were afterwards passed and he graduated with his Class in '49. - - - - - - 335

ILLUSTRATIONS.

DESCRIPTION OF THE GELATINE PROCESS OF PICTURE MAKING.

As the art of reproducing photographs by the gelatine process is quite recent and not yet very generally understood, a few words in explanation of it may not be out of place as an introduction to the description of the plates in this book, which have been made wholly by this process.

All photo-mechanical work depends on two peculiar properties of gelatine. 1st: Warm water readily dissolves gelatine, while cold water only soaks or is absorbed by it without dissolving any portion of it. 2nd: A mixture of a solution of gelatine with bichromate of potassa remains a simple mechanical mixture as long as it is kept in the dark; but when exposed to white light it becomes a chemical compound, hard and impervious to water.

In the first place then, a thin film of this mixture of gelatine and bichromate is spread over a square of plate glass in the photographer's dark room. A photographic negative is then placed in close contact with this film, and it is exposed to sun light. The film becomes hard and insoluble under the light parts of the negative, partially so under the half tints, and remains soft and unchanged under the dark shades. After sufficient exposure the plate is taken to the dark room and all the uncombined bichromate washed out by cold water. It is then in condition to print from, and may be taken directly to the printing press.

For each copy that is taken from it the plate is sponged with cold water and lightly wiped, leaving the hard parts dry, the semi-hardened parts more or less damp, and the soft parts quite wet. In this condition the ordinary "greasy" ink of the lithographers will adhere only to the dry parts of it and be repelled from the wet. Rollers coated with this thick ink, first of the quality called "coarse," then of "fine," are successively passed over the plate until the picture is brought out clearly in all its dark and light shadings. A specially prepared paper is now applied to the inked plate, passed through the press, and then carefully raised from the film, a perfectly printed picture. It is afterwards polished, if desired, as in the samples in this book, with talc and cotton batting.

Any color may be used in the printing. From three to five hundred copies can be taken from one film, and after that another film can be easily prepared from the same negative. An original and perfect negative will of course make the finest picture. The excellent reproductions here presented were made however, in all but two instances, the portrait and the diatom plate, from copies of the originals, and the most of them from negatives taken of the paper photographs brought from New Zealand. They are the productions of The Lewis Company, 15 Cornhill, Boston.

Plate I.— Frontispiece.
PORTRAIT OF THE AUTHOR.

Plate II.— Opposite page 8.
NEW ZEALAND "BUSH" SCENERY.

It is supposed that the New Zealand forest, or "bush" as it is there called, with its rank undergrowth of ferns and reed grasses, and its overhanging masses of parasitic growths, orchids, creepers, and climbing ferns, represents both in species and in luxuriance the vegetation which formed the coal beds.   Pages 298 and 303

Plate III.— Opposite page 32.
MITRE PEAK, MILFORD SOUND, NEW ZEALAND.

This sound is one of many remarkable inlets from the sea on the south-west coast of New Zealand, like the fiords of Norway. This one is nine miles in length and is walled in by snow-capped peaks which rise almost straight up from the water to heights of from five to seven thousand feet. On the left of the view is Mitre Peak, 5,600 feet high, so called from its resemblance in certain views to the double-peaked Cardinal's mitre.

On the right is Pembroke Peak, 7,000 feet high. Between the two is the narrow entrance to the sound, in one place only 500 yards wide. The view is taken from Fresh Water Basin on the inlet river at the head of the sound. Page 317

PLATE IV.—OPPOSITE PAGE 56.

TREE FERNS IN FERN TREE GULLY, HOBART TOWN.

Although this view of the indescribable luxuriance and beauty of the fern tree growths is in Tasmania (Van Dieman's Land), still it faithfully represents the borders and openings of almost every forest, or "bush," in New Zealand. These tree ferns, some of which are 40 feet high with a spread at the top of 20 feet, will not flourish except under the protection and partial shade of the taller forest trees. Page 303

PLATE V.—OPPOSITE PAGE 80.

MOURNING THE DEAD IN NEW ZEALAND.

The peculiarly heathen practice of wailing for the dead still persists among all the Maori (*Moury*) tribes of New Zealand. The dead body is laid out in the porch of the house, and the mourners come and bewail in a sad and moaning tone by the hour. I have heard a belated mourner going through his lugubrious wail in the door yard of a deceased two weeks after the burial. Page 305

PLATE VI.—OPPOSITE PAGE 96.

A SETTLEMENT OF CRAY-FISHERS NEAR HOT SPRINGS IN NEW ZEALAND.

This is the place where all excursionists to the celebrated Terraces of New Zealand are expected to stop and buy a bag of cray-fish, to be cooked for lunch in the hot springs on Lake Rotomahana. Page 310

PLATE VII.—OPPOSITE PAGE 116.

ARRANGED GROUP OF DIATOMS AND SPICULES.
(MAGNIFIED SIXTY-FIVE DIAMETERS.)

The original specimen is all comprised in one-thirteenth of an inch, about the size of the head of a pin, and contains 202 shells and spicules. The center and outside diatoms are *Coscinodiscus radiatus.* The first ring cluster is wheel plates found in the skin of the worm *Chirodota.* The second and fourth circles are the diatoms *Actinocyclus Ralfsii.* The third circle is the diatom *Arachnoidiscus Ehrenbergii.* The outside cluster is composed of the anchors and perforated anchor plates found in the skin of the worm *Synapta*, as also of the long diatoms *Pinnularia virides.* The negatives for this and the following prints of micro-photographs were taken for me by W. H. Walmsley, of 1016 Chestnut Street, Philadelphia. Pages 164 and 125

PLATE VIII.— OPPOSITE PAGE 128.

BIRDS HEAD POLYZOA — AVICULARIA.
(MAGNIFIED ABOUT THIRTY DIAMETERS.)

One of these illustrations is directly from nature, and the other is from a drawing of a stem of the zoophyte, showing the animals with tentacles extended, and the muscles which actuate the birds head attachments. These miniature heads, of no use or purpose in the colonial economy, so far as known, keep up a continual biting and snapping as long as there is life in the animal which they seem to guard. Page 126

PLATE IX.— OPPOSITE PAGE 136.

SPIRAL TISSUE IN LEAF STEM OF CASTOR OIL PLANT.

1st. Transverse section, magnified 12 diameters, showing the ends of the spirals in what are called the fibro-vascular bundles.

2nd. Longitudinal section, magnified 70 diameters, showing the spiral vessels as they lie in one of those bundles.

These little tubes, made, in the case of this plant, of closely coiled fibers, are the passage-ways through which the sap circulates to the extremity of the leaves and back again. In the leaf-stem they are laid away in small clusters between the wood cells and the pith cells. There are over 400 of these spiral vessels in the stem from which this specimen is taken. They are not larger than human hairs, and yet they are wound with a thread inconceivably smaller, and are as perfect as coils of wire around a form. Pages 135 and 145

ILLUSTRATIONS.

Plate X.—Opposite page 152.
THE ECHINUS AND ITS LARVA THE PLUTEUS.

1st. The Pluteus or nurse form of the Echinoids, magnified 20 diameters.

2nd. The Echinus, the spiny sea-egg or sea-urchin, reduced to $\frac{1}{2}$ natural size.

The Echinus which is here represented is found in holes that it has drilled near low tide in the surf-beaten rocks of the Bermuda coast. From its eggs is produced the Pluteus, an intermediate generation, almost microscopic in size, but an active swimmer by means of its numerous cilia-hairs. It is an entirely different animal from its parent, not having one point of structure in common with it. When this creature attains its minute growth a tiny saucer-shaped disk appears on one side of the stomach of the Pluteus, gradually growing at the edges into a globular form until it has enclosed the vital parts of its old nurse. It then forms a new mouth at the point last enclosed, discards all the external parts of the Pluteus, and sinks to the bottom of the ocean to begin the new life of the spiny Echinus. Page 124

Plate XI.—Opposite page 168.
TRANSVERSE SECTIONS OF SPINES OF ECHINUS.

Magnified about 30 diameters, making the largest section one-twelfth of an inch across. There is an infinite variety in the beauty, the structure, and the exquisite coloring of these thin sections. Pages 122–3

By request is here published the author's method of cutting and grinding these sections in quantity:—Imbed the spines in glue, making a stick of them. When nearly solid with glue and dry, cut into thin cross sections with a dentist's saw. Dissolve out the glue in hot water. Dry the sections and imbed them in Canada balsam on two pieces of glass. When hardened by heat, grind one against the other with pumice and water until level and smooth. Place another piece of glass in a saucer and cover with turpentine. Put one of the ground pieces on this with sections down. After one day the sections will all lie turned over on the lower glass. Carefully raise and imbed them as they lie in Canada balsam.

Treat the other ground glass in the same way, and when hard grind the two new ones together with pumice and water until the sections are as thin as possible. Then carefully dissolve them off with turpentine, and select and mount in balsam. Some will show best as opaque objects. Page 161

PLATE XII.—OPPOSITE PAGE 184.

PORTRAITS OF SOUTH SEA ISLANDERS.

There is nothing that pleases a native more than to make a display of his accoutrements and insignia of rank. The tattoo marks on the face, arms and breast of the New Zealanders indicate the tribe and rank of each person. A high chief is pretty well covered with them all over the upper part of his body. A married woman is tatooed on her chin as well as on breast and arms. These scarifying marks are put on in India ink, under some pointed instrument (formerly flint or bone), beaten into the skin by a light mallet. It is said that no person can bear the torture of it more than half an hour in a day. Some of these old cannibals must have had quite a foretaste of torment in this life. Page 298

PLATE XIII.—OPPOSITE PAGE 208.

WHITE TERRACES AND GEYSER, NEW ZEALAND.

In the central part of the North Island of New Zealand, about 100 miles inland by the road, is the remarkable geyser district which contains the hot lake Rotomahana, on opposite borders of which are the far-famed White and Pink Terraces. In each case, at a height of nearly 100 feet above the lake, there is an enormous fountain of boiling and spouting waters surcharged with silica. Inasmuch as only hot water will hold any of this mineral in solution, it must necessarily be deposited as the water cools. This is the cause of the formation of these splendid and spacious steps and basins of silicious sinter. A slight impregnation of iron in the waters of the Pink Terraces gives to them their beautifully variegated pinkish tinge. Pages 308 to 312

PLATE XIV.— OPPOSITE PAGE 224.

WHITE TERRACES WITH FOUNTAIN NOT FLOWING.

The natives say that when the wind blows strong in a certain direction, the waters recede from the fountain of the White Terraces, and they can look down into it as into a crater. This statement would be almost incredible without the evidence of this photograph. Page 309

PLATE XV.— OPPOSITE PAGE 240.

VIEW AT THE HEAD OF LAKE WAKATIPU, NEW ZEALAND.

Lake Wakatipu (*Wah-kah-teep*), 60 miles long, 1,000 feet above the sea, and said to be 1,400 feet deep, lying in the heart of the Southern Alps at the farthest end of New Zealand, is the wildest and grandest scenery lake perhaps in the world. From the end where the Invercargill railway reaches it, to the head where a single Irish family on one side and a single Scotch family on the other make the rival "towns" of Kinlock and Glenarchy, increasingly high and rugged snow covered peaks and ridges rise abruptly from the shores to heights of six to nine thousand feet. The terraces which are seen in this view, as sharply cut as if made by human hands, and which are over 400 feet high, are found at the same height and with the same shelves on all sides of the lake, showing the different elevations at which the water has stood in former times. Page 316

PLATE XVI.— OPPOSITE PAGE 256.

EUCALYPTUS FOREST OF AUSTRALIA, WITH TREE FERNS.

In these forests which cover so large a part of Australia, the enormous white trunks of the different."gum trees" (I have measured them over 17 feet in diameter) tower up 200 or 300 feet without branches, while underneath is an impenetrable growth of ferns and bushes. In the edges and more open spaces flourish the tall tree ferns, 30 to 40 feet high. Page 297

ILLUSTRATIONS.

PLATE XVII.— OPPOSITE PAGE 280.
HOUSE AND GROUP OF MAORIS, NATIVE NEW ZEALANDERS.

This is the scarcely varying model of all the Maori houses, a porch in front and one room back, all under a grass thatched roof, and with more or less carvings on the posts and cornices, according to the skill or rank of the occupant. The Maoris have found it easier to dress themselves in the cheap or cast-off clothes of the English than to make them from their native "flax plant" as they formerly did. Page 315

PLATE XVIII.— OPPOSITE PAGE 296.
PINK TERRACES AND BOILING FOUNTAIN, NEW ZEALAND.

Described under White Terraces—PLATE XIII. Page 311

PLATE XIX.— OPPOSITE PAGE 312.
HOT BATH BASINS IN PINK TERRACES, NEW ZEALAND.

The hot water in these basins is about breast deep, and one climbs up from one to another as he requires or can endure the hotter waters. Page 311

PLATE XX.— OPPOSITE PAGE 336.
SAILOR BOY "CHARLIE."

A copy from an old Daguerreotype, and the earliest likeness taken of the one whose latest portrait heads this volume. Page 338

BEYOND THE LIMITS OF VISION;

Or, The World Below the Microscope.*

Midway between two infinities lies the world that is revealed to our senses. A wide and wonderful world it seems to us, for within its range are all the forms and phenomena which are at the foundation of our knowledge, the arts and the sciences. Yet marvelous and almost infinite as are the scenes and objects unfolded to our sight, they form but an infinitesimal part of the boundless range of nature both beneath and beyond the limits of our perceptions.

The sharpest eyes, under the most favorable circumstances for observation, can see only about five thousand stars in all the sweep of the heavens. With the highest powers of the telescope it is estimated that twenty million stars are visible. Yet all these are only the brightest or the nearest of the suns which compose the great cluster of the Galaxy or Milky-way, to which system our sun belongs. In many parts of the Milky-way even the giant reflector of Lord Rosse discloses, beyond the stars which it resolves, only the same milky whiteness which we see every clear night in that marvelous girdle of the heavens. We have not yet seen even all the outlying lights of our own City of the skies. Yet this immense aggregation of worlds composing the Milky-way, numbering, with the dark planets which are doubtless circling about their suns, and the many unlighted orbs in their midst, probably thousands of millions, is only one of thousands of such star clusters that are within the range of

* A lecture written in 1884, and delivered before the Rochester Academy of Sciences and on various other occasions.

telescopic observation. Over five thousand nebulae have already been counted in the heavens; and every increase in telescopic power not only resolves more of the previously known nebulae into faint clusters of stars, but reveals others still deeper set in the infinitudes of space. Of the nebulous bodies which the Spectroscope has been able to examine, about two-thirds are proved to be clusters of stars, and the other one-third to be gaseous matter, nitrogen, hydrogen, and an unknown gas, imperfect or new forming worlds. Over three thousand star systems then, probably in every way similar to the one which lights our night skies, have already been located in the outlying regions of space. And still beyond are doubtless other systems teeming with their myriads of self-lighted suns. There is no boundary to the heavens. The mind of man cannot conceive of a limit to space. For if there is one, what limits it — what is there beyond?

The nearest fixed star to us is still twenty million million miles away. Light, which travels at the perfectly inconceivable velocity of 182,000 miles in a second of time, takes three and a half years to come to us from this star, Alpha Centauri. Sirius, the brightest star in the heavens, is separated from us by the light distance of seventeen years—or 100 million million miles. Sir. Wm. Herschel estimated that some of the light of the Milky-way is already ten thousand years old when it reaches us. Some of the infinite multitude of stars which appear as the hazy cloud-belt of the Galaxy, emitted the rays which strike our eyes to-night over ten thousand years ago.

But this is all within our own circumscribed world of worlds. There are telescopic star clusters so far banished in space that they are perhaps to-day receiving the last glimmer of the molten fire beds that once covered our earth. Were the entire stellar universe except our sun and planets swept out of existence at this hour, we would not know it — we would not even suspect it — for ages to come.

Such is the infinity of magnitudes. But I will have occasion to-night to speak to you of more startling infinitudes below our sight than there are above it. The world of the infinitely small is of vaster range and set off with far more inconceivable numbers than the universe of the heavens. We will follow it gradually down until it vanishes from all possibility of conception.

The limit of natural vision I suppose is not far from the one-hundredth of an inch. The volvox, which can be seen by the naked eye as a little green speck in pond water, is about the one-fiftieth of an inch in diameter. The largest diatoms, which are seen as the merest particles of fine dust, seldom reach the size of one-hundredth of an inch. The finest point of the sharpest needle is estimated at the one-thousandth of an inch across, and as you know can no more be seen than the edge of a razor. You can of course tell where it is, for it stops the passage of light; but you can see no dimensions about it whatever.

With the microscope the limit of resolving power is somewhere near the hundred-thousandth of an inch. The test rulings, known as Nobert's bands, are lines made by the point of a diamond on glass guided by the finest screws and machinery. The nineteenth band is ruled to the known fineness of 120,000 to the inch; and notwithstanding some claims to the contrary, I think it exceedingly doubtful if these lines have ever been clearly separated by the highest powers of the microscope.

One of the most interesting and complete illustrations of the use of the highest powers of the microscope that I have ever read, is in a monograph on one of the infusoria, by the Rev. Dr. Dallinger, a distinguished English microscopist. He has followed this animalcule, the greatest length of which is only the one ten-thousandth of an inch, through all the phases of its life history, comprised within ten to twelve hours. A full grown individual divides itself lengthwise into two perfect beings in about five minutes. In another five minutes, each of these go through the same operation again, and so on for hours. After from three to seven hours of this kind of multiplication, the older ones die off, while some of the younger and more vigorous attach themselves to each other in pairs. One entirely absorbs the body of the other into its own, and settles down to the quiet cysted state, as it is called. Then after a certain time there commence to ooze out of this body perfect little clouds of the minutest spores, until nothing is left of the parent organism but the shriveled skin. These spores, at first too small to be resolved by the highest powers that our microscopist could bring to bear upon them, soon however grew to be visible as distinct points, then to push out their little threads of locomotion, and at length to become the full grown monads, ready to commence the other kind of generation, that of self-division. You can any of you easily repeat at least some part of this experiment, by putting a bit of fresh meat into a tumbler of water and letting it stand for a few days. You will then have a crop of infusoria that literally "no man can number." They would not probably be the identical species experimented upon by Dallinger, but one no larger and having an entirely similar life history and modes of generation.

I have estimated in regard to Dallinger's monads that a hundred million of them, great and small, might be contained in a drop of water, and yet be no more crowded than I have seen bacteria in infusions. Theoretically the natural increase of one of these germs dropped into an infusion, and within twenty-four hours, would be numbered as the figure one followed by eighteen ciphers. Now as this would be as many as a good sized pond would hold, we must suppose that the cruel principle of the survival of the fittest comes into that community long before it is twenty-four hours old.

But we must hasten our steps. We have not passed below the microscope as yet, and we have a long journey downward still to make. I will first endeavor to give you some idea of Molecular Physics—of the conditions and sizes of the ultimate particles which compose the matter about us. I do not however dare to present to you the array of figures which are necessary to show the relations and dimensions of the molecules, without giving at least an indication of the methods by which they have been found out. You would not begin to believe me if I did not have some show of proof to offer. So at a risk of appearing a little abstruse, and perhaps of not being fully understood for a few moments, I will attempt to tell you how the scientists have been able to come at the ultimate molecules of matter, so totally below the reach of manipulation, or the highest powers of the microscope.

Plate II.—"BUSH" SCENERY IN NEW ZEALAND. See Page xiv.

Sir William Thomson has made some very ingenious approximations to the actual size of molecules from such entirely independent data as the following: *First*—In the dispersion of light in the spectrum—how small must be the original particles in the glass or the crystal of the prism, to retard light waves of 60,000 to the inch, which are the blue, and not much to retard those of 40,000 to the inch which are the red; for this is the true signification of the dispersion of the colors in the solar spectrum. *Second*—How many molecules thick must be the film of a soap bubble to resist the force and tension necessary to draw it out to an extreme thinness. And: *Third*—Knowing how much electricity or heat is developed by the application of thin plates of different metals as copper and zinc, how thin would they have to be to develop the same amount of heat which the same quantity of these metals produces when they are alloyed to form brass; for then they are applied atom to atom. In each of these cases his estimates of the probable size of molecules came to nearly the same uniform result, and furthermore, to the same result which is brought out by a far more accurate and reliable calculation, which I will more particularly describe.

It is now a well established principle that the molecules of any gas, as hydrogen, oxygen or the air we breathe, are in constant and rapid motion—one striking against another and bounding off to hit a third, and so on continually, precisely as billiard balls would act under the same impulse and without friction. This is the mode of motion known as heat; and the hotter the gases the swifter fly the particles.

The hydrogen that fills a balloon resists an outside pressure of fifteen pounds to the square inch; and it does it by this incessant bombardment of the atoms of the gas against the inside of the containing bag. Now the weight of a given volume of hydrogen being well known, it is only a matter of calculation to estimate with what velocity its parts must be hurled against the sides of any containing receptacle to resist such an outside pressure. It is found that its particles must fly about in every direction with the average velocity of 6,055 feet in a second, about 70 miles a minute. The particles of the air, being seven and eight times heavier than hydrogen, move with only about half that velocity. This is one element of the problem.

Again, if different gases are placed in communication with each other, they instantly commence mixing together. No matter how quiet they may be, or how different in weight within certain limits, after a certain time they are found to be thoroughly commingled. This is accomplished by the incessant knocking of particles against particles until they are finally scattered equally in every direction. Now it is by careful and repeated experiments on the rate of diffusion of the different gases with each other that physicists have calculated how many times in a second these particles must be hitting against each other to produce the observed results. It is found that the number of collisions which one atom of hydrogen must make in a second is on the average 17,700 millions. Thus we have the distance an atom travels in a second, and the number of hits it makes. From these figures we can very easily tell the average distance the atom travels between each two successive collisions, called the mean free path, and which must be about the actual distance apart of these atoms. You see we are beginning to get a little hold on these intangible and inscrutable things.

From the general principles of molecular mechanics there has been deduced the following simple proportion: As a given volume of any gas is to the amount of solid matter in it, so is the average mean path of any one of its molecules to one-eighth of the actual diameter of that molecule. Now a cubic foot of steam, which is water gas, when condensed makes almost exactly a cubic inch of water, which may be taken as very nearly the solid matter in that amount of steam. Therefore, the cubic inches in a cubic foot (1728) is to one, as the mean free path (about one-millionth of an inch), is to one-eighth of the diameter of a molecule of water vapor. The working out of this sum gives the size of the ultimate particle of any gas as about the 250 millionth of an inch. Here we have the problem solved; not perhaps with a perfectly accurate result, but certainly something near it. We have got at the approximate dimensions of the last unit of matter—and it is an exceedingly small thing—

perfectly inconceivable. The number of molecules in a cubic inch of any gas at ordinary temperature and pressure is the figure 3 followed by 20 ciphers. A drop of water contains about the same number—three hundred million million million. If that little drop of water were magnified to a globe as large as the whole earth, and its molecules were enlarged in the same proportion, they would still be no larger than apples. Now you may think of a pile of apples as large as a meeting-house, or a hill, or possibly a mountain, but it is beyond all possibility to realize the number that would be contained in a mass as large as the world we live on. If Mount Washington in the White Mountains were all sand, there would not be as many grains in it as there are molecules in a drop of water.

The cheese-mite is a perfect little spider, with all the parts and complicate organs of his order. This little insect, which you can scarcely see by the naked eye, disposes of a number of structural units represented by the figure 4 followed by 18 ciphers—enough, if they were the smallest beads you ever saw, and strung on a thread that was long enough, to reach to the bright star Sirius. If the body of an elephant were composed of only the same number of particles enlarged that go to make up the smallest living insect, the grained structure of the monster would still be finer than the finest dust of wheaten flour.

The smallest bacteria or infusoria, found so abundantly in foul waters, and which can only be seen under the higher powers of the microscope, are the proprietors each one of something like four million million molecules.

I have already mentioned the germs of the infusorium which Dr. Dallinger saw under a magnification of five thousand diameters as little clouds issuing from the cyst.* He tells us that he once watched these clouds two weeks before they had increased in size sufficiently for him to resolve them into discrete points—as the astronomer resolves the distant nebula into the faint glimmer of separate stars; both observations being on the extremest bounds of the power of magnified vision. From this point of first resolution, the germs gradually developed in about two days into

---

* Lecture before the British A. A. S., Montreal, 1884.

full grown ciliated monads, fifty millions of which, he tells us, could easily disport in a drop of water. Now these germs when they first became barely visible under the Doctor's famous 25th, could not have been much smaller than the one hundred-thousandth of an inch. Therefore they were composed of about 10,000 million molecules each. That is an aggregate of 10,000 million molecules is the vanishing point of microscopic vision. But even these, it strikes me, are enough to build up a very respectable little body. There are not as many parts in any house in the land, bricks, boards, tiles, nails and all.

The canning of fruits and vegetables is now a domestic art. Every house-wife knows that if the cans are properly scalded and sealed while hot, they will keep sweet for any length of time. But if opened to the air they will sour and spoil in a very few days. Now this last condition is simply the production in them of enormous numbers of what is called the Bacterium termo, about the smallest living thing that is known, somewhat oval or cylindrical in shape, with two cilia or minute hairs at one end, which lash the water, producing a rapid jerking motion. It is of a plant nature, or at least is so called, and increases by subdivision, in a short time completely filling the liquid and absorbing all the nutrient matter. Then follow the tribes of the infusoria, little voracious animals, which seem successively to devour the bacteria and then themselves. But whence came the bacteria and then the infusoria? They were not in the water nor in the fruit; for if they had been, the preparation that had been sealed up would have immediately spoiled. The first thing which the microscopist sees with his favorite 8th or 10th is a swarm of these full grown organisms lazily rolling or darting and frisking about. They must have come then either from spontaneous generation or from spores and germs let down into the infusions from the air. But it is now pretty well established that there is no spontaneous generation — no life except through antecedent life. Therefore the latter, or the air-germ theory, is the only true explanation. But no one has ever seen these germs in the air, and we must consequently suppose that they are beyond the reach of microscopic vision.

Epidemic and contageous diseases are now recognized and treated as produced and propagated by living organisms. Our systems of quarantine and disinfection are founded on this theory. In the case of most of these diseases, there has been discovered and described the veritable bacteria or bacillus which is the cause and virus of each. But still there are some, including malarial, yellow and typhus fevers, equally well known to be germ-diseases, the cause or contagium of which has never been discovered, although you may be sure it has been diligently sought for. These diseases have their regular periods of growth and culmination, of intermittence, or relapse and repetition. We know that there is something in them that grows and dies; but what it is no power of the microscope has yet revealed. In this case then, both the germs and the full grown product of the germs are below the limit of magnified vision.

Evidently the scale of life does not stop at or near the limit which the present state of the optician's art prescribes to the extent of our vision. And there is no assignable reason why it should. The smallest living creature that has ever been seen under the glass, has at least a million million units to work with. But it may be a million times smaller, and yet have the very respectable number of a million structural units, infinitesimal bricks, with which to build its simple little house of a single room.

So you see there is the easy possibility, and even probability, of another realm of the living kingdoms far below the reach of the microscope. And in strong corroboration of this conclusion, is the fact, as shown by the beautiful experiments of Professor Tyndall, that the blue color of both the sea and sky is produced by an infinite number of minute, and as he thinks organic, particles suspended therein, much smaller than the wave lengths of light, which are on the average about the one fifty-thousandth of an inch.

If you take a glass jar full of pure distilled water, which is perfectly colorless, and while stirring let fall into it a drop or two of a solution of resin or gum mastic in alcohol, you will have a liquid slowly passing from pellucid water into the most beautiful marine and ultra-marine blue, and then into a milky and opaque white. For resin, though perfectly soluble in alcohol, is insoluble in water; and by carefully mixing them as we have described, the particles of the gum are first in a state of molecular division, in which they are totally invisible; then by gradual aggregation they become large enough to chip off and scatter some of the blue rays of light, which are those of shortest vibration; and finally they become sufficiently large to intercept all light. This is the explanation of the colors of deep waters, verging from blue to dark green.

Again, there are certain gaseous compounds which sunlight is competent to gradually decompose into their original elements. One is sulphurous acid gas, composed of two atoms of oxygen and one of sulphur. It is the pungent gas one smells when a sulphur match is lighted. A beam of sunlight passing through a glass jar containing this gas, literally shakes the atoms apart, leaving the oxygen as a pure transparent gas, and the solid sulphur atoms suspended in it. For about two minutes no change of color is seen; after that time the sulphur atoms will have joined together into sufficiently large particles to affect the blue rays of light. Then for fifteen minutes the color of the gas is a gradually deepening blue, and finally a thick opaque white. This exemplifies in a beautiful manner the cause of the deep azure blue of our clear skies. There are scattered, through all the regions of the air, minute particles of matter, small in comparison to the length of light waves, which deflect and scatter some of the smaller and less energetic undulations of the sun-beams; and this light, left behind in the swift passage of the solar rays, remains as the ever-blue firmament of the skies.

That this light-scattering dust is mainly organic, that is, the product in some way of living things, is shown by the fact that it can all be burned out of any particular enclosure, and the air therein be left perfectly light pure. If sunlight is passed through a small apperture into a dark room, its passage through the air will be marked by a white streak, from reflection against the particles of matter which it meets. But if a platinum wire be raised to a white heat in this room by the electric battery, and kept there for a half an hour or more, every particle of reflecting matter in it will be burned out, and thereafter the track of a sun beam through this air will be as black as through a perfect vacuum. Now the inorganic material of our world has been long ago all burned up, and there is nothing now that burns except new formed, that is, organic substances. Therefore the sky dust is clearly of organic origin.

It is well known that the air which covers, and the winds which blow, over the regions of prolific life, and especially the busy haunts of men, are loaded with the germs and spores of every kind of infinitesimal organisms. The seeds of decay, of ferment, of disease, and of the myriad forms of infusorial life, must abound in the air which surrounds us. For not an animal ceases to breathe, or a plant to live, or a particle of organic matter to be exposed, but it is in a very short time invaded by the peculiar organism that seems to exist for the destruction of each.

Now this is not so on the heights of mountains, or even on our dry western plains. Meats may be preserved, and organic infusions kept sweet, when exposed in such localities, for a long time. Cattle that die on the western ranges dry up before decay sets in, and sealed cans of provisions opened on the higher summits of mountains will remain preserved for any length of time, showing that the germs of putrefaction and ordinary decay do not exist in the dry air of elevated plains nor in the upper regions of the atmosphere.

But organic matter is there in abundance, for the same deep blue skies are above the highest peaks of the Rocky Mountains, that are over us here to-night. Therefore it is probable that the germ life of the upper skies, whatever it may be, never develops into anything that becomes sensible to our means of observation.

But I propose, if you will kindly have the patience to follow me, to lead you down some long steps further into infinitesimal magnitudes, to give you an idea of one of the boldest speculations in regard to the ultimate constitution of matter, which the mind of man has ever conceived.

It is common knowledge that the chemists describe and give names to about seventy elementary substances, or forms of matter which cannot be further decomposed, or reduced to anything simpler, by any means known to them. Still there are few who really believe that those simple elements are the last and lowest condition of matter. The physicist who has not had his dream or his theory of the unification of all matter, must be the one who never thinks beyond the tables. I will endeavor to explain to you that one which has occupied such minds as those of Helmholtz, Maxwell and Sir William Thomson.

It is now no longer questioned that all space is filled with a highly elastic, all-pervading ether. Light and heat are simply wave motions, and it is impossible that they should come to us from the stars and the sun, except there were something to move, some material medium all the way from those bodies to the earth. Again, this medium retards light in coming from the sun to the earth just eight and one half minutes. Now one of the definitions of matter is, that which presents an obstacle to force. Therefore the luminiferous ether, which does present an obstacle to the passage of the light force, is material in its composition. It is perfectly elastic, that is, its parts move among themselves without friction, as is shown by the almost instantaneous passage of the radiant forces through it (182,000 miles in a second). It is beyond all conception minute in its structure, for it fills in between the ordinary particles of matter, so that light, which uses only this medium for its transmission, passes almost as readily through air as through space, but is a little retarded in the more solid material of glass and transparent crystals. Thus we have furnished us a material substance pervading all space, of the utmost tenuity and elasticity. Let us see if there is any way in which atoms and molecules could be manufactured out of it.

You have all probably seen a tobacco smoker make little rings of smoke from his mouth, or a steam locomotive, when just starting, puff up great black rings of smoke that ascend to considerable distances unbroken. I wish I could show you the beautiful illustration of this which Prof. Tait exhibits to his audiences. He produces by chemicals a dense smoke in a box some eighteen inches square, with a cloth stretched over one end, and a round hole in the opposite side. Then some smart blows struck on the cloth send out through the opposite hole ring after ring of the smoke, chasing and passing through each other, bounding and vibrating as they come into contact. These are what are called vortex rings, little whirlpools in the air. The particles of the smoke are rapidly revolving in the perimeter of the ring, and a constant current of air is passing through the center. You would feel this little blast of air quite sensibly if you placed your cheek in the way of one of these vortex rings.

Helmholtz has shown by mathematical demonstration that if the air were a perfect fluid, that is if it flowed in all its parts absolutely without friction, those rings once started would go on rolling forever, and no power could destroy them, for they instantly bound away from every thing that would touch them.

Furthermore, Helmholtz has shown that in such a fluid the form of the rings need not necessarily be circles, but may be figure eights, or any other continuous and knotted folds. And the form impressed on them at their birth will continue to be their form as long as matter lasts.

Now this is the essence of that bold conception which I told you about concerning the constitution of the ultimate atoms which go to make up our world. Minute portions of the infinitely fine and subtle matter of universal space are in some way set to whirling in innumerable little eddies and in certain stable forms, which by the incessant beating of the etherial particles, are compelled to approach each other, yet when they strike, their own vortex motion makes them rebound and react on each other in the manner constituting molecular motion.

I cannot tell you how the atoms were first started in this vortical whirl; nor why they are of certain constant patterns, and in a certain limited number of forms. Nor can I tell why they join together so capriciously to form the various substances which surround us. But this I know, that when once the atoms have been cast in their tiny moulds and emptied into space in the quantity and with the affinities they have, it is not a difficult thing to build a world out of them, nor to account for the laws which will govern it.

As to the materials of this world-structure, they fell into place as naturally as did the stones in Solomon's temple, for they were fitted for it from the beginning. They could not do otherwise. As to the laws, I will instance only two. And to explain the law of gravitation, allow me to use a homely illustration. If two balls were suspended near each other, and everybody was striking at them, they would naturally receive more blows on the outer and exposed sides than on the inner and somewhat protected sides. Therefore, they would of necessity approach each other. So the incessant beating of etherial particles against the unprotected sides of two atoms or molecules near each other would make them approach. And what is true of two, may be shown to be true of twenty, a million or worlds of them. The mathematicians say that the law of this approach would be exactly that of the attraction of gravitation.

Take again the laws of chemical affinity. We found in the case of the smoke-rings, that there was a constant suction of air through their centers. This might be called their polarity, for they would attract at one end and repel at the other. Now atoms have exactly this polarity; and if by any means, any two were backed up to each other, with their streams flowing in opposite directions, I think they would hold to each other, not quite in contact. A figure eight vortex ring might hold two simple rings. You see there is opportunity here for the play of any amount of ingenuity.

But I will remind you again that this theory of the constitution of atoms is only an hypothesis. It may, or it may not, be true. There is no doubt that the materials and conditions suited to it are in existence, and it seems to be a possible and even quite probable supposition. At least, so think some of the most thoroughly scientific men of the present time.

But if true, what an astounding conception does it give us of the infinitesimal world of matter! Every atom of the countless multitudes that make up even the smallest thing we know of, is itself composed of millions on millions of etherial particles, rolling in ceaseless flow and impelled by the same forces that move the rolling worlds of space.

It is such conceptions as these which have forced the scientist to the conclusion that there is no such thing as absolute size in nature. There is relative greatness or smallness, nothing more. Fix your minds on anything apparently great or small; there is still an infinite range of objects greater or smaller, above or below it. But the absolutely great or small is never reached.

There is another conclusion. However far we may carry our researches into the recesses of nature, however much we widen the limits of natural and explainable causes, we always come at last to the point where it is necessary to acknowledge the intervention of some will or potency beyond the powers of nature. Natural causes may construct a universe when the means and materials have been supplied. But no conceivable powers of nature can start into being the ever-rolling self-impelling microscoms that are to evolve this mighty structure. Matter and force may be eternal, and the units of matter may eternally have moved and clashed in obedience to that force; but when that molecular motion was transformed into the vortical motion of innumerable little atoms of exactest weight and measure, we know that a controlling will was there; for the atoms could never have measured themselves out, nor set themselves to rolling.

And when in two totally different moulds, two different atoms were formed which, in a myriad ages thereafter, were to unite to form the element of water, which alone could make the aggregations of the other elements fit sustainers of life, we know that a forecasting mind was there, for a far-reaching plan was formed.

The atoms themselves bear the stamp of a master workmanship. Each one after its kind is a perfect copy of every other. There is not the shadow of a variation in mass or weight or properties. Each kind is exactly fitted to attach itself to some other, either in pairs of atoms, or triplets, or some definite number. And the substances which each union brings out are totally different from every other, yet seemingly essential to the make up of our diversified world. Sir John Herschel has well said, that the atoms have the essential character of manufactured articles, and that this precludes the idea of their being eternal and self-existent.

Out of the myriad forms in which we must suppose it possible to have moulded the formative matter of the universe, only a few were chosen. Out of the infinite variation of quantities in which they might have been supplied, only that proportion was adopted which made a world that could be the home of living beings. To this end, that of life in nature, conspire a thousand coincidences in the creation and endowment of matter, each and all of which we would have no difficulty in imagining might just as well have been otherwise. The chances are then infinity to one against the concurrence of all these favoring circumstances.

What shall we say then? Is the world that bears us up, that feeds us, that delights our every sense, a fortuitous jumble of chaotic matter? Did the grim specter of chance preside at the birth of the little world-workers that have evolved this beautiful Cosmos? I am myself an unpretending reasoner. But every sense I have revolts at the idea of an uncreated machine that works a plan with never one mistake. For myself, I cannot but think that he who sees no intelligence back of all this amazing structure of the universe, must be the man whom "the gods have first made mad."

THE POLAR GLACIERS.*

The center of gravity of the earth is the center of the sphere formed by the surface of the oceans; or rather, owing to the flattening of the earth at the poles, it is a point equally distant, in opposite directions, from the level of the sea. The waters, being free to move, must of necessity conform themselves to this equidistance from the gravitating center of the whole mass. Inasmuch, then, as any plane which cuts the earth into two parts through its center of gravity, must equally divide the weight of the whole earth, it follows also that the same plane would exactly bisect the great spheroid of the oceans. In each hemisphere the sea-level in all corresponding parts would be at the same distance from this center and whatever land and mountains there might be above the ocean in one half would have to be counterbalanced by land, or an excess of weight of some sort, in the other half. And this counterpoising weight must itself rise above the level of the sea, unless we say that one side of the world is composed of heavier materials than the other, of which there is not the least evidence or probability.

If the plane thus dividing the earth be that of its equator, there will be found in the northern hemisphere about 44,000,000 square miles of land, and in the southern, so far as is known, about 16,000,000 square miles. Now, the great problem in physical geography is: What is there in the southern hemisphere to counterbalance this great excess of land in the northern?

Humboldt has estimated that, if the mountains and highlands of Asia were leveled down and made to fill up evenly the low places, the whole continent would have a uniform height of

* Published in Popular Science Monthly in April and June, 1876. The MS was in the hands of the Publishers some months before the appearance of Croll's work on the same subject, "Climate and Time."

1,150 feet above the sea. In like manner, South America would have a height of 1,130 feet; North America of 750 feet; and Europe of 670 feet. The average of the whole he estimates at 920 feet. Of the mainlands not included in the above—namely, Africa, Australia, the polar lands, and islands—about as much is north as south of the equator. So that we may safely estimate that there is in the northern hemisphere an excess of 28,000,000 square miles of land, of the average height above-mentioned, to be counterpoised by something yet to be found in the southern hemisphere.

If there is an excess in the quantity or bulk of water south of the equator over that north of it, then the difference of weight between this excess and so much land, which is about in the proportion of one to two and a half, must be added to the unknown quantity which we are soon to look for above the southern seas. As there is, of course, the same excess of water-surface south of the equator that there is of land-surface north of it, and as we may very safely assume that the oceans have a mean depth of at least 3,220 feet ($3\frac{1}{2} \times 920$) and that the southern waters average as deep as the northern, it follows that our unknown quantity is at the very least doubled by the above considerations. We have, therefore, to seek in the southern hemisphere what will balance 28,000,000 square miles of land at least 1,840 feet high.

We look over the map of the world, and down near the bottom we find some uncertain landmarks with many breaks, but on the whole tracing out very nearly the antarctic circle, and indicating that there is, covering nearly all that zone, an unexplored and scarcely discovered country. This impenetrable region is estimated to be as large as the continent of North America, about 8,000,000 square miles. A very little arithmetic will now prove the bold claim which I here make, that, even supposing the whole of this region to be land of the average continental height, there is still required over it all an average thickness of two and a half miles of solid ice to make the southern hemisphere equal the northern in weight.

This result of calculation is well confirmed by the information which all southern navigators have brought back from those most desolate and ice-bound regions. The zone of the antarctic has been encroached upon only in a small space south of the Pacific. On every other side, so far as has been discovered, mountains of ice block the way on and near the polar circle, which seems to be the great ice-barrier of the south pole. Discoverers suppose what they have looked upon to be land, but rarely have they ever seen anything but rolling ranges of ice and snow rising higher and higher as far as the eye could reach. In the most open of the south-polar seas, Sir James Ross, in 1841, sailed 450 miles along an unbroken cliff of ice from 150 to 250 feet high, and of unknown depth beneath the water. It was one of the vast antarctic glaciers pushing down into the sea, from which some of those southern icebergs were broken off, that navigators have frequently laid down for islands, while the next sailor that voyaged that way found open water where they were charted.

Not a sign of vegetation, not an indication of thawing, has ever been discovered within or near the antarctic circle, whereas there are aboriginal races and numerous settlements of civilized communities on every side within the arctic circle. The whale-boat or the dog-sledge has traversed the arctics and found the sea-level in almost every degree of high latitude. In the south no adventurer has yet penetrated within probably 1,500 miles of the center of greatest cold. Whence comes this great difference in the climate and ice accumulations of the two poles of the earth? It is the object of this article to inquire if, in the astronomical relations of our planet, there are found any sufficient causes for such differences.

The path of the earth about the sun once every year is an ellipse, with the sun in one of the foci or centers. An ellipse is a circular figure having two centers instead of one; that is, the circumference is everywhere equally distant from the two centers taken together—the sum of the two distances is always the same. Therefore, the sun being in one of these centers, the earth is nearer to it in one half of the year than in the other. At the present time the nearest approach, or the perigee, occurs about the 1st day of January; and the earth is at that time 3,200,000 miles nearer to the sun than it is on the 1st day of July.

It is a peculiar property of bodies revolving in elliptical orbits, that they travel faster when near the center of attraction than when further away. It follows, from the second of the three great laws of planetary motion discovered by Kepler, that the line connecting the two bodies must pass over equal areas in equal times. The earth passes through our winter portion of its orbit, that is, from autumnal to vernal equinox, in eight days less time than through the summer part of it. In the southern hemisphere of course the condition of things is reversed, and the winter there is eight days longer than the summer. Moreover, the sun is at its greatest distance from the earth during the long southern winter, and at its least in the short northern winter.

Of the two causes, I regard the first as of main importance. Distance from the sun, whatever theory may be, does not seem to have much effect upon climate. The southern summers, when the sun is over 3,000,000 miles nearer the earth, are said to be even some degrees cooler than the same seasons in corresponding localities of the northern hemisphere. And to take an extreme example, Mars, which is 50,000,000 miles further from the sun than the earth is, has snow-lines about its poles which reach no nearer the equator than on our planet in corresponding seasons. But the excess or diminution of eight days in the winters of climates which, even in their warmest seasons, barely balance on the thawing point of ice, is a true cause in polar conditions and differences. Considering that these days affect chiefly the period of briefest sunshine, it amounts to quite one-twentieth of the whole power of the sun on a hemisphere. This difference would not be apparent in the warm regions of the globe, where there is always an excess of heat which is carried off by evaporation and ocean-currents; but it would exert nearly its full force in polar regions which are unaffected by those influences.

It cannot be denied that it is the sun's heat which prevents the temperature of the earth from sinking to, or very near to, the absolute zero of cold, wherever in the thermometrical scale that may be. Chemists have produced a cold estimated at 257° below zero, of Fahr.* It is not by any means probable that this reaches

---

* The temperature of stellar space is estimated by Sir John Herschel and others at -239° Fahr.

the entire absence of heat. But on the supposition that it is so, and that polar regions are unaffected by the air or water currents of the tropics, then an excess of eight winter days would lessen a polar temperature 15°, and unquestionably amount to the difference of an accumulation of ice and snow year after year, instead of the annual thawing, during each summer, of the winter's increase.

This is precisely what is, or has been, taking place at the respective poles of the earth. Year after year, probably for a long period, there has been a steady accumulation of ice-material about the south pole, adding weight to that hemisphere. Then, in proportion to this increase, the center of gravity of the earth has moved a little toward the south; and the waters, always obedient to this controlling point, have gradually gathered into the southern seas, covering the lowlands and plains of islands and continents. At the same time the waters were drawn away from the north-polar regions, uncovering lands, and leaving bays and sounds and inlets innumerable. The geography of the countries fully corresponds to these inferences. The seas of the arctics are comparatively shallow and deeply cut up, and the lands are low-lying. In the antarctics the oceans are deep and bayless, and all the mainlands and islands are precipitous and craggy, as if they were the peaks and table-lands of mountain ranges.

It is now the question whether this state of things is a permanent arrangement—whether we of the north side are always to have the advantage of extent of territory, of fertile lands and healthful homes in middle latitudes, in short, of all that makes the rivalry of nations, and civilization a necessity. To answer this question it will be necessary to turn again to astronomy, and to study for a few moments some of its more abstruse problems.

In addition to the rotation of the earth on its axis once every day, and its revolution about the sun once in a year, there is also a slow rolling motion of the equator, caused by the attraction of the sun on the excess of matter in equatorial diameters over the polar. It is precisely as when one touches the rim of a top in rapid motion; there is set up at once a slow gyrating or tilting roll, and the upper end of the stem describes a small circle.

Just so the sun lays hold of the protuberant rim of the great terrestrial top, and immediately it begins to oscillate in the long secular period of 25,868 years; while the polar axis, extended to the heavens, describes in the same length of time a small circle of 23½° radius among the northern or southern stars. This is the motion which causes what is called the precession of the equinoxes. The plane of the earth's equator crosses the plane of its orbit; and when the earth is at the points of junction, the days and nights are equal the world over. These two points therefore are the equinoxes; and the earth passes through them about the 21st days of March and September. Owing to the rolling motion of the equator above described, these points, always in the line of intersection of the two planes, pass successively through the twelve signs or constellations of the zodiac, making slowly the entire circuit of the heavens. The vernal equinox, which now points to, or is on a line between, the sun and the constellation of the Fish, after about 26,000 years will have traveled the great circle of the heavens and come back again to point to the same cluster of stars, which is now overhead at midnight on the 21st of March.

But the time of this revolution, so far as it affects the climate of the earth, is modified by the following circumstance: The ellipse or oblong circle in which the earth revolves about the sun, is itself all the time slowly revolving. The long diameter of it, the major axis, makes a complete revolution in the heavens once in 110,000 years. Now as this revolution is forward, or in the the same direction among the constellations that the sun appears to move, while that of the equinoxes is retrograde, it follows that the extremities of the major axis, which are the perigee and the apogee, advance to meet the equinoctial points; so that the revolutions, or rather the conjunctions, of the equinoxes, which have to do with terrestrial climate, are accomplished in the shorter period of 21,000 years.

Now all this astronomy amounts to simply this; that in the year of our Lord 1248 the earth was at its nearest approach to the sun on the 21st day of December, our winter solstice; and that in 10,500 years from that time the same thing will happen on the 21st day of June, our summer solstice. In the period comprising the first case, our winters are short and mild, and our summers long and sunny. During the cycle which shall comprise the latter case, our winters will be rigorous and our summers short. The northern hemisphere is now having its great summer. In about 10,000 years it will be in the midst of its great winter; and whatever differences there may be between the two hemispheres, owing to astronomical causes, will then be in full force against the northern.

A distinguished Scotch mathematician, Mr. James Croll,* has estimated that the melting of a mile in thickness of the present antarctic ice would raise the sea-level at the north pole 300 feet, and at Glasgow 280 feet. We have calculated, from data which were intended to be under-estimates in every case, that there were at least two and a half miles of average thickness in what geographers call the great ice-cupola of the south pole. If therefore, not only this were removed, but an equal quantity of ice were deposited at the north pole, there would be a deepening of the sea at the arctic circle of 1,500 feet.

Thus it is seen that, as certainly as terrestrial revolutions continue, in the course of 10,000 years there must come an entire reversal of polar conditions. The southern waters must be drained off to make the oceans of an opposite hemisphere. New lands, enriched with the sediment of a hundred centuries, will rise up to extend the borders of the old south continents, and islands joining together, will expand into mainlands. At the same time the northern continents must be in great part submerged, and their summits and ranges become the bleak islands and bold headlands of a tempestuous ocean. Central Asia, with its broad table-lands, may still retain the name of a continent; but beyond a few outlying islands, there will be no Europe and but little of North America left. The Atlantic waters will stand five hundred feet over Lake Superior, and will wash the base of the Rocky Mountains in all their length. A new Gulf Stream may again, as it must often have done before, flow up the valley of the Mississippi, returning the deltas to the prairies, and re-

---
* The reference here is to an article published some years since in the *Philosophical Magazine.*

making the beds of the garden of the world. These are no idle or impossible fancies. Not only are they the results of rigorous calculation, but they accord perfectly with the unmistakable evidences which the ocean has left, all over our land, of its recent work and presence.

The time-honored geologist, Sir Charles Lyell, lays great stress on the quantity of land and the configuration of continents, as chiefly efficacious in the great climatic changes. But it may be pertinently asked, what becomes of his continents and configurations when the seas of one pole advance to the other, as they unquestionably do, as they cannot but do, every 10,500 years, obedient to the transfer of vast ice-weights from one end of the world to the other? On all the mountains of New England there are sea-lines at elevations of 2,000 and 3,000 feet, and Lyell himself has recorded the facts. When the ocean was that deep over Boston, there were no continents in the northern hemisphere. Undoubtedly the height and direction of mountain-ranges, the trending of sea-shores, and the course of the ocean currents, have much to do with local climates. But instead of the relative quantity or location of land and sea having any agency in producing the glacial periods, it is these periods which produce the land and the sea.

So much for the causes and conditions which pertain to the geography of the present and the future. When now we turn back a few of the leaves which tell us of the past condition of our planet, we immediately see that the same causes have been at work in recent geological times on a much more extensive scale—in fact, that they have been the chief agents in composing and modifying the present surface of the earth outside of the tropics. Over all the northern portions of Europe, Asia and North America, are found the unmistakable evidences of extensive and recent ice-work. Bowlders of every size, some worn and some angular, are scattered in immense quantities over all the country, on the hills, on the plains, in places where the only possible explanation is that they were lifted up, carried, and dropped, just where they are found; and the great iceberg was the carrier. The face of the rock-beds, wherever brought to view, in the valleys or on the mountains, is almost always found to be ground or polished, and over that, grooved and furrowed with nearly parallel scratches. The Alpine glaciers are doing exactly the same work to-day. Erratic blocks of foreign origin and sometimes of enormous dimensions, are frequently found perched on the very tops of hills, or stranded high up the mountain-sides; and the quarries from which they came are invariably found to the northward, sometimes fifty or even a hundred miles. It is argued that nothing but polar glaciers could thus have moved them in uniformly meridional lines. The scrapings of grounding ice-floes, the marks of ancient sea-shores, and marine relics and shells, are found at elevations of several thousand feet above the present ocean-level. There is no escaping the conclusion that the northern continents have been, in not remote ages, deeply submerged beneath an ice-laden sea; and that the entire polar and north temperate regions, extending in some places south of the fortieth parallel of latitude, have been capped with one massive covering of ice of great thickness. Precisely the same evidences are found in South America, and according to Agassiz, even much nearer the equator than in North America. We have again to search our astronomy for causes many times more powerful than any thing we have yet found, for differences of polar temperatures.

The earth is made to revolve in an orbit drawn out of the circular form by the combined attractions of the other planets, Jupiter carrying the controlling influence. When the average of all these forces for long periods is more in one direction than in another, our planet is drawn away from the sun on that side. Now it must occasionally happen, with the various periods of revolution of the planets, that they will unite at times to produce extreme irregularities. The present difference between the nearest and farthest distance of the sun from us is 3,200,000 miles. It is found, by calculating back the planetary orbits and conjunctions, that this focal distance has been as much as 14,000,000 miles. There was at such a time, an excess of thirty-nine winter days during each year of the great secular winter of either pole. This exceptionally high eccentricity occurred, according to the calculations of Mr. James Croll, about 850,000 years ago. But it is now generally thought that we have no need to go back as far as that for the period of the last glacial epoch. 200,000 years ago the focal distance was 10,500,000 miles, and the winter excess was twenty-eight days. This, on the supposition heretofore made of the absolute zero of cold being at least 257° below the freezing-point, would lower the mean temperature in polar regions, 50° Fahr., and would unquestionably extend the permanent ice-limits far into the temperate zone. From that time, down to 70,000 years ago, the eccentricity was continually from two to four times greater than now. Since about 70,000 years ago, it has been nearly all the time less than at present. Thus it may fairly be concluded that the great glacial period of the Post-tertiary era came to an end with the fourth secular winter in the past, or B. C. 67,000.

This is a very interesting date to us of the genus *homo;* for it must have been about this time, according to all accounts, that our forefathers made their appearance on the earth. Man, with the long-haired mammoth, the woolly rhinoceros, the huge cave-bear, the great-horned reindeer, and numerous other species now extinct, followed close upon the retreating ice-fields of the bowlder period. Our primeval ancestors were a race of hunters, and they subsisted on the most abundant and magnificent game that the world has ever seen. They lived in caves or under projecting ledges, and with only flint-headed weapons contested their lives and homes with savage beasts. They cracked the bones of animals for their marrow, or crushed them in stone mortars for the fats and the juices which they contained. It was the lingering carnivorous instinct to gnaw the bones of their prey. They had fires at their funeral feasts, but there is little evidence of their indulging often in the luxury of cooked meats. It was a rude life, and a hard struggle they must have had for it; but their history is read in the drift-beds and cave-deposits of Europe, as plainly as if there had been a Herodotus to write it.

The effect and bearing of the great ice periods on geological work and time will be further considered in a second article in continuation of this.

II.

The element of all others most sensitive to the changes and impulses of every kind of force is the earth's atmosphere. It is in a state of constant disturbance, and seems to be obedient to no laws or regularity. Yet, unstable as the winds appear, they are really, in their general movements, among the most orderly and effective agents in Nature. This is shown in a remarkable manner by their agency in impelling the great ocean-streams; and thence arises their important influence on glacial phenomena. In order to make this evident, it will be necessary to explain in brief the general laws of their circulation.

The earth turns on its axis from west to east, and with it rotates daily the enormous envelope of the atmosphere. The velocity of rotation at the equator is something over 1,000 miles an hour; at thirty degrees distance it is about 150 miles an hour less. In higher latitudes it is still less; and at the poles nothing. Therefore, whenever the air moves north or south on the surface of the earth, it will carry with it a less or greater velocity of rotation than the places it passes over, and will turn into an easterly or westerly wind, according as it approaches or recedes from the equator. In the region of the sun's greatest heat, the air, rarefied and lightened, is continually rising, and cooler currents come in on both sides to take the place of the ascending volume. As these side-currents come from a distance of about thirty degrees from the equator, they have, at starting, an eastward velocity many miles an hour less than the localities they will eventually reach. Consequently they will appear to lag behind in all the course of their progress to the equator—that is, they will have a westerly motion united with their north or south movements. These are the great trade-winds, blowing constantly from the northeast on this side, and the southeast on the other side of the equator.

But the heated air which has risen in immense volumes in the tropics, spreads out to the north and the south in the upper regions, passes entirely over the trade-winds, and comes down to the earth in the temperate zones. It however continues to have the velocity toward the east which it acquired at the equator, and when it strikes the slower-moving latitudes, it will be traveling much faster than the regions it comes down upon. Hence the winds blowing towards the east, that prevail almost constantly in the middle latitudes.

This is the normal order of the wind-currents, and that which would prevail with nearly perfect regularity if the world were a uniform globe of water or of land, and equally heated on both sides of the equator. But the continents, and particularly mountain elevations, produce great disturbances, unequal rainfalls and ever-varying atmospheric pressures. When also from any cause, one of the trade-winds, notably the southern, is increased in its violence so as to push a tornado tongue across the dividing line into the opposite system of winds, there is started one of those cyclones, or great circular storms, which ravage the tropics and whirl through the temperate zones, finally exhausting themselves in the higher latitudes to the eastward.

The southern hemisphere is at the present time colder than the northern, owing primarily to the fact that the winters there are eight days longer than the northern, and the sun, during those seasons, about 3,000,000 miles further from the earth than during the northern winters. The difference of temperature therefore between the warm air that rises at the equator and the cold air that comes in from the south, is greater than that on the north side. And as it is difference of temperature that produces the whole movement of the air-currents, of course the greater strength of that movement must be on the southern side. Hence the larger share of the equatorial current passes over to the south, and the southern trades are much the strongest. In accordance with this theory it is a matter of observation that the southern trade-winds reach across the equator and into the northern hemisphere in some places ten to fifteen degrees.

In obedience to and perfect accord with this great system of winds, the waters of the oceans move. The strong southeast trades blow up from Southern Africa, cross the equator, and drive the waters of the South Atlantic into the Caribbean Sea. The lighter northeast trades, blowing between North Africa and

the West Indies, assist and give direction to this movement, which finally impels through the Straits of Florida a tide of tropical waters a hundred times greater than the outflow of all the rivers in the world. This great flood of thermal waters spreads out in the Northern Atlantic, imparting to Europe a climate corresponding to countries twenty degrees south of it on this side of the ocean. There is of course an under-current from the arctics to the the equator, exactly compensating this enormous northward flow of the surface-waters. The same process and effect are repeated in the Pacific Ocean; and the great Japan Stream robs the southern hemisphere for the benefit of our Pacific States, only in a degree less than does the Gulf Stream for the benefit of Europe.

A change in the relative strength of the trade-winds, such that the northeast trades would blow across the equator into the southern hemisphere, would entirely reverse the course of the warm ocean-currents, and carry to the southern continents the heat abstracted from the northern. Such a change in the course of ocean-streams has unquestionably followed every change in the glaciation of the hemispheres from astronomical causes. The winds and the water-currents have always helped to increase the difference in temperature which a considerable eccentricity of the earth's orbit must always have produced between the northern and southern halves of our globe. It matters but little which of the two—the ocean-currents or the astronomical causes—have produced the greater effect, since it is certain that they have ever coöperated in one and the same direction.

On all the tropical seas, between the terminal lines of the two trade-winds, there is what is called the belt of calms, a tract averaging from 300 to 500 miles wide, in which whatever winds there may be are exceedingly light and unreliable. It is here, as we have seen, that the air and vapor, heated by the vertical rays of the sun, are continually rising and spreading outward in the upper regions. It is a complete dividing line between the climates of the two hemispheres. One may be frigidly cold, while the other is highly heated; the only difference being that the calm belt would be removed further into the warmer hemisphere. It now ranges from five to ten degrees of latitude on this side of the equator. In this belt of ascending air-currents is carried up the greater part of the moisture which afterwards descends as rain or snow far from the equator. Whatever excess of solar heat there may be in the tropics is here absorbed in evaporating water. To vaporize a pound of water, according to Prof. Tyndall, requires as much heat as to raise fifty-five pounds of ice-water to the boiling-point. It is manifest, therefore, that there must have been, during the glacial periods, an enormous amount of sun-power somewhere on the face of the earth to have supplied the vapor that buried one zone and half of another beneath a solid ocean of ice.

These facts effectually do away with all the theories, except the astronomical, which have been advanced by physicists to account for glacial phenomena; one, that our solar system has, during certain ages, passed through a colder region of space; another, that the sun in glacial times for some cause failed to supply his usual quantity of heat; and, as a consequence of either, that the glaciation of both hemispheres occured at the the same time. Equatorial heat is as necessary to a glacial period as polar cold. The one transforms the waters to vapor, and elevates it to the cloud-spheres, while the other sends in the cold winds beneath, which compel the vapors to come over to the frozen side and build up the glacier.

The system of the stratified rocks has been called the great geological book, with its uncounted leaves overlying each other. Now as it is a part of the glacial theory that each of these leaves or strata, at least in greater part, was the work of a glacial period, it is important for us to examine closely and particularly the course and effect of one of these great cycles of about 21,000 years. We will take for example, that one of the Post-tertiary glacial which was of the greatest extent and severity. Ten cycles back, about 210,000 years ago, one of the periods of maximum eccentricity had just commenced, the highest since four times that number of years. The perigee, or nearest approach to the sun, happened then as now, a few days after the winter solstice of our half of the world. It was the great summer of the northern hemisphere. But over the southern hemisphere at this time, almost if not quite to the tropics, extended one vast sheet of ice. It reached far into Brazil, it covered Southern Africa and lapped over on Australia. The marks are all there, scored on the solid rocks, to show how it crept up the southern slopes of the hills, and how far it pushed its icy arms. In South America at least, there is ample proof that the great glacier spanned the southern ocean to reach it; for the furrows on the rock-beds of Patagonia are from the pole toward the equator, whereas in any other case they would have been from the mountains to the sea. With such a state of things at the southern end of the world, with probably miles in depth of ice and sea in its higher latitudes, there could have been but little water left for the opposite northern regions. What is called the Atlantic-cable plateau, between Newfoundland and Ireland, was very possibly the north shore of the Atlantic Ocean; and probably no considerable bodies of water existed anywhere north of that parallel. The present continents were all mountain table-lands, far from the vicinity of evaporating surfaces. Like all such elevated regions, not exposed to specially moist winds, they were doubtless dry and arid deserts. However warm may have been the climate of the north temperate and arctic zones during this their great summer, their great elevation and the want of any kind of water-supply must have made them barren of all forms of animal or vegetable life. Consequently there would be, as is notably the case, but few if any traces of this part of the great season left in the geological records, at least above the present seas.

Five thousand years pass, and the perigee has advanced to meet the vernal equinox. The spring season is now the shortest of all; but as the autumnal is correspondingly lengthened, the average climate is about that of the present time. But it is the season of the great thaw—the breaking-up time—of the southern hemisphere, and the waters are returning to fill the northern ocean-beds. Imperceptibly a permanent white cap begins to fasten itself to the heights of the boreal zone, to extend its outline, and to increase its depth. Slowly the lands are being submerged and the oceans broaden out, till there comes a time when land and water are equalized in the two hemispheres, and the climates are substantially alike.

Another 5,000 years pass, and the perigee now coincides with the summer solstice of the northern hemisphere. This is the position there of greatest cold; the winters are twenty-eight days longer than the summers; and the extra days are in great part those of the briefest sunshine. Besides this, the earth is 10,500,000 miles further from the sun in winter than in summer. According to the most careful calculations, the temperature of extreme northern regions would be lowered 50°, and the mean annual range would be fully 60° below zero. This in all probability would carry the isothermal line of Labrador, South Greenland, and Iceland (32° Fahr.), down to Charleston and the Gulf of Mexico. The late Prof. Agassiz found ice-marks as far south as this, though it can hardly be supposed that the permanent glacier extended so far. There are however abundant signs of the permanent ice-layer all over the State of New York, and both east and west of it. The same distinguished authority was wont to claim in his lectures that all the beautiful north and south lakes of Western New York—the Cayuga, the Seneca, the Canandaigua—were ploughed out of the solid rock and walled around with their clay and gravel hills, by advancing and retreating glaciers. The rocky summits of New England are found to be grooved and scored all over their sides and tops with markings always in nearly a north and south direction. They have been traced on Mount Washington to within 300 feet of the highest point. There can be no doubt that, at the time we are writing of, about 200,000 years ago, there was one solid ice-stratum of immense thickness—Agassiz said from two to three miles—slowly being pushed from the northward by the power of freezing water, over all of New England and the Lake States.

Again the perigee proceeds to meet the autumnal equinox. The winter and the summer seasons have again become equal in length; and the sun is just half its time on the north side of the equator. The great ice-shroud is now being gradually withdrawn. Where it abuts on deep waters, enormous icebergs are broken off and float away to the south, carrying bowlders and soil and whatever it may have picked up in its slow course down to the sea. Where it terminates in shallow waters or on the land, its effect is to produce such an arrangement and diversity of soils and such a peculiar outline of country as no other agency could ever have brought about. So different is the nature and work of the great polar glacier from anything with which we are familiar at the present day, that it has seemed to me to require a few words of more particular description.

As is well known, the glacier is an accumulation of many winters' snows, consolidated by pressure into a clear blue ice. In this condition it manifests the peculiar property of viscous bodies—it is in continual slow motion in the direction of least resistance. Whether it is by the expansion produced by the repeated thawing and freezing of water in its interstices, as Agassiz claimed, or whether by the pressure of the mass and glacial regelation, which is the constant freezing together of ice-surfaces in contact, after breaking under unequal pressures, or crushing against obstacles, which is the theory of Prof. Tyndall, or whether by both causes combined, certain it is that large bodies of ice not only flow like a heavy lava-stream, conforming themselves to all inequalities of the surface, but they also scrape along in solid mass, as if pushed by some irresistible force from behind. Mountain-glaciers show both motions. But the great polar glacier, extending over comparatively level surfaces, seems to have been pushed bodily outward from its fixed polar base, and to have moved almost entirely under the mighty impulse of expansion. The parallel scratches and furrows which, in our hemisphere, mount straight up the north sides of mountains; the worn and rounded appearance of those sides and of the summits, as compared with the rough, unsmoothed southern slopes; the erratic blocks, or some peculiar specimens like the native copper of Lake Superior, carried almost directly south for scores or hundreds of miles, over heights, and even over arms of the sea—all show conclusively that the great glacier pushed its meridional course over all obstacles and to long distances.

Imbedding in its under surface the grit and gravel on which it froze, the mountain grindstone grated and ground the solid rocks over which it passed into the various materials of soil. Sand and gravel were the products from granitic rocks and sandstones, clay from the slates and shales, and loam from the softer lime-rocks. But the most striking effects which the polar glacier produced were the long ridges of gravel and bowlder-clay hills which it scraped up as it advanced, and left at the end of its journey, or at each halting-place of its retreat. For it must be borne in mind that the glacier was still pushing southward all the time that it was, on the whole, retreating. These terminal moraines are either the promiscuous gatherings of clay and bowlders and earths of all kinds, or, if they have been subjected to the sorting influence of moving waters, they are gravel hills with sandy bases, and clay flats extending usually to the southward of them. They run in somewhat parallel courses easterly and westerly, sometimes hundreds of miles. Great numbers of these concentric ridges may be counted in Western New York, between the long Lake Ontario ridge and the lake hills of the south part of the State. Several cross the New England States, one running along the coast of Maine, and westerly through the White Mountains. In addition to these are the lateral moraines, running in an opposite direction. These were, some of them, pushed out at the sides by outstretching arms of the glacier; others were formed by streams running down through breaks or fiords in the melting ice-sheet. So extensive and so marked are the traces of the great polar glacier over all middle latitudes both north and south, that it may truly be called the great landscape-gardener of the temperate zones.

But it is natural to conclude that, if there has been one glacial era caused by astronomical cycles, there must also have been others in earlier geological times. And, as we turn back the pages of the great earth-book, we find therein recorded the evidences of the vicissitudes of climate which we thus anticipate; but, if we mistake not, in continually lessening force and extent the further back we go. For long ages previous to the recent glacial epoch, through all the Tertiary era, the fossil plants and animals indicate the prevalence of a warm and genial climate over the greater part of the globe. Then come the chalk-beds of the Cretaceous period, in which are frequently found water-worn blocks of granite and aggregations of pebbles, proving that then, as now, the ice-berg floated down from the north over seas that were quietly depositing the chalk-shells. Still older, is found a long series of secondary strata, the Oölite, the Lias, and the Trias, which were deposited in at least sub-tropical climates. They are the burial-grounds of the enormous saurian reptiles that once had an age all to themselves in the world's chronology. Their remains have been found within a thousand miles of the north-pole, thus proving that warm seas covered every zone.

Between the great divisions of Secondary and Primary in geology, there lies a stratum found only in the higher half of the latitudes, and known as the Permian or New Red Sandstone. The scanty life-forms found in it, and the coarse grit and angular bowlders of which it is composed, evince the well-known glacial action. Geologists generally think that there elapsed between these great divisions a very long period of time in which, excepting this sandstone, but little was done one way or another to build up the crust of the earth, or to leave a mark in its records. This doubtless indicates periods of very small eccentricity. Such periods did occur, according to Mr. Croll's calculations, immediately before and after the great eccentricity of 850,000 years ago, in which we may perhaps conjecture the New Red Sandstone to have been formed.

Previous to this age were the long Carboniferous periods, during all of which a warm and moist climate prevailed over all lands that have yet been explored. Below the coal-measures are found again the grits and bowldery conglomerates of the Old Red Sandstone, which, with the great paucity of organic remains, would imply the alternations of somewhat glacial climates. The Silurian, Cambrian, and Laurentian systems preceded the Old Red in the order named, and reach back to the dawn of life on the earth. These formations are of vast thickness, and were deposited at the bottom of warm seas in all parts of the world.

It cannot be denied that, as we go back in the geologic records, we find more and more the evidences of greater heat and a more equable climate. It is certain that the astronomical relations which we have pointed out—the revolutions of the orbital points and the alternations of great and small eccentricity—have never ceased to exist. Therefore, if the world had been subjected to only the same solar heat in ancient as in recent periods, there must have been repeated glacial epochs; and we should find the bowlder, and the unsorted drift, and the scratched and polished rocks, all through the stone presentations. But very few, if any, such evidences have been found.

Again, for a warm and exuberant climate to extend into the arctic zone, there was necessary one of those great summers of considerable eccentricity, without the excessive drainage which an unusually large accumulation of ice in the opposite hemisphere would necessitate. Each summer cycle of coal forests, or of reptile monsters, implies, not only a long visit and a high evaporating power of the sun, but also the addition to the opposite polar regions, of a weight of ice only sufficient to draw the waters from a small part of the low and flat lands of the warmer hemisphere. We have seen that periods of warm, perhaps even of tropical climates in polar latitudes, intervened between the great winters of the last glacial epoch. But they have left scarcely a trace in the strata. They were the nearest approach possible, with the sun-power of recent times, to the conditions which of old brought out such a profusion of animal and vegetable life. But the only result in the later periods was, that the earth was unbalanced; all the waters were either turned into ice, or were following after it toward one of the poles; one side of the world was a frozen waste, while the other was a burning waste.

I think we cannot avoid the conclusion that the sun shone with a far intenser power on the Carboniferous swamps and the Oölitic shoals than on the gravel-hills of the Drift; that the oceans of early times were wider and warmer than now, and circulated more freely between the tropics and the polar seas; and that the heated and moisture-laden atmosphere retained the heat and equalized the temperature between the equator and the poles far more than at present.

With these conditions, that is, with a greater sun-power and a considerable eccentricity of the earth's orbit, I can conceive of a rational explanation, that which I have not yet seen in the books, of the formation of the coal-layers, alternated as they always are with marine deposits. These alternations are sometimes very numerous. There are as many as sixty distinct veins of considerable thickness, one over another, in the coal-mines of South Wales, as also of Nova Scotia. There must have been, in that case, sixty periods of dry land, each of sufficient duration to grow many forests, and each followed by a long-continued submergence, in order that each layer should become fossilized, and buried beneath a shale or a limestone, which could only have formed in the depths of a quiet sea. The books say there were so many upheavals, and a like number of subsidences, alternating with each other. As if Old Earth had bent her back, for her load of pit-coal, three-score times among the Welsh hills, and again as many more at Halifax. It is a far more reasonable explanation, that each considerable layer of coal indicates a cycle of long summers, and the withdrawal of a moderate depth of the oceans from one hemisphere to the other, by reason of moderate accumulations of ice in polar latitudes, and the return again of the waters after 10,500 years. In this way, and in no other that I can conceive of, can be fairly explained the constant mixture and alternations of terrestrial and marine relics, all through the fossil-bearing formations, and the hundreds, if not thousands of different and distinct strata which are found lying one above another.

Whoever, even cursorily, studies the phenomena of geology, must be impressed with the enormous length of time it has taken to arrange the terrestrial substructure, and prepare it for the higher forms of life. Even the comparatively recent period of the Bowlder Clay, which laid out the grounds of the present area of civilization, dates back for its commencement, as we have seen, probably 200,000 years. If it might be assumed that the Permian or New Red Sandstone was formed during the next previous period of extraordinary eccentricity, which was 850,000 years ago, then the Devonian or Old Red Sandstone would come in, very appropriately, at the next anterior era of extraordinary focal distance, which occurred 2,500,000 years back. The Carboniferous period, which came between these two, could not have been formed in less than 1,000,000 years, as most geologists concede; and by calculations previously indicated, those sixty Welsh layers of coal, if there are that many divided off by marine deposits of considerable thickness, would have consumed 1,250,000 years.

The average thickness of all the strata that lie above the Old Red Sandstone is not far from two miles. But this formation is itself, in many places, two miles thick. And the lower Primary systems will add at least ten miles to the vertical measure of the fossil-bearing rocks. It is estimated that "the fossiliferous beds in Great Britain, as a whole, are more than 70,000 feet in thickness;" and many that are there wanting, or nearly so, elsewhere expand into beds of immense depth. There are certainly fifteen miles deep of strata to be accounted for—the slow accretions of the ages—mainly ocean-sediment that has come down from the wear and washings of the solid rocks. It would be by no means a bold assumption to say that 20,000,000 years had elapsed since the eozoon first built its reefs in the warm Laurentian seas.

UNIVERSITIES vs. SCIENCE;

Or, Shall Science be Excommunicated?*

In the good old times when the Church had her own way, if any one proved refractory, he was threatened with excommunication, and he immediately came to his orthodoxy. This is what made old Galileo get down on his knees and renounce his heresies, and it kept back many a book of premature science from seeing the light of the early centuries. But after the great Protestant Reformation, and the loss of the hold which the Church had on the literature of the times, Christendom was inundated with books of men's wisdom, and strange doctrines which served only to unsettle the minds of the faithful.

It may be too late now to arraign science in this highly satisfactory manner, but we can at least show up some of the mischief it is working, and, for educational purposes, confine it to expurgated and approved editions of school books. With this view, I propose to follow up some of the most recent advances of scientific thought, as it is called, and to let all see where they inevitably land us.

Ever since the time of Luther and Calvin, the advocates of Christianity have been constantly engaged in contesting, and finally conceding, the claims of scientific investigators. The common-sense interpretation of those sublime verses in Genesis which tell the simple story of Creation, has had to be, in repeated instances, distorted and stultified to accommodate itself to the slow and toilsome processes of evolution.

---

* Written a few years since, on the occasion of the removal of Prof. Winchell from the Lectureship of Vanderbilt University, on account of scientific heterodox opinions.

As long as the contest was over the Old Testament account of the Creations, it would not seem to matter much whether the Church gained or lost in the controversy; for the truth of the Christian religion is not necessarily dependent upon either the cosmogony or the theocracy of Moses. The religion of the New Testament was a great and radical reform of the straight and highly anthropomorphic monotheism of the Hebrews. After this great Reformation was once established, it was no more important to it that the writings of the Mosaic priesthood should be retained, than it was to the reformed Protestantism of the sixteenth century that the bulls and encyclicals of the Popes should be longer regarded. In fact it is very much of a question whether the Christian cause has not lost rather than gained by incorporating the books of Jewish Mythology and Ritual among its sacred Scriptures.

In the first place the New Religion gave up at once the very primitive and human conception of God which was held by the Hebrews, as one coming down and talking with men, doing their battles and making laws for them, as one contesting his place with the gods of other nations, and governed by like passions as we ourselves. Again, the Christian religion first brought out the doctrine of future rewards and punishment, and the great theological tenet of the immortality of the soul. St. Paul says, "Christ came to bring life and immortality to light." Surely this is an entirely different religion from the unitarian theocracy of the Jews; and we cannot see how its eternal truth can be affected one way or another, though the beautiful verses of Genesis be shown to be figurative or fabulous, though neither the earth nor the sun is the center of the universe, though the world was created neither in six days nor in any periods whatever, and though neither Adam nor any portion of the human race was ever started off at once in the full tide of civilization and enlightenment.

But science does not stop when it would seem to have worsted the Hydra of ancient fable. It is every day putting forward bolder and more far-reaching claims, and it is now perhaps becoming a serious and important question whether some of the recent theories and discoveries of our scientific friends are not striking at the root of Christian theology as developed out of the New Testament—whether the time has not really come when Christian institutions of learning should discriminate against professors who teach or who meddle with these advanced theories of science.

I approach the further elucidation of these theories with great hesitation, because some may think they are subjects which should not be written upon. But how can we fight an enemy in the dark? How shall we know what to beware of, unless we expose it to the light? I therefore plunge " in medias res."

Late developments in what is called the kinetic theory go to show that all the forces in nature are only different modes of motion—transmutable one into another, but still motion and nothing but motion. If then all force is motion, and there can be no motion without something to move, the forces cannot exist except in connection with some form of matter. There is, and there can be, no impulse nor life nor manifestation, in the world or out of it, except through material substances. Under such a state of things, one can hardly understand how the spirit of man, which is certainly a force in his natural body, can exist separate from that body.

The life force of all the animal creation is a transmutation from chemical force, the materials for which are constantly supplied through the food we eat and the air we breathe. The moment the supply gives out, the life force ceases and the body becomes other kinds of matter, in most cases the food and substance of other animals. By far the greater part of all organic matter, the human organism included, passes the round of vegetable and animal existence time and time again. Therefore the body, once dead and eaten up and passed on to another generation of animated beings, can never be gathered together and animated over again. The resurrection of our bodies then would seem to be a physical impossibility, and under the kinetic theory there can be no spirits without corporeal bodies.

If we still maintain, as the most of us certainly will, that the soul of man is some mysterious entity independent of natural laws, and after the death of the body will animate forever some kind of an etherial form, we naturally inquire, where will be the habitation of such existences? We turn to the Holy Scriptures and we find the abodes of the blessed, the Christian's Heaven, described as in the upper sky, above the earth, outside of all its commotions, in regions of eternal day, where there is no night and the sun forever shines. Where else can this be than in the outlying regions of space? Now the scientists have lately been telling us that the temperature of the inter-planetary spaces is somewhere about 250° below zero, and that they are filled with shooting stars and meteors and fragments of iron, flying about in all directions with amazing velocities. Now this would not seem to be a very serene and tranquil location for the reunion of the saints.

The soul quits the natural body if its temperature is reduced to near the freezing point, which is 32° above zero. We can hardly suppose it would leave one body just because it was slightly reduced in temperature, and forthwith take up with another that had not the least last shiver of heat in it.

Again, the place for the eternal punishment of unbelievers is represented to be in lakes of fire beneath the surface of the earth, and we have always supposed there was no lack of that fluid in the bowels of our planet. But now comes forward the great geologist, LeConte, and tells us that the earth is solid from center to circumference, that even the volcanoes are only so many chemical retorts that are emptied as fast as filled. He has effectually forestalled the arguments of the Beechers, for there is now no longer a place for Hell.

But by far the most serious inroads yet made in the Christian intrenchments come from the Darwinian hypothesis, or that of the slow and gradual development of the human from the lower races of animals. We will present the main points of this theory as fairly as we can, for the purpose of seeing what inferences come with it. There can be no greater argument for development than the actual tracing or following of that development from either end to the other. We will attempt this kind of a showing, and will take for our example the nations of northern Europe, which now stand at the head of the world's advancement.

The native races of these countries can be followed back by authentic history through all the stages of civilization, feudalism, and barbarism, to the time when Julius Cæsar invaded the great Northland, and was everywhere met by hordes of fierce, half-naked and painted savages. Here we leave written history and follow up the abundant remains and traces which the prehistoric tribes have left of themselves throughout Europe.

First, we come to the builders of the mounds and tumuli scattered over all these countries, and containing the bones and the implements of an aboriginal people. They occupied Europe for a long period, in the same manner and conditions that the Indians inhabited North America for so many ages previous to its discovery.

Next, we come to the race of the lake-dwellers, who found their security against wild beasts, and an advantage against enemies of their own kind, in locating their dwellings on piers extending out into lakes and shallow waters. Their implements and the piles of their rude dwelling places have been found in prodigious quantity near the shores of the lakes of central Europe. Utensils and arms of bronze and polished stone, with some rude pottery, show that their period was the middle ages of primeval man. The unique location of their dwellings shows that even they lived long before man had dominion over the brute.

Lastly we come to the cave-dwellers. In late years there have been opened up in the bluffs which border the water courses of Europe numerous caves, nearly or entirely filled with river sediment, in which have been found great numbers of rough stone implements and a few human bones, mingled with quantities of the bones of the mammoth, the woolly-haired rhinoceros, the cave bear, and many other species of animals now extinct. Places where these early men gathered to chip and fashion their flint arrow-heads, axes, and hammers, have been found; and their location, always in or underneath the drift and gravel-beds of the Diluvial period, gives evidence of the great antiquity of these earliest known races.

The cave men lived on the flesh of all manner of wild beasts, which they probably ate raw, breaking up the bones for the marrow they contained. They were themselves but little better than carnivorous animals. Aside from their rude and unpolished implements, they have left no other marks of their presence and life in these dens than would have been left by a pack of hyenas. In fact, many of the caves give evidence of being alternately occupied by man and by wild beasts, whichever happened to have the mastery for the time being.

But man, at this period, had passed over the bounds which separate him from the brute creation. He had learned to make and use instruments to help him in his work. The Chimpanzee and the Gorilla build sleeping places, rude homes, for themselves with branches and sticks in the crotches of trees, and some monkeys use sticks and throw stones in defense and in fighting. But the cave-men had gone one step further. Some fortunate chance had taught some more than usually reflective individual that a well directed blow of another stone upon a piece of flint would split it into sharp-edged instruments with which he could cut off a larger branch than he could break off, or cut up his meat easier than he could tear it to pieces with his fingers and teeth. Then he learned that a few chipping blows on the end of a longer piece of flint would sharpen it to a point, and that he could throw this, fastened to the end of a stick, and wound a reindeer, with far greater effect than with a common stone. Here he had a knife and a spear, and he must then have names to distinguish them by. Thus, probably, arose first the rude arts of life, and then the rudiments of language.

We have said nothing thus far of the physical conformation of these cave-men. They have left exceedingly few remains of their own persons; probably from the fact of their burning their dead, or otherwise disposing of them out of their sight. They could live in the midst of any amount of the carrion of wild beasts, but they were very particular to remove every trace of their own dead bodies. However, two skulls of adult persons have been found, one in a cave at Engis, in Belgium, which, although denoting a person of low intellectual grade, does not differ materially in type from the ordinary cranium of the lower races of mankind; the other, found in a cave at Neanderthall, in western Germany, on the contrary, represents an individual more than half way down between our lower races and the anthropoid apes. The low and retreating forehead, the great development of the bony ridge over the eyes, so characteristic of the larger apes, the massive size of all the processes for the attachment of muscles, the enormous thickness and strength of some other bones of the skeleton found with the skull, all denote the powerful and terrible wild ape-man of the Rhine forests. There is no question of this creature being a link between man and the brute; and the finding of one such specimen is as conclusive of the former existence of an intermediate race as the discovery of a single fossil archæopterix was of an order of flying animals half way between birds and reptiles.

All further traces of primitive man end with those of the cave-dwellers. It is probable that no others will ever be found; because any condition lower than this would be simply animal. There is then no absolute proof that this lowest type of mankind originated from the next lower order of the animal kingdom, that is, from anthropoid apes. But this at least is certain, either the cave men did so advance out of the ape condition, or they were created in the semi-bestial state-in which we have found them. But the Bible account as well as every mythology of man's creation launches the first human family into the full tide of an advanced culture. Therefore no account that we have of any supernatural creation can by any possibility apply to the poor degraded cave-dwellers. The conclusion then seems unavoidable that they came up through still older and lower stages of animal being; that the succession must run uninterruptedly down and into some now extinct species of carnivorous apes.

Here we leave the argument of the evolutionists. I think no one can say I have not presented their case with fidelity and to the best of my ability. It remains to follow up these premises to their unwelcome but logical conclusions.

In all this long and slow progress from the cave-men or the ape men to the sovereigns of Europe, embracing a period, some think, of a hundred thousand years, there is no break in the chain. An exceedingly slow but constant advancement, worked out by the races themselves, spreads over the entire period. Where now, it may be pertinently asked, in this continuous line of progression from ape to kaiser, was the point at which immortal souls were introduced into the race? Brain capacity, intelligence, language, cultivation, were all slow and toilsome growths. But the attribute of immortality could hardly be a growth. Either the spirit of man has an eternal duration and destiny, or it dies like the soul of the brute. Neither has immortal life come with a certain upright stature, or with a certain weight of brain, or with the dawning of language or reflection, or with inter-breeding and contact with some favored race. By all the principles of logic, if the Europeans have immortal souls to-day, their forefathers had them when the Romans stocked the arena with wild beasts and barbarous Northmen—their prehistoric ancestors had them in the bronze age, in the stone age, and in the far distant ages of the gravel and drift beds—and their lowly progenitors had them when they were only gibbering apes.

I have had the pleasure of listening to the great apostle of scientific theology in his famous attempt to prove the immortality of the soul from the most advanced researches of microscopical science. It was ingenious and eloquent, but it turned out as all such theorizing outside of the Bible is apt to do, it proved too much. If there is an element of immortality in the mysterious life force that builds up, from undistinguishable germs, the lion after his kind and the man after his kind, then the lion is as immortal as the man, and all life is immortal. The distinguished lecturer himself realized the dilemma, and met it with a sublime expatiation on the delight it would afford the saints to have, in another world, the pleasant recreations and the domestic surroundings of this. The spiritual hunter would pursue spiritual game, and retrieve with spiritual dogs. It is the happy hunting grounds of our Indian aborigines over again. Religion as well as history repeats itself.

A noted Professor of Geology has attempted to bridge over the chasm between science and evolution by the hypothesis that

Adam was not the first of the human family, but simply the head of a subsequent and favored race. According to him, there were Adamites and Pre-Adamites, the first comprising the great Aryan race of Eastern Asia and Europe, the last comprising the aborigines of every country, which the Adamites have been constantly displacing ever since the dawn of history. The descendants of Adam received the divine blessings and all the benefits of the Promises. The aborigines struggled up as they could, on natural laws and the survival of the fittest. Now this was a most ingenious theory. It fitted into the rough edges of both sides of the great controversy, and gave to each a pretty fair division of the earth's inhabitants. The whiter races, of course, are given to the religionists, while the darker are consigned to the evolutionists, the former with immortality breathed into them by their Divine Creator, the latter—well! they are a little doubtful; they are in a kind of "no man's land." Still they may have a sort of improved brute soul. The Professor thinks if he were called to preach the gospel to the heathen, "his appeals to the negro would be of a widely different character from his appeals to the Aryan Hindoo or the Mongoloid American savage." The Professor is logical. He is to be commended for his honesty. For if the negro has a soul to save, neither he nor I, if this evolution is true, can tell when he got it or how he came by it.

It has thus far been our unpleasant duty to run down a few of the recent scientific theories, for the purpose of seeing where they would land us. If we have seemed at any time to present them as an advocate, it is only because by showing them in their most favorable light, could we discover their dangerous tendencies. We have found that, reduced to their logical conclusions, these theories are in opposition to the Christian's simple faith, and that they raise doubts and difficulties in respect to the scheme of salvation and future life. Can it then any longer be said that there is no conflict between religion and science. Is it not plain that Christian Institutions of learning should discriminate against all text books in which the development theory is made to explain the great facts of the Organic World, and that they should look with suspicion on all new Geologies, new Physics, or new fangled sciences of any kind? It would almost seem as if they would be equally justified in introducing among their studies the philosophies of Hume and Voltaire, as these latter-day sciences which tend to the subversion of the tenets they were established to maintain. As to calling professors, who are known to be tainted with these heresies, to lecture to pupils who have been confided to sectarian institutions, it would seem almost as absurd and out of place as it would be to invite Prof. Tyndall or Prof. Huxley to speak in a religious meeting.

One venerable President of a University has publicly stated that possibly the theories of evolution might be admitted and talked about "as working hypotheses." But we would kindly say, let him take warning; for they will surely work only mischief in any well ordered and orthodox institution. The only safety, as we suggested at the outset, is to excommunicate science, or expurgate the text books.

WHAT THE CHEMISTRY OF THE ROCKS TEACHES.*

It is a general rule that substances can crystallize only while solidifying from the liquid state of either fusion or solution. The only exceptions are, that some few substances crystallize directly from their vapors without passing through the intermediate liquid form. Now the older unstratified rocks of the geological formations, as the granites, are unquestionably fusible, are crystalline in their structure, and are practically insoluble. Therefore the evidence is conclusive that they were all at one time in a molten, fluid state.

Thus far, it would appear, geologists are agreed, since they have named these formations the igneous rocks. But whether the melted minerals were ever heated to a higher degree than fusion—that is to the condition of vaporized elements—is an inquiry either carefully avoided by the authorities in geology, or merely mentioned as pertaining to an ingenious hypothesis which, it is claimed, is unsustained by any sufficient proof. It remains to be seen, however, if this theory of the original gaseous form of the material elements does not follow as a necessary consequence from the chemical constitution of the rocks themselves; and if it does not explain and bear testimony in geological and cosmical sciences to such an extent as to make it absolutely essential to them.

The question here presented resolves itself into two alternatives: Either the materials of the earth's crust were formed according to chemical laws out of the simple elements preëxist-

---

* Published in Popular Science Monthly, April, 1874.

ing in gaseous forms, or they were created in the condition of melted and oxidized masses ready to cool into granite and limestone. The latter supposition will hardly be seriously entertained in these days of free inquiry into the natural causes of things. It is now not only conceded, but expected, that science shall have sole jurisdiction in every case where compound bodies are the subject of investigation. To follow them back to the primal laws and elements of their being, to reveal the cause and manner of their birth among the atoms, is now the highest aim of inductive research. On this border-line of inquiry where the known shades off into the unknown and the finite into the infinite, science has of late gained its most signal triumphs. And it scarcely requires a prophetic sense to discern that the groundwork of all systems of scientific knowledge will soon be laid in molecular physics.

In the constituents of the solid earth we have forms and conditions of matter of remarkable composition and complexity. The original materials of the ground, of the rocks, and of the mines, are found to be, in every case, fully saturated chemical compounds. Many of them, as the silicates, are adamantine acids neutralized by alkaline bases harder than the flint. They could not be made more stable, inert, and solid. They are materials that have apparently gone through stupendous changes, activities, and combustions, and at last have settled down to a rest that knows no waking. Science has no duty more legitimate or more imperative than to inquire how these rock-masses came to be where they are, and in the condition they are.

In pursuing this inquiry, since we find one of the alternatives to be inadmissible, it is necessary to accept the other, namely, that the matter which composes the geological formations preëxisted as simple elements, in a gaseous form. Oxygen, which makes up fully one-half the weight of the solid parts of the earth, is and always was a gas in its free state. In regard to the remaining elements that enter into the composition of the rocks, such as silicon, aluminum, calcium, and sodium, they could not all have existed on the earth at the same time as melted liquids; for the same heat which would hold one in fusion would evaporate others. Some therefore must have been contained in the atmosphere as simple gaseous elements. Inasmuch as granite is beneath all the other formations, if we show that this must originally have been in a gaseous state, we show that every other material must have been at the same time in like condition.

The granite rocks are by far the most abundant terrestrial substance that we know of. Geologists assign to them a depth of not less than thirty miles. And still below them there is the same or nearly the same chemical substance in fusion, as the fact and analysis of volcanic products sufficiently prove. The compound which is in excess in all granite rocks is silica, the oxide of the element silicon. The varieties are formed chiefly by small percentages more or less of the oxides, alumina and magnesia. This silica, or quartz, as well as the other components of the igneous rocks, is what has been termed "burnt material." It is the product of a most complete and tremendous conflagration; for the oxidation of silicon is as much and as powerful a combustion as the oxidation or burning of coal. To accomplish this burning, every particle of the silicon must have been brought into contact with oxygen gas. This would have been simply impossible if the mineral element had always been in a melted mass of miles in depth; for this, if for no other reason, that the oxygen could never have got at it—certainly not, if it was covered by other solid or liquid substances. Or, if it were conceded that silicon ever formed the surface of the earth, then all other materials of what is now the crust must have been gases above it; and as nine-tenths of the elements in vapor are heavier than oxygen—many of them more than ten times as heavy—this gas could never have even touched this imaginary sea of silicon. The oxidation then was only possible in the regions of the atmosphere, where oxygen existed and abounded. There only, among the free-moving gases, could the incalculable amount of heat evolved in the combination be carried off.

We confidently assume therefore that the whole of this most abundant mineral element once existed in the atmosphere in the form of a high-heated gas; and that some time and somewhere, on the confines of the enormously extended sphere of vapors, there was found a current sufficiently cool to condense a portion of it. If the vapor of silicon follows the general rule, that the density of gases is in proportion to their atomic weights, then it was but a fraction heavier than oxygen, and therefore not far below it in the atmospheric strata. The unceasing commotion of the elements would soon have brought this first cloud-mist of silicon into contact with oxygen, to which it has a strong affinity under high heat. Oxidized, and in molten drops of silica, or crystals of quartz, this new-formed material commenced its descent toward the center of gravity—the first creation from the primordial elements. As it fell into the more heated regions below, it was probably soon evaporated, and the vapor rising carried up with it the heat taken up in the evaporation. It was again condensed, its heat given up, and it descended for another charge of the internal fires. This in all probability is the epitome of the process of world-cooling.

At last the showers of melted silex reached the liquid surface of the nucleus which the force of gravity and compression must have formed, at an early period of the nebulous globe, of less or greater extent about its center. From this period the increasing torrents of silica, intermingled with the silicates which were forming at the same time, poured down through the heavy vapors, and filled up the furlongs-deep of granite ocean. On this vast deposit, and at about this stage of the gradual cooling of the earth, began, we must suppose, the first hardening and crusting over of the surface, since at this point, near the close of the granite age, first commences the division of the earth's crust into varieties and layers more or less distinct, as also the upbearing of the heavy metals which, without this surface-hardening, could never have floated on any molten sea of minerals. The slow cooling of the granite masses beneath this crust and under the enormous atmospheric or other superincumbent pressure, conformed them to all the acknowledged conditions of the formation of the igneous rocks.

There is found in the different beds of the granitic rocks every proportion of the admixture of silica with the silicates of alum-

Plate IV.—TREE FERNS IN FERN TREE GULLY, HOBART, TASMANIA. See Page xv.

ina. It is as if chances as variable as winds and storms had regulated the production and mixture. There is every gradation in the texture of granite, from the fine-grained blocks of the quarry, to the coarse compacted breccia so common among bowlders. It is as if the deeper beds had slowly cooled under great compression and consequent immobility of the particles, while the superficial layers had been worked up and closely conglomerated at the surface. There are specimens of granite composed of massive angular crystals that seem as if they had been thrown together and cemented. It is again as if they were the congealed *débris* of some terrific hail-storm of quartz, mica, and feldspar.

After the greater part of the silicious minerals had been deposited, and the cooler exterior gases had thus been let down to a nearer vicinity with the heavier vapors, we find that the metals proper began gradually to condense and fall. Those which have no active affinities for the other elements were deposited in their native purity. Others took on the forms of oxides or sulphurets, according to their first exposures or strongest attractions. Among the first of these cloud-productions, the rock records tell us, were the scanty rainfalls of gold and platinum, and the more plentiful showers of silver and copper. Rivulets of native ores ran along the hardening crust, filling the veins and crevices, or mingling with the liquid quartz that was seaming the granite and gneiss.

Then from clouds of condensing iron vapor that must have burned and scintillated with indescribable magnificence, fell the thick heavy storms of the black lodestone, the blood-red hematite, or the dark yellow pyrites. Possibly storm-centers were established, over which the cyclones were held concentrated and often repeated, by force of intense magnetic attractions which have left their traces in almost every iron-mine.

Following these, at times and places, came on the great snow-storms of the waxy flakes of zinc-blende and the pearly calamine, the red oxide or the white carbonate of lead and the gray galena, the beautiful crystals of the tin-stone, the gray plumes of antimony, and all the tinted and varied forms of the less abundant ores and alloys. Meanwhile through all the long ages of these metallic precipitations, there was continually falling over all the earth the white impalpable powder of lime—the element calcium condensed into cloud-mist and oxidized in the upper regions of the air.

These were the great chemical periods of our world; when the cooling vapors of the swollen sphere were struggling to unite and hold fast the embrace against the antagonist force of heat; when the conjoined elements were pouring down their fiery torrents, and the air was laden with the falling cinders and ashes of aërial conflagrations; when the vast workshop of Nature was forming and sorting its raw materials.

We do not however wish to be understood as insisting that all these minerals and metals came down in just the form and order that we have indicated, or that they were regularly deposited and left the orderly traces that perhaps our hasty sketch would seem to imply. There were unquestionably constant and profound commotions in the atmosphere, and the commingling of the most diverse elements. There were doubtless repeated meltings and chemical recombinations at the surface, and the rending and comminuting of the newly-formed crust by internal forces. The history of the earth's irregularities and disorders forms the greater part of geology.

But what we do claim as certain is, that all the constituents of the outer shell of our globe existed at one time as elemental gases above a sea of matter that was held in condensation by superincumbent pressure; that as the earth gradually cooled, these gases condensed somewhat in the order, inversely of their fusibility, and directly of their nearness to the outer bounds of the atmosphere, and fell to the surface like rain and snow from water-clouds; that they formed chemical combinations at the instant of their condensation or subsequently, according to the power of their affinities or the elements that were present; and that, excepting the more recent displacements by mechanical forces, they now lie in the earth as they fell from the heavens.

The silica and silicates which form the base and by far the greater part of the earth's crust, became oxides of their several eelement because oxygen was the superabundant gas in the earth's composition. There have been worlds made up apparently without oxygen; for the meteorites, which must be regarded as sample specimens from some stranger world however they may have been dispatched to us, are mostly composed of pure crystalline and malleable iron, which could have cooled into that condition only where there was no oxygen nor carbonic gases. If chlorine had been our superabundant gas, the silicon would perhaps quite as readily have united with it, and formed as stable a compound as with oxygen. But the product, instead of being the hardest of rocks, would have been a liquid, very much resembling water, a little heavier and nearly as volatile as the common ethers. In this case there could have been no dry land, and no living beings that we can conceive of. Eternal clouds and storms would have covered the face of the surging and boundless ocean.

Hitherto in our accounts of terrestrial phenomena, water has played no part. It is probable that it was early formed, and in the condition of vapor or steam diffused through the upper air. In this state it bears the highest degree of heat that we can produce, without decomposition. Hydrogen is the lightest of all the gases, and unquestionably took its place on the outer limits of the atmosphere. There it was brought into contact with oxygen by the commotion of the elements, and converted into steam as fast as its lowering temperature allowed of the combination. As we might expect from the respective positions of the gases, all the hydrogen which fell to the portion of the earth in the making up of its constituents was transformed into water-vapor. Hydrogen is found in no other combination that cannot be traced directly or indirectly to the decomposition of water.

The aqueous vapor being thus formed and lying in the upper and cooler regions of the air, it began after a time to condense and fall toward the earth. Meeting with warmer strata as it descended, it was soon evaporated and sent up with a load of heat that was set free by a recondensation. Then another and perhaps lower descent, for another charge of heat. Thus on the outskirts of the air, water-vapor was coöperating in the work of the heavier vapors of the interior. It was the great fire-carrier of the globe during all the time of the contraction and consolidation of the lower elements. When every thing else that was condensable had turned to dust and ashes and fallen to the earth, at last the waters reached the parched and scorious surface and commenced that grand series of aqueous transformations which made a new earth for the indwelling of life.

In the first place it was necessary that the upper crust should be hydrated, precisely as lime is slacked by pouring water on it. The material which had been last deposited was in reality this same caustic lime. In its lower deposits it was gradually intermixed with the sillicious compounds, until these latter formed without admixture the masses which are now the stratified granitic rocks. As every one knows, the slacking of quicklime absorbs a large quantity of water which is incorporated into the solid as water of crystallization, and great heat is evolved with enlargement of bulk. The pure silicious rocks do not take up water in this way, being what is termed anhydrous. All the rock-materials then that lie above the granite, must at some time have undergone this hydrating, reheating and swelling process. We accordingly find that all those strata which have remained in their original position, such as gneiss, the mica schists, the clay-slates, and the primary limestones, have the appearance of having been subjected to great heat and pressure, after having been acted upon by water and steam. In some instances they have been partially melted, in others strangely contorted, and in others partly dissolved. Under certain circumstances hot water and steam will dissolve small portions of silica, and if charged with carbonic-acid gas will dissolve lime quite freely.

The rainfalls of the primeval ages must have been fully saturated with the oxide of carbon which has played an important part in the making up of the strata. In this form it carbonated all the limestones, carried all the building-materials to the shell and coral land-makers, and furnished the supplies for the immense magazines of the hydro-carbons. And after all this there was enough carbonic-acid gas left in the air for the enormous vegetation of the coal-beds. But it was necessary that the carbon of this gas should be laid away in the earth in some form, either burnt or unburnt, before air-breathing life could come to any perfection. The solidifying of the carbonic oxide was the latest and slowest of the atmospheric changes.

It appears that during the epoch of the hydration of the lime-rocks there occurred periods when the waters were gathered into seas, and were sufficiently cooled for the existence of marine infusoria, mollusks, and corals. Life in some form has been ever ready to spring into being the moment that conditions and surroundings were suitable for it. After the deposition in those temporary oceans of considerable thicknesses of Cambrian or Silurian strata mixed with organic remains, some rent or upheaval has let the waters down to new beds of unslacked material, which have heated and as it is termed metamorphosed those first fossiliferous deposits.

The subsequent changes which the earth's crust has undergone — aqueous, volcanic, and organic — the working up of the conglomerates and sandstones, the depositing of the deep-sea beds, the overflowing of the traps and lavas, the storing away of the carboniferous treasures, are all the story of every hand-book of geology, and pertain no more to one theory than another of the origin of the rocks. When the quarries of the igneous rocks were once made and opened up to aqueous operations, the after-work was merely mechanics and masonry.

We have heretofore assumed that the gases which originally composed the aërial envelope of the earth, took up separate positions therein according to their specific gravities. This might seem to be controverted by experiments on the diffusion of gases, in which those of very different weights, as chlorine and hydrogen, will intimately commingle, even against gravity, when brought into contact. This may be true in the narrow compass of laboratory experiments, and yet not apply to any considerable thicknesses of the gases. Such a diffusion of one mile in depth of chlorine would be equal to lifting up to the hydrogen a shell of solid iron two feet thick. Whether we explain the distinguishing principle of the constitution of gases as a mutual repulsion of their molecules, or according to a late theory, as an incessant motion and clashing of atoms, there is nothing in either to warrant the supposition of the lifting or overcoming any considerable weight in the diffusion of gases. Under the first theory, diffusion to a limited extent would be accounted for by the small residuum of chemical or cohesive attraction that would remain between the atoms when separated as they are in the gases; and under the last theory, by the mechanical impulsion of the molecules, through their hitting against each other. Evidently it is a principle which operates only within narrow limits and in the lower temperatures of the gases. The sun gives no indications of such a commingling of its gaseous elements. Spectrum analysis, when applied to its outer edges, shows first hydrogen, then the vapors of sodium and magnesium, and lastly those of calcium and iron. The same fact and order of position are found to exist in the more condensed layers of the sun spots.

We have also further assumed that the elements in their gaseous states have specific gravities corresponding to their atomic weights. It is well known that all gases, whether simple or compound, at the same temperature and pressure, and not near to a condensing point or other change of state, contain precisely the same number of molecules in the same volume. Therefore it necessarily results that equal measures of the different gases should have weights corresponding to the weights of the molecules of which they are composed. Thus the atom of oxygen is sixteen times as heavy as that of hydrogen; therefore a cubic foot of oxygen gas will weigh sixteen times as much as a cubic foot of hydrogen gas. This is found to be experimentally true of all the gases that can be measured or weighed. The apparent but not real exceptions are, that in arsenic and phosphorus two atoms of the element unite to form one molecule of the gas, thus making it twice as heavy as it would be according to the general rule; while in the case of mercury and cadmium, the atom divides into two in forming their vapors. Hence we are not absolutely sure in regard to the vapor-molecule, and therefore vapor-density, of such elements as carbon, silicon, and calcium, which chemists have not been able to volatilize. But there is every probability, both from analogy and the position in which some of them are found in the photosphere of the sun, that the vapors of nearly all of them correspond strictly to their combining numbers. The following table therefore will show the relative positions in the atmospheric strata, of some of the most important elements, with the weights of their atoms in hydrogen units, their vapor-densities compared with air, and the solid specific gravities of some of them as compared with water:

GASES.	Atomic Weights. H = 1.	Sp. gr. of Gas. Air = 1.	Sp. gr. of Solid. Water = 1.
Hydrogen	1	.069	....
Carbon	12	.828	2.09
Nitrogen	14	.972	....
Oxygen	16	1.105	....
Sodium	23	1.59	.98
Magnesium	24	1.66	1.74
Aluminum	27.5	1.90	2.60
Silicon	28.5	1.97	2.40
Sulphur	32	2.22	2.
Chlorine	35.5	2.44	1.33
Potassium	39	2.69	.86
Calcium	40	2.76	1.58
Iron	56	3.86	7.80
Copper	63.5	4.39	8.96
Mercury	200÷2	6.97	13.60
Silver	108	7.47	10.53
Gold	196.5	13.57	19.34
Platinum	198	13.66	21.50

The atomic weight of any substance, simple or compound, multiplied into the specific gravity of hydrogen (.069) will give the specific gravity of that substance in gaseous form as in the above table, and which ought very nearly to agree with that found by actually weighing the gas when that is practicable.

It will be noticed from this table that the elements were arranged in positions most suitable for their combination and deposition, both in geological order and in the probable order of their condensation from vapors. Oxygen and silicon, which doubtless composed more than four-fifths of the entire bulk of the gases, were separated from each other only by the elements that were needed to make up the silicates. Their compound, silica, is involatile, and even infusible by itself, under any degree of heat that we can command. The same is true of lime and the earlier-formed silicates. Therefore it is impossible to decide from their volatility which of these substances would have first condensed and reached the surface. But as the vapor of silica when formed would still be of nearly the same specific gravity (2.07) with silicon (1.97), and would still separate by its immense volume the oxygen from the calcium below, we may suppose that in any case the silica would have to be condensed and deposited, in greater part at least, before lime, the oxide of calcium, could be formed.

Along with silica were formed and deposited the silicates of alumina—mica and feldspar; then the partially fusible silicates of magnesia, lime, and iron—hornblende, augite, and talc. Then followed a numerous order of complex silicates, in which the above-named ingredients are varied by small proportions of manganese, soda, strontia, zirconia, and many other mineral bases. With and after these, was produced the lime-deposit, the last of the minerals. The metallic vapors, which were all heavier than the mineral, were condensed and deposited chiefly during the later silicate period, and somewhat in the inverse order of their volatility, but locally and irregularly, as results of great perturbations or storms in the air.

It will further be seen from the last column of the table, that in no respect are the materials of the earth deposited according to their specific gravities as solids or liquids. There is in the superincumbent rock and ore masses, no order of position that would indicate in the least the floating buoyancy of the lighter substances. Therefore their arrangement cannot be referred to any origin from liquid conditions; and the only other theory is that of their gaseous origin.

There are many apparent anomalies in the deposition of the metallic and mineral compounds, which may require much study and perhaps further knowledge and experiment for their explanation. Thus there is in one place a carbonate of lime—marble—and in another a sulphate of lime—gypsum. There are in certain localities sulphuret ores of iron or copper, and in others oxide ores; while the metals of greatest vapor density, as mercury, lead, bismuth, and antimony, are found almost exclusively in sulphuret ores. It will perhaps eventually be established that sulphur was combined wholly into sulphuric acid gas, as carbon was originally combined only into carbonic acid gas; that both were brought to the surface of the earth in solution with rain-water; and that sulphur in this form united with the metals which had failed to be oxidized upon their condensation in the air, and also sulphated the quick-lime in the earth which had not been carbonated by the carbonic solution. Then there is the exceptional production in nature of the chloride of sodium—common salt. Apparently in this one instance the oxide is the less stable compound.

But if, as we have endeavored to prove, there is a necessity of accounting in accordance with this theory for the various compounds and phenomena with which geology makes us familiar, then it is in the highest degree essential that experiment and research be prosecuted in this new field. And there must be no hesitation in accepting the conclusions to which they lead. Should the nebulous origin of one planet be thus established by internal and inductive evidence, then the nebular theory of the formation of worlds, which has heretofore been received as only a provisional hypothesis, must be accepted as having a scientific basis. If the earth has once been a self-luminous body, in all respects excepting size like the sun of to-day, it follows from anology that the other planets have likewise been minor suns which have become extinguished by the burning out of their materials. To an observer on any unseen world among the stars, our sun should have appeared in those times as a brilliant double or multiple star, around which nine lesser companions have shone out for a season, and then one after the other folded themselves up in darkness.

Furthermore the study of this subject may throw light on many cosmical problems—may tell us in earth-periods if not in years, how old the sun is when his glowing vapors begin to condense into dark clouds, and perhaps too something of his future prospects as a luminary. It is remarkable that the spectrum has never shown any indications of free oxygen in the atmosphere of the sun. Is not the absence of this element further corroborated by the fact that the solar spots which, there is evidence to believe, are condensing clouds of iron and calcium, do not glow with fierce burning as they would if oxygen were present? Does not the enormous volume of the sun's uncombined hydrogen indicate that it has not found there the element of its strongest affinity? And is there not reason to believe that the heat and light supplies of our great luminary will last all the longer for the absence of this most extravagant fire-generator?

Again, the four outer planets of our system have specific gravities varying but little from that of water. Considering central condensation from pressure, it is probable that they are not more dense than they would be if composed of the lightest compound substance that we know of. If oxygen had been there in excess, it would long ago have burned and condensed their elements, whatever they might be, into most stable and solid forms. This gas therefore cannot have formed any considerable part of their constitution. Is it not then a probable supposition that these distant planets are composed of some non-combining and inactive elements like nitrogen, and that, undisturbed by combustions or elemental agitations, they have quietly stratified into gaseous worlds, retaining in great part their original heat? So far as the spectroscope gives any indications of their constitution, it shows them to be composed of gases unknown in the earth.

As we have stated, the four outer planets are very nearly of the specific gravity of water; then come the innumerable asteroids, filling the place of a missing planet, and of which we know but little; then three planets that are five and a half times as dense as water; and lastly, Mercury, over eight times as dense. Does not this increasing density of the planets from the outer to the inner, imply that they have been successively formed on the exterior of one great parent globe, and received each its proportion in the main of denser elements, as it was later born? That this effect should appear somewhat in groups of the planets, is owing probably to the absence or excess of oxygen among their components.

But if this is so, what shall we say of hydrogen, the lightest of all the gases, which seems to be most abundant the nearer to the center of the system? To explain this notable exception, might we conjecture that hydrogen is a more recent production than the worlds themselves? It has been observed time and again to burst up from the nethermost regions of the sun with inconceivable force, as if it were the pent-up product of a volcano, and to throw up columns of its flaming gas, in one case 200,000 miles high. And these great outbursts of hydrogen are always the precursors of the dark sunken spots in the photosphere. How came this almost imponderable ether to be imprisoned in the deep craters of the sun, if it is not a product that is constantly forming in the solar caldron?

But it is easier to ask questions than to answer them. And I will close, in the fear of having already been thought too free with the scientific imagination.

THE GENESIS OF WORLDS;

Or, World Creations.*

The New-World pioneers of the sixteenth century, when as first comers they looked on the sea-worn shores and giant forests of New England, had in reality no compelling reason for believing in the veritable old age of this new-found land. They had no "first order of proof" that the shores were not recently upheaved there for them to land upon, and with the growth of the centuries on them for the purpose of testing the manhood that was soon to reclaim them. But I think those sturdy adventurers, if they stopped at all to consider of scientific doubts, were not long in deciding that the scene before them was conformable to the laws and processes of nature, and therefore must have been the slow growth of time.

In like manner, the geologist, looking into the bowels of the earth and finding here and there the remains of a tree or a saurian, presumes that they once lived and grew in the same localities, and were buried and petrified under the rock-grindings of after-ages. But he really has no absolute proof of any such thing. They may have been created in the fossil state and laid away in the strata on the same day the earth was made. But I think the scientist, knowing laws of nature by which, with sufficiently long periods of time, all these geological results might have been gradually brought about, is justified in believing that they too were the slow product of nature and of time.

So we, finding that the world has certainly at some time been subjected to a heat at least sufficient to volatilize nearly every

---

*Published in Popular Science Monthly, April, 1877.

known substance, and that there are laws of nature by which, through periods of time immensely long, the earth and the planets might have been rolled up from a gaseous nebula and bowled off in their mighty revolutions, have just as much right to say that it was so, as we have to say that the American forests grew, or that the Triassic beds were deposited.

Geology has proved that the earth, up to the primary rocks, was once a molten mass. The crystalline structure of the unstratified rocks compels to this conclusion; for minerals insoluble in water can only become crystallized in large masses by cooling from a state of fusion. If then the earth was once an incandescent globe of melted rocks—for everything above the granite beds must then have been in a state of vapor—it is not unreasonable to suppose that it may have existed prior to that time in a still more highly heated condition—even volatilized and diffused through space as rare and attenuated gases; for this is the condition which all matter assumes under sufficient degrees of heat. In fact we must either suppose that the earth was created as a fiery liquid globe, for which we have no warrant, or we must follow back to the time when its vapors were scattered in space, unreflecting and impenetrable to light—when the earth was "without form and void, and darkness was upon the face of the deep."

Let us start then with that condition of things which is now very generally conceded must once have existed—the diffusion of matter in a nebulous form throughout all space. Calculations easily made show that the nebula must have been of extreme tenuity—such that the few grains taken up on the point of a knife-blade must have been expanded to fill several cubic miles. A heat so powerful—for we know of no other force which could thus hold apart the atoms of matter—would doubtless be sufficient to resolve every known substance into its simplest elementary constituents, perhaps into a very few primordial elements; for chemists are far from being satisfied that they have arrived at the ultimate forms of matter in their list of sixty-five elements. But however this may be, we know that the atoms, whatever they were, must have been held so far apart that no combinations could possibly have existed. Neither were they drawn more in one direction than another by their mutual attractions, for they were equally diffused through all space. Therefore heat, the great repulsive force, had overcome all the forces of attraction—cohesion, chemical affinity, and gravity.

Between such mighty contending forces we can hardly imagine a state of perfect equilibrium. Immense currents and worldwide surgings must be the long-continued if not the permanent condition of this state of things, especially if we conceive it brought about by natural causes. More condensed portions of nebulous matter would be formed—sections of space larger or smaller in which the forces of attraction counterbalanced those of repulsion. Each such section would then have its center of gravity, around which all the currents within its influence, by the law of the composition of forces, must eventually unite in one. This one flowing ever around and slowly toward the center, like a ball rolling down an inclined plain, goes faster and faster, until the centrifugal overbalances the centripetal force, and a part separates completely from the inner mass. Thus a ring is formed revolving around a central nucleus. Unless perfectly equipoised and of homogeneous material, this ring would sooner or later break up into a number of globes, which by the superior attraction of the largest, would ultimately coalesce into one. This globe still contracting might throw off satellites or moons, while the nucleus, also continuing to contract, would throw off other planets, all revolving in nearly the same plane and in the same direction. All these processes are in perfect accord, not only with the conditions of the heavenly bodies so far as discovered, but with known natural laws. Many of them have been successfully imitated on a small scale in experimental illustrations, as in the rapid rotation of oil suspended in water.

We have here given only the simple outlines of the famous "nebular hypothesis" of Laplace. In later years the discovery of nebulæ in the heavens in all stages of world-formation, the evidence of the spectroscope on the unformed material of the universe, and other proofs, have compelled for the proscribed hypothesis a recognized place in science. We do not stop to consider these subjects more fully because it is the purpose of this article to inquire chiefly concerning the forces that would be engaged in such a process of evolution; and firstly, how from the preponderance of the repellent forces holding matter in universal diffusion, there came the final mastery of the aggregating forces ever concentrating, combining, and working up the materials of the universe.

The first of the operations which comes to our notice in the progress of this evolution is the condensation of the gases. This according to all experience ought to evolve heat; but instead, we find only that the flow of the currents—the motion of the masses—is proportionately increased. Is there a connection of cause and effect between these phenomena?

All motion that we are familiar with requires the expenditure of heat. The combustion of coal supplies motion to the steam-engine. The evaporation of water by the sun's heat causes the rain-clouds and the mill-streams. The oxidation of certain elements in the food we eat is the combustion which supplies our bodies with power of motion. Recent discoveries have shown, not only that motion is heat transformed, but that to produce a certain quantity of motion an invariable certain quantity of heat is required.

Again, the cessation of motion evolves heat. It is well known that by skillful blows with the hammer a cold iron bar can be made red-hot. Two wheels revolving in opposite directions and touching at the circumference, become highly heated; and factories have been warmed solely by this transfer of motion into heat. Friction is but another name for the arresting of motion, and as we well know always produces heat. There is also here the same equivalence as in the other case. The stoppage of motion evolves just the amount of heat that was required to produce that motion.

The greatest triumph of modern science is the splendid induction that all the forces are correlative and indestructible. Not an impulse of motion, of light, or heat, or any force, is ever lost. It may be communicated from one body to another, or transmuted into some other form of force, or become for a time latent or imperceptible; but it always exists, and is reclaimable back again into the same in mode and quantity from which it started.

The grandest exemplification of these truths will be found in what we are now considering, the origin of the celestial revolutions. The condensation of gases gives out heat in direct proportion to the contraction of volume. The attraction of gravitation, not only between masses but between all particles of matter, increases in the inverse square of the diminishing distance. From these two principles it can be mathematically shown that in the contraction of each great world-nebula, heat would be set free in the precise proportion of the increase of atomic attraction; or in other words that it would take the exact amount of heat-force that had been released, to separate the atoms again to their original distance apart. But in this instance the heat-force is not really set free; it is transformed into the motion of the mass from which it came. Instead of holding the atoms apart, the work which it now has to do under the form of motion is to prevent the masses from falling into each other. It is this motion—the celestial revolutions—which keeps the worlds apart, and allows each to work out its destiny under the aggregating forces, without any interference from any other. Up to a certain point of condensation, which is previous to the radiation of heat into space, if this motion were at any time stopped, it would be resolved into just the amount of heat necessary to expand the mass again to its original dimensions.

The attractive forces, gravity, chemical affinity, and cohesion, whether these forces are many or one, are inherent properties of matter. Every atom has its definite capacity of attraction, which may be exercised or not according to circumstances. For it is evident that an attracting body may be at the same time drawing toward itself a million other like bodies, or none at all, without change of its power of attraction. In like manner the magnet has a definite lifting power whether it is actually holding up a weight or not. If this attribute of matter is not operative, or but partially so, it is because heat, or motion, or some repellent force, is holding the atoms or the masses at a distance from each other, and thus opposing the exercise of it.

The sum however of the attracting power belonging to the world of matter is as fixed as the quantity of matter itself. And I think it is in the highest degree probable that there is in the universe precisely enough repulsive force or heat to overcome all this inherent power of attraction. When all motion of the masses and of the atoms is resolved into repulsive energy, and brought to bear on the elements of matter, I imagine that they must completely fill the bounds or the infinity of space. Then if there were perfect equilibrium or rest, no further changes or effects could ever be manifested. Such a condition however could probably never result from natural causes, for the time necessary to the perfect balance of the forces must be as infinite as the space through which they extend, and to "set bounds to space" has puzzled philosophy from a very ancient date. If on the other hand the universe of matter was created in a state of absolute rest, we have the further and necessary provision that the Spirit of God moved on the face of his creation, and thus unbalanced the forces. But the equilibrium once broken, in whatever manner, from that moment evolution must inevitably proceed. For let there be an overbalancing of the aggregating force in ever so little or much, an equivalent of the opposing force must thereafter find some other work to do, and the field is effectually given up to the mighty agency that combines and constructs and brings order out of chaos.

So long and in proportion as the forming worlds continue to contract their dimensions, the rotations and revolutions increase in their velocity. Thus in the rapid and ever-speeding movements of the heavenly bodies there is stored up the ever-increasing reserve of heat that is liberated from the great contest with gravity. But in the progress of concentration there comes a time when the atoms of matter have approached each other sufficiently near for other forces of attraction, equally correlative of heat, to come into play—chemical affinity between molecules of unlike nature, and cohesion between those of like kind. Under the latter term are included all the changes of state which are the result of cooling, as liquefaction and solidifying. By these attractions heat is set free in such abundance and under such conditions that it cannot be stored away in the motion of the masses. It is then, probably for the first time, that heat becomes a wave force and is radiated into space as light and radiant heat—not however lost, for that is impossible, but moving ever onward and outward to the day and place of its final reclamation.

Our own solar system has already progressed far in this stage of aggregation. All the planets and satellites have become crusted over, and have ceased almost entirely to radiate heat. But the sun, the great central body, the one which should last of all become cold, is still in active combustion or chemical combination. Immense quantities of light and heat are still radiating from its surface—so immense that the little fraction which our earth catches as it flies through space, gives us all the motion and life and beauty which we enjoy. But the sun is not even now the glowing orb that once it was, as the rock-records of our globe testify. Its bright radiance is slowly but surely fading. Those huge black incrustations, often twice as large as the whole surface of the earth, that float awhile on its photosphere and then are suddenly broken up, were not always there. And if they have grown upon it, the uncomfortable conviction arises that they will continue to grow and darken more and more its life-giving face. Old age is certainly being written on the solar brow. It may be millions of years hence—for time is not one of the economies of nature—but the period will surely come when light and heat will both have departed from the sun, as they once ceased to be radiated from the earth and the planets and the numerous stars that have gone out within the records of astronomy. A pall of darkness will gradually overspread the universe as one by one the stars of the firmament shall fade away and sink into gloomy lifeless sleep. A day in the grand calendar of creation has passed, and a night has followed, cold and dark as the tomb of expiring nature.

But is there no awakening, no morrow to this night of the universe? Is the contest over, and never to be renewed? For answer, let us seek out in this case, as we did once before, the condition and movements of the great contending forces. Those of attraction have now in each world expended their utmost possible energy, and are holding all the forms of matter combined and compacted in a cold and rigid embrace. The forces of repulsion have entirely abandoned the contest, and are either vibrating through the unknown realms of space, or are locked up in the swift and complicated motions of the heavenly bodies. It is probable that by far the greater part of the repulsive forces thus exists in the form of motion. It has been estimated, no doubt with a near approximation to truth, that if by any means the earth could be suddenly arrested in its rapid course, its mass would thereby be raised to the enormous temperature of $23,360°$ Fahr.—a heat sufficient to vaporize and dissipate every known substance. If then, as would be the case, it should fall into the sun, this heat would be increased by the fall four hundred fold. Now it makes no difference in the aggregate evolution of heat whether this cessation of motion is sudden or gradual; and if we can find in nature any agencies tending to retard the revolutions of the planetary bodies, they must inevitably sooner or later fall into the sun. In such a case it can hardly be doubted that we have found a cause sufficient to produce again the disintegration and diffusion of matter.

The wave-theory of light and radiant heat presupposes the existence of an ethereal medium pervading all space. It must be a medium of material atoms held in equipoise by a balance of forces, for it is evident there could be no wave-motion unless there was something to move, and something too having the attributes of matter in a state of extreme mobility or fluidity. There is no other conceivable way by which light could reach us from the sun and stars except through this all-pervading form of matter. And if there is a material medium, of whatsoever exceeding tenuity it may be, it must present something of resistance to everything passing through it. It resists the passage of light eight minutes in 90,000,000 miles, thus proving its materiality by its resistance to force, which is one of the definitions of matter. If one could conceive of any force passing through an absolute vacuum, it could only be conceived of as passing instantaneously, for there is absolutely nothing to detain it. Again heat and its allied forces are only effects, and the subject is and can be only matter. There is no physical truth better established than that the forces can exist only where matter is in some form. It is not essential that this form of matter be subject to the ordinary laws of gravitation. The probability is that it differs entirely from anything that we have experience of. It would seem that the atoms composing the ether of space, instead of attracting each other like those of ordinary matter, must repel each other. At least this supposition would account for what there is remarkable in connection with the ethereal medium. But whatever theories we may adopt in regard to it, this is certainly true, that the revolutions of the heavenly bodies must be continually opening passages through it, and that a certain part of the force of those revolutions must be expended in pushing it aside. The centrifugal force is thus lessened, and the bodies are drawn nearer to the sun. In consequence, the periods of their revolutions are shortened. This has not as yet become noticeable in the case of the planets, from the fact that the slow contraction of their bulk by the loss of internal heat through volcanoes, thermal springs, and other sources, has the contrary effect of increasing the velocity of revolution, and thus counterbalancing the retardation by friction. The fact that the two effects are thus nearly counterbalanced, proves the retardation, for otherwise we know that the acceleration would be observable. In the case however of the light cometary bodies, it has been shown that they suffer a very considerable retardation in their passage through space. Encke's comet formerly came regularly back into the field of the earth's orbit once in every three years, but with a period shortened six hours each time. The whole planetary regions seem to be filled with collections of matter—star-dust and meteorites. They are all revolving about the sun in eccentric orbits, and are doubtless slowly circling toward it. The zodiacal light is supposed to be only an immense aggregation of this material. Thus the thickening stratum, as these strange bodies draw near to the sun, shows that they are all slowly gathering to that great center of attraction.

The evident effect of the fall of any of the planets into the sun would be the diffusion of highly-heated vapors far out into the spaces that surround it—probably far enough to reach the next outlying planet, and thereby to increase its retardation and hasten its fall into the mighty caldron. So one by one the planets dissolve and their elements fill the void of space. The expanding gases catch up the waves of radiant heat that have long been wandering from planets and suns and the nebula is again seething and surging with its mighty contending forces. Sun-system reaches out to sun-system, and star-galaxy mingles with star-galaxy, till through all the abysmal depths matter is again "without form and void, and darkness is upon the face of the deep." Chaos has returned once more, again to be breathed upon by the Omnipotent Spirit that reforms and recreates.

ON THE STRUCTURE OF ATOMS.

Chemists are now quite generally disposed to admit that the original and ultimate form of all matter is some single simple substance, and that what we call the atoms or simple elements, numbering now about sixty-five, are only different manifestations of this universal matter, depending on the quantity combined and the degree or complexity of its condensation. This theory accords so well with the first principles of chemical science, and with the tendency of all inductive knowledge, which is to bring facts and particular phenomena under more simple and general laws and conditions, that there is scarcely a writer on chemistry who has not somewhere shown a leaning toward this greatest of all generalizations—the unification of matter.

This field of inquiry is the great border land between the known and the unknown. As such, it has been so long the batting ground of the metaphysicians, that one feels almost like offering an apology for attempting to introduce a little common sense, or at least common language, into it. Still I have the courage to think that some clear reasoning may be held and some pertinent facts presented looking towards this great simplification. I will at least attempt to find how far we can go in this direction without abstruse speculation.

It is a well known principle of chemistry that all true gases, under the same quantity of heat and pressure, have precisely the same number of molecules or ultimate particles in the same volume. A cubic foot of oxygen or hydrogen or carbonic acid or any other gas contains in each case exactly the same number of atoms or molecules. Therefore the weights of the cubic feet of all the gases will correspond to the weights of their molecules.

A cubic foot of oxygen will weigh just sixteen times as much as a cubic foot of hydrogen, because the atom of oxygen is sixteen times heavier than the atom of hydrogen. It is immaterial then whether we say two atoms or two measures of hydrogen unite with one of oxygen to form water. In this case the three volumes of the original gases are condensed in the combination into two volumes of water-vapor or steam. If we were to suppose that these measures were cubic inches, and that each one contained 1,000 atoms, then the case would stand in this wise: 2,000 atoms of hydrogen have combined with 1,000 atoms of oxygen, and these 3,000 have formed 2,000 molecules of water-gas. Each molecule of the water therefore contains one atom of hydrogen and one-half an atom of oxygen. The oxygen atom has divided itself into two, and the hydrogen has not divided.

Let us take another instance. Three atoms of hydrogen unite with one of nitrogen to form two molecules of ammonia. The compression in this case is four volumes into two. Of course each molecule of ammonia contains one and a half atoms of hydrogen and one-half atom of nitrogen. Both hydrogen and nitrogen have in this case divided their atoms into two. Again, one atom of hydrogen unites with one atom of chlorine to make two molecules of hydrochloric acid, each molecule of the latter containing one-half atom each of hydrogen and chlorine. Now one molecule of ammonia will unite with one molecule of hydrochloric acid to form two molecules of sal-ammoniac or muriate of ammonia. Evidently a molecule of the latter is composed in the following manner: $(\frac{3}{4}H. + \frac{1}{4}N) + (\frac{1}{2}H + \frac{1}{2}Cl)$; and here is the proof of it. Reducing the above to their atomic weights: $\frac{3}{4} + 3\frac{1}{2} + \frac{1}{2} + 8\frac{1}{4} = 13\frac{3}{4} =$ atomic weight of sal-ammoniac. Now, any given measure of air being called 1, the same measure of H. will weigh .069, which is called its specific gravity. The atomic weight of any gas multiplied into that decimal will give the specific gravity of that gas. Therefore $13\frac{3}{4}$ multiplied into .069, which is .92, is the calculated specific gravity of muriate of ammonia gas. This gas has been carefully weighed, and the observed specific gravity found to be .89. The two are considered to correspond within the limits of error.

Plate V.—MOURNING THE DEAD IN NEW ZEALAND. See Page xv.

Let us take one more example. Two molecules of ammonia, $2(1\frac{1}{2}H+\frac{1}{4}N)$, unite with one molecule of sulphuretted hydrogen, $(H+\frac{1}{6}S)$, to make three molecules of hydrosulphate of ammonia. Therefore a molecule of this latter substance is composed as follows: $(H+\frac{1}{3}N)+(\frac{1}{3}H+\frac{1}{6}S)$, that is, $1+4\frac{2}{3}+\frac{1}{3}+5\frac{1}{3}=11\frac{1}{3}$, its molecular weight. This multiplied into .069 makes .78, the calculated specific gravity, while the observed is .79.

In this manner we have found that the atom of hydrogen divides itself into halves, thirds, and quarters; that of nitrogen into halves and quarters, and that of sulphur into sixths. In like manner it can be shown (see table appended hereto) that chlorine subdivides into halves, thirds, and quarters, phosphorus into eighths, carbon into sixths, and nitrogen and oxygen into thirds. Thus we see that atoms are far from being the indivisible things which their name would imply and the chemical books assert. They can be "cut up" at least into twelfths, which is the common divisor of the fractions named above.

When simple elements combine chemically, as oxygen and hydrogen to form water, there is always a product entirely different from either of the components. Ordinary mixtures of the gases, as oxygen and nitrogen in the atmosphere, although to all appearance as intimately associated as chemical combinations, yet still retain all the properties of the ingredients. On the other hand, chemical compounds will not show a trace of the qualities of the original constituents. The atoms themselves have been broken up and rearranged. There has been a new distribution of original matter in the molecules, and an entirely new substance has come out of it.

The alotropic states of oxygen in ozone and antozone, as also those of phosphorus, sulphur, carbon and others, where the same simple substances under different circumstances present entirely different properties, can be explained only on the supposition that there is some change or rearrangement of the internal mechanism of the atoms themselves.

Light is supposed to be a wave motion passing through space, by means of an all-pervading ethereal medium, at the rate of 180,000 miles in a second. Each color of the spectrum has its own determinate length of wave, though all colors travel with the same speed, and together form white light. In every inch of the progress of light there would be 38,000 waves of red and 59,000 waves of violet, and intermediate numbers for every shade of the other and intermediate colors.

Now in the passage of white light through the gases or vapors of the simple elements, as is the case with the light from the sun, certain colors are absorbed or held back, and the spectroscope, which simply spreads light out into its component colors, shows just what colors each elemental gas retains, by the dark bands which cross the spectrum. This is an infallible test by which any gaseous element may be known whenever interposed before any luminous substance. Some of the elemental gases cut out but few bands of colors, others a great many. Hydrogen for instance has but four dark bands, while in the spectrum of the vapor of iron there have been counted something like a thousand bands. Now each of these numerous bands indicates that some infinitesimal portion of the atom of iron has the power or the freedom to vibrate exactly in unison with the rays thus absorbed, and that these particular vibrations of the light are communicated to parts of the iron atom instead of passing on their way unobstructed. But it is impossible to suppose that a single solid atom has the power to, and does thus actually vibrate in a thousand different periods at the same time. This power can only be conceived of as belonging to a thousand or more sub-atoms or portions of which the atom of iron may be composed.

But if the elemental gases are in a state of incandescence, that is are themselves emitting the light, as is shown in the volatilization of substances in the electric arc-light, then they send forth only the same rays which by the former supposition they absorbed. That is, four bright lines would be all the light we should get from incandescent hydrogen, while something like a thousand very fine bright lines would represent the light from glowing iron vapor. In this case the thousand portions of the iron atom which have the power to vibrate in the same periods with certain light-waves, are the only ones that when set in motion by high heat can communicate motions to the ether which come within the limits of luminiferous vibrations. Hence we have the law of Angström, that a gas when luminous emits rays of light of the same refrangibility as those which it has the power to absorb.

Heat, which is a vibrating movement of greater amplitude than light, affects the individual atom, not in its parts like light, but as a whole, as will be seen from the following remarkable property of substances, known as specific heat. In all substances whether solid, liquid, or gaseous, a given quantity of heat will raise the temperature of an equal number of atoms or molecules the same number of degrees. Thus 9 lbs. of water, 56 lbs. of iron, 118 lbs. of tin, 200 lbs. of mercury, warmed by the same amount of heat, would each cause the thermometer to rise exactly the same number of degrees. These numbers, as is well known, represent the relative weights of the molecules or atoms of these several substances, and of course the quantities given above must contain each the same number of molecules. Therefore the mode of motion, or the force, which we call heat affects all molecules or atoms alike, no matter how light or how heavy they may be. Now it is contrary to all the laws that we know of, for a force to move a heavy body as easily as a light one. Consequently we must suppose the atoms to be constructed on entirely different principles from ordinary aggregations of matter. It is probable that motion, perhaps the vortex motion of minute portions of the ethereal fluid of space, is all we can predicate of them.

In all substances, simple or compound, there is a degree of temperature at which the particles are suddenly released from all cohesive attraction, and at once have a tendency to fly away from each other. This is at the transition from a liquid to a gaseous state, and the degree of heat at which this change is operated is called the boiling point of each substance. At this point there is a change in the balance of the forces lodged in the molecule—they now repel instead of attracting each other. The changes must be in the forces inherent in the particles themselves, for all we have done by the increase of heat is to remove them a little further apart, when all at once they burst away and endeavor to separate from each other. It is as if the atoms were made up of two kinds of sub-atoms, one kind attracting and the other repelling all others. If the one kind attracted according to the inverse square of the distance, as is the case in the attraction of gravitation, and if the other kind repelled simply as the distance, which is the law of the gases and probably of all repellent forces, then of course in the separation of molecules composed of these two kinds, there would always be a point where the repellent force decreasing simply as the distance would overbalance the attracting force decreasing as the square of the distance.

In organic compounds there are numerous series which increase regularly in the complexity of molecules by the successive additions of CH_2—such as the alcohol, the ether, and the ethyl series. Now it is found that with a considerable degree of regularity the addition of each carbon atom raises the boiling point of the compound from fifty to sixty degrees, Fahr., while each hydrogen atom lowers it about ten degrees, the average of the CH_2 group being about thirty-five degrees rise. Although variable and depending somewhat on the other elements in the compound, yet this change in the boiling point is so constantly in one direction and so nearly uniform as to indicate conclusively that there is a law connecting the two occurrences. The evident meaning of this fact is that carbon adds to the cohesive force of molecules, while hydrogen takes away from it. The balance of the force in the carbon atom is an attraction, while in the hydrogen it is a repulsion. This is in accordance with the nature or properties of each. Carbon has never been volatilized or even fused by any heat that it is in the power of man to control. There is seemingly no principle of repulsion in it. On the other hand, hydrogen shows no signs of atomic cohesion; there is no force which can press it or freeze it into close enough contact to make it take the form of a liquid or solid. The principle of atomic attraction seems to be wholly absent from its units. Hydrogen is the most electro positive of all the elements, and as is well known the positive or vitreous electricity is that which makes all light bodies repel each other. While carbon stands at the head of the electro negative solid elements, which form of electricity makes light bodies attract each other. All the other elements vary in their electric properties between these two, and the fact that they do vary shows that they are composed in varying proportions of parts or substances that attract or repel.

There is indubitable evidence that the earth was once a mass of melted rock material. The crystalline structure of all the primitive rocks shows this. They could not have crystallized except they had been previously in a state of fusion. There is also evidence that in still earlier periods all the matter forming the earth's crust was in a gaseous state. In no other condition could all the silicon and calcium and every other mineral have become completely oxidized. The chemistry of the rocks is a complete vindication of the nebular hypothesis. The moon has gone through the same fiery ordeal, as the volcanic nature of its surface gives evidence. The planet Mars is exactly like the earth in all its main features, and in all probability reached this similitude through the same cycle of changes that the earth has gone through. The sun is to-day still in the later stages of its gaseous state. Iron, calcium, magnesium and sodium are still vapors on its heated surface. Every indication goes to show that all the bodies of our solar system were once in gaseous or nebulous conditions.

Now either the material substances composing each planet and satellite were created separate from all the others and around each one's own center of gravity, or else the matter of the whole system was once equally diffused through all the space comprised within the planetary orbits, with but one center of gravity.

In regard to the first alternative we must of course acknowledge that it is impossible to argue against the assertion of direct creation; because certainly the Creator could, if he had seen fit, have spoken into being every part of the universe in fully developed conditions. But inasmuch as he has not done so in any single instance that has been closely investigated, but has left his purposes to be worked out by the laws which he has ordained, so I maintain that if we can form a reasonable and probable theory of the formation of the planetary worlds out of a more general diffusion of nebular matter, we are fully authorized to adopt it.

The nebular theory of LaPlace does this so completely that every physicist feels that it is a true one, whether it can be absolutely proved or not.

If it is true, and the matter of our solar system was ever thus expanded to fill the planetary spaces, then this matter must have been very nearly homogeneous; that is, all its ultimate particles, however small, must have been of nearly the same weight or attractive force. For if it had consisted of atoms of much different weights, like those of our sixty-five elements, many of which are over two hundred times heavier than the lightest, then the densest must inevitably have collected at the center of the mass. There would have been a very great increase in the density of the planets according to their nearness to the sun. The outer ones would have been composed of hydrogen; the inner ones perhaps of the minerals lime, silica, &c., and the sun would probably have retained all the heavier metals, as silver, mercury, lead, gold, and platinum. It is almost inconceivable that the earth should have really had such a mixture of the lightest and densest of the elements, ranging in comparative weights from 1 up to 230, or that the sun should be surrounded by such immense volumes of hydrogen, the lightest of all the elements, while underlying it should be the vapors of sodium, magnesium, calcium, and iron, belonging to the category of lighter elements.

The supposition which most fully meets the requirements of the case we have been presenting, is that at least some of the lighter and simpler elements of each planet and satellite continued in some manner to be formed and brought out during the cooling and condensation of each body. It is a very bold speculation, but after all it is sometimes necessary to form what are called "working hypotheses," and then work up to them, and ascertain what there may be of truth in them.

It is now an almost every day occurrence with the astronomers to watch through the spectro-telescope the eruptions of hydrogen gas on the surface of the sun. Enormous volumes of this gas are frequently seen to burst up through the chromosphere and ascend with amazing velocity to a height sometimes of 200,000 miles. These outbursts often carry up with them the glowing vapors of iron, magnesium, &c., showing that they come from beneath these low-lying vapors. Schellen says (Spectrum Analysis, p. 306): "It appears that eruptions of hydrogen take place from the interior of the sun; their form and the extreme rapidity of their motion necessitates the hypothesis of a repulsive power, at work either at the surface or in the mass of the sun, which Respighi attributes to electricity." Now how could this hydrogen gas get down underneath the vapor of iron, which is fifty-six times heavier than it is, unless it was formed and molded there?

We are to suppose that electricity has everything to do with these tremendous outbursts; for whenever they occur there is instantly sent out from them such an electric disturbance that the minute portion which the earth picks up creates auroral displays, electric storms, and terrific cyclones. Now the little manifestation of electrical action which we have in our thunder storms, brings about the union of nitrogen with oxygen, forming the nitrous acid compounds in the air, and of nitrogen with hydrogen, forming ammonia which is almost always perceived in the air after a near stroke of lightning; and it also changes oxygen into the alotropic state of ozone. Now if our comparatively feeble electric actions are able to accomplish so much in the way of chemical combinations and changes, what must the inconceivably more powerful action in the sun be enabled to perform in the way possibly of atom formation? I do not think it unreasonable to suppose that it might originate the vortical whirl of ethereal particles, which some of our most distinguished scientists think constitutes the elemental atoms. They conclude from certain physical principles and analogies that all atoms are only vortices of infinitesimal quantities of the ethereal matter that pervades all space, similar to smoke rings, only in far more complicated patterns. It might be supposed that in such a tremendous electrical laboratory as the sun, immense numbers of these vortices of various patterns were evolved, but that only a few forms and combinations would be able to withstand the powerful repellent force of heat, or in other words that it was a case of the survival of the fittest; and as hydrogen is the simplest and lightest of all the atoms, it would naturally be the most abundantly formed or preserved, as we see is the case at present in the solar workshop.

APPENDIX.

The proof of the correctness of the following figures is the multiplication of atomic weights into .069, the specific gravity of hydrogen, making the calculated specific gravity of each substance, and the comparison of this with the gases as actually weighed. The divisions of the atoms in the examples given are as follows:

Hydrogen—$\frac{1}{2}$, $\frac{1}{8}$.   Chlorine—$\frac{1}{2}$, $\frac{1}{8}$, $\frac{1}{4}$.

Nitrogen—$\frac{1}{2}$, $\frac{1}{8}$, $\frac{1}{4}$.   Phosphorus—$\frac{1}{4}$, $\frac{1}{8}$.

Oxygen—$\frac{1}{8}$.   Sulphur—$\frac{1}{4}$.

Carbon—$\frac{1}{2}$, $\frac{1}{4}$.   Iodine—$\frac{1}{4}$.

For an atom to be divided into both thirds and quarters, it must also be divisible into twelfths, the least common divisor of those fractions.

(See table on opposite page.)

ON THE STRUCTURE OF ATOMS.

Chemical Substances.	Composition of Molecule.	Same Reduced.	Atomic Weights.	Same Reduced.	Calculated Sp.Gr.	Observed Sp.Gr.
Hydrogen,	H	H	1	1	.069	.069
Nitrogen,	N	N	14	14	.97	.97
Oxygen,	O	O	16	16	1.1	1.1
Carbon,	C	C	12	12		
Chlorine,	Cl	Cl	35.5	35.5	2.45	2.44
Phosphorus,	P	P	62	62	4.28	4.32
Sulphur,	S	S	32	32	2.21	2.22
Iodine,	I	I	127	127	8.76	8.72
Ammonia,	$\frac{3H+N}{2}$	$1\frac{1}{2}H+\frac{1}{2}N$	$1\frac{1}{2}+7$	8.5	.59	.59
Hydrochloric Acid,	$\frac{H+Cl}{2}$	$\frac{1}{2}H+\frac{1}{2}Cl$	$\frac{1}{2}+17\frac{3}{4}$	18.25	1.26	1.25
Muriate of Ammonia,	$\frac{4H+N+Cl}{4}$	$H+\frac{1}{4}N+\frac{1}{4}Cl$	$1+3\frac{1}{2}+8\frac{7}{8}$	13.4	.92	.89
Chlorous Anhydride,	$\frac{3O+2Cl}{3}$	$O+\frac{2}{3}Cl$	$16+23\frac{2}{3}$	39.66	2.74	2.65
Phosphorus Anhydride,	$P+3O$	$P+3O$	$62+48$	110	7.60	
Phosphuretted Hydrogen,	$\frac{\frac{1}{2}P+3H}{2}$	$\frac{1}{4}P+1\frac{1}{2}H$	$15\frac{1}{2}+1\frac{1}{2}$	17	1.17	1.18
Phosphoric Chloride,	$\frac{\frac{1}{2}P+5Cl}{4}$	$\frac{1}{8}P+1\frac{1}{4}Cl$	$7\frac{3}{4}+44\frac{3}{8}$	52.4	3.62	3.65
Hydriodate of Phosph'd H.,	$\frac{4H+\frac{1}{2}P+I}{4}$	$H+\frac{1}{8}P+\frac{1}{4}I$	$1+7\frac{3}{4}+31\frac{3}{4}$	40.5	2.79	2.77
Hydrosulphate of Ammonia,	$\frac{8H+2N+S}{6}$	$1\frac{1}{3}H+\frac{1}{3}N+\frac{1}{6}S$	$1\frac{1}{3}+4\frac{2}{3}+5\frac{1}{3}$	11.33	.78	.79
Carbonic Anhydride,	$\frac{C+2O}{2}$	$\frac{1}{2}C+O$	$6+16$	22	1.52	1.53
Anhydrous Carb. of Am.,	$\frac{6H+2N+C+2O}{6}$	$H+\frac{1}{3}N+\frac{1}{6}C+\frac{1}{3}O$	$1+4\frac{2}{3}+2+5\frac{1}{3}$	13	.897	.9

EVOLUTION THE RESULT OF CHEMICAL FORCES.

According to evolutional theories the first great act in the formation of the world we live in, was the dividing off from the central nebula of the quantity of matter that was to belong to the terrestrial quota. This apportionment in the case of the earth contained some sixty-five different elemental gases, of exceedingly varying weights and properties, and in singularly unequal proportions. Some of these gases were more than two hundred times heavier than the lightest one, measure for measure; while one of them was more abundant than all the rest put together, and others were present only in mere traces. It was a strange and anomalous mixture; yet when in process of time these gases came to cool down and to consolidate into their most stable forms, it was found that this seemingly chaotic assemblage of most diverse elements had really been apportioned out in exactly the quantities, and the different gases had been endowed with precisely such dispositions for uniting with each other, that were necessary to make up a solid and habitable world. Any material variation in those affinities or in the proportions of supply would have entirely prevented the formation of an encrusted, well watered, and air surrounded globe.

For instance, if the element oxygen had not been both the dominant and superabundant material, the world could never have had a hard and permanent shell about it. Oxygen, so far as we know, is the only substance in nature that could have burned up the silicon, calcium, aluminum, magnesium, and other minerals, and laid them away in the rocks that form the crust of the earth. Silicon and carbon are two elements that are always classed together as having quite similar properties, and according to all analogy their compounds with oxygen ought to have been very similar. But if the oxide of silicon, instead of being the most solid substance in nature, that is quartz, had been like the oxide of carbon, a permanent gas at all terrestrial temperatures, the earth could never have been a solid globe. Calcium and sodium are two entirely similar elemental substances. But the compounds of lime are durable insoluble rock strata, while those of soda are salts and alkalies. If calcium had behaved in any manner like its compeer, sodium, the earth would have been covered with desolate seas of caustic solutions. If nitrogen had not been an exception to all the other elements in its inert and neutral character, if it had united with oxygen as readily as any one of all the others, the world would have had only seas of nitric acid and an atmosphere of the fumes of ammoniacal salts. Thus we might go on enumerating a thousand other contingencies, one as probable as another, in the happening of any one of which, our world, so far as we can judge, could not have existed in a condition suitable to living beings.

Ages on ages before ever there was a drop of water formed or a vapor cloud had floated in space, two gases existed which had the property or potency, under certain contingencies which up to that time had never happened, of combining together and forming the substance we call water. They were two out of sixty-five elemental gases. They had no resemblance to, and no property in common with, the vapor of water, except the gaseous state. They existed in such quantity relatively to the rest, that when the time came for them to combine, water should be one of the most abundant materials that were to result from the various chemical combinations. Now so far as human knowledge and experiment can determine, there were thousands of possible contingencies against the production of this substance which apparently alone makes this world or any world inhabitable. The union of oxygen with hydrogen, instead of being the most inert and neutral substance in nature, might just as well have been like that of oxygen with sulphur or phosphorus or nitrogen, or like that of hydrogen with chlorine or iodine or bromine, powerful and destructive acids. It might just as well have been like the compound of oxygen and carbon, a permanent gas, or oxygen and any of the minerals, a permanent solid at all ordinary temperatures. The chemical union of hydrogen and nitrogen is ammonia, of hydrogen and chlorine is hydrochloric acid, of hydrogen and sulphur is hydrosulphuric acid, and so on through a long list, all suffocating and destructive gases. Now all the compounds of hydrogen with any other element except oxygen, when they do freeze, which is only at very low temperatures, turn into solids that are heavier than their liquids and sink in them as fast as formed. So likewise all the compounds of oxygen with any other base except hydrogen, follow the general law of contraction in bulk through all stages of cooling. But water when cooling, as is well known, commences to expand from a few degrees above freezing, and the ice that is formed always floats on the surface of the waters.

I have stood on the brink of the great surging fountain of liquid lava in the volcano of Kilauea in the Sandwich Islands, and have seen it quiet down and freeze over like a lake of water, turning from glowing red to black. After a few moments, in some spot or along a crack, the crust would begin to sink downward, the edges of the huge blocks would turn up, and then disappear in the liquid, which commenced again to leap in columns and dash against the shore.

If bodies of water froze over and the crust sank in them as the lava in this caldron of melted silica, then all freezing lakes and rivers and seas would turn into solid ice. The inevitable final result would be that all the water of the world would accumulate in solid frozen masses in the regions of ice-forming latitudes.

Water is in all respects an exceptional product. It is exceptional in its abundance, in its being a liquid at ordinary temperatures, in its perfectly neutral qualities, in its solvent and hydrating properties, in its constant evaporation from liquid and even solid conditions, in its frozen form being a non-conductor of heat, and above all in its expansion in freezing so that ice remains always on the surface. On these exceptional facts, and especially on the last, depend not only the well being but the possibility of life on the earth.

When therefore out of myriads of possible and to all human conception equally probable states and conditions of matter, only those few and peculiar ones were selected which alone could bring about a certain result, I say unhesitatingly that such result must have been forecasted and provided for when matter was apportioned and received its attributes. I claim that the exceptional qualities of water in its various forms, subserving as they do special and apparently predestined purposes, are an unanswerable argument in favor of design in the original constitution of the elements out of which water is formed.

If then the elemental atoms were formed to bring about certain purposes in inorganic nature, why may not some of the elements have been formed to bring about a special purpose in organic nature? Why may not the successive evolution and advancement of life forms be as necessary a result of formative matter as the successive evolutions of the cosmical states that have finally resulted in a habitable and beautiful world? It is my purpose in the remaining part of this article to inquire if there are any direct evidences or reasonings leading to such conclusions regarding the organic kingdoms.

Carbon, the base and substructure of all living bodies, is a highly specialized and exceptional element. It has the capacity, which none of the other elements have, of yoking together its atoms in bands of hundreds and of taking on loads of some hundreds of other atoms, forming the exceedingly complex molecule of albumen or protoplasm, which constitutes the vital matter of all cells whether animal or vegetable.

The following are some of the formulae given for different specimens of albumen. But as all analyses of this substance differ, sometimes very widely, it is necessary to suppose that albumen is equally varying in its composition.

Lieberkuhn—Egg albumen $C_{144} H_{112} N_{18} O_{46} S$.
Wm. Gregory—Blood albumen $C_{216} H_{169} N_{27} O_{68} S_2$.
Wm. Gregory—Blood fibrin $C_{298} H_{228} N_{40} O_{92} S_2$.

Sun-light, acting on the foliage of plants, has the power to take the carbon atoms out of the carbonic oxide in the air, and to build them up into those wonderful molecules that are laid away in cereals and other seeds for the nourishment of vegetable germs. These substances, variously known as fibrin, glutin, legumin, &c., have thus become veritable reservoirs of sun-power. When taken into the animal system as food, they are carried through the digestive processes into the blood, and by the blood are laid away in the muscles, brain, and various tissues of the body, where as occasion requires they are burned up again in the oxygen of respiration, precisely as wood and coal are burned to generate mechanical power. This is the epitome of the history of all vital phenomena. The radiant energy of the sun builds up a frail and complex structure, which the animal economy tears to pieces; and as the atoms fall off from this microcosmic pile in the living organism, and yield up their forces to the body politic, there is life and impulse and intelligence. If it were not for the unique capacity of the carbon element to be thus enormously accumulated in the electric batteries of organic molecules, there would be, so far as we can judge, no possibility of life.

From the consideration of several facts in chemical physics it is reasonable to conclude that the atoms of all elemental bodies and the molecules of all compound bodies are very nearly if not exactly of the same size. Equal measures of all gases, no matter how heavy or how light, contain the same number of atoms or molecules. A cubic inch for instance of the vapor of aluminic iodide, which weighs 408 times as much as the same measure of hydrogen, contains just as many molecules as a cubic inch of air, oxygen, hydrogen, or any other gas, under the same temperature and pressure. Now the law of the equal contraction in bulk of all gases under the same weight of compression or lessening of heat, could not very well hold good if there was such an enormous difference in the sizes of molecules and atoms as there is in their weights. Again in solids, where the atoms are supposed to be nearly in contact, there is a very considerable correspondence between the atomic weights and the specific gravities of substances. Thus aluminum with an atomic weight of 27.5 and a specific gravity compared with water of 2.6, shows nearly the same ratio between the two (10.6) as silver with at. wt. 108 and sp. gr. 10.4 (ratio 10.4) and gold, at. wt. 197, sp. gr. 19.3 (ratio 10.2). If we take into account the comparative bulk of such weights of substances as are represented by their atomic weights, the correspondence is complete' all through the list;* showing that all ultimate particles in solids occupy very nearly the same space.

Now if it is really true that the last divisions of matter are all of about the same bulk, then the molecule of albumen, containing over 600 atoms and weighing more than 6000 times as much as the atom of hydrogen, is not essentially larger than that or any other atom. We can thus see what a tremendous amount of energy must be concentrated in the exceedingly minute molecule of the substance which makes up our lives. We can also see how readily may be explained, as for instance by the addition of an atom or the change of place of an atom, the infinite variations in life-forces that are necessary to account for all the infinite varieties of individuals or species or families of the organic kingdoms.

From the fact that all organic substances are formed on the same complex pattern as albumen, with carbon for their base, and that the nearer to the seat of life these compounds are found, the more complex they are, we are fully justified in concluding that the remarkable property which only carbon possesses of joining together its atoms in one molecule apparently without limit, is the true cause and condition of life. The carbon compounds that take active part in the life-processes never crystallize, but assume always when active the peculiar plastic condition known as the colloid, in which the dynamic forces, whether of the atoms in the molecule, or the molecules in the cell, or the cells in the organism, have full and free course to accumulate, and as we know do amount in the case of large sized animals to a very great sum of energy.

The constant repetition of muscular acts, or the practice of any skill or cunning, or the exercise of the memory or the perceptions or the reasoning faculties, become after a time habits,

---

* See full tables in "Miller's Chemistry," Part 3rd, page 957.

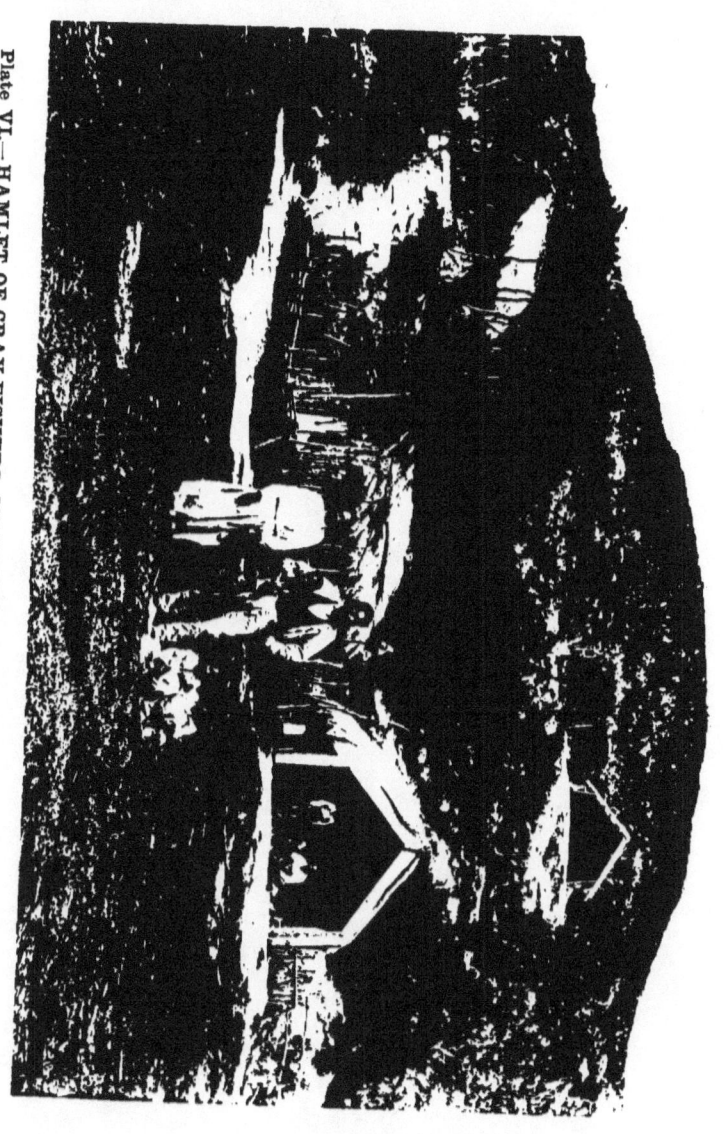

Plate VI.—HAMLET OF CRAY-FISHERS, NEAR HOT SPRINGS, NEW ZEALAND. See Page xv.

second natures, involuntary actions, and instincts. It is undoubtedly true that many of the effects of such acts and habits, and often the instincts themselves, are transmitted to succeeding generations. The modifications in any individual caused by the habitual exercise of any functions of body or mind will most likely be inherited by the descendents of that individual. This is without question a *vera causa* in the origination of variations in species as set forth by the evolutionists. But it must be remembered that disuse and atrophy are also hereditary, and that species often retrograde as well as advance. Indeed as far back as observation has extended it would seem that species in the wild state have deteriorated more frequently than they have improved. Therefore the principle of evolution through inheritance of slight changes does not necessarily mean progress, nor can it exercise any very extended influence on specific characters. It cannot in the nature of the case serve to explain great structural differences where there are no intermediate grades; for the first axiom of Darwinian evolution is "Natura non facit saltum." I am of the opinion that all the labored evidences and arguments in favor of natural selection and the survival of the fittest, prove nothing more than the application of these principles within the narrow limits of varieties and nearly allied species, and that the great advances that have been made from one order to another and from family to family are yet to be accounted for. These great generic steps, always from a lower to a higher standard, are never graded up but always bold and precipitate. The forms that ought to exist in order to show the gradual ascent are never found. The presumption is strong therefore that they never existed.

Let us for a moment make the attempt to apply the doctrines of modern evolution to the explanation of some one of the great structural transitions from one genus to another. Let us take as an instance the loss of one of the toes in any of the equine series in Prof. Huxley's famous crucial example of the development of the one-toed horse from the ancient Eohippus. This was a tapir-like animal about as large as a fox, with four hoof-toes to the fore feet and three to the hind feet. Its remains have been found in the Eocene or lowest Tertiaries in our western territories. Professors Marsh and Leidy have found in later strata the remains of other equine animals, with a gradually lessening number of toes, increasing size and horse-like appearance, and consolidation of the double leg-bones, forming connecting links through at least six hippoid forms up to the present genus, Equus.

The toes are got rid of in these successive forms by being withdrawn upwards, at first just clearing the ground, then drawn up into what are called dew-claws, then into splints on the metacarpus, then vanishing altogether. They are always removed in a regular prescribed order, in this as well as in every other case of the elimination of these members; first the big toe, number one; then the little toe, number five; then number four, or numbers two and four together, leaving two as in the ox, or only the middle one as in the horse. This regular order in the development of the ungulates precludes all possibility of chance being concerned in the operation. Chance makes no selections.

The fundamental doctrine of natural selection as set forth by Darwin is the perpetuation through inheritance of slight advantageous changes happening to any organism.* These must however be of sufficient advantage to enable the possessors of them, by reason thereof, to run out and supercede all the animals not possessing them; for otherwise the peculiarities would certainly be lost or merged by interbreeding. Indeed it is one of the great mysteries of natural selection in the wild state, how any slight variation happening to one individual is preserved for any length of time from being merged in the common characteristics of the race. However let us suppose that some one Eohippus of the ancient eras had been favored with a slight elevation from the ground of the fifth hoof-toe of each fore foot, and that this peculiarity had been successfully transmitted to a line of descendents. Three toes then touched the ground when running, but the little toe hung somewhat loose and failed to make a track. Now can it possibly be imagined that there was advan-

---

* "As natural selection acts solely by accumulating slight, successive, favorable variations, it can produce no great or sudden modifications; it can act only by very short and slow steps."—*Origin of Species*, page 409.

tage enough in this circumstance to enable those with the dangling toe to run out and supercede all those that had their four toes planted square on the ground? And then how many variations in this one direction, and how many exterminations of the race must have occurred before the Mesohippus came in with three clean toes on all his feet? It has always seemed to me that the commonly described processes of evolution, depending solely on the slow accumulation of slight advantageous variations, were entirely too inadequate, and the chances against their continued operation in one direction too infinitely great, to make them worthy of any consideration as a part of nature's means for bringing about the great advances in organic structure.

It will be shown subsequently that this same process of evolving races of one and two hoof-toed animals out of the five toed, was gone all through with by another and entirely independent order, the marsupials, long before the placental mammalia started out on the same course. Furthermore, at the same time that the one-toed horse was being evolved on the western plains of America, precisely the same development was going forward in the Tertiaries of Europe, with the Atlantic ocean rolling between. The Anchithere found in the Miocene of Europe was a tapir-like animal of the size of a sheep, with three hoof-toes to each foot. The Hipparion found in later strata in France and Germany, had grown to the size of the ass, and had the middle hoof much enlarged, with the side hoofs withdrawn upward and no longer serviceable. Besides the fully developed horse, these are the only hippoid forms that have been found in Europe; but they are sufficient to show that the horse was independently evolved on both sides of the Atlantic and at about the same time. It appears then that this slow and laborious task of constructing the most specialized and valuable quadruped in existence, is a process that nature has often gone through with. It seems to be one of the diverging lines that development is obliged to take, as if to accomplish some predestined purpose. And it is a little singular in this connection to note that all of man's useful domestic animals are of the single and double hoofed varieties. Moreover it has often been claimed that civilization would have been an impossibility without the valuable services of this fleetest and hardiest of quadrupeds, nature's common-carrier.

When we look back over the various geological eras, during which the earth was under the reign of different orders of the animal creation, we may very pertinently ask the question, why these were not each in its time sufficient for all the requirements of the great laws of food supply and the restriction of over-production? The races of the saurian reptiles ate up and killed off the redundancies of population as effectually as ever later races did it. The marsupial families that succeeded them were abundantly able to use up the food supply of their age, and to keep up the great balance of the producing and destroying forces of nature. But these again proved to be on an unsuccessful pattern, and they passed away, giving place to the quadrupeds of more recent times. These possessed the earth and fully filled their spheres until the tribes of mankind appeared, which have killed off and wasted the natural products until pretty nearly all balances are upset and there is but little of real nature left. Now what was there in the requirements of the ages or the laws of natural supply and demand that called into being the lowly marsupials to take the place of the gigantic reptiles, or the more delicate placentals to supercede the pouched animals, or finally the bipeds to exterminate the wild races of quadrupeds? It seems to me that nothing short of an inherent and independent principle of advancement in the races themselves can explain these anomalies of development.

It will be more fully shown hereafter that the great physiological changes occurring in the transitions from order to order and family to family of the living kingdoms, could not, in very many cases, have had intermediate stages, from the fact that anything less than the full and complete change would have been, not only of no advantage, but often a positive detriment or cause of destruction to the organisms. In these cases, as we might expect, no connecting forms have ever been found. It is as if nature had made a leap from one grade to another. I can explain in no other way the following instances of great and apparently sudden development. One is the transition from endogenous trees like the palms, that sprout from the ground with full-sized trunk and grow only upward, to the exogens like the pines, with bark and external rings of growth that often increase their bodies to an enormous size. This great change happened, to all appearance, suddenly in the Upper Silurian age. LeConte, in describing it as one of the steps of "rapid evolution," adds:* "When all the conditions are favorable for a great advance, the advance takes place at once, that is, with great comparative rapidity." Another instance is the transition from the boneless, soft-bodied, external shelled, invertebrates, to the internal skeletoned vertebrates, with an entirely different nervous system. This happened in the next succeeding age, the Devonian; and the same authority says of it:* "—the advance is immense. It is impossible to account for this unless we admit that, when conditions are favorable and the time is ripe for a particular change, it takes place with exceptional rapidity, perhaps in a few generations." Other instances are, the change from water-breathing to air-breathing organs, from the fish skeleton to the reptilian, from the oviparous orders to the mammalian, from marsupials to placentals, and so on.

There are definite and invariable lines of advancement in which both animals and plants develop, even in widely separated and independent provinces. All over the world are found similar and nearly identical forms of life, both living and extinct. Considering that impassable seas cover nearly three-quarters of the surface of the earth, it is simply impossible that all lands should in all ages have been so nearly connected that species could pass from one to another and intermingle. There must of necessity have been many centers of evolution, either partial or complete. Not to specify others, I will merely take the instance of the two polar regions. It has recently been very clearly brought out that life began in the arctic zone,† at least as one of the centers of distribution. But as the climatal and continental conditions of the northern and southern hemispheres alternate in certain long secular periods, and as there is an equal

---

* "*Elements of Geology*," by Joseph LeConte, pages 317 and 333.
† "*Where did Life Begin*," by G. Hilton Scribner, 1884.

necessity of accounting for the existence in the southern temperate zone of life-forms which could never have crossed the equator, it is rendered almost certain that the antarctic zone was once a center of origin and distribution of animals and plants as well as the arctic. Now if this was so, the two sources of life must have been, in the nature of the case, entirely independent. Yet they have evolved identical orders, families, and genera, and in some cases even species. Almost the only difference in the two hemispheres is that the southern provinces have not advanced in their indigenous productions to the same grade of development as the northern. Australia for instance represents almost accurately the life-conditions of Europe in the earliest Tertiary times, South America the later Tertiary, and South Africa the Quarternary. Now who will estimate the probability on the doctrine of chances of these hundreds of thousands of similar and often identical life-forms springing by fortuitous variation from two independent sources of origin? The chances against it are beyond the limits of figures.

All evolutionists have seen that independent centers of evolution would be fatal to their theories. Consequently they have exhausted their ingenuity in endeavoring to explain the anomalies of organic distribution. They have raised up sea bottoms to connect continents, have created imaginary islands for migratory halting places, and have stretched the great glacial bridges across the equator. They have been seemingly so afraid they would be obliged to acknowledge a supernatural Creator, that they have laid out miraculous sea-voyages for animals and plants, have sent them against winds and ocean-currents from north zones to south zones, they have loaded the whirlwinds with vegetable seeds and the feet of birds with living embryos. But notwithstanding the formidable array of the literature on this subject, I must think that if there is not an innate tendency to progressive development in living organisms, something that compels an onward movement along the entire front of the line, we might as well skip Darwin, Haeckel, and Spencer, and go back to Paley's "Natural Theology;" for this is the latest book that has given even an intelligible explanation of how animals and plants came to be what they are and where they are.

The earth had passed more than half of its life-bearing age before a single air-breathing animal had appeared. Up to about the period of the Carboniferous formation all animals had lived in the water, the highest forms being fishes of the shark type. undoubtedly the air at that time was loaded with carbonic oxide, and the profuse vegetation of those eras was needed to clear the atmosphere of noxious gases and render it fit for respiration. But about the time we have mentioned the record of the rocks shows the appearance of an amphibious animal, the labyrinthodont, with gills to breathe in the water and lungs to breathe in the air. It had feet with five toes, the double bones of the lower leg, the shoulder and collar bones, in short all the essential parts which make up the perfect mammalian frame-work. It was as different in its skeletal structure from any fish that then lived, as a beast is different from a fish to-day. The skeleton of the first amphibian was an immense advance on anything that had gone before it. It was the model on which, without the addition of a structural bone, has been constructed the varied frame-work of all air-breathing vertebrate animals.

There is no instance in the development of vertebrates above the fishes, where any structural bones have been formed anew or added to the frame. If there were any modifications to be made, they were simply changes in form and function, or more often the entire elimination of certain bones or members. The zebra, horse and ass, as we have seen, in the course of ages, by dropping successively the phalangial members, have finally come to possess only one, the middle toe. The ox and camel have got rid of all but two. The normal and original number however is always five; and man, as well as anthropoid apes, still retain the full complement. Therefore every species that has ever been in the line of man's derivation, back to the primeval batrachian, must have had the full complement of structural bones, the five fingers or toes, the double bones of the fore-arm or leg, the scapula and clavicle, and so on. But no fish that ever swam has any of these parts in any wise resembling those of air-breathing animals. For this reason I say that the production of the first lowly amphibian that crawled out of the water to live on land, was a miracle in animal creation. A genuine fish could never have developed into it by any manner of gradual selective changes. What benefit would it be to a fish to have simply a trace of an air-breathing lung, or any fraction of one not capable of sustaining its life out of water? What advantage would it be to a fish gradually to get rid of the numberless little bones in its fins, down to the five sets of phalangial bones, or gradually to develop jointed limbs with double bones in the lower parts, together with collar and shoulder bones? These are only useful for walking on land, and of course could be of no advantage to a fish until it had lungs for breathing air. The two developments must advance pari passu, and neither are of any utility until they are both in large measure perfected.

This amphibian order, the first development of land animals, and represented by some gigantic forms during the Primary epoch, seems to have been the prolific mother of races. But nearly all the offspring, including the saurians, the lizards, the flying reptiles, the dragons, the duck-billed monotremes, and the marsupials, proved to be failures in the great plan of life, and after a short but widely disseminated reign, either entirely or very nearly passed out of existence. From the very important fact that every family or order of the quadruped animals was started out with the full equipment of structural bones, and thereafter in its branchings immediately commenced to eliminate or to modify these skeletal parts, I think it amounts almost to a demonstration that each one sprung independently from the same line or stem of full-structured, undifferentiated, and primitive animals. This line, in the nature of the case, could have been no other than the great Carboniferous order of amphibians, which we know to have been the prolific parent of all the earlier orders of land vertebrates. Consequently the few living, and in all cases degraded forms, like the lancelets (amphioxus), the mud fishes (lepidosirens), and the duck-billed platypus (ornithorhynchus), which have been so often brought forward by evolutionists to represent intermediate classes or links, probably never had any connection whatever with other orders, but are merely the vanishing remnants of distinct and decaying families—the last relics of some of nature's numerous failures in the world-stocking enterprise.

The first departure from the egg-producing animals, for it is now known that the monotremes are oviparous, were the marsupials, which bring forth their young in an exceedingly immature state. The mothers take the little embryos, as soon as born, in their mouths and place them on nipples inside of a ventral pouch or receptacle, where they remain until they are large enough to run alone. The young of the kangaroo, which is an animal nearly as large as a cow, when first born are only about an inch long and quite worm-like. They have an embryonic life of only five weeks, and afterwards remain in the pouch about nine months. The embryos in this order of animals never have any connection with the circulatory systems of the parent. The gestation of the marsupials differs but little from that of some few genera of viviparous reptiles. But there is this great advance and difference, that the pouched animals nourish their young to maturity on the milk of the mothers.

A most singular structural peculiarity is found in the just born embryos of the marsupials. It is the elongation of the larynx, through which air is breathed, across the throat and into the nasal passage, where the end of it, which is like an inverted cone, is grasped by the membrane of that passage, so that respiration can go on freely and safely while the mother is at the same time forcing her milk down the throat of the helpless little one. In all other mammalia, including the mature of the marsupials, the larynx opens into, and is on a level with, the bottom of the throat; but it is protected by what is called the epiglottis, which closes when we swallow and prevents us from choking. Now here is a wonderful adaptive contrivance in a little formless embryo, the only thing that is at all developed in it, and without which it could not live a moment in the place where it is to mature. How will modern evolution account for such a structure as this, which is only of use in a complete and perfected form? The whole race of developing mammalia would have choked to death long before this absolutely necessary little device had been, by any slight adaptive changes, made effective.

As soon as marsupials became established in the animal kingdom they branched off into the different lines of development, the herbivorous, the insectivorous, the carnivorous, &c. There are marsupials corresponding with nearly every kind of quadruped that is described in our familiar books of natural history. When it is considered that undoubtedly from one marsupial species branched off all the various tribes of the pouched animals, and from one placental species divided off all the numerous races of our modern animals, it is certainly a most remarkable circumstance that they should so nearly agree in all their ramifications.

The original and primitive species of both orders, as we have often insisted, must have possessed the full complement of structural bones, because derived species never gain, but are almost always losing skeletal parts. Therefore we predicate a a common stem for the two orders, and that all the branches of each order descended from one individual or species of that order. Still if any should claim that each species or genus of the present order of mammalia had developed out of the corresponding species or genus of the marsupial order, then we would reply, that our point was gained without further argument; for it would be simply impossible that so many animals should independently and simultaneously pass through the great change from the marsupial to the placental organization, unless there were an inherent and irresistible tendency in the race itself toward that advancement; and this is all we are contending for.

The fact of this remarkable parallelism of species in the two orders was brought before me in the most striking manner when visiting recently the exceedingly interesting museums of Australia, particularly that of Melbourne. There are to be seen in those collections specimens of marsupial striped tigers and spotted leopards, marsupial wombat and climbing bears, pouched foxes, wolves, native cats, bandicoot rats, leaping rats and mice, marsupial rabbits, beavers, weasels, woodchucks, porcupines, phalanger squirrels and flying squirrels, ant-eaters, vulpine opossums, prehensile tailed monkeys, and many others that might be named. All these are of living species of marsupials, found in the Australasian islands. But there have also been found in various parts of the world and north of the equator, fossil specimens of a far greater variety of marsupial species. Among them are gigantic skeletons corresponding to the hippopotamus and rhinoceros, and to the large hoofed-animals and insectivora, to the giant sloth and armadillo, to lions and the ape-footed animals. Thus it is seen that there were at one time, spread all over the continents, classes of marsupial animals filling all the spheres and presenting all the similitudes of the quadrupeds of the present day. Why they were not sufficient for all the requirements of nature and did not persist to the end, are questions which natural selection does not answer.

But for some reason, whatever it may have been, the marsupial type was not found to be entirely satisfactory. Apparently it was not the best that nature could do, and so it was allowed quietly to pass away, and another order of animals, with improved methods of reproduction and a better quality of brain, was brought forward to take its place. The distinguishing quality of the placental mammalia is that the fetus has direct connection, by means of the membrane called the placenta or after-birth, with the circulatory systems of the parent, and is brought forth in nearly a full state of development. It was a great advance over the clumsy and imperfect processes of the marsupials, and it was at once accompanied by more graceful and symmetrical forms, by larger and more convoluted brains, and a much higher standard generally of animal life. But not the least trace of any intermediate races, or connecting links between the two orders, have ever been found. And it is impossible to conceive that there could be any. Either there must have been full uterine connection and sustenance of the fetus until mature, or there could have been none at all. A fractional or partial development of a placenta would have answered no purpose; for that would not have sustained the fetal life. Any gradual lengthening of the period of gestation, even if we could conceive of any means by which it could be brought about, would seem to be out of the question; for what possible advantage could it be to a kangaroo for instance to carry its unborn young six weeks instead of five?

If however, according to the theory of evolution, this most important of all the advances in organic nature was worked out in any way by the hereditary transmission of slight advantageous changes, the great question comes back to us: what was there in nature, or in the environment, or in the struggle for existence, to induce or start any tendency to any such change? The old marsupials were prolific enough, were apparently successful with their mites of embryos, were good feeders, well balanced in their orders, and filled satisfactorily every sphere in life. Although a little dull and lacking in brain capacity, yet they were physically a powerful race, and held their sway until the improved order came fully branched and developed to take their places. There was not only no necessity for the change, but no such advantage in its first stages as would cause them to be selected and perpetuated. Yet the great transformation came, according to the testimony of geology, suddenly and unheralded, just as many other changes in ancient life-histories have come. The great geologist and evolutionist, LeConte, has been obliged to specify this as one of his "critical periods," when life-forms were subject to sudden and most unaccountable variations. Writing of the era of the mammals, he says: "There is at certain geological horizons, a rapid and most extraordinary change in life-systems. This it seems impossible to explain on the theory of evolution, unless we admit periods of rapid evolution."

It seems to me very much as if these grand and radical advances came because they could not help it, because in the great plan of organic life the times had come when it was necessary they should rapidly develop. Just as in the life of the amphibian frog, the time comes when it must lay aside the habits and organs adapted to a water life, and take on the full-boned members, the lungs, and the sense organs necessary to a life on land. The hairy caterpillar, with a mandibulate mouth, with cutters and jaws and stomach for eating and digesting leaves or other vegetable food, after storing up a quantity of living matter, goes to sleep in its chrysalid case. In this condition all the parts of the caterpillar, the mouth, the members, the organs, the muscles and tissues and nerves, entirely disappear, and there is nothing left but formless protoplasm. Then, in this rich store of formative matter, there commences to develop an entirely new and different creature, with a suctorial mouth, a simple stomach for the nectar of flowers, a covering of gaudily colored scales, with two long articulated legs and broad wings, in short the airy and joyous butterfly. Now to my mind every metamorphosis of a larva into an imago is more of a miracle in organic development than the rapid transformation of a fish into a batrachian, or an amphibian into a reptile, or into a marsupial, or into the highest mamalian type.

One of the most striking instances of great and inexplicable changes suddenly supervening to the animal organization, is found in the remarkable difference in the sizes of the brains of the highest apes and the lowest races of men. From a great number of measurements and comparisons the following capacities in cubic inches of the crania of averaged human races and of individuals have been estimated.*

Finns and Cossacks, 98 cubic inches; Teutonic (German) family, 94; Esquimaux, 91; Negroes, 85; natives of Australia and Tasmania, 82; Bushmen (Hottentots), 77. The following are some individual or exceptional developments: Cuvier, the naturalist, 114 cubic inches; Byron, 110; Napoleon and Webster, 108; an Araucanian (south of Chili in South America), 115.5; an Esquimaux, 113; a Teutonic skull, 112.4; a Marquesan (South Pacific Islands), 110.6; a Negro, 105.8; an Australian native, 104.5. The skulls of prehistoric men that have been found are of the average brain capacity of modern savage races. Even that of the lowest cave man that has ever been found, the Neanderthall skull, is estimated at 75 cubic inches.

Now for the other side. The adult orang-utan, quite as bulky as a small-sized man, has a brain capacity of only 28 cubic inches. The gorilla, considerably above the average size of man, estimated by bulk and weight, has a brain of 30 cubic inches; the largest specimen yet known had 34½. The proportions average as follows: anthropoid apes, 10; lowest savages, 26; civilized man, 32. From these facts we deduce the following conclusions.

---

* Dr. J. Barnard Davis. Philosophical Transactions. 1869. Page 513. Alfred R. Wallace, in "Littell's Living Age." 1872. No. 1410.

1st. Large cranium capacity is not an unvarying index of high culture and intelligence; but such culture and intelligence never exist without the large averages of brain size. The case is like this: strong and powerful machinery is necessary to drive the mill; but if the power is not sufficient to drive the machinery, the mill will never run. The capacious brain that was given to the human race from its very inception, so far as we can judge, and which is in notable contrast to that of every other large sized animal, was a machinery that was absolutely necessary to the working out of any kind of civilization; but it lay dormant for untold ages, and only awakened in these later years under the spur of over-population, or rivalry, or of some master spirit. In all this the idea is unavoidably suggested of the original endowment of mankind with a surplusage of mind material—with an organ far above the then existing needs of its possessor, and designed for use only in long distant ages.

2nd. There is a gap between the brain-capacities of the lowest or most ancient races of men, and the highest known ape species, that natural selection does not and never can fill. If the principles of Darwinian evolution had anything to do with the case, we would have a right to expect that savage and primeval man would be furnished with a brain only a little superior in size to that of the larger apes; whereas he has one nearly three times larger, and but little inferior to that of races of the highest culture.

3rd. From the fact that whenever an adult European has a cranium less than nineteen inches in circumference, or brain contents of less than sixty-five cubic inches, he is invariably idiotic, we say confidently that man could never have sprung by any slow and ordinary evolutional gradations, nor probably by any relationship whatever, from anthropoid apes; because if he had, he would, with lessening brain or other abnormal conformation, according to the principles of reversion as exemplified in all derived species, become ape-like instead of idiotic. But so far as known there has never been a case nor an indication of any such reversion.

Throughout the whole race of the quadrumana, both living and extinct, the foot is prehensile, the thumb being opposed to the other fingers as in the human hand. In man there is a complete change in the bones and muscles of the foot, so that the power of opposability of the large toe is entirely lost, and the same is the case in the most ancient races that we know anything of. The structure of the organs of the voice in man is on a superior type to that of the apes; yet it is as perfect in the lowest savages as in the most cultured races of mankind. In the perfection of the human hand, its entire freedom from all locomotive uses, in man's erect form and the adaptation of feet and limbs to that position, in his naked and sensitive skin, demanding clothes and houses, and finally in all distinctly human peculiarities, man does not approach sensibly nearer the ape-condition even in the lowest or most primeval state in which he has ever been found. There are not only no intermediate forms between man and the anthropoid apes, but there is really no approximation to any relationship to them as we follow back the line of his descent.

The great cry of modern evolutionists is for "lost links"—the great complaint is, "the imperfection of the geological record." They find all the connecting links they want between species and perhaps nearly allied genera. But when it comes to intermediate forms between orders, families, and most genera, the findings have been in the highest degree unsatisfactory. Where in fact the most should have been found, there is really found the least or rather none at all. Intermediate forms, according to slow and gradual evolution, should have had as long and as prolific an existence as any others. Therefore the fact that they are not found in the geological strata, is the best of evidence that they never existed.

If now, after presenting the outline of the facts and reasonings which have led me to dissent from the promulgated doctrines of evolution, I might be permitted to indulge in a little exercise of the scientific imagination, I would say that all the facts and principles of the growth of life-forms would be readily explained under the hypothesis that every addition to the combining numbers of the molecules of germinal matter would necessarily produce higher and advancing orders of organisms. The great complexity of the carbon compounds in the life-centers, is quite certainly one of the conditions and causes of organic growth. It is natural therefore to suppose that the more complex those compounds are, the higher will be the development that proceeds from them.

All the higher forms of the animate creation, all in which there is any principle of progress or variation, reproduce by the union of two sexual elements. There is thereby added some mysterious force which starts cellular subdivision, and a new and independent life. The constitution of the fecundated nucleus is most certainly changed from the type of either parental germ, because an offspring is formed that always differs more or less from either or both sources of origin. It is then altogether probable that the molecules of one sexual element conjoin their chemical forces to the molecules of the other, thus creating a surcharged center of forces sufficiently powerful to start into being a new and self-unfolding life. Then whatever combinations of atoms, representing either parental ancestral or original traits, prove to be the stronger in the two-fold elements, will rule the subsequent differentiations. Sometimes from such unions have sprung remarkable and often valuable race varieties, called sports of nature, and differing from anything that has ever preceded them. As such variations occur most frequently among domesticated animals, which are in exceptional conditions of food supply and freedom from care or exertion, they may perhaps be naturally explained as springing from some extraordinary increase or superposition of atoms in the molecules of the impregnated germs which produced them.

In like manner in the geological ages, I imagine that when the suitable conditions have come about for a new step to be taken in the grand advance of life-forms, nature has provided for it in the simplest way imaginable, by merely piling a few more atoms on the enormously loaded molecules of germinal protoplasm. It might naturally be supposed that a higher quality of food would increase the formula of the vital compounds derived from it; and as a consequence the uniting germinal elements would form a higher combination in the ovarian nucleus, thus causing a rapid or perhaps sudden advance in the animal organization. At all events such advances have always come whenever changes have occurred in vegetable growths giving a greater supply or a higher grade of nourishment to the animal kingdom.

It is a strange and awe-inspiring thought that on the inconceivably minute atoms of carbon, was impressed the power of forming, in the slow progress of evolving ages, the highly organized beings who would one day take in hand these infinitesimal life-workers, and weigh them, and reason on them, and endeavor to find out in what manner they could so accumulate their wonderful centers of force as to build up this powerful and reasoning creature. And now I would submit the question: Which is the nobler thought; to conceive of man's exalted position in nature as arising from the God-given attributes of even the lowly carbon atoms; or to regard his origin and growth as the result of an infinity of slight and favorable variations that gave to their possessors in each case the upper hand in life and enabled them times without number to starve out or kill out their rivals that did not possess those advantages? To me it is not a satisfying reflection that each one of our ancestors, near or remote, has been the successful combatant in a deadly struggle for existence. I had far rather believe that the important organic advances have been made so rapidly that there has been no occasion for collisions and rivalries of races. The improved orders have come upon the stage of the world's progress precisely as the white men have planted themselves on the lands of the dark races, and the aborigines have vanished from before them imperceptibly and unaccountably, as is always the case with feebler races in the presence of the stronger.

THE MICROSCOPIST IN BERMUDA.*

Out in the midst of the Atlantic Ocean, directly east of Charleston, and over six hundred miles from it, or from any other land whatever, lies the little group of the Bermuda Islands. It is claimed that there are 365 islands in the group; but all told, there is not as much dry land in them as there is in the corporate limits of the City of Rochester. A mere speck in the wide waste of waters, it is a wonder that it was ever discovered, or being once discovered, that it was ever found again. In fact both these events were the mere chance results of shipwrecks. In the year 1522, Juan Bermudez, a Spaniard, was wrecked on these islands while on his way to the New World. He was glad enough to get away with leaving only his name on the stormy Bermudas. Nearly a hundred years later, Sir George Sommers, on a voyage from England to Virginia, ran against them and suffered shipwreck. This time the English took formal possession, and have held them ever since.

They are surrounded by dangerous coral reefs, which lie beneath the surface of the water, and on all sides except the south, are from ten to fifteen miles from the shore. These treacherous shoals, lying in a wind-beaten sea and in the track of the highways of commerce, have been the cause of innumerable maritime disasters. Some of the best fortunes of the island residents have arisen out of the poor mariners' misfortunes.

I do not however intend to give you either the history or geography of Bermuda; but only to illustrate some scientific facts and a few microscopic preparations, by its singular structure

---

* A Lecture written in 1878. Delivered in Canandaigua, and on several occasions.

and its abundance of marine invertebrate life. I went there with my little pocket microscope, to examine among the curious and interesting things of the ocean shore. It was almost my first lesson in microscopy, at least in the preparation of microscopic objects; and my story I hope will be an incentive to you to study nature and to gain knowledge, wherever you may chance to ramble or journey.

The Bermudas, in latitude 32° 15′, are the most northerly lands where the reef-building corals grow. These little tropical animals can flourish only in water which never falls below the temperature of 68°; and the clearer and salter that water is the better it suits them. In these respects the Bermuda Islands are admirably adapted to them. For while it never freezes there, there are also no fresh water streams to either muddy the ocean water or diminish its saltiness. These animals, belonging to the lowest order of beings that are provided with stomachs—the so called Gastrula type—have the power of secreting large quantities of carbonate of lime from the sea-water. And although so small individually as to be scarcely distinguishable by the naked eye, yet by the enormous increase of their numbers by budding, they are able to build up barriers that inclose continents and make islands. The branching species may grow to the height of six or eight feet; and the brain corals may make solid hemispheres 15 or 20 feet in diameter. These extreme sizes however are only found in more tropical waters. I have never seen them in Bermuda even the half of these dimensions.

The reef corals do not grow on bottoms deeper than one hundred feet, and never quite up to the lowest tide level. So that they are really confined to narrow vertical limits, and would never produce appreciable effects if it were not for the fact that nearly all shores are, in the long course of geological ages, gradually either sinking or rising. It is a mistake to suppose that the reef-building corals construct, directly from their growth, a solid wall of coral material. They only rear a forest of branching stems, into which the waves wash up shells and bones and broken fragments, which are all cemented into a solid mass by the deposition of carbonate of lime from the sea-water. And on

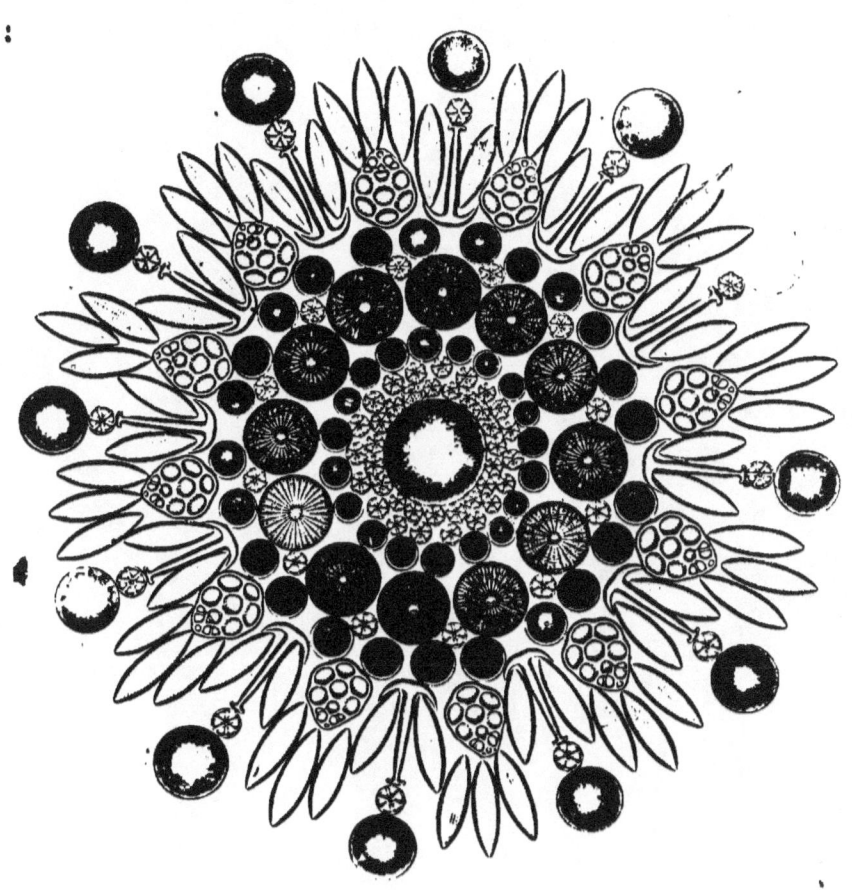

Plate VII.—ARRANGED GROUP OF DIATOMS AND SPICULES. See Page xv.
Magnified 65 Diameters. Original size of Group—○

this foundation they continue to build as long as they are uncovered by the lowest tides. Such a profusion of life as is found in the coral beds, requires a constant change and commotion in the waters which supply them their building material. Therefore these animals flourish best in the fiercest surf and on the stormiest coasts. The most dreaded of all the sailor's perils lie always concealed beneath the most tempestuous waters of the ocean.

The theory of coral islands is that there was once a much larger island—perhaps a mountain or a range of mountains—in the place where such an island now is. That the reef corals then built an encircling barrier around its shores, called in this case a barrier reef; and that, as gradually the island sank into the ocean, the corals kept on raising and narrowing in their reefs, until finally the main land entirely disappeared beneath the waters, leaving only the more or less circular reef about it. As any barrier, thus thrown up against the action of the waves, has a tendency to accumulate, and to raise into shore lines, the sand and shells of the ocean, so there is soon dry land where those barrier reefs once were. There are hundreds of these circular islands, called atols, in the Pacific Ocean. Some with a remnant of the old island still in the center, others with only water, into which, through a narrow opening that is usually left on the leeward side, ships can sail in and find a safe anchorage.

This is undoubtedly the condition of the circular reef about the Bermudas, except that the waves and the winds have made dry land on only a portion of the southern line of the reef. Outside the reef the bottom declines somewhat rapidly, and in a few scores of miles from it the water is almost unfathomable. There are further evidences of the gradual sinking of the islands during geological times, which I will not stop to enumerate. It is pretty certain therefore that there was once a larger and very different island in the region where the Bermudas now are and that as it gradually sank into the waves, the reef builders kept working in and up towards the surface, until finally every vestige of the old island disappeared; and there is now above the surface of the ocean only the material which the waves have washed up on the shore, and the winds have blown into the hills which so beautifully diversify the landscape of these islands.

Almost my first excursion was to the long stretches of sand beach on the southern shore, about two miles south-west of Hamilton. To my surprise I found the sand there composed almost entirely of minute shells; some perfect in form, others more or less worn by the action of the waves; but not a particle of the angular silicious grains which make up the entire body of our own sand both inland and on the sea-shore. All there was calcareous, carbonate of lime; and it was entirely the product of animal organisms. Back of the beach the winds have piled up a high hill of sand, which they are gradually rolling over on the valley beyond, thus giving an actual example of how all the hills were formed. I examined this sand in many places and found it identically the same with that on the shore. On the way back to the hotel, I examined the stone in the cuts through which the road passes, and found it composed entirely of the same shell substance, loosely cemented together by a deposition of carbonate of lime. Many times subsequently I saw masons—or carpenters, one hardly knows which to call them—sawing this same stone with our common hand saws into blocks and pannels and cornices and all kinds of convenient shapes. It did not dull their saws as much as an oak board would. This then is the material of which the whole islands are composed; for there is no other kind of stone found there. I saw also the same material which had been excavated from fifty feet below the level of the ocean, and which must of course have had that amount of subsidence at least; for this kind of rock forms only in the air. It is technically called Æolian Rock, from Æolus, the master of the winds, in ancient Mythology.

I ought perhaps here to tell you when and how to gather this sand, in order to secure the most perfect shells and the greatest variety of the finer and lighter spicules, corallines, &c. Go to the sea shore immediately after high tide, when there has been considerable surf coming in. You will find that the highest wave of high tide has left a little ripple mark along the shore, a mere skimming, not an eighth of an inch thick. But it is the gathering of that tide, fresh from the ocean and all cleaned and whitened. If you get there before the wind has blown away the lighter materials, and carefully scrape it together and bag it, you have the best samples which can be obtained.

Having studied thus far the problem of Bermuda, I was now even more anxious than ever to know the names and the life-history of the minute creatures which had built up, with the clothing of their bodies, a beautiful island, with its mass of rolling hills. By far the largest portion of the shells in the sand, I found to belong to the order called Foraminifera. Foramen is the Latin for a small apperture; and as you will see from the specimens shown to you later this evening, these shells are pierced with innumerable little holes, some of them not larger than the ten thousandth of an inch. But through these holes, no matter how small they may be, the animal pushes out parts of its body in minute threads, which may extend to several times its own length. These filaments, or pseudopodia as they are called, are both feeding arms, and means of locomotion. They feel around for food, and finding it, bring it by their natural adhesiveness up to the body and into the hole in the shell if this be large enough, or if not they envelop and digest the morsel outside. It makes little difference to this most simple of all living creatures where it takes in, or where it assimilates, the food which supports it. For its whole body is nothing in the world but a little albuminoid substance, just like the white of an egg, nothing more. There are absolutely no parts, no organs, about the creature at all. It seizes its food without members, swallows it without a mouth, digests it without a stomach, and sends the nourishment of it to the most distant parts without a circulating system. It moves from place to place without muscles, feels without nerves, propagates without organs, and builds an exquisitely beautiful house without a vestige of the senses.

I have taken these tiny specimens alive from the sea-weed at the bottom of the shallow bays, and placed them in sea-water in small vials. After a time I have seen them climbing the sides of the vial with a perfect forest of little threads thrown out from their margins. They had evidently realized that they were deprived of their customary food or supply of fresh water, and were trying to get out. A sea-weed or any senseless organism would have quietly settled down and died. But this morsel of structureless protoplasm has the same feeling, when deprived of the proper conditions of life, that an insect or a mouse has, and equally tries to escape. There is then sense and feeling in the first and simplest form of animated matter. Now so far as chemical analysis can determine, the body of the foraminifera is precisely the same albuminoid substance that fills the germ which originates, and the cells which make up, the body substance of every living creature. I can therefore readily conceive that as the scale of animal life ascends—as cell is added to cell of this already sensitive matter—as organs and members gradually appear, built up so variously and receiving their different functions from this same wonderful bioplasm—I can conceive that the combination of so many myriad batteries of electric sensitiveness might at last result in the complicate volitions and the high intelligence of the superior orders of creation.

Just in what way the foraminifera commence their little span of life, has not yet been fully determined. I have no doubt that the smallest morsel stricken off from any living individual, would go on growing and finally develop into the same form as that from which it was taken. This may in some manner be one mode of generation. But it is also probable that, in conformity with the law which seems to govern in all the lowest orders of the animal kingdom, separate individuals become merged in some way into one; and then the entire body thus united granulates into germs, which escaping become new individuals of the same species. Every shelled foraminifer, however generated, begins its growth as a little speck of jelly, around which it deposits a layer of carbonate of lime, leaving one or more openings for communication with the outer world. Then when the body substance has grown so that its shell will no longer hold it, the outside portion secretes and deposits another shelly layer about itself, inclosing the apperture into the first shell, and leaving others in the new. At the next stage of growth another or other segments are added. And according to the way in which these successive segments are added, will result the peculiar form which is characteristic of each species, whether a whorl, a spiral, a cone, a disc, or any one of an immense variety of shapes. There is a beauty and a symmetry about the foraminiferal shells that make them peculiarly interesting objects under the microscope. Some are exquisitely fluted, or dotted, or lined. Some are of the purest white, others like glass, and in the form of most beautiful vases or bottles, while others glisten like porcelain. The curves and the whorls are always exceedingly graceful, and the rulings beautifully regular. I have often wondered what all this display was for, when there were no eyes to see it. Why such a wonderful geometry of curves, when there was no mind to appreciate it.

But the class of animals we are now considering, derives perhaps its greatest interest from its past history. It was amazingly abundant in the old geological ages. The nummulitic lime stone of the Alps, which is made up in chief part of the coin-like shells of foraminifera, is in places ten thousand feet thick, and extends under nearly all of Southern Europe. The building stone of Paris is from its quarries, and the pyramids of Egypt are made out of it.

The Eozoan Canadense, which is the earliest trace of anything living found in the rocks, belongs to this class of animals. It is the largest of the foraminifera, sometimes several feet in diameter, made up of corrugated plates of carbonate of lime, between which was the sarcode body of the animal. On the bottoms of the earliest seas which covered the still warm crust of our globe, the Eozoan formed immense reefs, which are now the serpentine limestone so abundant in the Laurentian strata of Canada and other parts of the world.

It is singular that this simplest of all animal structures should have survived without change, except in its shelly covering, from the earliest dawn of life on the earth, through all the long eras up to the present time. It seems that evolution and the survival of the fittest, if they had any thing to do in the matter, could find no being that was better suited to live on shallow sea-bottoms than this undeveloped creature. I imagine that as long as the same conditions remain, there can be no material improvement made on the forms of animal life which nature first provides to meet those conditions.

In searching among the rocks at lowest tide, and in protected coves of the sea-shore, I found, hidden away in little round excavations just large enough to hold them, some fine specimens of the large-spined sea-urchins or Echini. It seemed to me that they had hollowed out and enlarged these secure homes for themselves as they grew, for I never could get them out without breaking up the rock in which I found them. They have strong spines all over their round shell, and strong muscles to move them; still it would seem to be a Herculean task for them to excavate into the solid rock. Yet there they were in their little round holes, so securely braced in that after pricking my fingers most unmercifully in trying to get them out, I soon gave it up and resorted to the hammer and cold-chisel.

The Echinus in its development is about midway among the invertebrates. It has a very fair digestive apparatus, and a little show for a nervous system. Its great peculiarity is that all its parts are arranged in divisions of five. Its mouth has five jaws, and five teeth that meet together in one point. It has five little red eyes on the opposite side of the body from the mouth. Five similar segments make up the shell in which it lives; and the plates of which they are formed are five-sided. The shell increases in size by these pentagonal plates enlarging at the joints.

The test or shell of the Echinus bears three different kinds of members. The first are the spines. Of course these differ in size, shape, and function in the different families. For instance in the Spatangoids, which live in the sand, they are spoon or spud shaped, for the purpose of digging away the sand and then covering the animal with it. But in the kind we are describing, the Echidna, they are strong and conical, running to a point, for the purpose of wearing away the rock. They are as beautifully fluted as an Ionic column. Each one has a socket at the base which fits on a little protuberance on the shell, forming a perfect ball and socket joint; and a set of external muscles moves the spine in every direction. The internal structure of these spines is most remarkable. Thin transverse sections of them make exceedingly beautiful objects under the microscope. Rays from the center pass outward through successive rings which seem to mark certain periods of growth, these all being formed of the finest net-work of calcareous glass, while every shade of color beautifies the pattern. I will have the pleasure of showing you some of these at the close of the lecture.

But another set of organs, not less numerous or wonderful than the spines, covers the test of these animals. Alternating with the meridional segments which carry the spines, are other segments pierced with minute holes. Over every two of these holes there is a fleshy tube, which can be extended to a considerable distance beyond the spines, and at the end there is a sucker which can be applied to any surface, and by drawing on the central part a vacuum is produced, by which the Echinus pulls itself about, or climbs the rocks beneath the water. The holes are for the purpose of admitting water, which the animal forces into the tubes to extend them. Muscular contraction does the rest of the work. Considering that there are as many as five thousand of these little elephant trunks on each sea-urchin, and that each of them seems to be under separate control, one would think that this small animal ought to be a pretty skillful operator to know just which one to extend and take hold with, and which one to draw in and to loosen. Yet it never makes a mistake.

There is still another set of organs, more strange and wonderful even than the two others. Scattered all over among the spines and tube-feet, are tiny upright threads of glass, covered with a muscular tissue, and surmounted at the tops, each with three minute prongs, toothed or spiked on the inner edges; and these triangular jaws are being continually opened and shut against each other, snapping and biting without a moment's pause as long as the animal lives. They were for a long time supposed to be little parasites on the Echinus, and received the name of pedicellariæ, which is the Latin for the louse parasite. They still retain the name, but are now known to be an essential part of the Echinoid economy, whatever that may be; for the utility or function of these snapping members has never yet been found out. We shall have occasion later to notice very similar organs belonging to another marine animal, and to speak of their probable use.

The Echinus produces a great quantity of eggs. In many maritime countries they are collected and eaten by the poorer classes. Now, what is very strange about these eggs is that they do not develop into the Echinus, nor into anything at all like it. The progeny is lively little creatures, almost microscopic in size, that swim about in the water by means of cilia, or minute hairs, on various parts of the body. Instead of being five-sided like the parents, they are two-sided like nearly all the rest of the world. They have two eyes, organs in pairs, a mouth, a big stomach, and eight spiny legs projecting downwards. After a time there begins to appear on one side of this creature's stomach, a flat round disk, which grows more and more dish-shaped, with the markings of five distinct segments. Then the saucer-like disk puts out five arms, then five clusters of rudimentary spines; all the while gradually enclosing the stomach of the poor Pluteus, which now begins to lose its legs, its mouth, and everything else that is of any use to it. Finally the parasite completes its little round shell, makes a new mouth on the side of the stomach last enclosed, discards now all of its old nurse, and settles down to the bottom to begin the new life of the slow creeping Echinus.

Here, it strikes me, is one of the strangest transformations in all the course of animal existence; one creature producing, in the ordinary course of generation, an entirely different being, perfect in all its life and parts, out of which, in the manner of an excrescence, grows the parent form again. If here is not a puzzle for the Darwinians, then I fail to appreciate the case. In accordance with what law of inheritance is it, that the Echinus lays eggs which hatch into another order of beings? By what principle of the natural selection of variations useful and advantageous, has it come about that the Pluteus develops in its vitals a little monster that literally eats it up alive? That a stationary animal like the Echinus should develop, in its mode of generation, some means of more widely scattering its progeny, I can very well understand. Other slow moving animals accomplish the same purpose by means of an intermediate and more active generative form. We shall even have a further instance of this before we close. But in all other cases the second or abnormal generation is a budding—a natural outgrowth from the first—like a flower bud from its stem. And it is the *second*, like the flower bearing its seed, which produces the eggs from which grow again the parent form. But in the case of the Echinus, it is the parent form which is the bud, the ova producing only the intermediary, or the nurse as it is called. One would suppose that if these slow and stupid urchins should happen to produce a being livelier than themselves, and better fitted to get a living on the high seas, this latter animal would repeat itself, perpetuating the variation; certainly not reverting to the original form in the clumsy way that the Pluteus does. However, I am not here to settle differences among the doctors; but simply to tell a few life histories of the lowly tribes of the sea-shore.

The Echinus has several relatives which live in the same waters with itself. They are however very strange relatives, being in no manner like it in external appearance; and they would hardly have been mistrusted to be of the same family, if they had not been discovered to have the same peculiarity of producing ova which developed into another kind of animal, out of which they themselves grew, in some way or other, like parasites. This is the case with the star-fishes, the feather-stars, the crinoids, the sea-cucumbers, and the worms called Chirodota and Synapta.

These latter are very much like large angle worms, and live in holes in the sand and under stones lying very near low-tide mark. They are of great interest to the microscopist, from the fact that in their skins are found, in great quantity, the wheel plates and the anchor plates which make some of the most beautiful specimens of his cabinet. The anchors of the Synapta I can imagine to be of some sort of use to the worm in making its way in and out of its hole in the sand. I have held it up by merely touching it with my finger. But whatever can be the use of those beautiful wheels of the Chirodota, with hub and spokes and rim, made of the clearest calcareous glass, and laid away in such profuse clusters in their skins, I have not the remotest idea. I will be pleased to show you these objects, under dark-field illumination, at the close of the lecture.

In rambling about the island I happened one day to meet my friend, Dr. F. M. Hamlin, of Auburn, N. Y. He was in the outlet of Harrington Sound, in his high rubber boots, searching for the rare little bird's-head Polyzoa, the Avicularia. On the sides or the exposed under surfaces of rocks where some strong tide current runs almost continually, will sometimes be found these little animal clusters attached and growing like a tiny bunch of sea-weed. Later at his room we had some of these objects under the microscope while still living and disporting in their native element. I do not think I have ever seen a more interesting sight than they presented when magnified by a low-power objective. Every branch of the shining white tuft was swaying and instinct with animal life. One above another on all sides of the stems were perched the little sea-anemones, with their vases of bright colored tentacles searching about in the water. Over the side of each polyp cup and about half-way down, was loosely attached a miniature condor's head, slowly nodding and at the same time snapping its enormous jaws with savage spitefulness. Without a moment's respite, and without any apparent connection with the animal within the cup, these singular appendages keep up their mimic show of battle as long as there is life in the cell which they seem to guard. Whatever can be the use or office of these strange members of the community, it is very difficult to determine. They are too far removed and too clumsily large to be purveyors of food for their host. However, that they subserve some important purpose is quite certain; for there are no useless members or wasted functions in the animal economy. Several observers have noticed that when these formidable jaws have happened to seize some passing object like a minute crustacean, they have held on to it with a death grip. So it has been conjectured that the office of the bird's-head attachments was to catch animal prey and to hold it until it died and its decaying body brought around those swarms of infusoria which are always present to feed upon decomposing matter; and that these minute creatures, which are in reality the peculiar food of the polyzoa, are drawn into the mahlstrom which the tentacles are continually creating in the immediate vicinity. If this is the true explanation, and it seems somewhat probable, we have here a strange and altogether anomalous provision for the feeding of these ever stationary colonies. The question then naturally arises: how came these singular members to be jointed to the cells of certain genera of Polyzoa, and to be endowed with the instinct of catching prey that their masters never ate?

The general theory of evolution is that an organism lays hold of all the slight modifications of structure which are in anywise useful to it, and by perpetuating them through inheritance, eventually comes to possess the perfected organs or peculiarities. But in the case we have presented, you will doubtless agree with me that nothing less than a perfect seizing instrument and a fully acquired habit of holding on to its captures until they died and decomposed, would be of any use at all to the polyzoan animal. There can be no intermediate links—no less useful processes for natural selection to lay hold of. We must therefore suppose that these remarkable appendages sprouted out at once and all perfect, as a sport of nature; or else that they grew upon the animal without cause or provocation. For myself I hold to the opinion that we have not yet begun to fathom the depth of nature's plans in the matter of perfecting its great families and orders of organisms.

There is often thrown upon the sea shore some matted tufts of fibers which look like clusters of fine sea-mosses. But the microscope shows at once that they are of animal origin and built up by the budding out of successive polyp-like animals one above the other. They have much the appearance of the Polyzoa just described, but are built up on a larger and coarser pattern, and are really of an entirely different family. They are the Hydrozoa, nearly at the bottom of the scale of animal life, with a simple sack stomach, and scarcely another organized structure in their systems. But they exhibit in their manner of reproduction the most characteristic example of what is called the alternation of generation; and it is for that reason that I bring them forward. Certain buds of this plant-like organism, instead of growing as usual into feeding members of the colony, become cells or capsules in which are formed and sent out one after another little animals bearing not the slightest resemblance to the hydroid polyps. In fact they are jelly fishes, medusæ, those inert umbrella-shaped masses of jelly which we have all seen lazily floating about in the sea, or lying stranded on the shore. Of course there has been a rapid and perfectly enormous growth between the microscopic forms first produced and the jelly fishes as we have seen them. After attaining this growth and maturity, the medusæ produce what are called ciliated gemmules, which are simply hatched eggs provided with vibratile cilia. By means of these swimming hairs the embryos move about in the water, but finally settle to the bottom, become attached to some shell or rock, and grow into perfect Hydra with tentacles and horny cups, from which other polyps bud off until we have again the plant-like tuft from which we started.

All the numerous individuals of a hydroid colony are connected to a common alimentary canal running through the center of all the branches. There is therefore but one animal, though having many heads, like the fabled Hydra from which its name is derived. Constructed on one of the simplest plans of nature, with only its feeding arms, and a stomach common to the whole community, fixed for life to its permanent base, this creature, apparently so uncared for, at the proper season, like the tree which it simulates, pushes out a profusion of flower buds, from which it detaches the flowrets one after another and sends them forth to bear seed and to disseminate far and wide its progeny. All its needs are thus wonderfully provided for. But it is at the cost of operating almost a biological miracle. For an animal of one form and habit and life has begotten another of totally different form and habit and life; and this one after swelling to enormous proportions and voyaging the ocean for a time like a water baloon, has finally produced—not its like, nor anything resembling itself—but a brood of little insignificant polyps, that take root and vegetate like the lowest things that live.

Plate VIII.—BIRDS HEAD POLYZOA. AVICULARIA. Magnified about 30 Diameters. See Page xvi.

It is not however the case that all the Hydrozoa produce free-swimming medusæ; for instance this Sertularia, which I will show you later under the microscope with its beautiful white-beaded reproductive capsules, retains the generative medusoid forms within these capsules, and emits only the ciliated gemmules which are produced from them. On the other hand some of the medusæ do not generate the branching Hydrozoa. There seem to be all gradations in the relations between these two kinds of beings. And it is a matter of surprise, seeing that the connection is not necessary either to one or the other, that natural selection, if it operated at all between them, has not long ago dissolved all connection whatever.

But I have not time to describe more of the marvels of the marine invertebrate kingdom. To me it is by far the most interesting province of natural history. The world had passed more than half of its living age before animals began to have a bony skeleton. The fishes of the Devonian strata, which is the formation next below the coal measures, were the first creatures that possessed anything like a bony structure. All the animals before these were invertebrates; and they abounded and held sway while the sea was depositing in places ten miles of the thickness of the earth's crust. All the rocks that are below us where we are to night, were formed before ever there was a vertebrated animal in existence. The invertebrates belong then to the most ancient families of the world. They are the last surviving representatives of the oldest inhabitants. While all the higher races have been progressing from grade to grade, these have always remained the same, except in a few changes of dress and externals.

They tell us of the prevailing conditions of life in the earliest geological ages; for the spheres they filled and were adapted to then, are the restricted spheres they fill and are best adapted to now. The same environments have followed them down in their gradually diminishing numbers from the Silurian age to the present time. They tell us of the earliest fashions of growth and of reproduction; when animals budded and sprouted like plants; when instead of pairs, it took triplets to carry out the great behest "to go forth and replenish the earth."

They flourished in the ages before man was formed; before the beasts of the field, the fowls of the air, and the great whales were created; before the earth brought forth grass and the herb yielding seed and the tree yielding fruit after his kind; before the waters were gathered together and the dry land appeared. There is no day set apart for the creation of these lowly tribes. Yet they had the seas all to themselves for a period longer than four of the creative eras, and have had more to do with bringing the land to the surface of the waters than any other agency. They were the silent workers at the marbles and the limestones while shoreless oceans covered all the earth.

MICROSCOPICAL COLLECTIONS IN FLORIDA.*

It has been my fortune during the past two winters to spend a few weeks in the regions of central Florida. Lake Harris is the most southern and the most beautiful of the cluster of lakes which forms the source of that exceedingly picturesque river, the Ocklawaha. With high banks, and surrounded by a belt of hummock land as rich as any that Florida affords, this lake is becoming settled upon, and its lands are fast being taken up by enterprising southerners for orange-groves and pine-apple plantations. The sojourner will find the society of this lake-settlement intelligent and hospitable beyond anything that would be expected in so new and pioneer a country. The vegetation of this almost tropical region is so full of interest to the microscopist, and the causes conducing thereto so peculiar, that I have thought them deserving of especial mention and illustration.

The absence, or at least the rarity of frosts injurious to vegetation in these lake districts, gives the longest possible season for the growth and maturity of such organs as are best or especially adapted to the exigencies of Florida plants. There is a period of rest, usually comprising about the three winter months, after which vegetation takes up and continues its growth again as if there had been no period of interruption; so that practically there is a continuous development of plant life, whether annual or perennial, from birth to death.

The soil of Florida, as of all the South-Atlantic sea-board, is sandy and naturally barren. No polar glaciers have ground up

---

* A Paper read at the Boston meeting of The American Association for the Advancement of Science (August, 1880); and published in its proceedings; also in American Monthly Microscopical Journal, October, 1880.

for these regions, as for the Northern States, a rich and abundant alluvium, sufficient in itself for the production of a rapid and vigorous vegetation. The South has apparently only the siftings of our northern soil, carried down to the ocean by rivers, and then washed up by the sea-waves to form its interminable sandy plains. But to compensate for this natural infertility of soil, the atmosphere, especially of southern Florida, abounds in all the elements of plant growth. The winds which come up from the Gulf on one side, or the Atlantic on the other, are charged with moisture, and bear also minute quantities of nitric acid and saline compounds; while the exhalations from the swamps and marshes furnish in abundance the salts of ammonia and carbonic oxide.

Now to utilize these precious products from the air, it is necessary for plants to have peculiar organs, such as absorbing glands, glandular hairs, stellate hairs, protecting scales, and a variety of other special appendages. All these have been developed by time and necessity in remarkable profusion and perfection in the vegetation of southern Florida. Although the meagre soil produces no nutritions grasses and scarcely enough of an honest vegetation to keep an herbivorous animal from starving, yet there is an abundant flora such as it is—air plants, parasitic growths, insectivorous plants, and strange herbs, all seeking a livelihood in some other way than the good old honest one of growing from their roots. It is this fact which makes the microscopical interest of botanical researches in central Florida. One can scarcely examine with a two-thirds objective the flowers, leaves, or stems of any plant growing there, without discovering some beautiful or striking modification of plant hairs, or scales, or glands, or other absorbing or secreting organs.

We will notice first the Onosmodium as found in Florida—*O. virginianum*. It grows from Virginia south, but is more glandular I think in Florida than anywhere else. It will be almost the first plant one would stop to observe on entering the pine woods—a dark green, narrow-leaved, biennial herb; its straight stem of the second year's growth, about a foot high, bearing a raceme-like cluster of flowers, coiled at the end, and straightening out as the flowers expand. The leaves of this plant are thickly studded on both sides with stiff transparent hairs, lying nearly flat on the surface, and all pointing towards the tip end of the leaf. At the base of each hair is a cluster of glandular cells, amounting sometimes to fifty or more, arranged in beautiful geometrical forms. When pressed and dried in the herbarium, the body of the leaf turns to a dark green, almost black, and on this back-ground, with a half-inch objective, the hairs stand out like sculptured glass, and the glands like mosaics of purest pearls. I think it is the most attractive opaque object that can be shown under the microscope.

That these glandular cells, covering as they do nearly half the surface of the leaves, especially the upper surface, and differing from all other vegetable cells, subserve an important purpose in the sustenance of the plant, there cannot be a doubt; but just what that purpose is, or at least what is the mode of operation, I think, has never been ascertained.

In the same locality will very likely be found the most beautiful of all the Croton plants, the *C. argyranthemum*. Unlike the other Crotons, which are bushes, this is an herb growing only about a foot high, with a milky sap which exudes when the stem is broken. The leaves are silvery, verging in some cases to a bronze color, and are thickly covered on the upper side with most remarkable and beautiful stellate scales. The flower-buds and stems when pressed, make much more beautiful opaque objects than the leaves.

The object of these scales is, without doubt, to prevent the too rapid evaporation of the moisture stored up in the plant. They are the exquisitely woven blankets which preserve the precious juices so laboriously gathered. The same kind of covering is spread over the leaves and stems of all the air-plants of Florida, and doubtless for the same purpose. The well-known Florida moss, although not a moss, but a member of the pineapple family, (*Tillandsia usneoides*), is an exceedingly beautiful object under the microscope. Each hanging stem is overlaid with filmy white scales, every one of which is fastened in its place by what would seem to be the stamp of some miniature seal on golden-tinted wax. This plant as ordinarily seen on the live-oaks near cities, is a dirty-looking and unattractive object, and goes by the name of "black moss." But in out-of-the-way places, removed from the dust and smoke of settled localities, it is pearly white, and exceedingly beautiful both to the naked eye and under any power of magnification. Florida moss should be preserved with only very slight pressure, just enough to make the threads lie straight. After it has dried in this way, small cuttings may be mounted in the ordinary cells for opaque mounting.

On the high banks of the lake, and in the adjoining fields, may be found the large-leaved and vigorous-growing Calicarpa (*C. Americana*), sometimes called the French mulberry, a bush growing some five or six feet in height. The under sides of the leaves of this plant are nearly covered with little round, yellow, sessile glands, flattened on top and marked off into eight or ten sections by ribs like those on a melon. They are in immense numbers—something like thirty thousand to the square inch—over half a million on a good sized leaf. Under a light net-work of branching glandular hairs, viewed with a two-thirds objective, these polished amber-colored disks glisten like a spangle of golden beads.

The same kind of glands is found on the leaves of many other shrubs in Florida—the sweet myrtle (*Myrica cerifera*), the low ground blueberry (*Vaccinium tenellum*), a certain bush or dwarf hickory (*Carya glabra*) and some others. These glands have been variously called resin dots, resin glands, and odoriferous glands. So far as I can judge however they are not connected with any resinous or odoriferous secretions. From their almost perfect resemblance to the terminal bulb of the mushroom glands of the Pinguicula and Drosera, which are known to be absorbing glands, the probability is that these also serve to absorb moisture and ammonia from the atmosphere and from rains. Although I am free to acknowledge that the position of the glands, being for the most part on the under side of the leaves, militates somewhat against this view of their purpose.

Great care will have to be taken in pressing and drying vegetable specimens in the moist climate of Florida. The little threads of the mould fungus will be sure to creep over the surface of the leaves, spoiling them for microscopical material, if they are not quickly and effectually dried. For this purpose it is well to have a good supply of the bibulous botanical paper, and to change the specimens every day to fresh sheets for at least four or five days. The sheets after being once used, should be spread out in the sun to dry. A weight of about thirty pounds may be used for the pressure.

The objects heretofore mentioned are all for opaque mounting. Almost every preparer of slides has his own favorite method for this kind of work. I myself prefer the use of the transparent shellac cells. Clarified shellac is dissolved in alcohol, and filtered through cotton-wool under a bell glass, and with the application of heat. The solution is evaporated down until it is so thick that it will only just run—almost a jelly. In this condition it can be put on a slide with a camel's hair brush, on the turn-table, and very quickly worked up into a ring with the point of a knife, used first on the inside to make the cell of the size wanted, and then on the outside to turn the cement up into a compact ring. Two or three applications of the cement, with intervals of a day or two after each, will make cells of sufficient depth for all ordinary specimens. These cells dry quite slowly; and if artificial heat is used, it must be increased only very gradually, otherwise vapor of alcohol bubbles will make their appearance in them. A small ring of Brunswick black may be made inside of the cell, to which when thoroughly dry, the object may be fastened with a very little liquid marine glue. In this case both sides of the leaf can be seen, which is often desirable. In all opaque mountings a minute aperture should in some way be left open into the inside of the cell, so that it shall not be hermetically sealed up. This little precaution will save an innumerable number of failures.

The collector in Florida will not fail to secure a supply of the leaf stems of the castor oil plant (*Ricinus communis*). In regions beyond the influence of frosts, this plant grows continuously from year to year and becomes quite a tree. It is only in such a growth that the spiral tissue of the fibro-vascular bundles is fully perfected. The castor oil plants grown in our climate during one short season, will furnish very little spiral tissue, mostly spotted ducts and scalariform cells. There is no more beautiful object for multiple staining than thin longitudinal sections through the woody fiber, the vascular tissues, and the pith cells of the castor oil plant. I will briefly describe my process of making these stainings. After being decolorized in chlorinated soda, the sections may be left for half a day or more in a solution of carmine in water containing a few drops of aqua ammonia; then for half an hour in a rather weak solution of extract of logwood in alum water, and finally 10 to 15 minutes in a weak solution of anilin violet or blue in alcohol. From this they can be carried through absolute alcohol into turpentine, and mounted in balsam at any time thereafter. If successful in this staining you will have the pith cells in red, the spiral tissue in blue, the wood cells in purple and the stellate crystals in green or yellow.

But the chief objects of interest to the microscopist in the vegetation of Florida, are the insectivorous plants. Not only are they more abundant and, as I think, more perfectly developed in the central lake regions of Florida, but some varieties are found there different, it seems to me, from any found elsewhere. I desire particularly to mention one which I discovered, and which perhaps might be entitled to rank as a new species.

In a lagoon-like basin at the side of a small lake near Lake Harris, in water from two to three feet deep, I found numerous specimens of the insectivorous plant known as the Drosera or sun-dew, growing thriftily and floating about among the scattered water-weeds, without any attachment whatever, indeed with very little root of any kind, the dead leaves that hung down in the water seeming both to buoy it up and to hold it upright. This plant differs from all the described species of Drosera, so far as I have been able to ascertain, in having an upright, leaf-bearing stem from four to five inches long, in floating free on the water, and in having unusually long, vigorous and numerous leaves. As I never found this floating Drosera in any other location, and as there was an abundance of the ordinary *Drosera longifolia*

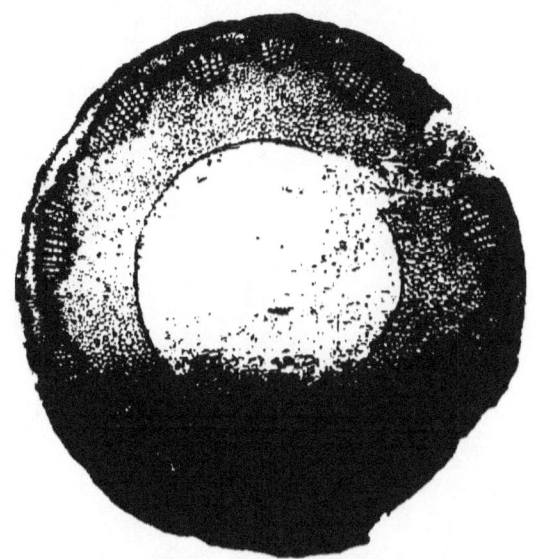

Transverse Section. Magnified 12 Diameters.

Plate IX.—SPIRAL TISSUE IN THE LEAF STEM OF THE CASTOR OIL PLANT. See Page xvi.

Longitudinal Section. Magnified 70 Diameters.

growing on the adjoining shore, I could not resist the suspicion that at this very spot in some past time a plant of the *longifolia* had by accident become uprooted, and floated out on the water; that finding it could capture insects even better on the water than crowded among shore plants, it adapted itself permanently to its new location and modes of growth. It appeared to me quite within the bounds of probability that here was an instance of the evolution of a species *in loco.*

The Drosera or "sun-dew" is found on the margins of nearly all small ponds and permanently wet places throughout the south. It is a small red plant, growing close to the ground, and glistening in the sunlight. Its little whorl of expanded leaves forms a circlet as beautiful as any flower, and often so very small that I have frequently mounted whole plants with flower-stalk and buds on an ordinary slide. Each leaf of the Drosera has, spread out on its upper surface and edges, from two to three hundred arms, called tentacles because endowed with the power of motion, and of such varying lengths that when naturally incurved, their ends just meet at the center of the leaf. Each tentacle has at its extremity a pad, like an extended palm, with a ridge raised lengthwise upon it; and in this palm is a bundle of spiral vessels connected with the same tissues in the leaf. Now all these tentacles secrete and exude from the glands at their ends a little drop of a very adhesive fluid; and the glistening of these drops in the sunlight on their usually bright red background, gives to the plant its beauty and its name of the "sun-dew." An insect attracted to and alighting on these leaves is inevitably held fast. The tentacles by which it is held very soon begin to bend towards the center of the leaf, carrying the fly with them. Then in some mysterious way, intelligence is communicated to the other tentacles, and they too begin to turn towards the center of the leaf, in the course of an hour or two completely covering the captured prey. If the insect is caught entirely on one side of the leaf, then only the tentacles of that side inflect. The glands after envelopment, exude a gastric fluid which dissolves the nitrogenous matter in the body, after which, by another change of function, they absorb and carry down into the plant all this nutritious little feast. In the course of three or four days the tentacles again expand and prepare themselves for another capture.

There are several reasons which lead me to believe that these unique and most wonderful organs of the Drosera are a direct and special development from the common simple mushroom glands, which are found on many plants, and which have for their primary function to absorb moisture and ammonia from the atmosphere and from rains. I found on the calyx and flower stem of the Drosera an abundance of these mushroom glands. Indeed the flower stem with its buds furnishes by reason of them an exceedingly beautiful object for the microscope, both in a natural state and when prepared by double staining.

I have found it quite a general rule as regards plants, that whatever organs, such as stellate hairs or glands, the leaves may possess, the calyx and stem of the flower will show them in far greater luxuriance and beauty. The stellate hairs of the Deutzia, the Crotons, and the Shepherdias, are far more numerous and striking on the flower buds than on the leaves. The mushroom glands which are found on the leaves of the Saxifrage and Pinguicula, are multiplied many fold in number and attractiveness on the calyx and flower stem of these plants. So I regard that this was once the case with the Drosera; and that the mushroom glands, which are now found on the flower, were then common to the leaves. A process of evolution has transformed them on the leaves into those wonderful motile arms adapted to the capture of insects, but has left them unchanged on the flower, where that function would be of no use to the plant. I occasionally find in my preparations a solitary mushroom gland among the tentacles of the leaf—a remnant of a race that has been supplanted. There is found in Portugal a plant very similar to the Drosera, the Drosophyllum, which has still only the mushroom glands on its leaves, and catches insects in great quantity by loading them down with the viscid secretion which these glands abundantly pour forth.

To exhibit the very delicate structure of the leaf and tentacles of the Drosera, it is necessary to color them slightly. The danger will be in over-staining; therefore, after decolorizing and immersing for a few hours in the carmine solution, the specimens should be exposed to only a very weak fresh solution of logwood for fifteen or twenty minutes. If the anilin blue is resorted to at all, it must be in a very weak solution. A mounting of a leaf and a stem with flower buds in one cell in camphorated or carbolated water, makes a very pretty and complete slide for the Drosera.

The Utricularia is a floating carnivorous plant which grows in the shallow water of quiet ponds. On the surface of the water from five to seven leaves are spread out like the spokes of a wheel, and from the center of these leaves the plant sends upward its flower stalk and downward its root-like branches, floating freely in the water. Among the thickly branching fibres of these long submerged stems, are perched innumerable little bladders or utricles, not much larger than the head of a pin, each provided with a mouth at the bottom of a sort of funnel of bristles, closed with a cunning little trap lid which opens inward, engulfing and imprisoning whatever minute creatures or substances may happen to be resting on it. In these sacks during the growing season, we will find numerous microscopic water fleas, mites and beetles, with grains of pine pollen and other floating particles. The organic bodies will be found in all stages of digestion, showing that the plant derives nourishment from such captured prey; and apparently its only means of livelihood is trapping.

When taken from the water and dried under slight pressure, the submerged portions of the Utricularia will be found literally covered with diatoms; and many very interesting chrysalids of water-insects will be found attached to them. These will all be washed off if the plant is bleached in chlorinated soda. To preserve them it will be necessary to remove the color in alcohol, and besides to handle very carefully. The staining can only be single; and I have found a weak solution of eosin in water, to be the best material for coloring, showing at the same time the structure of the utricles and the captures contained in them. Specimens of new growths, showing the just forming utricles and the peculiar circinate mode of growth, should be included on the slide. The mounting should be in camphorated water.

The Pinguicula, another of the insectivorous plants, is found abundantly on the more open plains, and not far from wet places. It is a compact rosette of very light green leaves, growing close to the ground, from the center of which rises a single flower-stalk, eight or ten inches high. The leaves have their edges turned up, forming a shallow trough, and on the upper surface are mushroom glands, which exude a viscid secretion. Insects are caught and held by this sticky substance until they die. The nutritious matter is then dissolved out by an acid secretion, and is ultimately absorbed into the substance of the plant by the glands on the leaf. The edge of a leaf when excited by a capture will bend over upon it for a short time, for the purpose of more effectually securing it, and of bathing it in the secretions. The calyx and flower-stalk, as I have already mentioned, are thickly covered with the same mushroom glands that are found more sparingly on the leaves. I have never seen any evidence that the flower appendages took any part in the digestion of insects. They seem to be rather in the nature of an ornamentation than of anything useful. For exhibition, therefore, or for double-staining, the calyx and flower stem will be found by far the most attractive part of the plant. The best way to preserve them, as well as all such small material, until wanted for use, is to put them green into a common morphia vial with a few drops of alcohol and water, and then to cork and seal them up tight with melted beeswax. To prepare them for the slide these objects may be treated precisely as recommended for sections of castor-oil plant, but should be mounted in a weak solution of glycerine in camphorated water.

If cells are made of rings punched out of the thin sheets of colored wax, used by artificial flower makers, and then coated with either liquid marine glue, or a mixture in equal parts of gold size and gum dammar dissolved in benzole, this method of liquid mounting may be as easily and safely performed as mounting in balsam. In very many cases simple water, made antiseptic in any manner, will be found far preferable to any other media, both for retaining the full and distended forms of minute organs, and for bringing out the delicate markings of vegetable structure which the highly refractive balsam would entirely obliterate.

There is only one other insectivorous plant found in Florida, the pitcher plant, (*Sarracenia variolaris*), a species growing only in the South Atlantic States. It is found in low and wet places among the open pine-barrens, but is not as abundant as the others which have been mentioned. The leaf is a hollow, conical or trumpet-shaped tube, with a flange or wing running up one side, and a hood which arches over the orifice of the tube. During the growing season this tube is usually more than half filled with water, which we must suppose secreted by the plant itself, because the hood effectually sheds all rain water from it. Crowded into the bottom of the tubes of mature leaves, we shall almost invariably find a mass of the hard and indigestible parts of insects. These creatures have been in some way attracted into that suspicious looking receptacle, and once in have been unable to get out again. A mere partially covered tube however, with a little water in it, is by no means a fly-trap. Not one insect in a hundred would fall into that well and drown, if there were not some special device absolutely preventing it from crawling upward. Now a microscopical examination of the inside of the hood and tube of the pitcher plant reveals the most skillful contrivance for securing insect prey that could possibly be imagined. In the first place, there are in the upper part of the receptacle and about the mouth, great numbers of sessile glands which secrete abundantly a sweet fluid very attracting to ants and flies. Further, there is on the inner surface of the hood and mouth, a formidable array of comparatively long pike-pointed spines, all pointing backward and downward. These grade off into shorter, more blunt, but still exceedingly sharp-pointed spines, which overlap each other like tiles on the roof of a house. This kind of coating lines the tube for a third of the way down, the spines growing finer until at last they grade off into regular hairs which line all the lower part of the tube; spines and hairs all pointing downward. An insect attempting to retrace its steps after its ambrosial feast, would find nothing which it could penetrate or grasp with the hooklets of its feet; and the wetness of the spines, from the constantly overflowing glands, would probably prevent it from making use of any other device that insects may have for climbing glazed surfaces. As a matter of fact no creature comes out of that prison house, unless it be with the single exception of one cunning spider, which in some way finds a safe and rich retreat under the hood of its great vegetable rival.

The bodies of the captured prey fall into the fluid in the tube and are macerated or decomposed, but without any signs of putrescence. Therefore the plant must at once absorb the animal matter, for otherwise this would cause the infusorial life which is called putrefaction.

In order to show the internal structure of the pitcher plant leaf, it will be necessary to separate the cuticle which bears the spines and glands from the rest of the leaf. To do this, pieces cut from the leaf, and preferably those showing the transition from one kind of spines into another, after being soaked in water, may be put into common nitric acid, and this brought up to the boiling point over an alcohol lamp. They should then be immediately washed in several waters, when it will probably be found that the cuticle, both the inner and the outer, has already separated from the parenchyma. The specimens will need no further bleaching, and may be stained either in eosin dissolved in water, or in anilin blue in alcohol. As there is only one kind of tissue to be stained, it will be impossible to get more than one color in them. They should be mounted or kept in water very slightly acidulated with carbolic acid.

I cannot but regard the pitcher plant as the most highly developed, and the most specialized in its organization of any of the insectivorous plants. It differs more widely from ordinary vegetation, and has more special and adapted contrivances about it, than any of the others. Now as I believe that the truth of the modern evolutionary theory will be eventually brought to a test by well-studied monographs, made by microscopists, on some such highly differentiated organic structures as this pitcher plant, I do not deem it a digression to present here briefly some inferences which seem to me to arise from the developmental history of this particular plant. Of course, if the pitcher plant was developed from other and ordinary plants, it had at one time the simple plain leaves of common herbs. It must have early commenced in some way to appropriate insect food on these leaves, because every subsequent change was for the betterment of the plant in this direction. The stem of the leaves soon began to put out flanges or wings on each side, the phyllodia of the botanists, which are not uncommon among plants. And these outspread wings must have assisted in the absorption of insect food that was washed down upon them. Then the edges of the wings turned up, and curved around towards each other, until finally they met and grew together, forming a tube and a much more complete receptacle for decomposing animal bodies. A South American genus, the *Heliamphora*, is just in this partly developed condition at the present time. Then from some unknown cause and in a way exceedingly difficult to explain, our *Sarracenia* commenced preparations for an entirely different manner of capturing insects. The leaf bent over the orifice of the tube, forming the hood, and those remarkable spines and tiled plates were developed on the inside of the hood and tube, growing backwards, contrary to the order of nature. When all this was accomplished and fully completed, but not before, our plant could commence its career as the most successful trappist of either the vegetable or the animal kingdom.

Now according to the Darwinian theory, all these transformations were the result of innumerable slight and favorable variations, each one of which happened to be so beneficial to the particular plant concerned, that it got the start of all the others, and every time run them all out of existence. One cannot tell how many million times this extinction and reproduction must have occurred, before our marvellously perfect little fly-trap was finally produced. Excuse me if I confess that not all the canonical books of Darwin are sufficient to make me put faith in the miracles attributed to natural selection and the survival of the fittest. I believe in the fact of the progressive development of the organic kingdom; for all science teaches it. But I believe it was governed and guided by forces more potent than chance variation and adaptive selection. The Being, or the First Cause if you will, who originated the simple elements of matter, and endowed them with the power and the tendency to aggregate into developing worlds, might equally as well have endowed certain of them with the power and the tendency to aggregate into ever advancing organisms. There is no element of chance in the myriad forms of crystalline and chemical substances; then why should there be in the scarcely more varied colloid forms of living matter? In a world that unfolds from chaos in one steady line of progress, that shows only design at every advancing stage, I must logically place somewhere at its commencement the almighty fiat of a Designer.

ON THE PREPARATION OF OBJECTS FOR THE MICROSCOPE.*

In the matter of microscopic objects and preparations, I acknowledge myself the advocate of the beautiful. In this new world which the microscope has opened up to us, I seek mainly, if not only, for that which is fair and lovely to behold. In the estimation of some of the professors of this science, I am afraid that this acknowledgment will place me in the class of those who make of the microscope a plaything, and who turn a means of instruction into a means of amusement only. But to me it seems that the field of microscopic research is so vast, and the harvest of instructive lessons so abundant, that I may be excused for gathering only the flowers.

The specialist and the expert, for the purpose of personal information and judgment, will have occasion, and ought, to examine the minutest and the dryest details in the line of his specialty. But he who would simply draw interesting lessons from nature, or instruction for the uninformed, need not go beyond the beautiful and the attractive in the list of microscopic objects. The facts of science and the range of discovery can be amply, and I think best illustrated by preparations which strike the eye and command the attention.

To illustrate my meaning, I will show you later this evening a longitudinal section through the fibro-vascular bundles in the leaf-stem of the castor-oil plant. It is, I think, one of the most beautiful objects in structural botany, and at the same time it opens up to us some of the most interesting and puzzling quest-

*A Paper read before the Rochester Microscopical Society, Dec. 11th, 1879.

ions in the history of plant growth. As you know, there is in plants almost as complete a circulation of fluids as in our own bodies. The sap travels up from the roots through the capillary tubes which are grouped in these fibro-vascular bundles, and from them passes out through the veins of the leaves. At the tip end of the veins it turns into another set of tubes underneath, and follows its course backward, gradually descending towards the roots again, through cells between the bark and the wood, where it leaves its deposit of formed material. The capillary tubes of the vascular bundles were first and originally formed as rows of large cells placed one on top of another. Afterwards the partition walls which separated the cells were absorbed and they became perfect tubes. Then on the inside of these tubes were deposited closely coiled spiral threads, sometimes rings, and sometimes again more open spirals, running in opposite directions and crossing each other, forming what are called the spotted ducts. But the spiral tubes, or tissues as they are called, are certainly the most remarkable structures in the vegetable economy. They are larger and more numerous in the castor oil plant than in any other that I know of. But even in that plant, it is as if wire, far finer than any silk or spider-web fiber, had been closely wound around a form more slender than the finest cambric needle, and then these coils had been laid away in groups or bundles of twenty or more in the woody tissues next to the pith cells. But now comes the puzzling question of how these spiral tissues or threads were formed. By what laws of growth, or by what natural process were these strange and complicate structures built up? The botanist has not yet been able to find it out.

I may show you also this evening the remarkable glandular organs, called the mushroom glands, of certain insectivorous plants, which glands are said to secrete a gastric juice that digests the bodies of insects, and which afterwards absorb the products of that digestion. They are found on the upper surface of the leaves, where they fulfill this extraordinary function. But what is very strange, they also follow up the stem of the flower, and are most beautiful and abundant on the outer leaves or sepals of the blossom, where it cannot be supposed that they ever have occasion to perform their peculiar office. But I have found it very generally the case that whatever appendages the leaves of a plant may have, the calyx of the flower will show them in much greater beauty and abundance.

I have said this much to explain in a measure my predilection for botanical subjects for the microscope. There is no end to beautiful things among them, both for artificial preparation and unprepared specimens, as opaque objects. There may be beautiful things among the preparations of animal tissues and growth, but I must confess that I have never yet seen many of them. Compare the plates of any animal histology, the illustration of Beale's work on the Microscope, for instance, with the elaborate drawing's of Sach's Botany. To use a rather gross comparison, the former might remind one of a German sausage shop, the latter of a French fancy store.

Now the only way in which vegetable preparations can be made available for the microscope—that is, to be seen by transmitted light—is to remove the green chlorophyl, or other coloring matter, by either soaking in alcohol or immersing for a time in the Labarraque fluid, which is the same as the chlorinated soda sold by druggists as a disinfectant. Alcohol merely dissolves out the coloring matter, leaving the cell contents, or the protoplasmic matter, still in the specimen. Therefore an object decolorized in alcohol will be somewhat more opaque than if decolorized in chlorinated soda, which destroys all the softer parts, leaving only the frame work, or the cellulose. Sometimes the alkaline soda in this preparation is not fully saturated or neutralized by chlorine. In this case vegetable substances will be eaten up and destroyed in it, as they would be in any alkali. This fact has given the preparation a bad name with some microscopists, who say that it is unsafe to use. But I have never experienced any trouble in the use of that which has been made by reliable chemists. The preparation should be kept in the dark as much as possible, as light causes it to precipitate. Thin objects such as ordinary leaves and thin sections will be decolorized in this solution in from twelve to twenty-four hours. They must then be thoroughly washed in several waters to remove all trace of the crystallizable solution.

Now in order to bring out and to contrast the various tissues, as the woody fiber, the cell walls, the ducts and spiral vessels, it is necessary to recolor these objects; and it is highly desirable, if possible, to color the various parts differently. Now it is a singular and fortunate fact that certain colors, or at least certain pigments, will either go to certain sets of tissues and leave the others entirely unaffected, or they will color certain tissues quicker and more readily than they will others. Thus carmine dissolved in water with a few drops of aqua-ammonia in it, will color only cell contents. Therefore, for carmine to have its best effect, or indeed any great effect, it is necessary that the leaves or thin sections be decolorized in alcohol, which does not remove the albuminoid matter. Again, the extract of logwood, dissolved in weak alum water, will color first the woody cells or fibers, then other cell walls, as the pith and leaf cells; and finally, if the specimen is left in it long enough, it will color the spiral and other vascular tissues. It is therefore well to remove the objects from this dye before its work is complete—say in from fifteen to thirty minutes. And if it has then colored them too far or too deeply, they may be soaked in pure alum water, which will remove the color in the reverse order already named above. Lastly, aniline blue dissolved in alcohol will color spiral tissues, hairs, glands, resin dots, leaf veins and generally all that is left uncolored by the other pigments. I have not however been able to color the stellate hairs of Deutzia, Croton, Shepherdia and others, with aniline blue. Aniline green will color them; but it is not always a permanent color. It is very powerful in its action and requires only a minute or two to do its work.

A general formula for double or multiple staining may then be given as follows: Carmine one day, logwood half an hour, and aniline blue an hour. But it is nevertheless true that each kind of objects, as for instance sections of stems, thick leaves and thin leaves, leaves to show crystals, and those to show hairs or glands, will require a somewhat different treatment one from the other. It is very desirable that experimenters in this field should record their experiences, thus giving us a literature on the subject which shall be a guide to future operators for all similar preparations.

Now in regard to the mounting of double stainings; balsam is undoubtedly the best medium for all such as will bear this mounting. An object mounted in Canada balsam is sure to improve with age. If we can say of other media that they will preserve their objects without change, it is the highest excellence that can be expected from them. But a preparation in balsam will be brighter and clearer the more the volatile elements are evaporated from the medium—that is, the older it is. It is however a fact that high refractive media, such as balsam and, less so, glycerine, will obliterate, or render indistinct, the fine and delicate markings of objects. There are very many vegetable stainings which in balsam are without character or interest, but which in carbolated or camphorated water are veritable beauties; all the fine cellular markings and the smallest hairs or glands appearing plain and distinct. I think it is safe to say that more than half of the vegetable preparations you will have to do with, if you exploit this field, will appear to better advantage in water than in any other medium.

So it has been quite a study with me for some time back to find a means and a mode of fluid mounting both expeditious and reliable. I am happy to say that I have found a method which, so far as I can judge from the limited time that I have used it, seems to be fully satisfactory. At least I have yet to discover the faults of it. Our worthy member, Mr. Streeter, has been lately making a very neat and ingenious set of punches by which circular rings, five-eighths and three-fourths of an inch in diameter, can be cut out of the colored sheets of wax used by the artificial flower makers. Several colors of this wax are made in sheets double thick, and if a still greater thickness is desired, two or more sheets may be laid on top of each other. These rings, if cemented in any way to the slide, make very convenient cells for opaque mounting. But it occurred to me that if they were covered with a coating of some cement, such as marine glue, which is unaffected by any of the liquids used for preserving objects, they would be exactly what is wanted for fluid mounting; for the great requisite in fluid mounting is a cell that is a little soft or yielding, so that the thin glass cover will come down into close contact with the cell all around. When this is the case, you can quickly take up the fluid that runs out, with a camel's hair brush, and at once apply a coating of cement to the edges of the thin glass, and your slide requires no further care. But if the thin glass cover does not fit closely to a cell, the air will be very apt to get in while you are drying it; and when you come to put on the cement, that will be almost sure to run in.

The marine glue, with which I thought to cover the wax cells, is a composition of equal parts of India rubber and shellac, dissolved in mineral naphtha. It has long been considered the most adhesive and permanent cement that can be made; and from the large quantity of rubber in it, it would seem as if it ought to be impervious to all the liquids used in mounting.

In applying these wax circles to the slide, a little care is necessary, that no air bubbles remain between the wax and the glass, nor in the cement which covers the cell. First, make a ring of cement on the slide, with a small camel's hair brush, of the same size of the wax ring. Then lay on the ring, accurately centering it on the turn table, and press it down under a piece of writing paper held on it in such a way that the ring underneath cannot be displaced. It is well to let this dry for a day. Then cover the top and the edges of the cell with one or two coats of liquid marine glue, and in two or three days it can be trimmed with the point of a knife blade, cleaned and used for mounting.

As a preservative fluid, one can use carbolated water—four or five drops of carbolic acid to each ounce of filtered water—or camphorated water—that in which a little fine camphor has been mixed and afterwards filtered—or any other preparation of water which will prevent fungoid growths, or in other words preserves the objects. Put enough of the liquid in the cell to fill it full, immerse and arrange the objects in it, and then let a thin glass cover of the proper size come gently down on the liquid. It will infallibly press out all the air and settle gradually on the cell ring, pushing out all superfluous fluid. A gentle pressure around the edges will make the glass attach itself to the cell so that it can hardly be moved. Then, with a small camel's hair brush, take up the outside fluid, squeezing the brush between the thumb and finger to dry it. When as dry as the brush will make it, apply a coating of the marine glue around the edges of the glass cover, and the slide is finished, so far as its safety and durability is concerned.

In looking over and arranging my cabinet of specimens not long since, I was greatly surprised at the great number of slides that were merely opaque mountings—fully one-half, I should say. Now this implies that I have found as much beauty in natural unprepared objects as in those which have been in some way carried through a process of preparation, such as staining, cleaning in potash or acids, carrying through alcohol and turpentine into balsam, etc. There is an exhaustless field of attractive objects in the scales of the insect tribes, the feathers of birds, the shells of the protozoans, the spore cases of mosses and ferns, the hairs and glands of plant leaves, in seeds and pollen. All these require mounting as opaque objects; and, in my view, the best way to do it is to make cells either of shellac cement or of the wax sheets, as I have already described, and in the center of them paint with Brunswick black a round disk three-eighths or one-half of an inch in diameter. On this disk, when thoroughly dry, fasten the object with a minute drop of marine glue, and fasten a thin glass cover on the cell with the same cement. With this form of mounting, the Lieberkuhn can be used or not, as one may desire. I have found it necessary in almost every case of dry mounting to leave a small opening into the cell, either by filing a little notch on the ring and leaving this open when the cover is cemented on, or by afterwards pushing a small cambric needle through the ring. If the cell is hermetically sealed, the expansion and contraction of the air within, by changing temperature, seems to cause a slow movement in the cements that are inside of it, no matter how much they have been previously dried. The walls of the ring or the finishing varnishes will work inward and spoil the mounting, or the object will be slowly immersed in the black cement that forms the background. All these troubles seem to be obviated by the minutest aperture opening into the cell.

I have on several occasions, both here and elsewhere, recommended the shellac cement, which is now made by Mr. G. H. Haass, the druggist, on East Main Street, as the best material for building up cells for dry mounting. I have never yet seen occasion to change my opinion in regard to it. The cells are beautiful, durable and tough as horn when thoroughly dry. The cement is so easily managed, can be so readily worked up into a ring with the point of a knife blade on the turn table, that I would think almost any one could easily acquire the skill or knack of making the cells. I have made many hundreds of them, and I know they cost me less labor and time than any other cell that is made. I always carry along two dozen at a time, first laying the foundation of the rings, making them of the right size in diameter and breadth, then afterwards, with a day or two of interval each time, making successive additions to them until they are of the required depth. One hour's time is sufficient for each operation with the whole two dozen; and four times going over them would make the deepest cells that one would ever have occasion to use. Thus it takes me only ten minutes in all, and at the most, for the making of each cell, and it does not require any subsequent painting or fixing up. After the mounting is completed however, I usually finish around the outside with balsam, turning it up trim and true with the knife point on the turn table.

As I desire these remarks to be a pretty full expression of my views and experience in the higher forms of mounting, I cannot omit speaking a few words in regard to a certain cement which has been recommended to you for cells for fluid mounting, on the authority of Dr. Hunt, of Philadelphia. It is white zinc mixed with gum dammar dissolved in benzole. Now every preparer of slides would hail with delight a white cement that was safe to use in all cases, but unfortunately no cement can be made white without the mixture in it of solid particles, particles that do not dissolve, that settle to the bottom of your vials. It is a mechanical mixture, and no cement is safe to use in contact with liquids

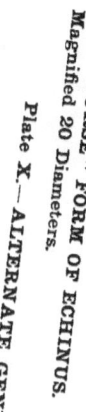

THE PLUTEUS, OR "NURSE" FORM OF ECHINUS.
Magnified 20 Diameters.

THE ECHINUS, OR SPINY SEA-URCHIN.
One-half Natural Size.

Plate X.— ALTERNATE GENERATIONS OF ECHINUS. See Page xvii.

of any kind, that is not a thorough and complete solution in all its parts. This is the experience of all microscopists. Dr. Carpenter, who as you know is no mean authority, says: "The varnishes used for mounting objects in liquid should always be such as contain no mixture of solid particles. This is a principle on which the author from an experience of many years is disposed to lay great stress." He says, "that he has always found that such cements (mechanical mixtures), although they may stand well for a few weeks or months, become porous after a greater lapse of time, allowing the evaporation of the liquid and the admission of air." White zinc cement may answer for finishing purposes, if used with great caution; but it is at best a very treacherous material, insidiously working its way into places where it has no business to be. It has caused more failures than any other material we work with. I know that nine-tenths of my lame ducks have white feet.

In conclusion I would remark that there is a strange fascination in the art of the microscopist. It has been the life work of many men of cultivated and superior minds. It has been the recreation of a vast number of scientific and professional men. Those who have once taken it up in the love of it, have seldom laid it aside. There is in it the widest field for the display of ingenuity and artistic taste, together with the fullest scope for research and new discoveries. To the gratification of accomplishing a new process or of finding a new object of interest or beauty, there is added the highest incentive which is now left to the man of science—that of searching out the secrets of nature on the border-land of the invisible. Be assured that the field of labor and research to which this evening I seek to incite your exertion and your emulation, is at once the most fascinating, the most important, and the most honorable of the occupations of cultured minds.

THE PREPARATION AND MOUNTING OF DOUBLE STAININGS.*

There is no art of the microscopist more beautiful and interesting than that of bleaching and re-coloring vegetable tissues. In no other way can the wonderful processes of plant growth be made manifest under the microscope. Therefore, any suggestions tending to simplify the art and make it more generally practicable, will be of interest to all workers in microscopic preparations. In my experiments with double staining I have found that different colors, or at least different pigments, vary greatly in the activity or penetrating power with which they affect vegetable substances. Thus, an object prepared for staining may be left in a strong solution of carmine for a day without having all its parts colored; whereas in a logwood or analine dye of equal strength, it would be colored perfectly opaque in less than an hour. By taking advantage of this fact and immersing objects, first in the color having the slowest action, then in another of greater activity, and so on, double or even multiple staining becomes a simple process, instead of the very difficult and complicated one which has been published in our magazines.

I will give the general details of the operation as I have now practised it for some little time. I do not claim that exactly the same formula will answer for all kinds of plant specimens, or that all the colors given below should be used in all cases. I merely give a general formula, which each operator will find it necessary to vary somewhat according to the results of his experimenting. If I succeed in stimulating others to more detailed work, by showing how simple the process is in most cases, I will have accomplished my purpose. All vegetable preparations, whether parts of leaves or sections of stems, should first be fully decolorized in the common chlorinated soda solution,

* A Paper read before the National Microscopical Congress, held at Buffalo, August, 1878, and published in its Proceedings.

sold by all druggists as a disinfectant. This result will be accomplished in most cases in about one day. Then, after being thoroughly washed in pure water, the preparations should be placed in a solution of carmine of about the consistence of common carmine ink; and they may remain in this for a day. Pure carmine will readily dissolve in water with a few drops of aqua-ammonia in it. After being washed in two or three changes of pure water, the objects may now be placed in a somewhat weaker solution of extract of logwood in alum water. A small quantity of alum in the water is sufficient to effect, at least with the aid of heat, the solution of the logwood. This should be filtered, not old at the time of use, and of a strength not more than half that of common writing ink. In this solution the objects may remain from fifteen to thirty minutes, according to the delicacy of the specimens. If the color should appear to be too deep or opaque, it may be partly removed by soaking in pure alum water. Then, after washing again in several waters to remove all trace of the alum, place the objects in alcohol for a short time, and then into a weak solution of aniline blue in alcohol. In this they may remain an hour or two, or until all the parts not previously stained are colored blue. If on trial the blue should appear to be too deep, it may be partially removed by soaking for a time in pure alcohol. It sometimes happens that even aniline blue will not color all the parts of vegetable substances, such as large glandular or stellate hairs. In this case an immersion for a minute or two in a very weak solution of aniline green in alcohol will accomplish the work. Green is the most powerfully absorbent color that I know of; and should be used with caution, as it would soon spoil a staining.

From alcohol the objects may be removed directly to turpentine. I do not like the action of oil of cloves. It shrivels up the tender tissues and gives them the appearance of being burned. Besides, it is not necessary as an intermediary between alcohol and turpentine. After a day's immersion in turpentine the preparations will be ready for mounting in Canada balsam. Vegetable preparations have quite an appreciable thickness, and unless some special care is taken of them after being mounted in balsam, it will be found that air will quite often work in under the cover. Therefore, as soon as a balsam mounting is dry enough to have the superfluous balsam cleaned off with the point of a knife around the thin glass cover, which will be in two or three days, especially if aided by heat, a light coating of shellac cement, colored with aniline blue or red, not green or yellow, can be spread with a camel's hair brush around the edge of the cover, and the next day another coating, and perhaps the third day another still. In this way the cover will soon be firmly set and can be cleaned; and the slide is a permanent mounting in much shorter time than if left simply for the balsam to dry hard; and there is no risk of air working in from the drying of the balsam. Canada balsam is by far the best and safest medium in which to mount all stained preparations that will bear this mounting. But there are many, such as those with delicate hairs or glands, or with fine cellular markings, that will not show to advantage in so refractive a medium as balsam. These may be removed from alcohol into water containing three or four drops of carbolic acid to the ounce of water. It will be necessary also to mount them in the same fluid in the cells. Well dried shellac cells may be used; and if the tops are made perfectly level by holding a bit of fine sand paper on them while being turned on the turn-table, the thin glass cover will fit closely, pressing out the superfluous water, which can be taken up with a camel's hair brush. When well dried in this way, a little gold size can be applied to the edges with perfect safety against its running in. A very simple and almost universally applicable cell I have recently made in the following manner: My friend Wm. Streeter, foreman in the works of Sargent & Greenleaf, of Rochester, makes a neat little double punch for the purpose of cutting out narrow circles from the thin colored sheets of wax used by artificial flower-makers. Either single, doubled or three-folded sheets can be used, according to the thickness of cell that may be required. These circles may be fastened on the slide, either by shellac cement or by simply warming the slide. Then over all the cell, both inside and out, a coating of gold size or of marine glue dissolved in coal naphtha, must be spread with a camel's hair brush. When this is dry we have a cell beautifully colored, and proof against all the fluid media which one may have occasion to use in mounting. Besides, the cell is always soft enough to have the thin glass cover pressed into perfect contact with it all around, which is the great requisite in all fluid mountings. It should afterward be finished on the outside with Brunswick black or shellac cement to form a firm support to the thin glass cover.

REPLY TO THE QUESTIONS RAISED IN THE DISCUSSION OF THE PAPER.

In answer to the objections which have been made to the use of chlorinated soda, on the ground that it is liable to destroy the structure of tender vegetable substances, I would say that if leaves are dried and pressed, or stems are first dried and then soaked before cutting into sections, they will not be injuriously affected by the soda solution. At least that has been my experience. I am informed however that there are preperations sold under the name of chlorinated soda, which are imperfectly saturated with chlorine; and consequently are still strongly alkaline. These would naturally have the effect to destroy organic structures. Moreover, if this solution is exposed much to the light there is a precipitate formed and deposited, which may leave the fluid more strongly alkaline and therefore more destructive in its effects upon vegetable tissues. The preparation known as Labarraque's fluid, imported from France, is perhaps the most reliable for bleaching purposes, though somewhat more expensive than the home-made chlorinated soda solution.

In regard to decolorizing vegetable substances by soaking in alcohol, this may be very well with thin and tender specimens, and where the object is to exhibit the cell contents; but where the object is to show the cellular structure or the fibro-vascular tissues, I think that the results will be more satisfactory in the use of the stronger chlorinated solution, which removes entirely the cell contents, and makes the specimen more transparent, and in my view far more beautiful.

SOME NEW FORMS OF MOUNTING.*

I have the pleasure of offering, as my contribution to the Microscopical Congress, a brief description of some recent methods which I have used in the preparation of slides. The cement which is essential to these processes, and which I regard as the most important working material of the microscopist, is shellac varnish, prepared in the following simple manner: The white clarified stick-shellac is dissolved in alcohol, and filtered through cotton once or more times until it is quite clear and transparent. As the filtering is a somewhat difficult operation, it will probably be best for most persons wanting it, to let the druggist make this preparation for them. With this cement I build up a cell as deep, and perhaps as quickly, as one can be made with a curtain ring, painted up as it usually is. As much as one or two drops of the cement can be put on a slide with a brush, using the turn-table, and then slowly worked up into a narrow ring with the point of a small knife-blade held on the turning slide. When this has dried a day or two, another layer can be put on and worked up in the same way. Three or four such layers will be sufficient for almost any cell, and it can then be dried in the heating oven and laid aside for future use. By carrying along a dozen or two slides at a time, one will find great economy both of time and labor. These rings, being transparent, are admirably adapted for opaque mountings that may be used with the Lieberkuhn.

If common curtain rings are cemented to slides with the shellac cement colored with aniline blue, the joined edges of the brass film of which they are made being on the glass, and then

---

* A Paper read before the National Microscopical Congress, held at Indianapolis, August, 1879, and published in its Proceedings.

subjected to a slowly increasing heat until the cement begins to burn, a very beautiful appearance is given to the under side of the ring, a circle of minute golden links, as seen in the specimens which I offer for your inspection. These rings can then be painted on the turn-table according to one's fancy, and used as cells for any kind of mounting.

I use this cement, colored with the various aniline dyes which are soluble in alcohol, for painting and finishing slides. These colors are far superior, for all purposes of ornamentation, to any other materials or devices of painting. They dry quickly, and adhere to glass with greater tenacity than any other cements that I have ever used.

For a cell that will perfectly withstand the action of Canada balsam or turpentine, I make use of shellac cement colored with aniline blue, in the following manner: After a cell of the required depth has been made on the slide, and pretty thoroughly dried in the usual way, it is heated on the heating table, lightly at first, in order to avoid bubbles, then gradually increasing the heat until the cement commences to smoke and the color to burn out. By heating one side of the ring a very little more than the other, as may be done over an alcohol lamp, a part may be left blue, while the rest is yellow or reddish, which has a very pretty effect under Canada balsam. These cells are hard as bone, and can scarcely be cut from the glass. Balsam has no effect on them whatever. Slides may be finished off outside with liquid balsam, made true and circular with the point of a knife on the turn-table. In a few days, or in a shorter time by using the oven, they will be ready to clean and lay away. The cells which I have described are the only cement cells that can be used with Canada balsam. They are particularly adapted to vegetable stainings, algæ, and other preparations, either too thick or too tender to be mounted in balsam without something to sustain the thin glass covers.

In opaque mountings, where cements of any kind are used either for backgrounds or to hold objects in place, I have found it highly advantageous to leave on or in the lower part of the ring, a minute aperture opening into the cell, not necessarily larger than a fine cambric needle would make. With this provision both the cell and the cements go on drying, and there is no sinking in nor moving about of the objects in the cements which hold them. But if the cell be hermetically closed, one may almost certainly expect that the beautiful shell or other object will sooner or later be overwhelmed in a black sea. I have lost in this way scores of foraminifera and coralline specimens on which I had expended a great deal of labor. If curtain rings are used for the cell, a little notch can be filed in the under side of it, and this be left open on the lower side of the slide when finished.

If the opaque mountings are for dry objects, I make in the center of the ring a disk of Brunswick black, or white zinc, according as the object to be shown is white or dark. It may be 5-16 of an inch in diameter for the Lieberkuhn of the $1\frac{1}{2}$ inch objective, but not over a quarter of an inch for that of the two-thirds objective. After the cement is dry and quite hard, a slight coat of balsam is spread over it, and the objects placed in this and arranged, if necessary, under the microscope. The slide is then set aside to dry, and may be covered safely the next day.

If the objects to be mounted will bear immersion in balsam, as shells, plant seeds, minerals, etc., I pursue the following plan: The thin glass covers are cemented to some old slips, which are kept for that purpose, by two or three touches of balsam applied at the edge of the cover. Care is taken in this, and in all cases, to accurately center all work on the slides by means of the self-centering turn-table. Then, on a light coating of balsam in the center of the cover, the objects, whatever they may be, are placed and arranged. When quite dry, and the objects are thus securely fastened, they may be completely covered by balsam, and put into the drying oven until thoroughly hardened. Then, over the balsam, Brunswick black, if the objects are white, or white zinc cement, if they are dark or high colored, may be spread, by thin layers at first, each being dried in the open air for a day before the next is applied, until there is an opaque covering to the objects. The thin glass cover is now to be thoroughly cleaned around the objects and then removed from the slip by a slight heating, just sufficient to loosen it. It can then be turned over and mounted on the cell designed for it.

The best preparation for fastening the cover to the cell is gelatine, dissolved in water, with enough alcohol added to liquify it from the jelly state. I place the thin glass on the cell, and then apply the gelatine solution with a brush around the edges, leaving the little opening on the lower side. Just enough of the water cement seems to run in under the glass, and to dry just where it is placed. Afterwards the cell may be finished with liquid balsam, carefully avoiding the little aperture, and the outer edge gathered up into a neat trim little circle, with the point of a knife on the turn-table.

The last and most important recommendation which I have to make, is the strict observance of every rule and precaution tending to neatness and cleanliness. There is a world of beauty and delight in the revelations of the microscope; and there is a peculiar fitness that all the surroundings should be likewise lovely. Whenever I receive a mounted object disfigured with dirt or fibres, with ragged or unfinished settings, I write another name in the already very considerable list of "Exchangers to be avoided."

THE MICROSCOPE AND ITS PREPARATIONS.*

The more I study the wonderful revelations of the microscope, the more I seem to realize that there are two distinct worlds of vision, with a well-defined line of demarkation between them. The one is the world of our natural vision—the beautiful display of nature which is ever before our eyes. The other is the world which the powers of magnified vision have in these latter days unfolded to us. The things which are beautiful and interesting to the unaided eye, are not the things which are beautiful and interesting under the microscope.

The exquisitely colored plumage of some birds, even the brilliant feathers on the breasts of tropical humming-birds, are coarse and unattractive objects when magnified sufficiently to bring out their true structure. Not that the feathers of birds do not furnish some very beautiful microscopic objects. The structure of the fibers of the minute down feathers of some birds, composed of little cones, the black point of each just inserted into the white mouth of the one next below it, the exceedingly minute hooklets and barbed fibrils which unite the edges of the vanes of common feathers, are striking and interesting objects. But they are not the things that contribute to the visible attractions of the feathered tribes.

The gaudy colors on the wings of butterflies are among the coarsest and most ill-defined of objects under low powers of the microscope. But the exquisitely wrought and beautifully painted scales which the high powers bring out, regularly laid like tiles on both sides of the wings, and which the naked eye fails to

---

*Lecture written in 1881, and read before various societies, with exhibition of specimens.

discover except as the finest dust, are objects which once seen will never be forgotten.

The ever varied and delightful colorings of the flowers have no beauty under the microscope. But if you examine those gaily colored stamens and pistils under a magnifying power of about a hundred diameters, you will see, adhering to them in myriads, minute grains of pollen of exquisite pattern and beauty. They are the object of all the growth and the display of the flowers; but are things which no eye had seen, save as an impalpable powder, until the microscope revealed them.

So through all the list of objects in nature, with hardly an exception, the things which strike our eyes and that we call so beautiful, are not the things which will bear the enlargement of microscopic vision. And it seems to me that there is a natural boundary—a line of demarkation—between these two realms of vision; as if each had been produced for its own particular and separate purpose. We can readily understand the reason of the development of that which through all time has pleased or served the eye of man. Every thing in nature, it is said, at least in organic nature, has its utility, its adaptation to some useful end. But of what use could be the production or development of colors or forms or beauties, other than such as can be seen by ordinary eyes? And there are no indications, so far as we can judge upon optical principles or by comparative anatomy, that any other eyes see images much more magnified than do ours. I may then propound the questions which have so often puzzled me: "Why was this nether world, this microscopic world, which is vaster in its limits and more wonderful than the other, which no eye had seen or could see, before the invention of compound lenses some three hundred years ago, why or how was this world ever brought into being, at least in such beauty and marvelousness? Why the almost inconceivably minute and accurate rulings and curves and radials on the shells of the lowly diatoms, when there were no senses that could perceive them? Why the complicate dottings and etchings on the almost invisible scales of the insect tribes, when there was no vision in the world that could see them? But children can ask questions which the philosophers cannot answer; and so far as I know, I have just been asking precisely such questions.

There is a lively little insect, the largest of which is not more than the tenth of an inch long, called the Spring-tail or Podura, found in damp saw-dust in wine cellars, or in any moist and protected places near decaying wood. You may catch or collect them by sprinkling a little flour on a piece of paper and placing it near their resorts. The body of this insect is covered with minute scales, remarkable for their almost infinitesimal markings. The finest line that can be made, visible to the unaided eye, is about the 250th of an inch in breadth. The rulings on writing paper are at least five times as broad, or about the 50th of an inch in width. Now across that finest line, which you can only see as a mere mark without breadth at all, as many as four or five of these Podura scales could be placed side by side. And across each scale in waving lines are rows of forty or fifty dashes, like exclamation points, side by side. This makes them, as you may readily figure, about 50,000 to the inch. This Podura scale used to be the test for the highest powers of the microscope; but now object glasses are made of such perfection that test objects of double that number of lines to the inch are required. These are found in the shells of a certain diatom, the Amphipleura pellucida, found quite common in almost any pool or rivulet. The rulings or striæ running across the frustules of this diatom are as fine as anything that has as yet been found in nature, exceeding in some cases 100,000 to the inch. Yet Dr. Woodward, of Washington, has repeatedly photographed portions of this shell, showing distinctly and clearly markings so fine that 400 of them might be drawn lengthwise on the finest line that you can see with the naked eye.

But I did not come before you to-night to speak of the most difficult of the objects which this instrument resolves; but rather of the beautiful and interesting preparations, requiring not nearly so high a power and satisfying something more than curiosity. I am myself inclined to search for the attractive and the beautiful for exhibition with the microscope; and whenever I find anything that satisfies in those respects, I am very apt to make a study of it—to find out all I can of its intimate structure, and of the life history connected with it if it is an organism. So if there is anything of interest to you in my talk this evening it must come from these special studies.

When I came home from Florida last winter, I brought with me some herbarium specimens of nearly all the insectivorous plants —those which catch and digest insects in some way or other as a part of their food. Among them are these leaves of the Pitcher plant, some species of which you have probably all seen. This is the Sarracenia variolaris which grows only in the Southern States that are on the Atlantic coast. The leaves are composed of a hollow conical tube running down to a point on the stem, of a projecting wing or flange which follows all the way up on the inner side of the leaf, and of a hood which in this species arches over the entire opening of the tube. This tube during the growing season is usually nearly full of water, which we must suppose to be secreted and furnished by the leaf itself, because the hood would effectually keep out all rain water. At the bottom of the tube is a perfect mass of the hard and indigestible parts of insects—heads by the hundreds—a veritable Golgotha of skulls. Now it is evident that there must be something about these leaves that is very attractive to insects, in order to make them go in under that suspicious looking monk's-hood; and then some further peculiarity that makes them fall in such numbers into the well below. Insects do not drop into ordinary receptacles of water in that way; for if they did there would soon be none left to fall into anything.

Mrs. Treat, of Vineland, N. J., who is quite an observer and writer on the insectivorous plants, says that the edge of the wing secretes a sweet and intoxicating fluid which, as the flies drink it, and at the same time crawl up the blade, gradually inebriates them until, as they rise over the lid of the tube, they tumble headlong into the well beneath. I do not myself think it is necessary to suppose anything more than an ordinary sweet secretion from the glands which are specially numerous under the hood and all around the mouth of the tube. When I show you, under the microscope, the formidable array of bristling spikes and pointed scales which lines the whole inside of the tube, all pointing downwards, and especially the strong pike-pointed lances which are thickly set under the hood and on the inner margins of the lid, all pointing backward and downward, you will not wonder that when a fly has once entered those horrid portals he is inevitably lost. There is only one way for him to go, and that is straight downward. I could not imagine a more perfect fly-trap, a more dangerous den for an unwary insect to get into. And I have no doubt that many a poor fly at the bottom of that charnel house has recalled his Virgil:

> "Facilis descensus averno est;
> Sed revocare gradum—hoc opum, hic labor est."

To help you that are not versed in fly-talk, shall I give you Dryden's beautiful translation of that passage?

> "The gates of hell are open night and day;
> Smooth the descent, and easy is the way:
> But to return, and view the cheerful skies—
> In this the task and mighty labor lies."

In order to make the structure of the inside of the pitcher plant leaf at all apparent and in condition to be seen, I was obliged not only to remove the original coloring matter of the leaf by soaking in chlorinated soda, but also to separate the inner cuticle or skin, which holds all the hairs and spikes and glands, from the rest of the leaf by immersion for a time in a weak solution of potash. Of course the cuticle, thus prepared, has to be again artificially colored in anilines or other colors, in order to make the different parts and structures distinguishable.

The Utricularia, or Bladder-wort, is another very singular insectivorous plant. It grows on the water, on the surface of shallow ponds, but is not rooted to the ground. It spreads out from five to seven leaves, like the spokes of a wheel, on the surface of the water, and these are buoyed up by numerous little air bladders. From the center of these leaves the plant sends upwards its flower stalk, and downwards its root-like branches. These latter bear, among their finely branching fibers, great numbers of little egg-shaped bladders or utricles, not larger than the head of a pin. These bladders have at one end a cunningly arranged mouth, or rather lid, opening inwards, and surrounded by some bristling branching hairs. Through this mouth and into the cavity of the utricle, quantities of microscopic insects, water fleas, and animalcules, in some way or other find their way, and are there digested and absorbed with the exception of their hard parts. What brings so many of the tiny denizens of the water to crowd themselves into these uninviting little prison houses, is I think still a good deal of a mystery. The prey caught is indiscriminately animal and vegetable eating organisms, and even larvæ and floating pollen grains. So that it cannot be a secretion of any kind which attracts so various an assemblage of aquatic animals and things. The bristles around the mouth are so arranged as to form a kind of open-work funnel, conducting directly to the valve which closes the mouth. The writers on the subject, Darwin and others, seem to think that chance and curiosity alone conduct the prey to and into the orifice. I hardly think that these would account for the presence of all and so many of the things which, as you will have an opportunity to see for yourselves, are found within the bladders. I think that the lid is sensitive to the touch or irritation of anything lying upon it, and opens with a quick motion, engulfing whatever may be near it. We have plenty of instances of such sensitive movements in other plants of similar habits.

But how strange it is that down in the water there should be this little carnivorous vegetable, lying in wait for its prey, and like a great shark ready to turn up its mouth and swallow anything and everything that happens to come along. Really our ideas of the distinction between animals and plants are quite disturbed by the performances of these animal-eating plants.

I have here a preparation of a small portion of the fruiting stalk of a greenhouse fern, called Aneimia Mexicana. It produces its spores on a stalk which grows up from the top of a leaf stalk, and the spores are like the pollen grains of the mallows and abutilons; in both which respects it is quite unique and remarkable among ferns. It makes a very beautiful object under dark field illumination, as I will show you later in the evening. It is a very pretty experiment to place the spores of a fern on a piece of porous sandstone, partly immersed in a saucer of water,

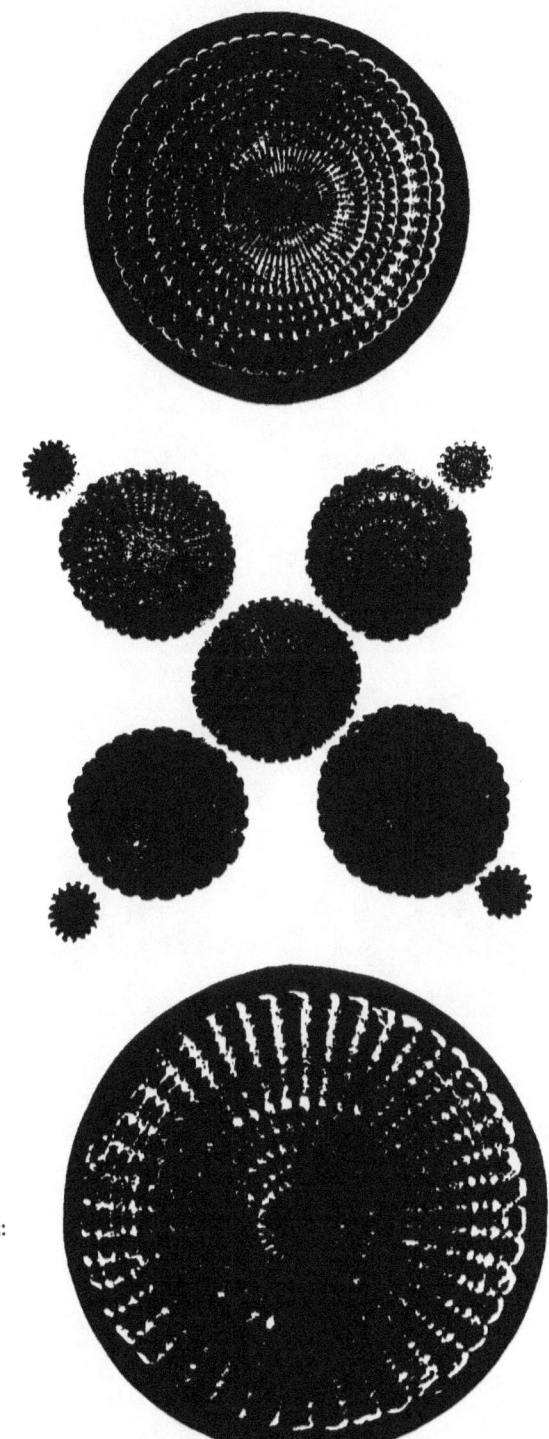

Plate XL.—TRANSVERSE SECTIONS OF THE SPINES OF THE ECHINUS. See Page xvii. Magnified 30 Diameters.

and to watch their growth. You would be surprised, if you did not already know the fact, to see that the spores did not, like seeds, produce ferns or anything like them. They produce what is called "the nurse" of the future generation of ferns. It is a plant resembling another and a lower order than the ferns themselves: a little flat leaf with a tiny stalk and root immediately under the middle of it. On this leaf when mature, little projections arise, in a certain number of which are developed minute spiral sperm-cells with vibratile cilia at one end of them, which finally leave the cases in which they were produced and wriggle about in a lively manner over the surface of the leaf. In the meanwhile another but much smaller number of the projections develop into stationary germ cells; and into these germ cells the active little motile cells eventually find their way, thus fructifying the germ, which immediately commences to throw down a separate root and to develop into the true fern. It is a case of alternate generation among plants; and it is the same kind of reproduction which is so common among the lower orders of animals, the invertebrates, in which one kind of animal produces another entirely unlike itself, which in its turn produces the first kind again. Both the plants and the animals which undergo this strange kind of generation, lived and flourished together, and possessed the earth all by themselves, in that far olden time when the coal beds were being made. And up to this time there had not been an "herb yielding seed" nor a "tree yielding fruit after its kind" on the earth. Apparently the sublime narrative of organic creation given in Genesis, commences at this point.

It has been objected to the method of preparing such specimens as I have described to you—that is by decolorizing them and then staining them in various colors—that they are unnatural, that there are no such things thus colored in all the realm of the vegetable kingdom. This objection formed the burden of a very caustic article published some months ago by a distinguished microscopist. He was immediately replied to by such a number of infuriated preparers that, so far as I know, the distinguished microscopist has never opened his head since.

The fact is, that in order to display at all the internal structure and modes of growth of vegetable tissues, and the delicate glands and organs which make up the vegetable economy, it is necessary to make the specimens transparent by dissolving out, in some way, the green chlorophyl. Alcohol will do this, but it usually takes quite a long time. The chlorinated soda solution, sold by druggists as a disinfectant, will do it much more effectually, and in a few hours time. After this operation, we have an object which is certainly translucent, but the parts are of such uniform brightness that they are not readily distinguishable one from the other. It is necessary again to slightly color them, in order to obstruct some portion of the light, and to contrast one organ or tissue with another. Here comes in the art of the microscopist. Without effacing a mark or destroying the faintest tracing in his picture of nature's work he can give it to you in oscuro, in monochrome, or in varied and contrasting colors. And when you see that beauty of coloring in no wise detracts from the naturalness of organs or tissues, or from the true representation of vegetable growth and processes, I think you will accord to the enthusiast of this art, the painters' freest license.

My friends, I have given you a brief introduction to one of the most interesting of the sciences—one which lies at the foundation of all the natural sciences, for the microscope is now the indispensable instrument in all physical research—one which opens up more vistas of knowledge and of exploration than any other branch of experimental physics—and one the merits of which, I am happy to say, are being every day more appreciated. I even cherish the hope to live to see the day when its claims as a distinct and worthy science shall penetrate the incrusted helmets of the heads of our learned universities—when its manipulations, its processes, and its investigations shall be considered equally important teachings with the reactions of chemical agents, and the work and handicraft of the laboratory.

DIVERSITY OF RACES.*

There is a problem yet to be solved in the history of man, which is now the occasion of much uncertainty and mystery in its records. It is the problem of the origin of races—a question, the solution of which alone will account for those strange diversities in organization, in civilization, and in character, which so distinctly divide the families of mankind. It lies then at the very foundation of the philosophy of history. But so involved is it in mythical fable and allegory, so obscured by dark and varying traditions, that he who, in history and nature, would search out data for conclusions, must content himself with only arriving at probabilities, or perhaps merely indicating a course for further investigations. And that we are authorized, and even called upon in seeking out the origin of races, to look beyond revelation, will be readily conceded by those who consider the very different construction from the popular one, which science has placed on the Mosaic account of the world's beginning. Nor are we forbidden to reason on this subject because we may not as yet be able to establish the correctness of a different and better interpretation. It required ages to explain the allegory of inanimate creation; and it will yet require years of laborious research to remove all the mystery of man's origin.

---

* Written in 1849 for one of the Senior prizes of Yale College. The writer was called up by President Woolsey and Prof. Larned, and told that the Faculty adjudged the essay worthy of the prize in a literary point of view, but could not award it in this case because they did not consider the article orthodox, and could not do anything to encourage such writings. It was at once demanded by the students and published in the Yale Literary Magazine for April, 1849.

To him who looks out on the world with an inquiring eye, it would seem that there could remain no longer a doubt in regard to diversities in the human family, independent of climatic and sectional influences. For over all the earth, wherever man is found, he beholds the unvarying marks of species; but not a trace of any uniform effects from either heat or cold, fertility or barrenness. From the bleak and inhospitable regions of Terra del Fuego, through the torrid Pampas and forests of the Amazon, as far as to the icy abode of the Esquimaux, the American Aborigines are physically the same.* The negroes of Van Dieman's Land † and Caffraria ‡ are even darker in complexion than the Abyssins,§ the Gallas,‖ and numerous tribes of Ethiopia, which roam beneath the scorching sun of the Line. The white man possesses the same organization on the cheerless mountains of Caucasus as in the loveliest valleys of the Rhine. And the black man is the same, whether on the arid wastes of his native Nigritia, or the exuberant fields of the American States. Local influence may affect its subject for a season or a life; but it has never wrought an hereditary change. The same sun in his round of ages could never have bleached the European and blackened the African, or tinged the Asiatic with yellow and the Indian with red. Uniformity without variableness is the offspring of nature; and when we find this following not in the train of extraneous causes, we must turn to race itself as the key to the mystery.

Behold then the world divided not less into continents than it is by families of men. Australia, and South Africa whither the roving Arab has not fought his way, present a species of the most distinct character, stamped as it is with the impress of its own degradation. The Aborigines of the New World bear every mark of a peculiar people. As the beings of a day, in their slender proportions and delicate hue, they exhibit the signs of their own evanescence. Asia teems with its countless myriads,

---

* Malte Brun's "Univ. Geog." Boston Ed. of 8 vols., vol. 5, p. 15.
† Malte Brun, vol. 1, p. 547.
‡ Prichard's "Phys. Hist. of Mankind," 3d Ed., Lond., vol. 2, p. 289.
§ Prichard, vol. 2, p. 136. ‖ Prichard, vol. 2, p. 156.

and, though varying somewhat among themselves, yet all together bearing a sufficient resemblance to distinguish them from every race besides. Europe too appears proudly exhibiting its characteristic species. And what is yet more striking, under similar circumstances and the same climate in which is found every variety of mankind, this continent alone affords the spectacle of an aboriginal white man.

Such are the physical diversities of races. But there is a still more marked distinction appearing in their psychical characters; between which and the former, there is an obvious but strange connection. One race seems as it were set aside by the hand of Providence for a doom of the most dismal degradation. Another appears sadly fated to grope ever in mere conceptions of wild sports here and hunting grounds hereafter. A third, amid all the elements of progress, is bound down under an immutable conservatism. While yet another seems equally destined, and rapidly speeding on, to the highest perfection of humanity. Those lands of the Negro to which the dim light of Islam or the rays of foreign culture have never penetrated, present the gloomiest picture of man. It is there that he has arisen in no sense above an instinctive existence. Without a letter or symbol of language, barren and blank in intellect, aroused from habitual stupor only by the clang of horrid dissonance, like the brute he lives, and seems like the brute to pass away. The American Indians are a people of unique character, having many noble traits, but wholly incapable of permanent civilization or improvement. They seem to have been created merely to be the tenants of an unoccupied territory, till in the fullness of time it should become the home of a mightier race. That time has come, and now before the white man they vanish like a breath of air, and soon will be numbered only by their bleaching bones on our plains. Wide over the continent of the orient dwells another race, midway in the ascent of civilization. It is here that man, with every incentive of a bountiful nature and of rich discoveries, as it were with the thread of his own destiny in his hands, has plodded on for untold ages in the same profitless round. Nations here have sprung up in a day, have swept like the stormking over all the East, and again as speedily have disappeared. Here unceasingly, since the earth has been tenanted by man, has been witnessed the spectacle of myriads jostling against myriads, of empires clashing with empires; yet Asia is Asia still, a vast sea of humanity that stagnates over half the world. From these sad contemplations we turn to Europe, the birth-place of progress, the home of refinement. Select from the chart of earth that spot, the blackest with mountains, the most jagged with stormy seas, and every way the most unpromising of any the sun beholds, and you have marked the land of civilization's nativity. In this bleak corner sprung up those fair favorites of nature who have ever gloried in advancement as the state alone congenial to them, and who are nobly bearing onward all that is enlightened in humanity.

Who now will say, what, other than native character, produced these astonishing differences? What, but the impress of the Creator's hand at their origin, made the white man civilized, the dark man half civilized, the red man savage, and the black man brutish? It is no answer to say that education or state of society might gradually have wrought the diversity; for the question again reverts back upon those very influences; and we ask, what occasioned *their* existence, or what brought them to affect separately each species as a whole, distinguishing it from every other?

Again, who will show the external causes which have made the European, from the very infancy of his being, the lord and arbiter of earth? Behold the monuments of the Macedonian, reared on the Indus and on the Nile. Behold Asia and Africa cowering before the resistless Cæsars. The hosts of Persia cross into Europe for conquest, but scatter in fright and dismay when the bold Greek comes out to battle. The Saracens make the sweeping circuit of the "midland sea," and plant the crescent of Islam in the heart of Europe; but speedily again recoil before the chivalrous Franks. The Spaniards' rude cannon is heard on the plains of the Aztecs, and forthwith the conquest of the "White Gods" is extended wide as their terrible fame. While the dark races have ever bowed a willing neck to the most abject ‘despotisms, and while every revolution throughout the East has but reproduced this same sad feature of enslavement, the European has unceasingly fostered the principles of freedom, and every governmental change, from the earliest times to the present, has served but to make more republican his civil institutions. This same democratic element we find in the municipal structures of the Greek and Roman republics, as also in the laws of the ancient Briton and German; and beyond this race the world presents no other such spectacle. Men in early stages of society have wrought out for themselves two distinct forms of natural religion; and these, if any thing can, must indicate original character. We find then the most prevalent to be a symbolical idolatry, a gross materialism, which formed the cumbrous machinery of the worship of the brutes, of "stocks and stones," or of the celestial orbs. Such are Fetichism, Shamanism, Boodhism, and the varied forms of Pantheism and Sabeism. The other is a personified mythology, a beautiful idealism; in which alone is recognized the existence of an extra-mundane God. This religion, whether figured under its Saturn or Zeus, its Odin or Veli-bog, is the only and peculiar creation of the white man.* Over all the East, the South, and the West, polygamy and sensuality have reigned with unbridled license. How different, how chaste and pure comparatively, has been society in Europe from the very infancy of its nations! Here too, on the soil of this small continent, mind has cast off its shackles and widened its realm, till now the very elements of nature and the attributes of force are subservient to its uses and pleasure. By the beautiful art of stamping thought, the dead live on in all their former greatness. By simply poising the magnet, the trackless ocean at once lost its terrors, and New Worlds loomed up beyond it. The lawless vapor of the sky is bolted in, and made to bear man's burdens. The sun stoops to paint his image, and the lightning does his errands. The recesses of thought, too, open to the light of day their own dark caverns, and mind explores the mystery of mind. But beyond his native home, wherever the white man has appeared to assert his supremacy of intellect, the spectacle is still the same. Long ages back he mys-

* Prichard, vol. 3, p. 12.

teriously came to the wilds of this Western Continent, and started into magic being a beautiful but frail civilization; and long did the red man worship his "white and bearded god." * The fair sons of Circassia have formed for centuries the ruling castes of Egypt and either Turkey ;† and many a once humble merchant on the Thames or Zuider Zee, is now basking in oriental state.

Such is European superiority. And we say again, let him who can assign it an impersonal cause. It is vain to point to any tendencies in the natural world; for these cannot produce genius; nor often have they favored its development. Equally vain is it to refer the cause to a concurrence of circumstances; the chances against which, even if any could be conjectured sufficient to the effect, would be beyond computation. Again must we revert to native character. And, as we behold a Newton born to greatness, so must we regard this race as created to its supremacy. At intervals down through the generations of men, the Creator has seen fit to send forth some giant mind, whose capacities should astonish, or whose might awe, the wondering pigmies beneath it. So likewise, to vary the monotony of ages, has He ushered into being a powerful race, a master-piece of His mysterious workmanship, whose Titan arms should wield the destinies of a benighted world. Why He has wrought in His Creation so incomprehensibly, it may not be for us to inquire. The Lord God made it so, and it is good.

It is an opinion quite common in regard to the origin of races, that it is referable to a period immediately following the Deluge, and to those descendants of Noah who received divine blessings or curses. This however is founded, we think, on no direct authority of Holy Writ, which, in that connection, specifies only what may be explained more plausibly by events comparatively local and immediate. Thus, the malediction on the son of Ham was fulfilled in the subjection and enslavement of the Canaanites to Israel; and the blessing of Shem, in the prosperity of the Israelites. Surely the assertions that " Japheth shall be enlarged,

---

* Prescott, "Conq. of Mex." vol. 1, p. 60; Bradford, "Am. Antiq." p. 301.
† Blackwood Mag. for 1849, vol. 28, p. 134.

and shall dwell in the tents of Shem, and Canaan shall be his servant," are very far from having received their verification in any past or existing order of things, if these patriarchs were the authors of races. Again, that the scriptural account of the Deluge does not necessarily imply its literal universality, we have very clear evidence, as well as high authority.* And that it was not in fact universal, is now generally maintained by scientific men and conceded by most divines. For, to the geologist, the physical appearance of the earth presents no indications of a flood prevailing over all lands at one and the same time; but on the contrary every presumption against it. The natural historian affirms that the dissemination of animals from one common center is not only impossible, but contradicted by innumerable facts. The theologian perceives the necessity of such an unparalleled combination of miracles, in the collection, storage, and sustenance for nearly a year, of over a hundred thousand zoological species, in an Ark of but an acre's area, that he also is compelled to assign a comparatively limited extent to the Noachian Deluge.† Nor can this tendency of modern science to modify and explain, by the intervention of natural causes, the phenomena of Bible history, with the exception of avowed miracles, be regarded as in the least heretical. So far from it, it must give us the noblest conceptions of a Deity, to reflect that the wondrous machinery of the universe, moved and regulated solely by a few grand laws, works out, of itself, His own eternal purposes. There is then no necessity, arising either from the Mosaic records, or the universality of the Flood, for accounting Noah as the second progenitor of all the human family.

In the days of Abram, the tenth in descent from the patriarch of the Deluge, Egypt was a populous country, the seat of a flourishing empire. On the other side, Assyria "of the Chaldees" was on its march of refinement and magnificence; and on every hand we read of "kings of nations," and "captains of hosts," coming out to battle on those ancient plains. Before the time of Moses, in the tomb of Osiris far up the Nile, the Egyptian was

---

* John P. Smith's "Relation of Scrip. and Geol.," London, 1839, p. 304.
† John Pye Smith, p. 159.

painted with all the peculiarities of the Copt at the present day, and with him were represented the white and blue-eyed stranger from the North, and the sable sons of the South.* Long back in time, in the cave of Elephanta, of which not even the ancient books or traditions of the Brahmins have preserved an account, were placed the sculptured images of the Indian, the perfect statues of the modern Hindoo, and of the crisp-haired African.† Thus to the earliest date of history must we refer the existence of permanent nations, as also the existence in them and around them of permanent races. And no one will gravely say, that either through or from Egypt there went out a tribe which was so soon found to be the ill-formed Negro, from India another branch which immediately stood forth as the fair Caucasian, and from China another which appeared as the red race, while the original families remained of the same dark hue and peculiar organization.

If now we turn to the researches which have been made in relation to the antiquity of the old Empires of Asia, we will find that all antiquarians, without giving the least credence to the pretensions of those nations to a prodigious age, but judging from their literature connected with accidental astronomical observations, have dated back their origin to a period coeval with, and in most cases long anterior to the scriptural era of the Deluge. They are united, so far as I have been able to find, in fixing the dawn of reliable history, in Egypt,‡ in either India,§ and in China,‖ between the first century after and the fifth before that epoch. And beyond these comparatively authentic periods, traditions and dark mythologies tell us of wonderful demi-gods, of dynasties of the sun and moon, of silver and golden ages, reaching back in time to the day when the fiat of the Omnipotent spoke man into being. When now we consider that in those remote ages, many centuries must have been

---

* Creppo's "Researches of Champollion," p. 264.
† Asiatic Researches, vol. 4, p. 431 and 433.
‡ Prichard, vol. 2, p. 199. Creppo's Cham., p. 82
§ Prichard, vol. 4, p. 105 and 106; also p. 107, note, and vol. 2, p. 195 and 196. Heeren "On Anc. Nat. of Asia," vol. 3, p. 291 and 304.
‖ Prichard, vol. 4, p. 474–477.

requisite for nations to have wandered so far from each other, over vast tracts of country equally inviting with those they eventually chose, and with no necessity whatever impelling them on, and that many more must have been required for them to have established in those seats, two thousand leagues apart, splendid and well adjusted monarchies, and to have attained no inconsiderable advance in science and literature, it verily seems counter to all probabilities, if not possibilities, to ascribe their origin to that lone Ark which rested but forty-two centuries ago on the summit of Mount Ararat.

Thus have we traced the characteristics of races back through all historic time, and in all probability beyond the age when righteous Noah was selected to be the head of a favored line. It remains for us to consider if even further we may not peer into the dark night of antediluvian ages.

All history, sacred and profane, as well as tradition running far back of this, establishes the fact that from time immemorial there has reigned from the Nile to the Hoang Ho, over one-fourth of the earth's circumference, the same peculiar culture, stamped with such a striking unity as to be remarked by every antiquary from Herodotus to the present time. Throughout the realms of China, India, Assyria, and Egypt, they have found, ever prevailing, the same dogmas in philosophy and religion, the same institutions and superstitions, the same knowledge in the sciences and advance in the arts.* Not only were years and cycles similarly apportioned in many of those nations, but even weeks were divided alike, and days named after the planets ranged in precisely the same arbitrary order.† Such coincidences have compelled all to assign to ancient civilization a common origin. Is then this origin indigenous or foreign?

That there has been no intercourse between these nations since the earliest records of history, we have abundant evidence. And that there was none previously is shown by the fact, that while the languages in common use in the Old Empires had no similarity whatever and the literature in those languages was wholly

---
* Prichard, vol. 2, p. 103.
† Tytler's Univ. Hist., Harper's Fam. Lib. ed., vol. 5, p. 67.

distinct, the elements of their civilization were almost identical.*
Yet however, many of their sacred books, as the Vedas of the
Brahmins and the Zendavesta of the Magi, were written in
foreign and similar tongues, but understood only by the priests.

Again this ancient civilization itself bears the marks of a foreign origin. It is such a strange composition of refinement and barbarism, of exalted ideas mingled with the lowest conceptions of sense, such a peculiar combination of the most refined truths of religion and philosophy, with a mass of childish superstitions and ridiculous notions, as to be accounted for on no other supposition. The Chinese have at the present day implements of science of the use and application of which they are totally ignorant. They have been acquainted with the art of printing for thousands of years; yet even now it is but a laborious system of wood-engraving. For ages they have used the magnetic needle but to gaze at in toys, and have compounded gunpowder but to blaze in fire-works. The Indians have had many beautiful specimens of sculpture, but valued them only for filling the dark and loathsome caves connected with their superstitions. The Chaldees were conversant with many sublime truths in Astronomy, which they brought into use only in reading destinies in the horoscope. The Egyptians applied a superior knowledge in architecture only to rear huge pyramids and obelisks to cumber the earth. In short, over all this vast region, from the Pacific to the Great Desert, we find the vestiges of a progress far beyond the genius of the people, the elements of a civilization which, from their present inferiority, from the history of the past, and more than all from that eternal immobility which has stamped its identity on the annals of four thousand years, we must infer, they never were capable by themselves of acquiring. It seems as if in remote ages the fragments of some noble and perfect machinery had been carelessly scattered over Southern Asia, which a wondering race had preserved as toys or as relics.

The existence of permanent hereditary castes in all the Empires of the East, from the first faint glimmerings of their history,

---

* Prichard, vol. 4, p. 480 and 556. Creppo's Cham., p. 207. Malte Brun, vol. 1, p. 567.

would seem to indicate a peculiar foreign agency; since every such institution in modern nations, of which an origin has been recorded, is known to have sprung from the advent of foreigners, superior either in authority or in native powers. That such was the case in at least one of the ancient nations, we have the clearest evidence in the distinctive character of the sacred caste of the Hindoos, which is acknowledged to be of foreign extraction.*

But further, all the traditions of the East refer the origin of its literary and religious castes to the distant North. Thither the Magi and the Zendish priests of Western Asia point as to the home of their heroes and their gods.† From thence, in remote antiquity, came down the Brahmins of India, diffusing throughout the South a foreign culture.‡ The Chaldeans are said to have been strangers in Assyria, whose native land was far among the Highlands of Upper Asia.§ The priests of Lao-tseu, from whose system the great Confucius drew the elements of his practical philosophy, trace back the wanderings of their sect to the same regions of the North.‖ That the same early teachers found their way to the Nile as to the Ganges, is shown from the fact that, of all nations, no two have ever had more dissimilar languages, or a more identical cultivation, than Egypt and India.¶ Hence we conclude that the ancient civilization of the East was there introduced by foreigners, who were so few as to be unable to change the native tongues of the lands they civilized, as also that it emanated all from those same lofty table-lands of the bold Tartar, from which Asia has recruited its dynasties from time immemorial.

To this tendency of tradition to assign to oriental advancement, dating back with much certainty to diluvian ages, a still more ancient original in the regions toward the Arctic, the accounts of travelers who have penetrated thither add much corroborative evidence. They tell us that over the vast snow-fields of Siberia and the bleak uplands of Tartary, where now roam a

---

* Heeren's Asia, vol. 3, p. 279 and 280.
† Prichard, vol. 4. p. 12 and 49.
‡ Ib., vol. 4, p. 244.
§ Ib., vol. 4, p. 563.
‖ Ib., vol. 4, p. 485.
¶ Ib., vol. 2, p. 217.

few scattered savages gleaning their bare sustenance from a sterile nature, are to be found the vestiges of an ancient people which once was numerous, refined, and powerful. Here have been discovered in countless numbers ancient mines, quarries, and tumuli, of which the barbarous tribes which now behold them with a careless look or a vacant stare, have preserved not the slightest account or tradition.* In the Ural and Altai Mountains, are mines so long since abandoned that nature has even already progressed far in the tedious process of filling them again with the original materials. Quarries also are found, deeply excavated, and in them the implements of the workmen; but the constructions, for which these doubtless afforded materials, exposed to the elements, have, with but few exceptions, crumbled to dust. Of the mounds which are scattered up and down on the banks of the Irtish and Yenisei, many contain ornaments of gold and copper, beautifully embossed and of exquisite workmanship; but others present only the rude relics of a people who had lived out their day before art was known or mines were wrought. Would we now follow up the stream of time to the era when this polished people, from unknown causes, deserted their primeval seats, and still on to the far more remote period of their origin? We pass from age back to age, from the fall to the rise of mighty empires and religions; we trace back the tribes chosen of God, to the patriarchal family of the Deluge, and yet we have not probably arrived even to the decline of this ancient race. But a nation springs not, Minerva-like, into refinement in a day. And we have yet to allow for the slow progress of man into the arts and inventions of comparatively civilized life. Who then, on that scroll of time which counts its cycles of ages back to those when the giant creatures of a tropical clime roamed over exuberant plains where are now the wastes of Siberia, will venture to mark any but a darkly distant period for the origin of this long since extinct nation.

Again, in Europe, we find the same peculiar phenomena, its traditions and early history pointing ever northward; while

---

* Prichard, vol. 4, p. 281; also vol. 5, p. xvii. Malte Brun, vol. 2, p. 304. Tytler's Hist. vol. 5, p. 73.

there, profusely spread, are found the vestiges of ancient and unknown races.* Those strange mounds, called "giant's tombs," which have long been the wonder of the Northmen, have opened up for antiquaries a field of most interesting research. By the differences, not only in their structure, but in the relics they contain, there has been made a chronological division of them into three distinct classes. In the most recent are found various implements of iron, which metal is known to have been in use among the tribes of the North long before the Christian era. Other tumuli, different from these, present only relics of gold, bronze, and copper, which, before the age of iron, were long the materials on which was exercised the ingenuity of a polished race. But in a third series of barrows, by far the most numerous, appear only ornaments of amber and weapons of stone. Not a trace is here found of any remains that would indicate the knowledge of metals among the tribes which deposited them. Both the numerousness of the rude relics of this class, and the wide extent over which they are spread, bear evidence that the people who wrought them were for long ages the sole inhabitants of Northern and Western Europe. What then must be the extreme antiquity of the original race which there began to work its slow and toilsome way into the advanced state which it occupied even at a very distant epoch from the earliest date of its history or traditions?

Thus have we attempted to thread a few of the windings in the labyrinth of the past, and have shown, we think, that from such researches may be deduced the strongest probabilities in favor of several distinct centers of distribution, and consequently of the original diversity of races in the human family. Nor can such a supposition be justly construed as at variance with revelation. That the history of creation in Genesis, so beautifully and appropriately written thus for the imaginative Jews, is allegorical, science is daily proving more and more conclusively, and the learned are now agreed in the belief that the true beginning of things is but darkly figured forth in the work of those six days. Then why select from the very midst of an otherwise continuous

---

* Prichard, vol. 3, p. 294, also p. xvii—xxii.

allegory, a part only on which to impose a rigidly literal construction. And Moses himself, so far from recording anything inconsistent with the supposition that there were cotemporaries with Adam, has related many circumstances which can be explained on no other whatever. The fear of Cain, as he went out from his father's home, lest those who found him might slay him; his marrying and founding a city in the land of Nod, while yet he was the only child of the primeval pair; the circumstance of "giants in the Earth in those days," ere it was possible for the human organization thus to have changed; the marriage of the "sons of God" with the "daughters of men," which made the renovation of the chosen people necessary; all imply the existence of races coeval with the Adamic creation.

This hypothesis moreover explains much that has been mysterious both in nature and in history. It alone accounts for those distinguishing marks in organism which so plainly divide the world of man; and also for those distinct traits of character which are deeply impressed on each several kind. It tells how the American Indian, sequestered from all the world besides, became the only and ancient tenant of this Western Continent, and how the European, environed by thronging myriads of a constitution and capacity totally different, grew up alone and distinct to his high preëminence. It explains why the Negro in his benighted home has ever contested sway with the wild roamers of the forest, and never yet has asserted his right of "dominion over the brute," and why the dark race of the Orient has groveled on in its childhood of ages, as if man had no goal of destiny in his career through time. It adds the lacking links to that chain of gradation which is at once the beauty and wonder of terrestrial creation. And it perfects the range of that beautiful economy of living existences, that whatever variations nature calls for, the Creator provides.

But beyond the analogies drawn from inferior orders of beings, there is another and a higher analogy, which seems to force upon us this theory. No one doubts that the providences as well as the revelation of the Omnipotent, proclaim man to be an originally distinct and superior order of animal creation. No one now

Plate XII.—PORTRAITS OF SOUTH SEA ISLANDERS.   See Page xviii.

supposes that he to whom all nature is made subservient, whose manor is the Earth, whose realm of thought the Universe, is but a favored chimpanzee, and undistinguished from it by the creative hand of the Deity. But there is a particular race of men in which have always centered His most marked providences. Yet we are told that this is but a chance variation from the rest; as if, while in one case providental agency was applied in aid of creative power, in another and for the attainment of the same grand result, He could combine it only with accident. On the bounds of Europe were erected those mighty barriers of mountains and seas which have ever kept within their own allotted homes the hordes of Tartary and the nomads of the South, while that favored land rested in quiet until the dawn of its glorious day. During more than twenty centuries Jehovah instructed and watched over His chosen tribes. But when, by His agency, the civilization of the East had been borne to the classic shores of Europe, and all things were adapted according to His eternal purpose, He compelled even reluctant Israel to deliver over to the favored race the trust of His sacred religion. And again, when the time had come that the nations of Southern Europe must be renovated, or Christianity and man's advancement become extinct, He stirred up the countless tribes of the North, whose incursions beyond the Alps gave the grand impetus to modern progress. Surely the hand of God has marked the course of the white man. There is a glorious destiny to which He is guiding him, and for which He created him. Providence then, as well as reason and research, indicates an original diversity of races.

CHILDHOOD OF SCIENCE.*

In the middle centuries of the Christian era, between two ages of promise and of progress, occurred the gloomiest period in human annals. The thousand years that ended with the fifteenth century have been named, by the common consent of historians, the dark ages of the world. All the lights of ancient civilization were extinguished in the growing darkness of that period. The grace of Grecian culture and the charm of classic literature relapsed into ugly wranglings and the empty war of words. The amenities of social life and the peaceful sway of civil law sank into the misrule of passion and the lawless reign of feuds.

It was a strange and unaccountable relapse, for the records of noble civilizations were on the shelves of the monasteries, and under the dust of ages lay the volumes of the teachers of antiquity, of Plato and Socrates, of Euclid and Archimedes, of Pythagoras and Aristotle. With many of the elements of knowledge and the revelations of nature, with the unlit lamps of science and philosophy in their hands, the scholars of the middle ages groped and stumbled through the night of a thousand years.

In the year 1346, on the famous battle-field of Crecy, in the heart of France, thirty thousand Englishmen under Edward the Third and his son the Black Prince, gave battle to a French army of four times their number. But from the English vanguard, we are told, the booming of cannon for the first time broke in on the clang of spears and the twang of crossbows. The mail-clad archers were stricken with terror as they saw their

---

* A Lecture written in 1860, and delivered at various places in Illinois.

ranks plowed by unseen and resistless missiles. One of the finest armies that France ever raised was that day beaten with the most fearful slaughter on record. The use of artillery was the fatal blow to ancient chivalry; for it rendered useless the brute courage of hand to hand conflicts, and made the issue of battles to depend on the element of numbers and guns.

A hundred years later (1450), in the German town of Mentz, three humble artists,* with the utmost precautions for secrecy, were working at the mystic art of book making. The unwieldy but neatly printed folios which they issued were the superstitious wonder of Christendom. Indeed the pious Parisians burned their first consignment of books as the work of witchcraft. But no art was ever more eagerly seized upon by the nations of Europe than was that of printing. This was a second and a greater blow dealt at the institutions of the dark ages; for it carried knowledge to the fireside of the lowly hamlet, and enabled the people to form a public opinion, which is the greatest counterpoise of bigotry and oppression.

The fifteenth century, the terminating period of the dark ages, closed with the announcement of a series of most splendid geographical discoveries. The Portuguese had boldly pushed out into the Atlantic and added to their charts the outlying islands. Columbus from over the western ocean brought the tidings that he had found the golden Indies. Vasco de Gama crept around the stormy cape of Africa and reached the Indies of an opposite hemisphere.

The opening up of new worlds at the same time opened up new spheres of thought and judgment. The bursting of the boundaries of the old-world geography had much to do with the overthrow of the old-world boundaries of creed and opinion. Within twenty years the heroes of the Reformation were storming the hoary castles of Romanism. Erasmus was hurling his satire against monastic ignorance and grimace. Martin Luther was launching his denunciations against the trafic of indulgences. And immediately came Calvin and John Knox to sweep up and clean out the rubbish of Popery.

---

* Johann Gutenberg, Johann Faust, and Peter Schöffer.

In the last half of the sixteenth century literature had its most flourishing period; when Queen Elizabeth (1558–1603), as well from her own elevated tastes as from a peculiar spite at the Puritans, extended the patronage of royalty to talent, especially the dramatic; when Sidney paraded his heroes in the "Arcadia," and Spencer sang the allegory of the "Faerie Queen;" when Shakspeare new-vamped kings and immortalized them in tragedy, while "rare Ben. Jonson" did the same for their fools in comedy.

But the brightest constellation of genius was seen rising on the world in the year sixteen hundred. It was then that Francis Bacon was preparing the canons of his new philosophy; that Napier, the Baron of Merchiston, was following up that splendid mathematical induction which ended in the discovery of Logarithms; that Tycho Brahe was just closing at Prague his memorable observations on the planets. It was then that Galileo was wrestling with the forces of nature, making himself strong for the great contest with the schools, and the fiery Kepler was searching in the heavens for the unwritten laws of creation. Thus was science the last-born of the brotherhood of Letters—the latest but the mightiest leader in the second march of civilization.

The first and by much the hardest task of every new instructor is to unteach the errors and unseat the prejudices which have found a lodgment in the universal mind. For the purpose therefore of bringing out the earliest struggles of the school of science, we must first unfold the errors and prejudices with which it had to contend.

In the scope of the sciences dependent on observation, astrology was the great and universal error of the early ages. It was observed that the sun regulated nearly all the phenomena of nature, as the growth and death of vegetation, the changes of seasons and climate, the life and habits of animals. The moon also had her influences, directly in the ebb and flow of the tides, indirectly, as was generally thought and as many still think, in the determination of the weather, and in all the critical conditions of plant and animal life. From such premises the leap to the conclusion that the planets and the stars had much to do with the affairs of men and of kingdoms, was as nothing for the logical vaulters of those days. In accordance with this theory, the fixed stars in the zodiac, or sun's path, were divided into twelve signs, each supposed to preside over a particular part of the body, as Aries the head, Taurus the neck, and so on. In this circuit of the heavens were also distributed life and death, marriage and children, riches and honors, friends and ememies, and the entire catalogue of human interests and affections. Then that star of zodiac which rose in the east at the moment of the birth of any child, became the controlling influence of that life, and predictions were made for it in all after time according to the approach of this, its "first house," to the influences of any planet, the sun or moon.

Through the long night of the middle ages the only observer in the unexplored realms of nature was the astrologer, who catalogued the stars only to fill a fortune-teller's tables, who calculated the intricate problems of siderial time and the precession of the equinoxes only to cast back the horoscope, who configured the mazy paths of the planets only to forecast their influence on some "star of destiny." Yet so fascinating were the pretensions of judicial astrology, so sweeping its generalities, and so vague its proofs, that it held captive the strongest minds of the age. Roger Bacon, Kepler, and Francis Bacon consulted its divinations; Tycho Brahe was extremely credulous of its presages; and Cardan, the great algebraist, died to accomplish an astrological prediction.

In experimental science, the only workers of the middle ages were the alchemists. In dark and smoky cells, retired or hidden from the sight of men, untold numbers of these so called chemists wore out their lives at the furnace and smelter. With the simple furnishment of mortar and crucible, of alembic and aludel, of quick-silver and amalgams, of aqua fortis and aqua regia, the old alchemist experimented with untiring iteration for the three phantoms of the gold-seeker—the grand alkahest or universal solvent, the philosopher's stone or the quintessence of the metals, and the grand elixir or the universal panicea. With the solvent all the baser metals were to be reduced to their primal constituents. With the philosopher's stone the contaminating elements were to be separated out, until gold the refined and subtle essence of matter remained as the residuum. The grand elixir was to conquer infirmity and confer upon its imbibers the immortal youth. On these lofty but futile abstractions the old enthusiast labored until he was borne from the laboratory to the cemetery—from the grave of his genius to the grave of the tomb. So numerous were the votaries who squandered their fortunes and devoted their lives in these absurd vagaries, that the Catholic Church found it necessary to fulminate its bulls, and the State to enact penal statutes against them.

The few mysterious truths of the universe which the astrologers had discovered, and the few secrets of nature which the alchemists had elaborated, strange, isolated, and inexplicable, made even the learned of the dark ages credulous of almost anything. Physical science was magic; and chemistry especially seemed to have an elective attraction for all that was illusory and mystical. It was the ghost-time of philosophy; and all nature seemed wrapped in a weird portentous shadow. Hence sprung the dreamy tenets of the Cabalists, the arrogant pretensions of the Rosicrusians, and the pantheism of the Theosophers.

The first feeble light of science that appeared in the gloom of the middle ages was Roger Bacon, who figured during the last half of the thirteenth century. He was acquainted with the composition of gunpowder, and treated of the wonderful properties of lenses. He was however accused of having fabricated a brazen head according to the prescriptions of occult philosophy, which uttered oracles to him when consulted by magical incantation. He used his new powder to such noisy purpose and his dark arts with such fearful effect that he became the terror of the community. He worked also in alchemy, and supposed he had discovered the great medicine which was to carry him over the centuries; but at the age of seventy he was poisoned by his brother Gray-friars, and the grand elixir proved to be a failure.

However, notwithstanding this tinge of folly and superstition, Roger Bacon had many of the elements of the true philosopher. He was learned in the languages and in all the physical knowledge of the day. He dared to appeal from the authority of the schools, from the dicta of Plato and Aristotle, to the guidance of nature and of reason. For this and his denunciation of their immorality, he drew upon himself the hostility of the monks and clergy. On an accusation of studying and practicing magic he was summoned before a high Council of the church, his writings were condemned, and he was sentenced to ten years confinement in his cell.

Roger Bacon was the first to declare that observation and experiment must be at the foundation of all science, that from facts we must reason up to principles, a doctrine which was diametrically opposed to all the reasonings and practice of scholastic philosophy. And it was not until four hundred years later that these canons of inductive science were successfully established by his more fortunate and illustrious name-sake, Francis Bacon. But had the times been ripe for the truth, it is more than probable that the friar would have superceded the chancellor.

Two centuries later in a Benedictine cell the child-worker in chemistry, Basil Valentine, was experimenting in search of that fifth element which was to decompose and transmute all the metals into gold. But while he toiled his life out over this great delusion he seems to have discovered some of the most important medicines and chemicals of the early pharmacy. His chief exultation however was in what he called "the triumphal car of antimony"—anti-moines—the anti-monk medicine. Tartar emetic is one of the preparations; and it was said that the old Doctor once experimented on a convent of monks, and that he left not a shaven crown of them all. No wonder they thought that antimony did not exactly agree with monks.

Early in the sixteenth century Bombastes Paracelsus, the last of the alchemists, was called to a professorship of chemistry in the University of Bâle—a strange erratic man, whose genius like a meteor flashed across the morning sky—a man of extremes, on the one hand so learned and eloquent that he carried his audiences whither he would, on the other so vain and boastful that the word "bombast" has been derived from one of his high sounding names. His success as a physician bordered on magic, his insolence as a professor bordered on madness. He did not stop with contemning the time-honored authorities in learning, but he harangued his crowds of hustling students around fires that were fed with the books of the schoolmen. With an unsparing hand he laid bare the tricks of pharmacy, the delusions of astrology, and many assumptions of alchemy. With an insight as clear as Chancellor Bacon's, he exposed the sophistries of scholasticism, the futile methods of inquiry, and the utter emptiness of all the philosophy that had gone before. But high above his practice of physic, his experiments in science, and his criticisms of the school systems, there seems ever to have flitted that vague wild conception of something yet unattained—some potent, dark-hidden essence of matter, which once found would compel nature to deliver over her riches.

Such was the man who for a time, with his fascinating eloquence, his inane egotism, and his mad pranks, kept up such a storm in poor little Bâle that the magistrates were forced to banish him from his chair. Having soon after abandoned himself to vice, he sank into infamy, and died wretched and forsaken at an obscure tavern in Salzburg. But his work was done; his errand as a public agitator was accomplished. He was the lump of acid thrown into the crucible of alkali that had been filling up for a thousand years, and which ceased not to effervesce till all was neutralized and purified.

As we approach the dividing line between the old-school and the new-school philosophers, it will be well to understand fully the difference between the principles and the modes of thought that characterized each. We will therefore for a moment compare and contrast the new or inductive method with the old or deductive system.

It is now well understood that there is but one true way of prosecuting physical research. Facts, observations and experiments must first of all be gathered together and classified. From these, conclusions may be formed such as explain or comprise each different class of phenomena. From these conclusions, more general principles may be predicated; and from these principles we may step, it may be, to the one law that binds them all in harmony. This is the great secret of induction, of the a-posteriori reasoning, from facts up to general principles. The opposite method is deduction, or a-priori reasoning, from general principles down to particular things.

To this latter method the ancients obstinately clung. It is true that the old Greek mathematicians, reasoning from a few axioms and general truths, proving each proposition by more simple demonstrations that had gone before, had deduced a perfect system of Geometry. But there the utility of the method ended; and so far as science is concerned there might just as well have been a blank from Euclid to Kepler, from Archimedes to Galileo. Yet who has not read in his classics how those vaunted philosophers of old labored and struggled to discover the great axioms of nature, by which to explain the phenomena of the world about them, on which to build their Geometry of common life? One makes "fire" the essential matter and origin of the universe; another "air;" a third discovers the key to every difficulty in the "infinitude of things;" while a fourth can invent nothing more unintelligible than "entity and non-entity." At length came the great authority which was to sway the opinions of men for two thousand years. Aristotle constructs his universe on "matter, form, and privation;" and the phenomena which he cannot bring under this senseless triad of words are handed over to "occult causes," about which it is forbidden us to reason. The highest efforts of deductive philosophy served only to raise standards of profitless phrases, about which argument and disputation continually revolved. It was the dizzy dance of error and delusion, in which those who entered, ended where they began.

In order to show how different was the result when inductive philosophy was installed in the place of the ancient, allow me to unfold a few of the steps by which one of the early and most important discoveries of science was reached, the fact and the law of the attraction of gravitation. Scarcely two hundred years ago, Sir Isaac Newton in his garden,* watched with

---

* During his retirement to Woolsthorpe in 1666, where he went to avoid the plague.

thoughtful eye the fall of apples from the tree. Objects fall in the same manner from the highest elevations on earth, and meteors fall from unknown heights in the sky. Why then may not this gravity be a tendency which reaches beyond the earth, even to the moon? A stone attached to a string and whirled in the air, is kept from flying off by the tension of the string. Why may not gravity be the chain that holds the moon in its sweep of thousands of miles? Light which emanates from a central point was known to decrease in intensity in the inverse proportion of the square of the distance. Analogy would teach that gravity if it reached out into space would be in accordance with the same law. If now he could know accurately the moon's distance and how much it weighed, he could easily figure out the force which was necessary to hold it in its orbit; and if it was the same that the known mass of the earth would exert at that distance, then his hypothesis would be a proved fact. It was some years before accurate estimates were made on the elements of his problem. But ultimately his figures realized his most sanguine expectations; and thus was seated on the throne of science the most potent ruler of the world of facts.

It would be ungenerous to pass on to the child-workers in science without paying our tribute to the illustrious father of inductive philosophy. The Novum Organon of Francis Bacon,* I do not hesitate to say, contains more original thought than any other book that ever sprung from the genius of man. The world of literature at the time when he wrote, less than three hundred years ago, was a dreary waste; yet this lonely traveler, unaided, with scarce a finger-board to point his way, has given us the guide-book of knowledge from that day to this.

With a boldness that startled those rude ages he declared that philosophy had been going wrong from the foundation of letters; that men had sought to make a world from their own conceptions, and to draw from their own minds the materials which they employed. They had totally disregarded the facts of nature, and without any intermediate steps had leaped at once to the most sweeping and absurd generalizations. The way that promises

---

* Born in 1561—Died, 1626.

success, said he, is the reverse of this. It requires that we generalize slowly, going from particular things to those that are but one step more general, from those to others of still greater extent, and so on to such as are universal. He then points out the various methods of inductive reasoning, their comparative importance, and the manner in which they are to be used. Not only does he thus new-create his philosophy, but he is compelled to originate the examples which illustrate and make it intelligible, to start in their onward paths the very sciences, then unknown, whose manual of discovery he was writing. He is as it were the inventor of some intricate and wonderful machine, but totally useless until he shall also have discovered materials and commodities on which to set it at work.

The Novum Organon was the work of a life-time. Throughout a busy and illustrious career of high professional, literary, and political successes, it was the ever recurring subject of the author's thought and labor. Revised and rewritten twelve times, it received year by year the increments of his maturing and creative mind. It was the work of a seer, of one who forecasted the future. The founder of the new philosophy wrote for ages that were to come. He did not expect to be appreciated or understood in his own time; neither was he. The king said it was a book past understanding. Another said it was such a work as a fool could not write and a wise man would not. Sir Edward Coke wrote this distich on the title page of his copy:

> "It deserveth not to be read in schools,
> But only to ballast a ship of fools."

Such a reception of his most labored effort called out that touching expression in Lord Bacon's will: "I bequeathe my name to posterity after some time be passed over."

A hundred years before science had its great expounder, away on the banks of the then lonely Vistula, a young Polish student was poring over the astronomical system of Ptolemy. The problem which Copernicus* had set before himself was one of peculiar difficulty. It was none other than to rearrange the wheel-work of the stars, to bring order and symmetry into the

---

* Born in 1473—Died, 1543.

jumble of machinery and clashing spheres which the ancients had piled up in the heavens.

According to this labored and complex system, the starry vault was arched over by a series of spheres of the clearest crystal, sliding one upon another in grooves or furrows parallel, serpentine, or spiral. No less than twelve of these spheres, or deferents as they were called, thus spanned the firmament. The outermost one, the blue empyreal realm of the gods, was the "primum mobile" or the chief mover, within which the others grated, slid, or clashed according to the requirements of the motions they were set to produce. The fixed stars twinkled in one of the furthest spheres. Saturn had one all to himself; so Jupiter and Mars. The sun was borne onward in another, and the moon appropriated the lowest. But after all this comfortable arrangement it was found that the planets would not keep their places in the circles. The sun was much nearer to the earth in winter than in summer; and the moon strayed into all manner of devious paths. To arrange for these irregularities, other circles were framed into the spheres, and the planets and luminaries revolved, each its own way, on epicycles whose centers were carried forward in the deferents. Again, as new variations were discovered, other wheel-work was added, new grooves were notched in the solid arches, cycle on epicycle, centric on eccentric were piled, until the heavens were such an orderless mass of running gear as would have put to shame the genius of any modern wheel-wright. Yet this was the time-honored astronomy of the early centuries, the fondling of philosophy and the dogma of the church.

On it Copernicus, a traveled and accomplished scholar, labored for fifteen years, till only getting confusion worse confounded he finally abandoned the entire system of Ptolemy, fixed the sun in the center of the universe, and set the other worlds revolving about it. He gave to the earth the double motion of rotating on its axis and following the other planets in almost inconceivable distance and rapidity about the central luminary. It was a bold and startling hypothesis; so far beyond all conception that it did not even disturb the watchful censors of the church of Rome.

The work which expounded the new doctrine, the "De Revolutionibus," lay unpublished in the study of its author for thirty-six years; and even then remained unnoticed for more than fifty years longer. The fact was, the theory of Copernicus was only an hypothesis. It could lay no claim to being an inductive discovery, and, until Galileo took hold of it, was no more a proved fact than were the absurdities of Ptolemy's Almagest. The discoverer himself, so said Kepler, did not seem to know the worth or extent of his own discovery. He gave the earth's axis an extra revolution to maintain its parallelism among the fixed stars. He retained the cumbrous notion of epicycles and eccentrics; and only differed from the old masters in idealizing their solid superstructures, in removing the center of operations and enlarging their boundaries. He took great credit to himself for so arranging his running gear as to do away with one set of Ptolemy's balancing wheels known as the equants. Evidently the time had not yet arrived for the new school of science.

Fifty years after the death of Copernicus, Kepler* had commenced his Herculean labors. Through a mass of figures that would have terrified a score of other men, he brought to light the three primary laws of planetary motion. Seemingly simple and easy of discovery, these laws, which have been of such inestimable service in the advance of knowledge, were yet arrived at through severer toil and more disheartening failures than have characterized the establishment of whole sciences since that time. The only method of calculation that Kepler knew anything about was, like the process of the school-boy ciphering by "trial and error," to guess at the answer and then work out the sum as if it were the true one, then guess again, mayhap a little nearer correct. Thus did this man of indomitable perseverance, but of moderate mathematical talents, erect for himself a most stupendous monument of figures and of errors. Thirty ponderous volumes record his blunders and their proof. A few choice pages establish the most fortunate discoveries of science.

And in this I would not be understood to say anything derogatory of the remarkable genius of Kepler; but simply to imply

---
* Born in 1571—Died, 1630. Würtemburg, Germany.

that he failed to grasp the true method of discovery. The time had not then arrived for the systematic researches of induction. The great school-master of the new system was not yet abroad. However we cannot but admire the frank unresting mind, the great honest heart, and the fiery questioning spirit of this medieval philosopher. His writings tell us the whole story of his mistakes and his successes, his troubles and his rejoicings, his struggles with thought and his struggles with hunger; for a life of bitter want and disappointment had fallen to the lot of this devoted disciple of learning. "If God stand by me," would he say, "and look to the victuals, I hope to perform something yet." His treatise on the perturbations of Mars reveals greater perturbations in his domestic economy. While he searches in vain for the laws of dependence between the planets and their great parent the sun, he bemoans equally the feeble dependence between himself and the numerous little satellites that revolved about him. His great work, "The Harmonies of the World," showed far more the harmonies of a noble spirit that, over the hardships of poverty, the mortifications of failure, and the persecutions of the Würtemburg doctors, could look calmly and cheerfully to the glorious meed which posterity would award to his labors if successful.

Kepler seems to have had a Heaven-born intuition that there was some law of harmony regulating the movements of the solar system. But what was the nature of it, or how he came by the notion, he had no more idea than he had of Newton's Calculus. Yet he set himself to testing by actual figures and trial every conceivable relation that a genius peculiarly fertile in hypotheses could suggest. From Tycho Brahe's observations he calculated the path of Mars through seven oppositions, figuring out each ten times. In the absence of logarithms and the aids of algebra the figures of each calculation covered ten folio pages, making seven hundred pages in all; an enormous labor in itself, but it was only the first step in his tentative process. His object being to discover what device or complication of curves would agree with the true observed places of Mars, he tested the circle in every possible variation of eccentric and epicycle. But none of them would give him the true place within eight minutes. Ten of the best years of Kepler's life were thus spent in trying to reconcile the planetary motions to the mystic and divine properties of the circle. At last, from the simple circumstance of his happening to use the ellipse to facilitate his calculations, came his first great discovery, that the planets all revolve in elliptical orbits, with the sun in one of the foci or centers.

The second law of planetary motion discovered by Kepler, which is, that a line connecting the sun with any planet would pass over equal areas in equal time, was rather in the nature of a mathematical corollary from the first law, and therefore did not require much time or effort for its discovery.

But the intuitions, the almost inspirations of Kepler's mind, that there were definite relations between the distances from the sun and the periods of revolution of the planets, were not yet realized; and so long as those "harmonies of the universe" were unascertained, he accounted all his other discoveries as nothing. He therefore commenced at once and over again his dreary wanderings in the fields of conjecture. He followed up each shadowy indication of a relation, till hope was exhausted in that direction, then turned off to another with the simple regret that the last had been such a sad thief of his time. He ran down to their farthest absurdity the vague conjectures of Greek philosophy, dozed with Plato and dreamed with Aristotle. For a long time he held by the numerical harmonies of Pythagoras; then by the five regular geometrical solids of Plato. But his longest, dreariest wanderings were in the endeavor to fix the musical gamut in the skies, to guage the motions of the planets by some relations of concords of sounds.

Over twenty years were thus spent in these baffled efforts, till at last it occurred to him to compare the various powers as the square and cube of the planetary elements. He eventually hit upon the very relation which afterward became the law. But this time, with his usual ill-luck, the poor man made a mistake in his figures, and was again tossing on the sea of uncertainty. Months afterwards, however, he was induced to recur to the same figures, namely, the ratio of the squares of the periodic times and the cubes of the mean distances of the planets. That is, taking, for instance, the earth's revolution about the sun as one (year), and the distance from the sun as one (radius), the square and cube of which are still one; then, as the periodical time, say of Saturn, is about $29\frac{1}{2}$ years, one is to the square of $29\frac{1}{2}$ as one is to the cube of Saturn's distance from the sun in radii of the earth's orbit. The sum worked out gives $9\frac{1}{2}$ radii for Saturn's distance; that is, Saturn should be $9\frac{1}{2}$ times further from the sun than the earth is. In this second trial, Kepler found to his infinite satisfaction and delight that the rule would hold exactly true in the case of all the planets. It was in reality a capital discovery; for it was the one column on which was constructed the whole science of celestial mechanics. It was the foundation of all of Newton's demonstrations; for it gave the only absolute proof of universal gravitation. It was the germ from which have sprung more physical truths than from any other discovery that has ever been made. Yet at the time when it was made I can hardly conceive how it should have been regarded as more than a curious relation, a freak of the Great Artificer. At least so thought those who came after Kepler; and seventy years passed before the Principia of Newton gave to the world the first sign of its true importance. Yet Kepler, with a scientific instinct, a sublime, inexplicable foresight, records the 8th of May, 1618, as the day of the most important discovery of his life and of the age; and he bursts forth in that ever memorable rhapsody: "Nothing holds me. I will indulge in my sacred fury. I will triumph over mankind by the honest confession that I have stolen the golden vases of the Egyptians to build up a tabernacle for my God far away from the confines of Egypt. If you forgive me, I rejoice. If you are angry, I can bear it. The die is cast; the book is written, to be read either now or by posterity; I care not which. It may well wait a century for a reader, as God has waited six thousand years for an observer."

The last and the greatest name I have to mention is that of Galileo the Florentine, who in the year 1600 and at the age of 36, had just commenced his eventful career as the first experimental philosopher and the sturdy creed-questioner. Up to this time the crudest and vaguest notions had existed on the subject of motion and force. Aristotle had divided all motion into natural and violent, and had taught that it was a kind of disposition residing in and exercised by the moving body. If it fell towards the earth, that was natural motion, and in accordance with its disposition. All other motion was unnatural and soon exhausted itself. Levity or lightness was supposed to be just as much a property of substances as color or density. Thus smoke ascended because it was endued with absolute levity. Air did not press or gravitate on water because it was in its proper place above it; but stones and earth sank in water because their proper place was beneath it. Water rose in a pump or siphon because nature abhorred a vacuum; but very unaccountably it abhorred it only thirty-two feet. It was taught that two pounds of lead would fall twice as far in a minute as one pound would; and that a body would fall twice as far in two minutes as in one. In short, the whole school philosophy was but another name for error and confusion of ideas; to dispel which Galileo enunciated his three laws of motion, the laws of fluids, of falling bodies, of pneumatics, in a word the established science of mechanics.

But far less for these discoveries than for the wit and argument with which he combatted the errors of scholasticism and the inveterate opposition of the church, is he entitled to the tribute of the greatest champion of science. Aristotle had taught and the sacred scriptures implied that the earth was the fixed center about which the heavens and the celestial bodies revolved. The hierarchy of Rome had staked its infalibility on the geocentric hypothesis, and the dreaded inquisition had arrayed its terrors against the heresy of disbelief. Yet Galileo had the hardihood and the genius, at a time when but little was known of the laws of motion, and nothing of the revelations of the telescope, to declare himself the supporter of the Copernican system, and prepared to prove it against all the world. Its opponents argued that if the vast earth rotated daily on its axis, everything movable on its surface would be hurled into space like water from the rim of a revolving wheel. Galileo replied that they had entirely mistaken the nature of gravity, which was nothing more than the balance of opposing forces, the surplus of the attraction of the earth over the centrifugal force from its rotation. But, said he, if you see an objection in the centrifugal force on the surface of the earth, what is going to become of your own system when that force is carried out to the distance of the sun and moon and stars? What conceivable power can hold them in a daily revolution about the earth? The school-men again declared that the amazing rapidity of the flight of the earth through space, a thousand miles in a single breath, would soon leave its fragments strewed in its wake like the wreck of a storm-driven ship. Galileo objected to this the inertia of matter, the first great law of motion. If a body is once set in motion it will continue in that motion until stopped by some other force. Thus we as safely ride the flying world as the flying chariot. Again they said, and it was the argument most strenuously insisted upon, that if the earth was in motion from west to east then a ball dropped from a high tower should fall, not at its base, but to the westward of it, which was not the case. It was taught in their books that an object let fall from the mast-head of a vessel in motion would strike the deck at a certain distance behind the foot of the mast. Much more then should the ball from the tower fall away from the base. To this Galileo replied that their quoted experiment would give no such result as was claimed. The object while falling from the mast-head would continue to have the same forward motion that the ship had, and would drop exactly at the foot of the mast; and to convince them that this was so, the experiment was actually tried on a vessel in the harbor of Marseilles.

Thus did this sturdy philosopher, while establishing the fundamental principles of mechanics, at the same time uproot the errors of scholasticism and overthrow the dogmas of creed philosophy. But in all this time he was gradually arousing against himself the implacable enmity of that power which for a thousand years had been dealing out law to kings and creeds to states, and had furnished as well opinions for the high as indulgences for the low. Already he had been ordered to desist from his bold teachings. But for the unresting mind of Galileo to cease its work was as much an impossibility as for the sun to hold back its rays. Come what might in the bitter end, his call was to think, to experiment, and to teach.

It was in the year 1609 that a report came to Galileo that Metius, a Dutch optician, had succeeded in so combining two lenses as to make distant objects seem near. More was not told, nor needed. The next day Galileo had a telescope that tripled the breadth of objects; and in a few weeks he had constructed one which magnified thirty-two diameters. This wonderful tube he first pointed to the moon; and with what amazement he saw for the first time those rugged mountains and chasms, those deep fissures and lava streams sweep across the field of view, you who have ever sat down to the sight may faintly conceive. Here was another world like the one we tread on, vast and mountain-girt, circling on in its unsustained flight about the earth, at once the long desired analogy to the earth revolving about the sun, and a final answer to the old dogma of the schools that the heavenly bodies were divine and therefore beyond the sphere of reasoning or of causation. What could be more unspiritual than mountain chains and crater vortices?

Again he turned his magnifying gaze to Venus, and with a joy that was well nigh ecstacy he beheld the horns and the crescent, as Copernicus had predicted a hundred years before they should appear to an enlarged vision. Could he longer doubt that Venus was one of the children of the sun? Pushing still outward his gaze he saw for the first time the four moons that wheel obedient to the influence of Jupiter. Might he not call them the grand-children of the same great parent of light and of life? Mars in his telescope waxed and waned as the moon in full quarters. While Saturn with its rings seemed like three vast worlds overlapping each other. Is it strange then that this great world-discoverer should arise each night from his sublime disclosures more and more convinced of the comparative littleness of this globe of ours, of the insufficiency and the arrogance of that philosophy which made it the center of the universe and the sole object of creation? Is it a wonder that his mind was exalted above the bigotry of a creed-bound faith to the worship of that majestic God to whose power neither vastness nor space nor time present the shadow of a limit.

But a still greater surprise awaited Galileo when he turned his telescope to the fixed stars. Expecting to find them greatly enlarged as all the planetary stars had been, he was startled to behold them the same glistening points of light that greet our eyes each cloudless night, brighter yet still of no sensible magnitude. But where to the naked eye a few only could be discerned, there burst upon his lens-eyes tier upon tier of twinkling orbs, countless and unending; so deep set in the limitless void, so infinite in distance, that no breadth of vision could in the least enlarge them. Could it be possible they were also so immeasurably remote that even the diameter of the earth's orbit formed no sensible angle with them? The Ptolemaists had been hitherto unanswered in this their last argument, that the earth's axis, being always unchanged in direction, should, by the new system, in a revolution whose diameter was near two hundred million miles, point successively to a circle of stars in the northern sky, instead of pointing to that single Pole star the whole year round. Yes, Galileo could now answer back that it was no longer an uncertain hypothesis that the North Star was so vastly remote that it would not seem to have changed its place by a hair's breadth, though viewed from opposite bounds of the earth's stupendous journey.

Thus did this single-handed philosopher beat back his opponents step by step; and Dialogue succeeded Dialogue as new truths were to be established or further errors combatted. He is now an old man of seventy years. His hairs are blanched by study and watchings and benefits to mankind. He is already preparing for the rest of the faithful servant whose work has been well done, when a summons reaches him to appear before the tribunal of the Inquisition and answer to charges of heresy and blasphemy. In the dark chambers of that secret court, with all the insignia of intolerant power and the appliances of torture before him, the old man is solemnly called upon to renounce the great truth which his whole life has been consecrated to reveal and maintain, "the motion through space of the earth and planets around the sun." Then came the sentence of the tribunal, banning and anathematizing the doctrine that the sun is the center of the system "as a tenet philosophically false and formally heretical." And then they sentenced that old and infirm philosopher—this band of infallibles! They bade him abjure and detest the said errors and heresies. They decreed his book to the flames, and they condemned him for life to the dungeons of the Inquisition.

And did Galileo yield at last? Broken down by age and infirmity, importuned by friends more alarmed than himself at the terrors of that merciless tribunal, he signed his abjuration, yielded all his judges demanded, echoed their curse or ban as their superstition or their hate required. He is not the martyr of science. But as he arose from the floor on which while kneeling he had pronounced his great perjury, a spark of the old fire of his manhood came back to him, and he stamped his foot and exclaimed to those about him, "e pur si muove"—"and yet it does move." Yes, thou wronged and persecuted philosopher, it moves—it will move till the eternal day. And each rotation that lifts the bright sun in the east, each revolution that brings again the glad spring, shall attest thy sturdy but over-tried faith, and bring honor to thy venerable name. It was the last of the old man's teachings. Thenceforth he made haste to the bourne which divides us from care.

THE HUNS OF ATTILA.*

Only a few seasons have passed since tidings reached us of commotion and conflict on the far off banks of the Danube; and the tale of the wrongs of Hungary aroused a lively interest in every land.† Then came the stirring news of battle and carnage. The brave Magyars had stood forth to breast the tide of leagued oppression, had nobly and for a time successfully striven in the fight for liberty. Every liberal heart throbbed with pride and sympathy in those manly aspirations and gallant struggles. But soon came the sad accounts of disaster and defeat. Again the nations mourned another Poland fallen—buried beneath the crushing weight of Cossack tyranny.

Two years later, a war-steamer, floating a strange banner of stripes and stars, steamed up the Strait of Bosphorus to the seat of the Moslem empire, and presented to the Sultan an order from the civilized nations of the world for the release of the Hungarian refugees from Turkish prisons.‡ The patriot exiles, who were at once a burden and a menace to the effete monarchies of the old world, received a glad welcome in our last born of nations. Soon in all our temples was heard the voice that had been the soul and center of the Hungarian struggle, sounding forth with thrilling magic, though in a tongue but recently acquired, the thoughts that kindle and the words that burn. The patriot of his father-land toiled while among us, with all the

---

* A Lecture written and first delivered at Skaneateles, N. Y., in 1852.

† The last Hungarian Revolution and struggle against Austria and Russia, with Kossuth, Gorgey, and Bem, as leaders, occurred in 1849.

‡ The steamer Mississippi was sent to Constantinople in the Fall of 1851, and brought away Louis Kossuth, his family and friends to our country as the guests of the United States Government.

power of a mighty genius, for aid in the cause of his downtrodden country. Doubtless it was inexpedient for us to adopt the measures he advocated. Yet for his unfaltering honesty I respect the man; for his giant intellect I honor him; for his devoted patriotism I revere him. He failed; but steadfast in his purpose, he now awaits on the borders of Europe the awakening of the oppressed. While to those in whom his hopes have been disappointed, he sends the significant message that his days of declaiming are ended, that the only speech he has yet to make is, "Up, soldiers, and follow me."

These national events and the presence of its great chieftain and champion among us, have given to whatever relates to Hungary an especial interest. Even the legendary stories of the early founders of this nation, comprising the long and eventful wanderings of the hordes of the Huns and the achievements of Attila their first known king, sufficiently interesting in themselves, will impress us the more vividly that now the voice of him who was wont to glory in such rude ancestry has scarce yet lost its echo on our shores, and the memory is yet fresh of the desperate strife for independence of those who claim to be descended from those barbarians, and "ambitiously insert the name of Attila among their native kings."

Of the doubts of some historians respecting this martial genealogy, we need not stop here to consider. It is sufficient to know that even in the time of Attila* the Huns had given their name to Hungary; and when, four centuries later, Arpad with another body of Huns came down from northern Europe he was joined by the descendants of the Huns of Attila, and these were the undoubted ancestors of the Magyars who constitute the chief part of the population of Hungary.

If one should seek by the dim light of ancient history and tradition the spot from which diverged the first migrations of the tribes of human kind, he would always be led by undeviating lines to the lofty table lands of Central Asia. Thither are merged and lost the earliest traces of the swarming tribes that in ancient times successively peopled or overspread the eastern

---

*Attila fought the great battle of Chalons in A. D. 451.

Plate XIII. WHITE TERRACES AND GEYSER, NEW ZEALAND. See Page xviii.

continents. As we shall soon find this to be the native land of the Huns, it will be interesting for a few moments to look in upon these rugged home-lands of races, and to search out the influence which they have had on the destinies of the world.

Stretching centrally across the immense continent of Asia from west to east is a wide belt of uneven table-lands, averaging between one and two miles in height above the level of the sea. It is about five hundred miles in width and perhaps three thousand in length. On the north side are the lofty ranges of the Altai mountains and the sources of the great Siberian rivers. On the south side are the stupendous peaks of the Himalayas, from which arise the sacred rivers of India and China. But the mountain-locked valleys between have no water outlets in any direction. Large streams and even rivers run down through them, emptying into salt lakes and basins, and there end. Evaporation is the only known discharge. Over the eastern half of this singular belt extends the great desert of Gobi, the most inclement and desolate tract on the face of the globe. Yet in all times, and to-day, along the streams and oases of this bleak and storm-beaten desert, roving tribes of Mongolians pitch their tents of felt, and pasture their thriving herds. The western half, known as the great Steppes of Tartary, abounds in rich grazing lands, in fertile valleys, and in hunting forests. The climate, although somewhat rigorous in winter, is yet of surpassing healthfulness; and there seems to be, in all the surroundings of these romantic regions, just that element of ruggedness and hardship that brings forth the most restless, daring, and prolific races of mankind.

"These inaccessible regions," says Gibbon, "were the ancient residence of a powerful and civilized nation which ascends by a probable tradition above forty centuries." There is no doubt that these mountain highlands have been overflowing with nomadic races, of various states of culture, from times beyond the reach of tradition or mythology. They have supplied the dynasties and the ruling caste to the races of southern Asia since oriental nations have had an existence. From thence have issued the innumerable hordes of the Tartars which in the earliest times so often ravaged the plains of the south. Here were produced the prolific swarms of the Calmucks, or Black Huns, that menaced and overran the Chinese borders from a period of twelve centuries before the birth of Christ. From the high regions of the north came also the White Huns in later times, a polite but warlike people, whose monuments of victory dotted the plains from the Caspian Sea to the mouth of the Indus.

Beneath the metalline mountains of the Altai, the race of the Turks forged at their anvils, the basest slaves of the great Khan of the Moguls. About the middle of the sixth century of our era, it suddenly came into the minds of these stalwart smiths that they might just as well use the weapons they were forging, as to hand them over to their task-masters to use. And thereupon they rose up against their oppressors, established themselves in their place, and forthwith commenced a series of conquests which ended in the founding of the grandest empire of the middle ages.

In the twelfth century the terrible Zengis Khan led from these Highlands the myriads of the Moguls, and we are told that the crowded hosts of the Southrons were mown like hemp before his conquering blades. A world of shepherd barbarians bowed to his sway, and the Mogul dynasties were seated on the thrones of Asia.

But we return to the race that has been styled the Black Huns of Tartary, whose character and wanderings and conquests we have undertaken to present before you this evening. Perched then on their mountain-girt uplands, twelve centuries before the Christian era, we find this rugged and untamed race becoming the terror and the despoilers of Asia. A nation of herdsmen, they subsisted almost entirely on the milk and flesh of their flocks and herds, as also of their horses. Their habitations were rude tents, or at best small huts which might easily be mounted on wagons, always ready, whenever choice or necessity bade them, to move to other pasture grounds. Their sports were the boldest feats of horsemanship or the dangerous chase of the bear and the boar. Constant practice had seated them so firmly on horseback that rider and horse seemed to have grown into one animal; and the old Greek historians related that they ate and slept and lived on the backs of their steeds. Every circumstance of their habits and surroundings contributed to make them bold in battle and rapid on the march.

The earlier chieftains of the Huns had extended their conquests and dominions so widely that, at the time when they became formidable to the empire of China, they were found to be the rulers of the entire northern part of Asia. On the one side the Pacific Ocean, and on the other the Ural Mountains, had stayed their conquests. On the south they were bounded by the empires of China and Persia; while on the north their arms had pierced the frozen regions of Siberia as far as it were glory to conquer or resistance had been met with.

In the third century before the Christian era (B. C. 215) the incessant forages and incursions of the Huns had come to be such a terror to the timorous Chinamen that it entered into their wise little heads to build a high wall of defense from the sea to the farthest mountains of the west. So they set to work, and for fifteen hundred miles, over hills and ranges and every obstacle, they reared a cemented wall of brick and stone, 20 feet high and 23 feet broad, with towers and parapets and a highway for armies on the top, the most stupendous work ever accomplished by human hands. But it was a vain and delusive security. The myriads of the horsemen of the north, whose impetuous march had never been stayed by the chasms and precipices of their mountain land, found but a feeble barrier in the Chinamen's rampart of stone. It seemed rather to invite attack than to repel invasion; for we read that within a few years after its construction the stately armies of the empire had all been surrounded, cut off, or defeated, by the restless and resistless cavalry of the Huns.* For more than a century then did the rude warriors of the mountains levy their tribute on the luxury and handicraft of the foremost nation of antiquity. Not only bales of silks and embroideries, but bevies of fair maidens from the south, found their way yearly to the rude and unaccustomed service of border chieftains.

---

* In the reign of the Chinese Emperor Kaoti. B. C. 201.

At length there came to the throne of China an emperor who proved himself able to cope successfully with these barbarian conquerors.* He bought over some wild Tartar tribes of the north, and recruiting his army with these hardy mountaineers, he sent it out to hunt up and give battle to the unsuspecting Huns. This army pierced many hundred miles into the northern wilderness, and at the dead of the night, while the stupor of riot and drunkenness was brooding on the camp of the Huns, surprised them in their tents and left fifteen thousand slain as the mark of their victory. Though the Hunish chieftain bravely cut his way through their murderous army and escaped, it was only to renew the contest with the same bloody issue and disastrous result. From that ill-fated night the power of the Huns in Asia began to wane. Long years they struggled against their fate. But at last the time came when they were forced to bow to the yoke of their ancient tributaries. With stern and haughty reluctance were they whose Tanjous had reigned for thirteen hundred years the sovereign lords of Upper Asia, compelled to draw the bow and rein the steed with the mouthing soldiers of China. The spirit of freedom that was fostered by the wild life of the herdsman and huntsman, could not long brook a servitude like that. With these rovers it must be absolute independence at home, or a lawless and nomadic life in other lands.

In the one hundredth year of our era the spirit of migration broke out on the Highlands of Asia. The wild and unknown regions of the west were open to nomadic adventure or conquest; and westward trended the wanderings of the greater portion of the Huns, till they were lost on the tablets of history and their journeyings were noted only by their results. For as in their relentless march they expelled one tribe of barbarians from their ancestral pasture grounds, these drove out a neighboring tribe, who in their turn pressed upon another, till Europe received the mighty impulse, and the world of barbarism was set in westward motion. Tribe after tribe rolled on along the frontiers of the Roman Empire, or pealed their war-songs at the gates of the city that from its seven hills had ruled the world. The dismal bell

---

* The Chinese Emperor Vouti, of the Dynasty of Han. B. C. 90.

of fate which then was ringing in the clang of passing millions, tolled out to old Rome the periods of the progress of the Huns.

The first of the tribes whose movements startled the quiet of those early ages, was the Franks, a confederacy of the clans that in their wild independence had roamed unmolested amidst the Black Forests of Lower Germany. The dictator Cæsar had found them there and vainly attempted to track them in their inaccessible wilderness; and there they had continued to defy the Roman legions. But now (about 175 A. D.), driven out from this retreat by some resistless impulse from the regions beyond, the Franks made haste to spread their desolating warfare and plant their name on the plains of France.

Next came down the tribes of upper or northern Germany, confederated under the name of Alemanni—all-men—that is, men of all races, and all fighting men. These with incredible swiftness and in overwhelming numbers, overspread the northern provinces of Italy, and celebrated their barbaric orgies almost in sight of Rome. The city itself was preserved only by the most energetic measures. The aged senators rushed to arms; the artisans and the populace hastened with one accord to swell the unaccustomed army, and the tide of this appalling irruption was rolled back on the forests of the north. For many years the Alemanni hovered on the confines of the Roman territory, the defeated of many a bloody battle, till at last they were scattered and merged among the Franks of Gaul.

Following hard upon these, came the ruthless Goths, the most wide-spread and far-famed of the barbarians of the north. They issued from the regions of the Baltic, and suddenly their countless hordes confronted the Romans on the banks of the Danube. What may have been the original impulse of this eventful migration, we are now unable to say. It may have been a famine or a pestilence; or more likely it may have been some terrible defeat inflicted by the on-pressing myriads of the north on some battle field now hidden beneath the gloomy forests of Russia. For it must have been about this time, near the year 250, that the Black Huns of Tartary poured down the Ural mountains into Europe; and through the chain of the tribes of

Sarmatia the shock may have been communicated to the dwellers on the Baltic.

How strange and grand on the chronicles of the past are these nomadic irruptions! A nation with its unnumbered millions starts up by one common impulse, and moves on over mountains and deserts and river barriers, from one climate to another, from continent to continent. Without a regret or a backward look, they leave the familiar scenes of home and of country, the spot where lie their buried dead, and carelessly roam, they know not whither. We look upon such movements with amazement, who have been wont to witness the never dying attachment of our own aborigines to the home of their childhood, the land of their fathers. And nothing more clearly disproves their common origin with the wild Tartars of upper Asia, than these diverse instincts of their natures. The Indian, whose all of future hope and religion lies centered in the earth-mound where, with his tomahawk and scalping knife by his side, his blanket and his trophies around him, he shall rest from the toil of the hunts and the dances of the spirit land, turns with a longing stronger than the instinct of life to the hillocks in the forest which he has reared for burial mounds. But the Celt or the Tartar cared little where bleached the bones of his ancestors, or where over his own unheeded body the carrion beasts should hold their revel. His religion taught him to dread only the death of the coward and the craven—that only the souls of the brave are the care of their gods.

These rude nomads tilled no soil and gathered in no harvests. Their sustenance was their flocks and herds, their only domestic arts the cure of meats and the preparations of milk. Their dwellings were tents and wagons, a perpetual encampment, within which were nightly gathered their numerous animals. For amusement they hunted the hare, the deer, the stag, and the elk. But no chase was so welcome as to rouse the angry boar, to grapple with the hungry bear, or to encounter the fierce tiger of the northern forests. They worshiped only the god of war and him whose voice was in the thunder. And for these stern divinities the altars often reeked with the blood of human victims. In each succeeding year as summer approached, these herdsmen and shepherds were wont to seek fresher pastures on the hill-sides in the distant north. Again, as winter drew near, they sought the protected valleys of the south, ordinarily herding back and forth by the beaten tracks of former seasons. But anon, as the herd-boy's call sounds on the eventide to gather in his flocks, a rumor is borne to the startled camp, that tribe after tribe, in the far reaches of the east and the north, on the war-horse and the car, are sweeping on in the course of the setting sun. Sharp and hasty sounds the note of preparation to the bustling throng; and ere the morning dawns the warrior mounts his steed, the women and the children scramble to their seats on the wagon, the oxen are inspanned, the flocks and the herds are started on, and the driver whoops his shrill cry for the march. Thus,

> "Oft o'er the trembling nations from afar,
> Has Scythia breathed the living cloud of war;
> And where the deluge burst, with sweeping sway,
> Their arms, their kings, their gods, were rolled away,
> As oft have issued, host impelling host,
> The blue-eyed myriads of the Baltic coast.
> The prostrate south to the destroyer yields
> Her boasted titles and her golden fields.
> With grim delight the brood of winter view
> A brighter day and heavens of azure hue,
> Scent the new fragrance of the blushing rose,
> And quaff the pendant vintage as it grows."*

Four hundred years had passed away since the wise men of the east had hailed the rising star of the Babe of Bethlehem. Christianity from its feeble beginning had come to be a religion of state. The pontiffs of Rome then ruled in temporal matters, and the mandates of the church went forth to curb and to unseat kings. The tribes of Gaul (or France) had become Christianized and were the allies of Christian Rome. The empire itself had lost as yet but little of its nominal power, though governed by two emperors, the one having his seat in the east on the Bosphorus and the other in the ancient capitol on the Tiber. But in

---

* From a fragment of a poem by Thomas Gray. Mason's Life of Gray, p. 196.

the mind of the Roman there were strange forebodings of coming evil. The twelve centuries of the duration of Roman sovereignty, foretold in the twelve vultures that appeared to Romulus, and which had ever been regarded as a prophecy of destiny to Rome, were now near to their eventful close. An earthquake of more than usual terror had recently sent the sea careering high up into the land, had toppled down stately castles, and caused wide-spread desolation among the sons of the south. This to Roman superstition had betokened some direful calamity. All southern Europe was at this time anxiously scanning the horizon for some signs of alarm; when lo, on the far off bounds of its geography, there suddenly loomed up the dark masses of the Huns. Their coming was heralded from end to end of Europe; and rumor catching up their ferocious habits and ungainly proportions, magnified them into odious monsters sprung of "midnight foul and hideous hags." With a shrill piercing voice, uncouth in mien and gesture, with beardless face and sunken but flashing eyes, with a massive head crowded between broad brawny shoulders, well might they be hailed as savages by barbarians of other worlds than their own.

But little time however was given for fright or fables. Like a tempest the Huns swept onward, deluging the land with indiscriminate slaughter, or drawing into the vortex the tribes which stood in their way. On the banks of the Tanais they encountered and vanquished the wide-spread Alani. The Ostrogoths, who held sway from the the Euxine to the Baltic, bowed to the storm. The Visigoths, who came next in turn, fled frightened and trembling upon the tribes of the west and south, and ere long, cowering on the summits of the Alps, stood gazing on the majesty of Italy.

The chieftain of these now driven and fugitive Goths, the renowned Alaric, had once, upon some occasion of defeat, like Hannibal of Carthage, sworn upon the altar of his gods eternal enmity to Rome. And now, six hundred years later and in the very track of the mighty African, he was leading the desperate myriads of the north in one of the grandest irruptions of ancient times, either to retrieve his fortunes or bury his name and his race beneath the walls of the "Eternal City." Host upon host of Gothic clans poured down on the plains of the Po; and almost before the rumor of the approaching deluge had reached the capitol, its roar was heard from the watch-towers, and Rome, whose sacred walls had never known till now the unhallowed contact of barbarism, looked out upon a raging sea of north-men. Cut off from all supplies, the besieged were soon reduced to the vilest extremity of famine and pestilence, and were compelled to purchase the retreat of the barbarians at the price of tons of gold and silver and silks and spices. But in the absence of impending danger, the old Roman haughtiness returned, and the revolting conditions of the truce were spurned. Again Alaric stood at its gates and summoned the proud city to surrender. Again he dictated the terms of capitulation and retired, having seated on the imperial throne a Roman of his own choosing. He was soon however recalled again by another, the last faint flickering of a flame that had once blazed brightly on a universe. For the third time the stern Alaric sat down before the gates of the queen of cities, his anger aroused by the childs-play of his fickle enemies. Treachery speedily opened the gates to his army; and at the still hour of midnight, suddenly the clang of barbarian arms rang out on the silent streets, and the lurid glare of conflagration burst on the appalled city. For six days was the seat of ancient wealth and classic beauty given over to the licentious pillage of the hordes of the northern forests; and the track was now broadly beaten, in which, as shortly closed its twelfth century, the last vestige of the might and majesty of old Rome was trampled out beneath the iron tread of barbarism.

In the fifty years which succeeded their first appearance, the Huns had become the masters of northern and eastern Europe, as of old they had been of northern Asia. The Russian and the Finn brought down to them their furs; the Eastern Empire sent tribute of its wines and its money; and the hardy warriors of Germany and Scandinavia bore the bow and the battle-ax in their lines. It was then, as the chieftain of these savage hordes, that Attila appeared, a leader courageous, resolute and relentless beyond any whose deeds have been recorded in history. His appearance is well described in these lines of Herbert:

> "Terrific was his semblance, in no mould
> Of beautiful proportion cast; his limbs
> Nothing exalted, but with sinews braced
> Of Chalybean temper, agile, lithe,
> And swifter than the roe; his ample chest
> Was overbrowed by a gigantic head,
> With eyes keen, deeply sunk, and small, that gleamed
> Strangely in wrath, as though some spirit unclean,
> Within that corporal tenement installed,
> Looked from its windows, but with tempered fire
> Beamed mildly on the unresisting. Thin
> His beard and hoary; his flat nostrils crowned
> A cicatrized swart visage. But withal
> That questionable shape such glory wore
> That mortals quailed beneath him."

It was the great absorbing desire of this ambitious man to make of all Europe, from the midland sea to the frozen ocean, one wide domain of anti-Christ, and himself the barbaric monarch. To this purpose bent all his aims and his energies. He styled himself "The scourge of God;" and with Heaven-daring zeal he strove to make good the impious appellation. His predecessors had achieved for him the conquest of all but the western Roman Empire, with Gallic France and the Peninsula. For the subjugation of France then did Attila gather together his clans and his native armies, swelled by the accretion of numberless tribes and levies; and westward again swept on the flood of irruption. The track of the Huns as heretofore was one broad scene of havoc and slaughter, until in the heart of France they laid siege to the city of Orleans. But the unexpected appearance of the allied armies of Italy and of Gaul compelled them to raise the siege and for a time to retreat.

One midsummer day, in the year 451, on the banks of a little rivulet in the north-eastern part of France, a traveler paused to rest him on his journey and to look out on the broad plains of Chalons. Through all this champaign country, extending a hundred miles around, which was in later years to be beautified by countless vineyards, could now be seen only the desolate waste left by the barbarian armies in their recent passage southward.

But now not a sound stirred the air; not a moving thing relieved the monotony of ruin. Again the wayfarer looked; and far on the western horizon a low dark shadow seemed rolling up from the space beyond. Could it be a cloud mounting so clear a sky, and betokening a coming storm? Again he looked; and lo, as far as the eye could see, there darkened against the setting sun the living masses of innumerable cavalry. Startled from his rest, the traveler sped frightened over the plain; and soon where he had stood beside that brook the war-horse of Attila pawed the ground. Poising a javelin above his head, the chieftain sent it whirling through the air, till far in the distance it quivered in the sod. "Thus far," said he, "retreats the monarch of the Huns. Pitch there my tent; for here will we stay yon proud Roman, or leave our bones to whiten on these plains."

In a circle of many miles circumference, the cumbrous wagons of the Huns were interlocked with each other in double lines, forming a strong fortification, and having one only opening in the front. Within this enclosure were soon collected a million horses and a countless swarm of human beings. Close upon their rear came the Roman general Aetius, with his Gothic ally Theodoric, who had followed the Huns from the siege of Orleans, and now encamped on the opposite side of the brook. There within the compass of a few leagues were assembled the nations of all Europe; on the one side the barbarians of the east and the north, and all who hated Rome and Christianity alike with an intolerant hatred; on the other side the legions of the Roman Empire with the vast armies of the Christianized Visigoths and the tribes of Gaul. Heathenism and Christianity, barbarism and civilization, had there met for deadly and exterminating conflict.

Night came; but with it came no quiet to that vast multitude preparing for the coming battle. The sound of the sledge and hammer, the clanking of arms and armor, the wild blast of the trumpet, the loud and startling laugh, and the native war-songs shouted in savage dissonance, the clatter of thousands hurrying to and fro, the voices of sentinels and officers rung out in many a discordant tongue, all raised on the air of night so hideous a din, that naught was noted beyond the passing sight. An accidental encounter of some divisions of either army occurred within half a mile of the Hunish camp for the possession of a ridge which would command the flank of either side in the coming battle. But in the uproar of the night it was unheard or unheeded, although fifteen thousand were left dead on the hill-side before Torismund, the valiant son of Theodoric, had occupied the eminence for the Roman army.

It was well past the mid-hour of the following day, when all preparations were completed, and the two vast armies were arrayed against each other on opposite sides of the little rivulet. On one side Attila at the head of his brave and faithful Huns occupied in person the center of his line. These grim-looking warriors, dark and hard-featured, mounted on wild unbridled horses, with the bow and quiver slung at their shoulders and in their hands the huge naked sword, presented by far the most terrific appearance in all that line of battle. While far away on their right and their left, stretched the myriad tribes and nations of the barbarous north. There were the Gepidæ, the Heruli, the Geloni, the Scyrri, the Rugians, Burgundians, Thuringians, and Belonoti, and the thousand hordes that roamed the wilderness from the Rhine to the Volga. On the extreme left were posted the tall commanding Ostrogoths, next to the low ridge which here extended along the ranks. On the other side of the stream, Aetius commanded the left flank. The center was filled with tribes of doubtful constancy or valor, the robust Alan, the sturdy Armorican, and the gaudy Frank. While on the right, and opposed to the Ostrogoths, were stationed the blue-eyed light-haired Visigoths, led on by their aged king Theodoric.

On this battle field of the early ages, were thus gathered one and a half millions of warriors. It was the grandest and completest armament that the world of those times could furnish. The trained and selected fighters of a continent were facing each other on that day of destiny. The Roman legions, skilled in all the tactics of antiquity, the Scythian archers, the most noted marksmen of all times, the dexterous spearmen of Gaul, the powerful wielders of the Gothic battle-ax, and the Hunish horsemen, beyond question the most daring riders in the world, swelled the squadrons of a field the most momentous in the annals of history.

The charge to the conflict was given by Attila, who ordered Valimer, the giant king of the Ostrogoths, to seize on the eminence occupied by the Visigoths. And by the rancorous struggle of these rival tribes of Goths was commenced the sanguinary battle of Chalons. Not an uplifted arm was stayed by the ties of brotherhood; not an arrow shunned its mark for kindly memories of the olden time. Fierce and remorseless was the contest, as is always the warfare of kindred tribes or nations.

For a time the remainder of either army paused motionless at sight of such deadly strife. But not long could the warriors be restrained, now panting for the carnage. No longer could the restless chargers be curbed, as they snuffed the battle afar off. On came the Romans and their Gallic allies. On swept the Huns and their Scythian horsemen. A cloud of arrows darkened the sky and fell pattering like a storm of hail. At length the long spears reached opposing spears; swords clashed against swords; and all were mingled in one vast mêlée of carnage.

In the action we have undertaken to describe, there was little of military skill or generalship to relieve the story of blood, since the battle was decided by the blind impetuosity of barbarians. The Huns, almost with their first charge, pierced through the ranks of the Alans and Sicambres, and wheeling by a rapid movement to the left, encountered the Visigoths. While the Romans, cut off from their right wing, were left almost alone in conflict with the barbarians of Attila's right. Although they bore themselves bravely that day, and the gallant Aetius was seen riding the foremost wherever the strife was the fiercest or danger the most imminent, yet night closed on the scene while the issue on this side was still undecided. The main interest therefore, as well as the decision of the battle, rested with the opposite extreme of the armies, where the Huns and the Goths side by side were toiling up that low hill, a task made difficult by the disadvantage of the ground and the ferocious obstinacy of the Visigoths who defended it. Again and again the dark masses of warriors charged up the ascent; again and again they rolled back as they met the resistless tide from above. Yet still the fight waxed fiercer, and deeds of single handed daring and brutal passion were there enacted which the chroniclers even were loth to tell. The riderless horses, it was said, of these gipsies of the orient were seen dashing away into the ranks of the enemy, and there with more than human ferocity fighting and tramping among the dense columns, till at last their dying shriek told the tale of both horse and rider. A Hun and a Goth on the hill-side, wounded to the death, crawled on to each other, and with their teeth in their expiring agonies tore each other's flesh till life went out in this horrid death strife. Such was the animosity in battle of man and beast among these savage hordes.

The closing hours of the day thus passed, while still the battle raged and the carnage was unabated. The sun was already sinking below the western sky, and Attila was now almost exulting in the victory. The old man Theodoric, his white hair streaming on the wind, was riding heedless of danger before his warriors and urging them on to yet another charge, when in mid-career he was struck by a javelin from a noble Ostrogoth, and falling from his horse, was trampled beneath the feet of his own cavalry. The youthful Torismund from the hill-top beheld the brave chieftain, his father, borne to the ground; and with a wild cry of anguish he rushed down with his followers on the Huns, like an avalanche started from its fastness by some wind gust of the Alps. It was not a charge, nor any species of human warfare, but the savage onslaught of wild beasts. They fought hand to hand, without mercy asked or quarter given. Each blow of the battle-ax felled some victim to the ground. Each plunge of the steed trampled out some luckless life. The hill-side became clogged and hideous with its burden of the slain; and the stream below flowed sluggish with its swollen current of blood.

But the boldest champion of that fearful struggle was the leader Attila, who everywhere conspicuous on his powerful black charger, seemed to court every danger and to know no fear. The spirit of battle now possessed him. Over his brow there darkened that hideous scowl, and from his eyes shot forth the living fire of the demon of war. Before his gaze the bravest cowered, and by his resistless arm the foe were leveled like grain before the reaper. He seemed, like Ajax, to carry the battle on his own gigantic shoulders. But all in vain the hero fought.

No will or might of man could resist the fateful doom. For the decree had gone forth; and by the side of young Torismund there was a spirit mightier than man's which guided the closing struggle.

At length, as night drew over the scene its thickening veil, Attila commanded the trumpets to sound a retreat. And soon, defeated and pursued, his weary warriors gathered within the circle of their wagons. Torismund and the Roman too retired from the field; and darkness spread its gloomy pall above the ghastliest scene on earth.

The number of killed in the battle of Chalons has been variously estimated by historians from 162,000 to 300,000, according as they have included those left dead on the field of battle, or those who died of their wounds, or were otherwise missing. But it was a sufficient number in any case to show that this engagement was the most sanguinary that the world has ever witnessed. As the chronicler of the time has most quaintly remarked, "There was nothing to be compared with it in all the annals of antiquity; and it shows how the madness of kings may thus in a few hours sweep away whole generations of men."

During the night Attila caused a huge funereal pile to be erected of the wooden saddles of his cavalry, on which he placed all his trophies and his captures, resolved that if the Romans stormed the camp on the following morning they should fail of their most coveted prize, the person of the barbarian king. But for unknown, or at least unrecorded reasons, Aetius chose to allow the now desperate remnant of his enemy to retire without further worrying. He may have thought the wounded lion more dangerous than in fresh and open fight; or he may rather have thought that another such a victory as he had already won would be enough to 'ruin any army or any cause. At all events the Huns soon broke their encampment and retired unmolested to the dark forests of Hungary. And when two years after, on the death of Attila, his wide empire was dismembered and dissolved, Christianity drew a long breath of relief, and rested for a time from the perils that had so closely beset it.

Had the "Scourge of God" been victorious on the Catalaunian plains, who will estimate the influence it would have exerted on the destiny of the world? From the merciless and exterminating warfare of the Huns, and their inveterate hatred of the Roman's new religion, it is but reasonable to suppose that the Bible had been buried beneath the chaos of barbarian riot; that none had been left to repeat the story of the prophets and the apostles, or to worship any spiritual God. On the valleys and hill-sides of Europe had gloamed the increasing darkness of heathenism. The soothsayer, on every mountain top, had scraped the bones of animals slain, to divine the presages of futurity; and the altar, reeking with the blood of human victims, had sent its odious incense up to an angry Heaven. The sun it may be had risen and set on a hemisphere, and again had risen and set on another, but had looked in all his round only on benighted millions of paganism.

But this dismal panorama was never to be unrolled on earth. The arm of the arrogant Attila was stayed in the moment of victory; and lo, along the paths of pagan conquest the lights of Christianity blazed forth. The Holy Book, the germ from which was to spring the giant oak of civilization, was scattered on the farthest wilds of Europe. Refinement sprung out on the rude impress of barbarism. Sage wisdom stepped forth from the turmoil of savage passion. Wealth, at the Midas touch, poured its full horn into the lap of diligence. Science began to dawn on the night of ages. Invention teemed with its multiform enginery. And the elements bowed down at the bidding of man. In every dell where rises the hamlet of the husbandman, the sound of the school-call gathers in the truant and the student; and from every hill-side rings the echo of the church-going bell. On every land of the white man there are loud cries for liberty and self-government. While on all the lands of the dark races the voice of the preacher is heard amidst the jargon of idolatry. The heart of every freeman swells with the proud boast of civilization's heritage, of the glories of his father-land, and of the endearing ties of home. And still sweeps on this majestic tide of prosperity, whose tiny source lies in the far distant past, when the champions of progression and of retrogression stood marshaled on the plains of Chalons, and for the first time the brawny arm of old might fell palsied before the power of the right.

Plate XIV.—WHITE TERRACES, FOUNTAIN NOT FLOWING. See Page xix.

PREFACE TO LECTURE ON ANCIENT PAINTING.*

The old and the new! Words that sum up all there is of human achievement in the world. The old are the memorials of the grand struggle of man's development. The new are the achieved results of all past efforts.

It has always seemed to me that the works and discoveries which have marked the stages of the world's progress ought to be subjects of interest to every one. But mine is not the universal conclusion. There are many who look upon the accomplishments of the past as vain and wasted efforts, because they do not equal the splendid results of the present. The world of observers is clearly divided between those who take interest in the old and the antiquated, and those who care for none of these things.

In the latter category is perhaps the majority of the enlightened classes of our own country. In America our growth and wealth are mainly of the present generation. A man's family dates no further back than his father and mother, and his fortune scarcely ever as far back as that. Every thing in our habits and culture leads us to value only what runs with the current of our immediate and absorbing pursuits. Those of our people who travel abroad, where there is only the old to show, are quite often discontented and disappointed tourists. They have the restless longing to put life into the lifeless, and novelty into the antiquated. If they could have their way, they would "mighty soon clear out the old rubbish, and slick up things generally." One may hear, almost any day, in presence of some

---

*A Lecture written in 1878, and delivered before the Rochester Art Society, and on various other occasions.

noted relic of the past, such characteristic remarks as these: "How very, very clever! Now isn't it?" "C'est magnifique! Mon Dieu, c'est un ouvrage splendide!" "Well now, I can't see anything there to make a fuss about." This last speaker has somehow gotten the name abroad of being excessively practical, of reducing everything right down to its present value of merit or utility. He is pointed out as the "cui bono" man—the one who is forever asking, "What is it good for?"

Now, my friends, there is a world of interest and of attraction in things that are good for nothing—in old castles and ruins, in old statues and paintings, in old histories and legends. It is in the endeavor to make this appear to you, that I am to speak to-night of things long since passed away—of the Rise and Fall of an Empire of Art more wonderful and impressive than the Empire of Arms which Gibbon has immortalized.

I have had the opportunity and the pleasure to give my dissertation on the more modern art of painting, in the Catalogue of the Gallery in our City, which the liberality, aided by the gifted taste, of one of our foremost citizens, has already made the richest collection of the Fine Arts in America. But further back than anything there shown—more ancient than the old, grander than the grandeur of artistic Italy—there is another realm of art dimly rising out of the dawn of nations and of languages. In this cloud-region of the classics I have gathered this evening's subject, which is "Ancient Painting as among the Lost Arts."

ANCIENT PAINTING AS AMONG THE LOST ARTS.

It would seem as if the world's progress had always been made by starts and sudden bounds. The Genius of cultivation has visited the earth like the rare and uncertain returns of a comet. After each appearance it has departed again for unknown regions; and when or how or where it would return from its roaming, no man could tell. Who could have foretold or supposed that the spirit of letters and literature would have made its first appearance on the rugged sea-girt peninsula and islands of Greece? Then, five hundred years later, on the classic hills of the capitol that boasted to rule the world? And again, after a dreary absence of fifteen hundred years, to have alighted on the islands of Britain, afar in the Northern Seas? Sometime, away back in the ages, science has come very near dawning upon the earth. We have no certain knowledge when or where, for we only know of the fact by the fragments that have been left. The races of Eastern Asia have, for all historic time, known how to calculate eclipses, to figure the revolutions of the planets, to divide and measure the seasons and years, together with many other elements of knowledge implying an intimate acquaintance with astronomy. They have made gunpowder, used the magnetic needle, created power by steam, and printed with types, for thousands of years. But as they never made any worthy use of this information and these discoveries, we must suppose them to be the relics of a lost civilization.

So also the beautiful arts, as painting and sculpture, have been twice discovered, and twice have grown independently, and by almost identical stages, to a remarkable state of perfection. First in the small Republics of Greece, about 400 years before Christ; and last in the States of Italy, and 1,500 years after Christ. But between the two periods every trace of the first era had entirely disappeared. Painting was for more than a thousand years one of the Lost Arts.

The causes that brought about this total extinction of one of the brightest lights in human progress, will be that of which we will discourse mainly to-night. But first we must tell the story of Grecian Art, in as few words as possible, and gather from the scattered accounts given in the old authors, as clear and correct an idea as we can of the process, materials, and varieties of Grecian painting.

It must be borne in mind that all we know of these things comes from the incidental allusions of ancient writers, who had not the remotest thought that their works would outlast the beautiful specimens they were praising, or that the time would ever come when their writings would be searched to find out what was that mysterious handicraft called Grecian painting. Therefore it never occurred to them to say, whether their artists used canvas or wood, oil paints or water colors, brushes or sponge or stylus, colors or sketches or outline. No more would a traveling correspondent in Europe at the present time think to tell the same things about the pictures he saw. Why, every one knows that paintings are made on cloth, with brush and oil paints and all varieties of colors. But unfortunately these are the very things that we are most in doubt about, that we cannot reconcile, in regard to ancient art. The more one studies, the more is he convinced that the modes and materials of picture making in the olden times were essentially different from those of the present, that the process of Grecian painting is to this day a Lost Art.

It is probable that for portable pictures the Greeks painted mainly on wood. In the early stages of the art the wooden tablet was stained black or white, a covering of wax was spread over the surface, the picture was drawn in outline with a stylus or pen, and then burnt in. Afterwards colors mixed with wax and oil were put on with a brush or sponge, and then burnt in. All tabular pictures on wood were what was called *encaustic*, that is, the wood was made in some way by heat to absorb the color vehicle, thus blending the colors and softening the outlines, producing what from all accounts must be conceded to be a marvelous attainment in painting. But this art, whatever it may have been, has never been rediscovered. There was also, without doubt, a method of painting on canvas. The colors, dissolved in water, were thickened with glue and put on with brushes. When the painting was dry it was heavily varnished with a mixture of warm Punic wax and oil. This was called "distemper."

Mural paintings were in part, like those of modern times, in *fresco*. That is, water-colors were used on fresh walls, or on a coating of mortar not yet dry, the plaster thus taking up the paint and rendering it very permanent. But as lime destroys many colors, which consequently cannot be used in fresco, the ancients adopted another and a peculiar practice for wall paintings. As fast as the picture was made on any dry wall, with water colors mixed with some kind of gum or glue, it was varnished with Punic wax and oil, heated by fire from a chafing dish "usque ad sudorem," up to a sweat, when it was rubbed with wax candles and polished with white napkins. In this way the wall paintings had all the beauty of finish, the harmony and tone of amalgamated outlines, and the splendid varieties of coloring, of the tabular pictures; and more than all, they were as enduring as the walls themselves. The frescoes of Pompeii are mostly, if not all, of the kind we have just described. None others would have lasted as they have done, preserving their freshness of color and distinctness of outline through a burial of nearly eighteen hundred years in damp and destructive earths. This method of painting is also another instance of ancient discoveries passing forever from the role of the Arts.

With these remarks on the materials and processes, we can now relate what were the accomplishments of ancient art. Five hundred years before Christ, painting was in a very rude and primitive state in Greece. According to one author, it was the custom as well as a necessity for an artist to write under his productions: "This is a bull;" "This is a horse;" "This is a tree." Shortly after this time, Cimon, the Cleonian, is mentioned as being able to paint the sexes so that they could be distinguished, and faces looking side ways or up or down, and could make folds in drapery, and show the veins and muscles. He was the first one apparently who could dispense with the labels on his works.

Then followed Panænus, the brother of the great sculptor Phidias, who painted the battle of Marathon, and introduced the portraits of the chief leaders on both sides, so well executed that they could be recognized by those who had ever seen them living.

Polygnotus was the first who painted with more than one color. He used four, red, yellow, blue and black. He flourished about 450 B. C.; and his great triumph was that he put expression in the face, and kindled up the fire of life and passion in the human form. He was the Prometheus of art. Under his hand the bright smile of beauty, and the lovely form of woman, veiled with flowing or transparent drapery, first appeared on the painter's tablets.

We have now reached the time when the famous pictures of antiquity began to be produced. We will mention and describe some of them, in order to show the high advance in art.

Apollodorus painted Ajax defying the lightning. On the night of the downfall of Troy, Cassandra, priestess and daughter of Priam, fled for protection to the temple of Minerva. But despite the sacredness of the place, she was there exposed to the brutality of Ajax, the boldest and the rudest of the Grecian chieftains. To punish him for this sacrilege, Minerva borrowed the thunderbolts of Jupiter, and pursued him returning to his home. His vessel was wrecked in one of the wildest of storms; but he swam to a solitary rock in the sea, and there in his wrath defied all the lightnings of Heaven. Minerva carried him off in a whirlwind. We are told, and may well believe, that this was a magnificent painting.

Zeuxis painted the infant Hercules strangling the serpents. This valorous demi-god was the son of Jupiter and Alcmena. Juno, always jealous of these side issues, sent two serpents to destroy the infant while he was yet in his cradle. But nothing daunted, the child seized them in both his hands, and squeezed them to death. The terror of the mother and the fright of the attendants, contrasted with the fearlessness of the infant prodigy, made this a long noted painting. Zeuxis also represented Jupiter seated on his Olympian throne, and all the other gods doing him reverence. It was as grand a subject as some of the gorgeous scenes of Paul Veronese. A Helen, a Penelope, and an Alcmena, were some of the minor works of this same master.

There was once a contest between him and Parrhasius, which should produce the most life-like picture. The two brought their productions—Zeuxis, a vine and some clusters of grapes, so perfectly natural that when exposed the birds flew and pecked at them for genuine fruit. Elated with his success, he called to his rival to remove the curtain from before his picture. But when he found that this curtain was only a painting, he acknowledged himself fairly beaten; for he had only deceived the birds, whereas Parrhasius had deceived an experienced artist.

Zeuxis once painted a boy carrying a basket of grapes. The birds also in this instance, when they saw it, flew to the basket for the fruit. The painter, exulting in his triumph, was however a good deal mortified when his rivals reminded him that the boy had not deceived the birds, else they never would have dared to fly to his basket.

Parrhasius is acknowledged to have made notable advances in what was always the great aim and strife of the classic painters and sculptors, that is to endow the forms of their gods with such a perfection of human excellence, each in some one direction of development, as clearly to show them superhuman. He it was who could prescribe the limits of variation from the ordinary type of mortals, that heros and gods might take on both in picture and statue. His canon of proportions was the law for all subsequent artists. As one instance, it is mentioned that he gave to Jupiter that peculiar inclination of the head, a certain higher elevation of the neck behind, a bolder protrusion of the front, and an increased perpendicular of the profile, so that he seemed actually to be giving the awful nod which shook the universe, and made gods and men alike to tremble.

Parrhasius painted an allegorical representation of the Athenian demos, or democracy, which Pliny said expressed at the same time all the good and bad qualities of this versatile people. One might trace there, he says, at once the changeable, the irritable, the kind, the unjust, the forgiving, the vain glorious, the proud, the humble, the fierce, the timid. Just how all this could be got into one painting, it is impossible for us to conceive. But the ancients certainly had a gift for doing these things. We never could have believed that the whole story of the Nile could be told in one piece of statuary, if we had not actually seen it.*

Timanthes, one of the most gifted masters of Greece, was most noted as the painter of the Sacrifice of Iphigenia. On the way to the siege of Troy, the Grecian fleet was detained at Aulis by adverse winds. At this place, Agamemnon the leader having in some way offended the goddess Diana (by killing her favorite deer, I think), he was informed through Calchas, the soothsayer, that he could appease the divine huntress, and raise the wind embargo, in no other way than by the sacrifice of his beloved daughter Iphigenia. Reluctantly he sent for her, and she was placed for the immolation, when by some legerdemain human or divine, the girl was snatched away, and a hind was left in her place. What was most remarkable about this painting was, that after exhausting all the expressions of grief that he could invent on the countenances of those present, the artist had not yet touched that of Agamemnon. Then, as if to signify the utter inadequacy of human power to represent the father's anguish, he covered that face with a mantle, and there left it. Singularly enough this famous painting was found copied on the walls of the House of the Poet in Pompeii.

Timanthes seems to have been skilled in ingenious expedients to represent his ideas. In a painting of ordinary dimensions, where he wished to show the enormous size of a sleeping Cyclops,

---

* This colossal group is in the Vatican Museum at Rome. The giant figure of the god of the Nile is partly reclining and leaning against the Egyptian Sphinx. Sixteen cupids are climbing up on him, or sporting with ichneumons and crocodiles, representing the sixteen cubits of annual overflow of the Nile. There are also humorous battles of the pigmies with crocodiles and hippopotami. This piece of sculpture was found in the excavations of an old temple of Minerva near the Church of Santa Maria in Rome, in A.D. 1513.

he introduces a group of satyrs trying to measure his thumb with a common walking staff.

We come now to Apelles, a painter in the age of Alexander the Great (B. C. 330), and exalted by the united testimony of all antiquity to the highest rank in his profession. One of the most celebrated of his paintings was the Venus Anadyomene—Venus rising from the waves—born from the foam of the sea. It was in after ages carried to Rome, and still existed in the time of Nero. Another famous painting represented Alexander grasping a thunderbolt. And Pliny says that the fingers which held the bolt, as well as the bolt itself, seemed to project from the canvas. This picture sold in its time, and in that age of dear money, for what represented over $200,000. In a grand contest for the prize in paintings of horses, Apelles, seeing that favoritism was going to rule against him, demanded that all the paintings should be exhibited before a troop of live horses. And these animals, disregarding the others, neighed as they passed before his own picture of their kind. This impartial judgment could not be got over.

These things do seem almost incredible, and I would not wonder if there should be some skeptics here. But I think that these and similar stories are related too often and too seriously in the old authors for that there should not be some grains of truth in them.

Cotemporary with Apelles was Protogenes, also famous in the art. He spent seven years in finishing a great national painting, a hunting scene, which was to commemorate alike the founder and the founding of his native City of Rhodes. He had occasion to represent in the picture a dog panting, and the froth running from his mouth. But he never could paint, with any satisfaction to himself, the foam at the mouth. Finally out of all patience, he threw his sponge at the dog's head, and then found to his surprise, that he had by this act painted exactly what he wanted. Whatever a sponge has to do with painting, is one of those inexplicable things that we are continually meeting in the stories that have come down to us descriptive of ancient art. There is another mystery connected with this same painting. Pliny says that Protogenes painted this picture with four layers of colors, in such a way that, when one was destroyed by the hand of time, the layer underneath would reproduce the piece in all its original freshness and beauty. This is entirely incomprehensible to us, and we must revert again to our theory of Lost Arts.

It was between Protogenes and Apelles that occurred that remarkable trial of skill in sketching, which gives us some ideas of Grecian Art not otherwise obtainable. Apelles, who was an Athenian, having heard much of Protogenes who lived on the island of Rhodes, bethought him at one time to make the voyage, and thus to form his rival's acquaintance. Arriving, he called at the house of Protogenes, and learned that he was absent. Being shown into the studio, and finding a canvas and brushes placed as if for work, he took the liberty to draw a figure thereon, and then left. Protogenes returning saw the sketch, and at once said that no one but Apelles could have done that. But he immediately took the brush and drew a figure over the first, correcting or bettering some of the outlines. He then directed his housekeeper that, if the stranger came back, she was to show him again into the studio. It happened as he foresaw, and Apelles seeing himself outdone in the second trial, seized the brush and over all drew a third figure, still more perfect than either, and cutting both. Protogenes now confessed himself vanquished. He ran to the harbor, sought out his rival, and the two became thereafter the warmest of friends. Now, that this trial brought out some extraordinary results, is shown by the fact that the canvas containing it became highly prized, and at a later day was taken to Rome and preserved in the Palace of the Cæsars. Art writers, both ancient and modern, have had much to say about it. Michael Angelo thought without doubt that the figures were outlines of the human form, and that they embodied some of those exquisite perfections which make the Grecian statues, which have been dug out of Italian ruins in the last few centuries, objects of study and wonder to all who see them.

To illustrate this fact, and to show wherein consists that excellence, allow me to relate an incident connected with our own most distinguished countryman and artist, Benjamin West.

A little more than a hundred years ago this young painter went to Rome for the purpose of perfecting himself in his art. There was great curiosity among the acquaintances he had made on his arrival, to see what would be the first impressions of the quaker artist on beholding the renowned statues of the Vatican. So there was quite a company who attended him on his first visit to that museum. When brought before the Apollo Belvidere, he at once exclaimed, "My God! how like it is to a young Mohawk warrior." Well, the Roman friends were a good deal astonished to hear their most famous statue compared to an Indian savage. But there was a truth and a praise there which they little realized, as a few words of explanation will show.

For unknown ages previous to their contact with civilization, the Indian tribes of North America had been almost constantly in active hostilities with each other. Every man's life was every day in peril, and he only who was the swiftest of foot, the quickest of sight, and the most enduring on the war path, stood any chance of arriving at man's estate, and transmitting his powers and prowess to a line of descendants. It was preëminently the survival of the fittest. And we may rest assured that all that nature could do to endow that Mohawk warrior with fleetness, acuteness, and endurance, with the exact muscles, and sinews, and weight, and length of limbs, and prominence of sense organs, necessary to the highest display of agility, of quickness, and of vital force, had been given him. What praise then could be greater for the nameless sculptor of this relic of Grecian art, found four hundred years ago in the ruins of Antium, than to say that he had formed the god of the bow, the god of all high feats and adventure, the god that was the embodiment of manly beauty, courage, sagacity, and strength, on the same model that nature was using for her hero and Apollo in the forests by the Great Lakes?

I have now placed before you, in brief outline, a few of the many noted examples of ancient painting, which the classic authors are unanimous in praising to the full extent of the powers of language. But they do not praise them more than at the same time they extol the beauty and the excellence of the *statues* which adorned their temples and public halls. They all unite in saying that the arts of painting and sculpture were equally advanced. They had no more occasion or motive to deceive in the one case than in the other. For they never could have imagined that the time would come when sculpture would be represented by some of their most beautiful and wonderful specimens, while the sister art of painting would be represented by absolutely nothing. Therefore if we find that they told the truth in one case, we are bound to believe that they did so in the other.

Now what are the facts in regard to Greek sculpture? Leaving out of the question all the rest of Greece, we will only take notice of the small island of Rhodes, some forty miles long by fifteen wide. When the Romans took it, in the year 42 before Christ, they carried away 3,000 statues, among which, mere chance preservations we must suppose, were those remarkable groups of the Laocoon and the Farnese Bull. If there were many of them like these, what a proof of the amazing richness of art in the ancient times! There is not, in all the realm of sculpture, a more elaborate and splendid work, than that called the Farnese Bull, found among the ruins in the Baths of Caricalla at Rome, and now in the Museum of Naples. It is carved out of one solid block of the purest white marble, and contains four life-size figures, besides the wild animal to the horns of which Dirce is attached and dragged by her long hair. It represents the pitiless vengeance that one woman can take upon another for wrongs endured. Antiope, the mother of the two youths who are holding the plunging bull, had been persecuted, and for a long time confined by her relatives, because her early affections had not chanced to run in the line of family interest. But now, by a turn of fortune, she has in her power the chief instigator of her persecutions; and she stands there as cold as the marble, to witness the most atrocious vengeance that ever yet was executed.

The Laocoon, also according to the testimony of Pliny, from one block of marble, was found in 1506, beneath a vineyard in the ruins of the Baths of Titus, and is now in the Vatican collection. Laocoon, the priest of Neptune, had strongly urged the

Trojans not to admit into their city the huge wooden horse which the Greeks had offered them on the eve of their pretended departure. And for this, Minerva is fabled to have sent two enormous serpents from the sea, which folded and crushed in their horrible embrace the priest and his two sons. For agonized expressions, as well as anatomical contortions, this is justly considered the great masterpiece of sculpture. These two examples, if there had been no others found in the ruins of Rome, would have been sufficient to establish the fact of Grecian superiority in the line of statuary, over all nations and times, ancient or modern.

The art of painting involves the same principles, the same knowledge of form and proportions, and the same skilled hand and eye, that sculpture does. It is impossible to imagine the successful cultivation of the one, without that of the other. For these reasons I think we cannot avoid the conclusion that the painter's art has never since, not even in the palmiest days of art in Italy, arrived at such a state of perfection as in the flourishing periods of ancient Greece.

And for this superiority there was necessary exactly the condition of things which we find in Grecian culture and civilization. Here was a nation of hero worshipers, of refined idolators, whose religion was the adoration of the beautiful, whose highest aspirations were to represent their divinities under the most perfect of human forms. Was it the chaste Diana, the goddess of hunting? Then her resemblance must be that which, not one life, but generations of huntresses would develop. Was it a Hercules to be represented? His type can by no means be made up from ordinary wrestlers and pugilists. It must be the outcome of a line of warrior athletes, whose very existence for generations may have depended on their power to carry the weightiest armor and to wield the heaviest battle-ax. It will never answer for a criticism, to say we never saw such length and slenderness of limbs, together with such fullness of the vital organs, as the old artists have given to their Apollos and Dianas; nor such swollen and knotted muscles as seem almost to disfigure the Farnese Hercules. We may be sure that their models have existed, or might exist under favoring circumstances. Benjamin West found the Apollo in the Mohawk warrior of a hundred years ago. The fabled Amazons might have had a Diana for their Queen. And I have no doubt that the brawny Saxons, in their early fighting days, have had a veritable Hercules for a King. These then are the lines in which ancient delineators were immeasurably superior to the modern. And in so far their art and genius have passed away.

Before closing the account of ancient art attainments, I should perhaps say a few more words in regard to the wall paintings that have been uncovered, within the past 120 years, in Pompeii. Previous to the year 79 of our era, when it was suddenly buried by a shower of ashes and gravel from the first recorded eruption of Vesuvius, Pompeii was merely a small provincial city, with never more than 30,000 inhabitants. But from its delightful situation, near the Bay of Naples, and on the fertile slopes of the extinct volcano, it had come to be somewhat of a resort for Romans of moderate means. There was in it however nothing of special elegance or pretension, its best house belonging to one of its wine merchants; and it was as far from being an art center as probably Sorento is at the present day. That it should have contained any specimens of the fine arts, is a wonder. That it did have so many and such remarkable ones, is a most striking evidence of the inseparable connection of the arts with all the tastes and necessities of ancient every-day life. The houses of Pompeii were in reality profusely adorned by decorative artists and painters imported from Greece. There was an almost infinite variety of subjects and scenes illustrated on their walls, from flowers and fruits to dancing genii and floating nymphs, from representations of homely and comic life to heroic legends and the myths of the gods. In fact we have here a most charming and complete illustrated journal of the first century of the Christian era.

Many of the prominent pictures, we know, were copies of more ancient ones; and it is probable that none of them evince a higher grade of talent than that of the copyist. There is really no good reason to suppose that the decorations of this retired city compared more favorably with original works of the great masters of Greece, than the frescoes of the hotels and villas of Nice compare with the Stanzas of Raphael in the Vatican or the ceilings of the Sixtine Chapel. Yet there are in these fragments, as it were, of another world of art, elements of beauty and form and color that have made and always will make them the study and admiration and wonder of all lovers of the beautiful. Another thought. Here are wall-paintings that have preserved their fresh and lively colors for two thousand years; while those of the old Italian masters of 250 years ago have had to be retouched and repainted to keep them from becoming unrecognizable. Could there be a more convincing proof that, not only the modes and the skill, but the color materials, the pigments, of the ancient painters are among the Lost Arts?

Rome succeeded Greece as the depository, but never as the creator of the wealth of the fine arts. Rome conquered the whole known world, and gathered in the spoils of conquest to beautify or encumber the masses of bricks and stones which made her capitol. The quantity of art material that was brought over from the neighboring peninsula of Greece was perfectly overwhelming. The despoiling commenced in the time of Julius Cæsar, was continued under Augustus, Caligula, Nero, in fact as long as there was anything to carry off.

If now we seek the causes which destroyed or buried the art treasures of antiquity, and which finally wiped out from the face of the earth all knowledge of practical art, we come directly upon the causes which made of Rome a heap of ruins, which in a thousand years reduced a proud city of two million souls to a miserable huddle of twenty thousand, and which buried alike the trophies and the aspirations of a mighty civilization.

In the first rank of destructive elements we must enumerate that of fire. And, as the conflagration most disastrous to art, we may mention that of the year of our Lord 64. Nero, desiring to clear off a space on the Palatine Hill for a golden palace that he had in his mind, set fire to the interiors of the marble structures which Augustus had reared there. But the work of the incendiary did not stop where he intended it should. It soon passed all control, and raged for nine days. When it was over, the greater part of Rome was in ashes; and it is probable that half the art specimens brought from Greece were destroyed in those few fatal days.

Another cause, which has served perhaps more than all others to bury the marble and stone works of Rome, is the inundations of the Tiber. This is one of the rivers that come directly down from the Appenines, and like all mountain streams is peculiarly liable to overflow. Repeatedly has the Tiber spread itself through all the lower parts of the city, and swept or dissolved into ruins every building that was not on a hill or the sides of a hill. All the valleys, and the bed of the river itself, have been filled up and actually raised from twenty to thirty feet. Visitors to day go down into an excavation of at least twenty-five feet to get to the old floor of the Forum and the paved streets of ancient days.

The famous hills of Rome have been raised to nearly the same extent by successive layers of ruins, arising in this case from alternations of periods of destruction and decay, with those of activity and reconstruction. On the Palatine, one descends first into the marble palaces of the Cæsars, then underneath to the plainer brick structures of the ancient Republic, and finally down to the tufa-stone foundations of the original "Roma Quadrata."

The great and wealthy city and center of Christian civilization offered tempting rewards to the hungry and rude barbarians who swarmed on the northern confines of the Empire in the early centuries. In the year 410 of our era the Goths, under Alaric, besieged and took possession of the city, pillaging it for five days. Forty-five years later, the Vandals, under Genseric, plundered and ravaged it for fifteen days. Again in 546, the Goths, under Totila, starved the city into surrender, and then enforced the extremest extortions. It is said that in some of these sieges, the broken arms and limbs of statues were hurled at the enemy from the walls like any other rubbish.

But worse than all the barbarians, as the iconoclasts of art, were the Christians themselves. When from poor and persecuted hiders in caves and catacombs, they could at length proclaim

Plate XV.—VIEW AT THE HEAD OF LAKE WAKATIPU, NEW ZEALAND. See Page xix.

themselves masters, what could be more natural than that they should hold the objects of desire or worship that belonged to their enemies, or pertained to the old idolatry, in hate and abomination? No decree of a time-serving or Christian Emperor was more welcome to a fanatic populace, than one giving license to destroy the art remains of heathenism. We read that the early converts used to put ropes around the necks of marble Apollos and Venuses, and try them publicly as criminals. Of course they found them guilty, and then they pounded them to dust. Eusebius informs us that in the early and rapid spread of Christianity, whole towns arose and destroyed the temples in which they had just worshiped. The air echoed with the noise of hammers, the crashing of pediments, the breaking of pillars, and the shouts of a maddened and frenzied populace. The finest works of Phidias and Praxiteles, and all that were left of Polygnotus, Apelles, and Zeuxis were demolished or burned, and their ashes were danced upon with fanatic exultation. So great had been the destruction that when, in the year 400, Arcadius and Honorius issued a fresh edict to go on destroying, they added, as well they might, "if any pictures or statues are still left."

After foreign enemies had destroyed or carried off everything that could any longer attract them, the Romans themselves, as if struck with the madness of destroying demons, began fighting and ravaging in civil wars and domestic contentions. For five hundred years in the midst of the dark ages, Rome was perpetually torn and wasted by the sanguinary quarrels of the nobles and the people, the Guelphs and Ghibbelines, and the factions of the Colonna and Ursini families. From one time to another, all the massive structures of the old city have been transformed into fortifications—the Coliseum, the Pantheon, the mausoleums of Hadrian and of Augustus, and the enormous Baths; while towers and strongholds were erected in every part, to serve the purpose of robber chieftains or lawless factions. The venerable ruins were recklessly plundered of all that could be used in masonry or fortification, while the marble of columns and statues and costly ornaments were burned in lime-kilns to supply the materials for mortar.

Then famine and pestilence took hold on the doomed city, and the malaria of the marshes, from neglect of drainage, crept up from the low grounds, and seized the stragglers of the ever contracting populace, until from the proud and teeming capitol of a world, it came at last to contain only the miserable remnant of twenty thousand inhabitants. In this fact alone is largely explained the vast and wonderful ruins of Rome. For ages there were not inhabitants enough to occupy the hundredth part of the buildings that had been reared. Of course they fell into decay. The falling roofs and walls of the upper half buried and preserved the lower. The work of time and decay leveled the surface and disintegrated the soft materials, till eventually the needy descendants of Roman conquerors planted their vineyards or herded their cattle over the ruins of Forums and Palaces.

Like many another pilgrim to the great cemetery of a past civilization, I have followed the tourist's track to the ruins of Rome. I have wandered among the gloomy and wasting remains of a power and a culture that flourished nineteen centuries before. I have gone down into the excavations, and seen marble relics disentombed from beneath thirty feet of the accumulated debris of ages. I have groped my way under ground through dark and dripping passages that were once the gay and airy halls of a palace. But I must confess to you that I have failed to be impressed as I ought with the mighty changes, the awful destruction which these ruins would indicate. They are so encompassed and crowded upon by modern improvements, so carefully repaired and abutted by recent masonry, so evidently kept for show, that my imagination could not get beyond the eager lives and the begging hands that are ever reaching down from the New Rome into the Old Rome. I do not say this to find fault. It is commendable to preserve, by all means and at any sacrifice, treasures as unique as these. But it is none the less true that the modern surroundings and appliances, and papal tablets, and the devices of the artful showmen, destroy the illusion of antiquity and the impression of overwhelming vicissitudes.

To get away from this influence, I have climbed the Capitol Hill, and stood on the brow of the lonely Tarpeian ledge, the only spot that has remained unchanged through all the mutations of Roman fortune. And I have there endeavored to transport myself five hundred years into the past, to see before me only the wide and mournful scene of desolation which was there unfolded in the gloomiest hour of the night of ages. On all the seven hills, that once sustained the seat of an empire that seemed as eternal as their foundations, there could then be seen only the specters of ruin, grim and unrelieved. Half buried in wild and brambly commons, were the massive piles of the Baths of Diocletian, of Titus, and of Caricalla, the dismantled Colisseum, the triumphal arches, the dilapidated columns of some heathen temples, and innumerable mounds and monuments that had long ceased to commemorate anything. Over the Palatine Hill, where were buried one under the other, the remains of three periods of national architecture, were then only vineyards and gardens. On the valley within the amphitheater of the hills, enclosures for swine and buffaloes occupied the ground beneath which, deeply buried, were the pavements of the Via Sacra and the floors of the Comitium of the Roman people, where their Scipios had brought the trophies and received the appellations of conquered continents. Such was the desolate grave from which the new culture was soon to arise—such the mournful spectacle which preceded the Renaissance of Art.

SKETCHES OF THE "OLD MASTERS" IN PAINTING.*

There is every reason to believe that the art of painting was carried to a high degree of perfection by the ancient Greeks. We cannot judge of this by any specimen paintings that have been preserved, for these are things that do not endure. But the ancient writers say that Grecian art was equally advanced in painting and sculpture; and in regard to the latter there have been found in late years, buried in the debris of cities and villas, statues and groups in marble that would substantiate the most extravagant claims. We are authorized to conclude therefore that their claims in regard to painting were not exaggerated.

In further corroboration there is the remarkable, almost miraculous, preservation of the frescoes of Pompeii. This was a small provincial town of Italy, a place little likely to have even a fair sample of ancient art; yet there have been opened up in this buried city frescoes and wall paintings that have been studies and models for painters from the day they were discovered.

But with the incursions of the northern barbarians and the closing in of the dark ages, all art culture absolutely died out, and until about the year 1300 painting was one of the lost arts. It had to be re-discovered and worked up again to perfection by slow and toilsome labors, as much as if it had never existed. We can best point out this growth by sketching, though ever so briefly, the lives and work of those who have been laborers in this field; and first we must mention,

Giotto.—GIOTTO DI BORDONE was born near Florence in 1276. His occupation as a boy was to tend sheep. When ten years old

---

* Written in 1875 for the Catalogue of Powers Art Gallery, Rochester, N.Y.

he was noticed sketching one of his flock on a stone. His genius was appreciated, and kind patrons gave him instruction in all that was then known of art. It was not long before he led all his instructors. These were the times when they made those rigid expressionless Christs and Virgins and Saints, with their heads surrounded by hoops, and painted on wood, usually the inside of case doors, which priests threw open on occasions of great devotional exercises. Giotto made the first faces that had life in them —the first Christ on the cross that looked at all like a suffering Saviour. He lived in the time of the poet Dante, and was his friend and companion. Each one has in his own way made the portrait of the other; and both pictures are of the kind that are immortal. When he died in Florence, in 1336, and was buried with great pomp in the Cathedral, it was recognized that the poor shepherd boy had become a power and a leader among men. He was without question the father of painting and of the mosaic art. Some of the oldest frescoes in the Campo Santo of Pisa are by his hand. The mosaic of the Disciples in the storm, called "Navicella," in the portico of St. Peter's, is his. His works were very numerous and his pupils were very many; so that his influence was carried down for many generations. But the next great advance in painting was made more than a hundred years later and in the time of

Leonardo da Vinci (*Vin-che*).—He was born at the castle of the Vinci, near Florence, in 1452; was the natural son of Pietro da Vinci, but brought up with all the advantages of wealth and of the best instruction. He had a wonderful and versatile genius—was a poet, musician, mathematician, mechanic, sculptor and painter. As an artist, he introduced the element of the ideal into painting. Grandeur of design, harmony of expression, united with the minutest finish—the poetry of the art—may be said to have originated with Leonardo. He is best known by his fresco paintings; and the best of these is "The Last Supper," in the convent of Maria delle Grazie, in Milan. This has long been in a bad state of preservation from the fact that the artist was experimenting in the use of oil paints instead of the usual water colors for wall paintings. Leonardo, although brilliant and the most attractive man of his age, yet lacked application—the concentration of his energies on any one line of effort. He was therefore the inferior of the younger and rising genius, Michael Angelo, with whom he was often brought into rivalry and jealousy.

Michael Angelo Buonarotti, was born also near Florence, in 1494, was from an influential family, and received all the advantages of education. His marvelous talent for both painting and sculpture was early developed. When it is considered that throughout his long life of nearly ninety years he was patient, laborious, virtuous and indefatigable, his great influence on his age, on the arts and on all who came after him, is easily accounted for. Michael Angelo lived in troublesome times, when political changes were sudden and violent, and states were continually passing from one hungry possessor to another. This ablest of men had not however the continence or the wisdom to keep aloof from political entanglements; so was he continually flying from one city to another, now basking in favor, and now hiding himself from his pursuers. He was never married, and was past sixty years old before he met the first woman who seems to have exercised an influence over him. The accomplished and highborn Victoria Colonna gave him her friendship, and the poems and sonnets that passed between this elderly pair were at one time the amusement of all Italy. During the last twenty years of his life he was the architect of St. Peter's church; he made all the plans, but did not live to see it completed. He died in Rome in 1564; his body was taken to Florence, and buried with unusual honors in the church of Santa Croce. Sculpture seemed to have been his preference, and numerous works, especially his David in Florence and his Moses in Rome, attest for him the highest place in the art. It was with great reluctance that he undertook the decoration of the Sistine Chapel. The ceiling, which is the most complete and wonderful series of Biblical illustrations that ever was painted, was accomplished by his own hand in twenty months, and when the artist was thirty-five years old. The Last Judgment was executed twenty years later and was the labor of six years. These monuments of painting have placed the name of Michael Angelo at the head of the list of perspective painters.

Titian.—TITIAN VECELLIO, (born near Venice in 1477, died at Venice in 1576), began at the early age of ten to show indications of the surprising talent that was in him. He lived a long and active life, and was a life-long painter. It is not strange therefore that his always beautiful productions abound in every old collection. It is hard to specify his best, since everything from his hand is so highly prized. His loving countrymen have selected and carved in relief on his tomb "The Assumption of the Virgin," and on each side the martyrdoms of St. Lawrence and St. Peter. The last is the one which is generally considered his best work. The Venetian School is noted for its mastery in colors, but is accused of being faulty in design. Titian as a colorist is unexcelled. As the delineator and painter of the human form he is matchless. His portraits are perfectly magnificent. Those that go by the name of "Titian's Mistress," as the Flora in the Uffizi and La Bella di Tiziano in the Pitti, are masterly productions. At the age of thirty-four he married a Venetian lady, by whom he had three children. He lived to be almost a hundred years old, and then may be said to have died before his time, for he was carried off in the midst of his work by the pestilence that has so often ravaged Italian cities. Those who died of this disease were not allowed the honors of burial, but an exception was made in his case, and he was buried in the church of the Franciscans in Venice. His monument is one of the finest works in marble that has ever been made.

Raphael.—RAPHAEL SANTI was born at Urbino, a city on the opposite side of Italy from Florence, in 1483, and died in Rome in 1520. Like nearly all the geniuses of painting he developed very early, his father teaching him in the art before he was ten years old, and at sixteen he was filling orders. He entered the Vatican at twenty-five and died twelve years after. His time was short, but he accomplished a glorious work and left an undying name. He was unquestionably the first of the Italian painters, and withal so gentle and lovely in his character as to make only friends wherever he went; as Vasari said of him,

"He was full of the might of a noble nature." Raphael was never married, but during the last ten years of his life his labors were lightened and his genius stimulated by the love of "La Fornarina," whose picture is the gem of the Barbarini Palace in Rome, and for whom he provided liberally in his will. He was buried, according to his own singular desire, in the Pantheon of Rome, and with magnificent ceremonies. The power of Raphael as a painter lay in his perfect mastery of the passions. There was no shade of emotion or thought that he could not portray on his canvas. Every face and every scene tells its own story better than words can express it. The Sistine Madonna at Dresden, is a marvel of spiritual power and sublimity. But the Transfiguration of Christ on the Mount is now thought to be the finest painting in the world. It was unfinished when the great painter died, and when they laid out his body in state, they placed this picture, such as it was, beside it, as the saddest evidence of the untimely work that death had made.

Andrea del Sarto—so called from his father's trade, that of a tailor, his real name being ANDREA VANUCCHI—was born in Florence in 1487, where also he died of the plague in 1531. He earned a great reputation, both in oil and fresco, and was called "the faultless." He is best known by his frescoes in the convent of the Annunciata, in Florence; the Madonna del Sacco being the best. He was led into many errors of character and even into a serious embezzlement by an unworthy wife. But he bitterly repented, and it is charitably supposed that evil was not in his nature.

Correggio.—ANTONIO ALLEGRI—called Correggio from his birthplace, a small town between Modena and Parma—was born in 1494, and died of a fever in his native place in 1534. But little is known of his life beyond the fact that he was one of those men who are always in need, no matter how much money they earn. It is probable that he died in poverty and on account of privations. The greater part of his work was done at Parma. There are those wonderful paintings in the domes of San Giovanni and the Cathedral, which show the extreme effects of foreshortening, an art in which this painter has the highest reputation. He was asked what he expected to do with those myriads of frogs up there. But when seen in the right light and position, the Assumption of the Virgin in the cupola of the Cathedral is one of the grandest scenes that was ever painted. Apparently all the heavenly hosts are there; and no words can convey the richness and boundlessness of the effect. Correggio is the greatest master of what is called chiaro-scuro, the grading of light and dark shades into each other. His management of light was certainly wonderful. In this it may be said that he was the founder of his own style, for nothing went before him that was at all like him. In his pictures all is life and motion, poetry and grace. Some of his best are "La Notte" or the adoration of the Shepherds at night, and the reclining Magdalene, in Dresden, also the madonnas Della Scala and Della Scodella, at Parma. "La Zingarella" (the Gipsy), so called from the turban worn by the Virgin, is the portrait of his gentle and lovely wife, who died shortly before him.

Tintoretto—so called from the trade of his father, who was a dyer, his real name being JACOPO ROBUSTI—was born at Venice in 1512, where also he died in 1594. When young he was for a few days a pupil of Titian; but for some unaccountable reason he was summarily dismissed. It has been said that Titian discovered his genius and feared his rivalry; but we can hardly believe that. At any rate this rebuff did not discourage the young learner. He became an indefatigable worker and has left some canvas paintings that are perfectly astounding for their magnitude and the amount of work upon them. His Paradise, in the grand hall of the Ducal Palace, is the largest oil painting in the world, being 74 by 30 feet. His best work, "The Great Crucifixion," in the School of St. Roch in Venice, has fifty-seven different personages, in every conceivable position and expression, some on horseback, many of life size and bearing the likeness of men then living, as Bassano, Paul Veronese, Titian, &c. It is a magnificent theatrical representation; and if it did not take place as represented, we can only say that it would have been a splendid pageantry for the occasion.

Paul Veronese—Paolo Cagliari—was born at Verona in 1528, and died at Venice in 1588. This always pleasing painter excelled in the representation of grand architecture, gorgeous draperies, varied costumes, and generally in imposing scenes and striking effects. He had a most noble fancy and the utmost fertility of invention. Whatever he undertook became a masterpiece in its way, and he executed a great number of oil paintings. No collection seemed complete without some of the large and splendid works of this great painter. There is the Adoration of the Kings in the Dresden Gallery, the Feast of the Levite in the Venice Academy, the Marriage at Cana in the Louvre of Paris. This last is perhaps the best and most elaborate of his works. It is a colossal painting 32 by 21 feet, and contains one hundred and twenty figures, many of them portraits of distinguished persons of the time, Queens, Emperors, and Painters. It is a wonderful instance of executive power. But after all it is only a Venetian feast. Instead of the scene being transported to Galilee, Christ is brought down to Venice and the sixteenth century.

Caracci.—Annibale Caracci, was born in Bologna in 1560, died in Rome in 1609, and was buried in the Pantheon near Raphael. He was the painter of the remarkable mythological frescoes in the Farnese Palace in Rome. He, with his brother Agostino, and uncle Ludovico, formed the celebrated Caracci school, which was the middle link between two great lines of painters. Raphael, Michael Angelo, Titian and Correggio preceded, and were coruscations of genius. What they accomplished for art seemed in no wise dependent on labor. The Caracci, while they were extraordinary men, were nevertheless great only as their predecessors were great. With them all was labor and imitation. But they were the teachers of a new race of painters who were to carry the glory of Italy to its second culminating point. The most distinguished of the pupils was

Guido Reni (*Gwe-do Rá-ne*).—Born near Bologna in 1575, died at the same place in 1642. He has left about three hundred paintings to testify to his ability and application, and they are scattered through all the galleries of Europe. The Crucifixion of St. Peter with his head downwards, which is in the Vatican, is called one of the best of his oil paintings. The fresco of Aurora strewing flowers before the chariot of the sun, is much the finest ceiling work of this master. The aim which Guido set before himself in early life, was to rescue and elevate art from the decline into which it had fallen under Caravaggio and the Naturalistic School, by which is meant the selection of subjects from common life, or as it has been called, "The Poetry of the Repulsive." Guido, on the contrary, brought into his representations the highest order of grace and beauty. But it was a standard drawn entirely from his own ideals. As he said of his St. Michael, "it was in vain for me to search for his resemblance here below; so that I was forced to make an introspection into my own mind and into the idea of beauty which I have formed in my own imagination." Therefore, as a very natural consequence, all his personages are in a great measure repetitions of the same ideal. Whether it be a St. John, or Niobe, or Paris, or Christ, or Cleopatra, there is the same general resemblance. Guido Reni must have been at one time in receipt of a princely income from his works; but all great men have their failings, and singularly enough that of this man was gambling. He was reduced to such distresses for money to feed his ruling passion that he used to sell his time by the hour for the manufacture of Madonnas, and of pictures unworthy of his genius. Poverty and debt at last brought on the fever of which he died.

Albani.—Francisco Albani, son of a silk merchant, was born at Bologna in 1578, and died at the same place in 1660. He was a fellow pupil and friend of Guido Reni, whom he followed to Rome. There in the Borghese Palace are his most famous pictures, "The Four Seasons"—landscapes with mythological accessories. His excellence was in mythological and fanciful subjects. Lanzi thus compares Albani as a painter, to Anacreon as a poet. "Like that poet with his short odes, so Albani with his small pictures acquired great reputation, and as the one sings of Venus and the Loves, and maids and boys, so does the artist hold up to the eye the same delicate and graceful subjects." His pictures would seem to be but the repetition of his home life; a lovely and sightly villa, presided over by his beautiful wife, who bore him twelve children, so lovely that they were sought for as models in sculpture and painting. Another friend of Albani was

Domenichino (pronounced kéno), real name DOMENICO ZAMPIERI. He was born at Bologna in 1581, and died at Naples in 1640. He was a man of eminent genius, but timid, dependent, and ill-fitted to make his way against the rivalries that raged in his time among artists. He left Rome and went to Naples, to avoid the persecutions of rivals; and there he is supposed to have been poisoned at the instigation of three painters, notoriously known as the cabal of Naples. He excelled in design, in composition, and in expression. His masterpieces are quite numerous, but the best is his "Last Communion of St. Jerome" in the Vatican; this is generally called the second best painting in the world, and was executed for the pitiful sum of about fifty dollars.

Guercino (Gurchéno), so called from his squinting, his real name being GIOVANNI FRANCISCO BARBIERI, was born at Cento, near Bologna, in 1590, and died in Bologna 1666. He was of very humble origin, and when a boy had to take care of his father's cart, as he delivered wood and faggots about the town. Almost the only one of the great painters who was self-taught and self-made, he yet arrived, by force of an original and commanding ability, to great distinction and affluence. There is a grandeur, life-likeness, and brilliancy of coloring in his works, which, after Raphael, and with a century between them, formed the second crowning point of Italian art. Guercino painted two hundred and fifty large pictures, besides his frescoes and numerous smaller works. His best production is probably the famous Saint Petronilla in the Capitol Gallery in Rome. It was painted for one of the chapels of St. Peter's where there is now a mosaic of it. The saint is being held up in her tomb to be seen by Flaccus, her betrothed.

Carlo Dolci (Dol-che), a native of Florence, was born in 1616, and died in 1686. His best works were those of a devotional character, Madonnas and penitent saints. To these subjects he gave great beauty and grace; and among the enthusiasts of sacred pictures this painter has many passionate admirers. His Mater

Dolorosa, his Ecce Homo, his Magdalene, his St. John sleeping, are all beautiful, and have been many times copied and imitated.

Carlo Maratti—Was born at Camerino, up in the mountains from Ancona, in 1625, and died at Rome in 1713. He was a very pleasing painter, but not a very original genius. Having had the good fortune to secure the favor of the Popes of his time, he became very popular in Rome, and has been called the "Last of the Romans." His best works, like those of all the last painters, were Madonnas and Holy Families.

Here ends the list of the old masters in Italy. We have mentioned all those who have any claims to originality and inborn genius. They have had no successors among their countrymen. Outside of Italy we have occasion to mention, for the purpose of completing the list, only one name, that of

Murillo—born at Seville, in Spain, in 1617, where also he died in 1682. In his early life he was harassed by poverty, and his pictures were frequently sold for what they would bring on the street. But at the age of thirty he married a rich and noble wife, and from this time he took rank among the first in Seville. His earlier works were largely from common life, as beggar boys, peasants, &c. Later he painted almost exclusively religious subjects. In this field he is probably without a rival. Although it was said that he had covered more canvas than any other painter, yet in all the vast number of his paintings there is no sameness, no tiresomeness. Every repetition of the sainted Mary has that in it of varied beauty and tenderness and purity, that touches even the unsuperstitious heart, and that, in those days of saint worship, must have stirred the very depths of religious emotion.

It is often a matter of great surprise to visitors of foreign galleries to see such countless numbers of Madonnas, and scenes from the life of the Virgin Mary. The truth is that these paintings have all been at one time objects of worship in some church or private chapel. In Catholic countries the votaries kneel down and say their prayers before pictures of the Blessed Virgin. A beautiful painting, from which the Mother of God looked down upon the worshipers with the ineffable sweetness or the mournful sorrow of Murillo's Madonnas, inspired transports of devotion in those who believed that she was the great intercessor between them and the more august and unapproachable personages of the Godhead. There was then, through all the years when art flourished, a constant demand for these devotional paintings. They were almost the only remunerative subjects. And it is a sad truth that too many of the gifted masters were compelled to exhaust the wealth of their genius on altar-pieces which have now lost their peculiar significance, and are attractive only as they are beautiful pictures.

Plate XVI.—EUCALYPTUS FOREST OF AUSTRALIA, WITH TREE FERNS. See Page xix.

THE STORIES OF NOTED PAINTINGS.*

REBECCA AT THE WELL.

She is admiring the presents that have been given to her by Eliezer. Original, supposed to be by TINTORETTO (1512–1594), is in the Gallery at Parma. Abraham, when quite a young man, emigrated to the west, and became very rich. But he was among strangers and did not desire his boy Isaac, who had now come to the marriageable age of forty, to take him a wife not of his kindred; so he loaded up ten of his camels with valuable presents, and told his chief steward to go down into Mesopotamia among his relatives, and look up a wife for the lad. After a journey of about a thousand miles the old servant arrived near his destination and stopped by the well where the family of Nahor, who was Abraham's brother, were wont to go for water; and he said to himself,—the first damsel that comes and who, when I ask to drink, shall offer to draw also for the camels, shall be the one whom the Lord has chosen; and while he was yet speaking, there came out a damsel very fair to look upon, and went down to the well and filled her pitcher. Then he ran to her and asked her for some water to drink, and she made haste to give him to drink and also to draw for the camels. And it came to pass as the camels had done drinking that the man took a golden earring, of half a shekel weight (a shekel is about half an ounce), and two bracelets for her arms, of ten shekels weight of gold; and he said—"Whose daughter art thou? Tell me I pray thee;" and she said, "the daughter of Bethuel, Nahor's son, whom Milcah bare unto him;" and he put the earrings upon her face and the bracelets upon her arms. Is there need to say, after this, that when those camels returned to the land of Canaan, they carried back the fair Rebekah and her damsels?

* Written in 1875 for the Catalogue of Powers Art Gallery, Rochester, N.Y.

THE SHOWER OF GOLD.

By PIETRO LIBERI (born at Padua in 1605, died 1687). Away back in the dateless periods of ancient Greece, as the fable runs, a certain King of Argos, seeing no signs of a son to succeed him, consulted the oracle thereon, and was told that he himself would have no male issue, but that his daughter Danäe would bear a son who would one day kill and succeed his grandfather. To prevent this unpleasant contingency the king locked up his daughter in a brazen tower and kept her there for years. But the cry of a little four year old at last opened the prison doors, and the startled king demanded whose child that was. Danäe said that Jupiter had descended to her in a shower of gold, and that she had borne the semi-divine offspring. The king, who was evidently a wholly irreligious man, refused to believe any such story. He boxed up the mother and child and pushed them out to sea. They were carried by the winds and waves to a certain island, where they were found and hospitably received, and Perseus grew up to manhood. He went through adventures too numerous to mention, till at last, being engaged in the public games in some distant place, he accidentally pitched a quoit into an old man and ended his days. This old man proved to be Acrisius, his grandfather. Moral — (according to the Greek narrator) — It is in vain for man to fight against the gods.

ST. CECILIA.

By RAPHAEL — (born 1483, died 1520). St. Cecilia, with a "regal" in her hands, is listening to the heavenly music in an ecstatic trance. She is surrounded by the four patron saints of Bologna, (commencing on the left) St. Paul, St. John, St. Augustine and Mary Magdalene. There are many who think this the finest painting in the world, and it would be hard to prove them much in error. St. Cecilia lived in the third century, and was the daughter of a noble and wealthy Roman who, with his family, secretly embraced Christianity. Her husband was beheaded on account of his faith, and she, being also suspected, was ordered to worship Jupiter. On her refusal she was condemned to be thrown into a bath of boiling water. The story relates that this did not hurt her at all, and an executioner was sent to slay her with the sword. His hand trembled so that he inflicted three wounds on her neck and breast, and yet did not kill her. She lingered three days. She gave her money to the poor, and desired that her house should be made a church. She died sweetly singing, and was buried beside her husband. The Church of St. Cecilia-in-Trastevere, in Rome, consecrates the place where she suffered martyrdom, and contains the treasured remains of herself and her husband St. Valerian, as well as other martyrs.

THE THREE FATES.

By MICHAEL ANGELO—(born 1475, died 1564). In the old mythology the Fates or Parcæ were the daughters of Erebus and Nox, and were supposed to preside over the birth, life, and death of mortals. Clotho, as the arbiter of births, holds in her hands a distaff, from which the thread commences to run. Lachesis, disposer of the events and actions of human life, twists the thread between her fingers. And Atropos, the inevitable destiny, holds herself ready to cut it off with her scissors. They were considered powerful godesses, and were worshiped with great solemnity.

MARY MAGDALENE.

By TITIAN—(born 1477, died 1576). Mary Magdalene, the most interesting of the women of Bible history, the loving sister of Lazarus, she of whom the Saviour said, "She has chosen that good part which shall not be taken away from her," she who bathed the feet of the Lord at the feast of Simon, she who was first at the sepulchre on the morning of the Resurrection—this was the favored name under which the painters, each and all of them, lavished the wealth of their genius in depicting all that was tender and loving in woman.*

---

* In describing the paintings of this subject by the old masters it is appropriate and even necessary to follow the legends of the church, which make Mary Magdalene and Mary the sister of Lazarus one and the same person. The beautiful pictures of the Magdalene in a cave (see the story following) would have no meaning on any other supposition. Modern commentators, however, make two distinct persons of these scripture Marys. There is nothing in the Bible to contradict either of the hypotheses.

THE PENITENT MAGDALENE; OR, THE MAGDALENE IN A CAVE.

By POMPEO BATTONI—(born at Lucca 1708, died at Rome, 1788). The original is in the Royal Gallery of Dresden. The legends of the primitive church form a sequel to the New Testament, which has influenced catholic worship and Christian art almost as much as the sacred narrative itself. According to those legends, Lazarus and his sisters Martha and Mary, and the blind man who was restored to sight, and two others, were set adrift on the Mediterranean, shortly after the crucifixion of Christ, in a boat without sails, or oars, or rudder. They were wafted at the sport of the winds and waves, till finally they were driven into the harbor of Marseilles. Here they preached to the heathen and did miraculous works, until a little church was started, over which Lazarus became bishop. But Mary, always bewailing the sins of her early life, retired to a cave between Marseilles and Toulon, where in her need she was ministered to by angels, and from which, after many years of solitude and expiation, she was carried to Heaven by the same ministering hands. Some of the loveliest scenes in all the realm of painting are those which present this fair penitent in her solitary cave life.

DAVID WITH THE HEAD OF GOLIATH, MEETING THE DAUGHTERS OF SAUL.

By ANDREA DAL FRISO—(born 1551, died 1611). Of all the champions of the Philistines, that most persistent and prolific enemy of ancient Israel, Goliath of Gath seems to have been the most remarkable and terrible. He was near 12 feet in height, his coat of mail weighed 150 pounds, his spear "was like a weaver's beam" and carried a 20 pound point of iron. The engagement which brought this monster to the front was one of forty days duration; and morning and evening of each day he had come out between the hosts defying any man of the Israelites to single combat. It happened on the last day that young David, who had been taken from his flocks to be sent to the army with provisions for his elder brethren, heard the challenge and offered at once to go out against him. The offer, unequal as it was, was only too gladly accepted by his terror-stricken countrymen; and David, armed only with his staff and sling, met the mail-clad giant in mortal combat. At the first throw the practiced slinger felled his foe with a stone well implanted in his forehead. On his way to Saul bearing the trophy of the bloody head, he met the king's daughters, singing "Saul has slain his thousands and David his ten thousands."

CLEOPATRA.

By GUIDO RENI—(born 1575, died 1642). Cleopatra, the Queen of Egypt, and the last of the royal race of the Ptolemies, killed herself, it is supposed, by the bite of a small but exceedingly poisonous serpent, called the aspic. After the famous naval battle of Actium, B. C. 31, the city of Alexandrea fell into the hands of the Romans. Marc Anthony, who for the love of this fatal woman had been fighting on her side against his country and kindred, on receiving a false rumor that the Queen had committed suicide, fell on his sword with a like purpose; but had, after all, the mortifying consolation of dying in her arms. Cleopatra then tried to cast the spell of her charms over the new Roman conquerer, Augustus, as she had so often done on other occasions; but failing in this, and seeing all empire lost, this most fascinating woman perhaps that ever lived, at the age of thirty-nine, enclosing herself alone in her castle, thus died the painless death of the asp-poisoned, to avoid the humiliation of being taken to Rome to grace the triumphal procession of Cæsar Augustus.

THE ANGEL REFUSING THE GIFTS OF TOBIT.

By GIOVANNI BILIVERTI—(born at Florence in 1576, died 1644). The story of Tobit is told in one of the Apocryphal books of the Old Testament. He was a rich Jew who, with his wife Sara and his son Tobias, was carried into captivity by the Assyrians. He lived a just life and gave freely of his goods to help his brethren. In one way and another his misfortunes were increased, and he became blind, and nothing was left to him but his wife and son. In this strait the angel Raphael was sent to him, who, in the guise of a servant and a guide working for stipulated wages, brought him by various devices out of his poverty, restored to him his sight, and obtained for his son a fair and wealthy wife. When, however, they called Raphael before them to pay him his wages, and further to give him the half of all the wealth he had helped them to obtain, the angel refused the gifts, pointed them to God as the source, and informed them that he was "one of the seven angels who go in and out before the glory of the Holy One." "Then were they troubled and fell upon their faces, for they feared. But he said unto them, fear not, for it shall go well with you. Praise God therefore. And after a few more words he vanished, and when they arose they could see no one."

THE RAPE OF EUROPA.

By PAUL VERONESE—(born at Verona, 1528, died at Venice, 1588). The original is in the Gallery of Paintings in the Palace of the Conservatori, at the Capitol in Rome (No. 224). There are also paintings of the same subject by the same master, very similar in composition if not copies, in the Ducal Palace at Venice, and in the National Gallery in London. Europa has just seated herself upon the bull, who has lain down to receive her; her attendant women are arranging her dress. She is again represented in the middle ground as going down to the sea; and in the extreme distance the bull is swimming with her towards the island.

A very ancient legend relates that Europa was the daughter of Phœnix, the founder of Tyre, and first king of Phœnicia in Asia Minor. Jupiter, becoming enamored of her, changed himself into a beautiful white bull, and approached her, "breathing saffron from his mouth," as she was gathering flowers with her companions in a field near the sea-shore. Europa, delighted with the tameness and beauty of the animal, caressed him, crowned him with flowers, and at length ventured to mount on his back. The disguised god immediately made off with his lovely burden, plunged into the sea, and swam with her to the Island of Crete, where he resumed his own form, and under a plane tree made love to the trembling maid.

THE HOSPITALITY OF ST. JULIAN.

By CHRISTOFANO ALLORI—(called il Bronzino—born at Florence in 1577, died in 1621). St. Julian "the Hospitaler" (died A. D. 313), was of noble family, and when young given only to hunting and feasting. One day as he was chasing a deer, it turned on him and said, "Thou who pursuest me to the death shalt cause the death of thy father and mother." Affrighted, and to avoid fulfilling the prophecy, he fled from his home to a far country, where he married and established himself. After a time his father and mother, led by a strange fatality, set out to find their son. They arrived at his house in his absence, were received with all kindness by his wife, and put in her own room and bed to sleep. The husband coming back in the early morning, and entering his chamber, saw in the dim light two persons in his bed, and one of them a bearded man. In a transport of jealousy he drew his sword and slew them both. When immediately the truth was made known to him, in despair he fled again from his home; and to expiate his crime he built a hospital at the ferry of a dangerous mountain torrent, and devoted himself, without reward, to the succor and safety of passing pilgrims. At length one winter day of storm and swollen waters, there was brought over at great risk a poor leprous youth almost dead from cold and exhaustion. In spite of the disease he took him in, and he and his good wife tended him until morning. Then the leper rose up, and his face was transformed into that of an angel, and he said, "Julian, the Lord hath sent me to thee, for thy penitence is accepted, and thy rest is near at hand;" and he vanished from sight. Then Julian and his wife fell down and praised God for his mercies; and soon they died, for they were old and full of good works.

LINDA OF CHAMOUNIX.

By FERRARI. The original is in a private collection in England. She was a beautiful Savoyard girl, and her home was among the highest peaks of the Alps. Like many another, she had the irresistible longing for something better—for dress and city life and luxury. Secretly she left her mountain village and found her way to Paris. Her father soon followed after her, and in the guise of a beggar, sought her from door to door. At last he found her as the richly attired mistress of a young nobleman. They recognized each other at the door, and she offered him a purse of gold which he refused, but besought her to go back with him. When he found that it was in vain for him to urge, he returned to his home, and sent back in his place the young lover of Linda. This one sings under her windows the beautiful songs of Savoy and of the early love, till every home instinct is stirred in her heart and the old ties lead her back to duty and repentance. This story has been wrought into one of the most interesting of the French operas, in which the wanderer, having lost her reason, is led by the power and associations of music all the long way back to her home and friends. The painting shows the handsome Savoyard thus conducting her, and they are "almost there."

LUCRETIA, THE ROMAN.

By Guido Reni—(born 1575, died 1642). The original is in the Capitoline Gallery of paintings in Rome. The story of Lucretia is told by Livy in manner as follows: Now it happened, in the year of Rome 242 (510 B. C.), that Sextus, the eldest son of King Tarquin the Proud, was seized with a wicked passion for Lucretia, the wife of his cousin, Tarquin of Collatia; and one night while her husband was away to the wars, he gained entrance to her room and by cowardly threats compelled her to submit to him. Immediately that she was at liberty. Lucretia sent in haste to Rome for her father, and to the camp for her husband; and when they came she told them of the wicked deed of Sextus, and she said, "If ye be men avenge it." And they swore to her that they would avenge it. Then she said again, "I am not guilty, yet must I too share in the punishment of this deed, lest any should think that they may be false to their husbands and live." And she drew a knife from her bosom and stabbed herself to the heart. From this affecting tragedy sprang the revolution which banished the last tyrant from Rome and made Junius Brutus and Tarquin, the husband of Lucretia, the first Consuls of the new Republic.

RUTH GLEANING.

Supposed to be by TITIAN. The original is in the Palazzo Communale, Bologna. In the middle of the Old Testament, in the very midst of the wars, and the laws, and the genealogies of that stern old race of Israelites, comes the little book of Ruth, telling one of the most delightful episodes of family life and love that ever was written. The story is too long and too well known to be related here. It is only necessary to say that Ruth, being a fair young widow, but a stranger in the land, being of the race of the Moabites, and being restricted by the severe customs of the Jews to marrying only the nearest of kin to her husband who would or could take her to wife, found herself obliged to resort to certain ruses in order to excite the attention of her relatives. This gleaning in the barley fields, then, was only one of the innocent devices that she practiced to bring herself to the notice of the rich uncle Boaz, who was gathering in his harvests there, and who was seemingly a very good party for the beautiful widow if he only could be awakened to a sense of his duty in the matter. It is hardly needful to add that Ruth, assisted by her mother-in-law, Naomi, succeeded in every point.

BEATRICE CENCI IN PRISON.

The portrait of Beatrice Cenci (*Bā-a-tre-cha Chĕn-che*) is from the original of GUIDO RENI (born 1575, died 1642), in the Barberini Palace in Rome; but the combination is the original of a young and promising artist now living, ACHILLE LEONARDI—52 Via Babuino, Rome. The beautiful girl having been imprisoned in the Castle of St. Angelo and forbidden all intercourse, the young Guido has been obliged to steal into the cell, concealed by the Judge's robe, and to take his sketch from this almost back view. Beatrice Cenci was beheaded in Rome September 11th, 1599. Her father, Count Cenci, was notorious for his crimes, his violence and cruelty. He had purchased pardons of the Papal priesthood so often and by such enormous sums that he was called "a certain and copious source of revenue." He had a walled and moated castle called "Petrella," in a most desolate region on the Neapolitan frontier, to which he retired during the summer with his family, three children and a second wife, and where he indulged in every species of wanton cruelty with impunity. Here the surpassing beauty of Beatrice excited his unnatural desires; and to violence and barbarity was added the crime of incest. These accumulated villainies finally aroused his wife to conspire with the steward and others to destroy their common tyrant. He was assassinated and his body thrown from the wall. Suspicions were excited; the family were thrown into prison; Beatrice was particularly persecuted, was hung up by the hair, and finally forced to say that she committed the murder. Family rivalries and property considerations incited the persecution. She was condemned to death by Pope Clement VIII, was beheaded, and buried in San Petro-in-Montorio, in Rome, before the High Altar. Her portrait was taken by Guido Reni just before her execution.

THE SAMIAN SIBYL.

By GUERCINO—(born 1590, died 1666). In an open book, on which the Sibyl places her hands, one reads this Latin verse: "Salve casta syon permulta que passa puella"—welcome, Virgin divine, who hast passed through many trials! The Sibyls were ancient Greek prophetesses, who, as the early Fathers claimed, foretold the coming of Christ to the Gentiles, as the prophets did to the Jews. They were consulted as oracles, were regarded as holy virgins, and lived in caves and grottoes. Varro, a Latin author, B. C. 100, mentions ten of them, named from the localities of their habitations, of whom the Samian Sibyl was the sixth. She is supposed to have lived about the time of Isaiah, and to have prophesied to the Greeks who came to see her on the Island of Samos.

CUMÆAN SIBYL.

By ROMANELLI, a painter of the Bolognese School, and of the 17th century. Original in the National Museum at Naples. The Sibyl has in her left hand a book with the inscription, "*Ut non confundar,*"—Let me not be confounded, or misunderstood.

The Cumæan is the most ancient and most celebrated of all the Sibyls. The legend is that Apollo fell in love with her, and offered her anything she was minded to ask for. She immediately picked up a handful of sand and demanded to live as many years as there were grains of sand in it. But it was a boon which brought no good to either party; for she refused in any way to favor his suit; and he refused to add continued youth to the gift. So the prophetess kept on growing old and withered, till when the allotted time of some thirteen centuries had passed, there was nothing left of her to die but her voice. "Vox preterea nihil." She had lived one hundred years when Æneas came into Italy, whom, according to Virgil, she conducted into the infernal regions. Three hundred and fifty years later she appeared to Tarquin, the last King of Ancient Rome, with nine books of prophecy which she desired to sell. But he treated the matter lightly, and she went away and destroyed three of them; then she came back and demanded the same price for the six remaining. He still refusing, she went away and destroyed three more. When last she came back demanding the same sum for the three that were left, surprise and curiosity induced the king to look into them; and he was then only too glad to take them at any price, and to preserve them as among the most precious archives of Rome. She never afterwards appeared in history or fable. The painters, with a very excusable license, have always represented this Sibyl as young—not more than fifteen years old. She is believed to have foretold the event of the birth of Christ in a stable in Judea.

THE MADONNA DELLA SEDIA.

By RAPHAEL — (born 1483, died 1520). Original in the Pitti Gallery, Florence, No. 79. This painting is of the exact size of the original; and the beautiful circular frame is the exact copy of the one which frames the original picture.

A very interesting story is told connected with the inception of this painting. There was an old hermit, called Father Bernardo, who lived up in the Florentine mountains, and whose solitary hut was under a great oak tree. Now there was a Mary, the young daughter of a vine-dresser, who used to visit the old man, and bring him both presents and kindly words to cheer his loneliness; so that he was wont to say that he had two daughters, two angels of comfort, the old oak and the lovely girl. At the breaking up of one terribly severe winter the hermit found himself surrounded by the mountain floods, and was obliged to take refuge in his oak tree, where he remained three days, and was finally rescued, almost perishing, by Mary and her father, who had come up as soon as they were able, to see how it had fared with the recluse. Everything that he had was swept away, and they took the holy man home with them till they could fit him up another hut in his favorite retreat. Then Father Bernardo blessed his two daughters, his preservers as he called them; and it was ever his prayer that the two might be together distinguished in some remarkable way. Years passed on; the hermit was gathered among the faithful, and the old oak was made up into wine casks for the vine-dresser. One day as Mary, now a wife and a mother, with two beautiful boys, was sitting near one of these casks, and wondering how the holy man's blessing could ever be fulfilled, there came along a young man whose great heavenly eyes seemed to be searching for the beautiful. It was Raphael Sanzio. He stopped, and, struck with the marvelous beauty of the mother and children, he asked to make them the models of a madonna picture which he had long desired to paint. He had only his pencil and nothing to draw upon. Turning to the smooth head of the cask near by, he sketched on it the likeness of this lovely family, took it home, and there brought out the famous Madonna of the Chair, probably the best known of all the representations of the Virgin Mary.

THE APPIAN WAY.

The Via Appia was commenced, as a military road, by Appius Claudius, B. C. 212, and subsequently extended to the south of Italy. In the vicinity of Rome it is lined, almost encumbered, with the ruins of ancient tombs. It seems to have been a conspicuous and favorite burial place for the old Romans. Pope Pius IX had it dug out and opened up as a road again, in 1850–3, as far as the eleventh mile stone, and it is now one of the most delightful drives out of Rome.

THE CARNIVAL IN ROME.

By BARTOLOMEO PAGANI, a Roman artist. In all Catholic countries the week before the commencement of Lent is given up to all kinds of diversions and follies and masquerades. In Rome this celebration takes place on the Corso, one of the principal streets of the city. Every balcony and window is occupied, while lines of masqueraders go up and down the street during all the afternoon and evening. The chief amusement is throwing bouquets and comfits. These comfits, or confetti in Italian, used to be small candies mixed with flour, but now they are sifted gravel of small size and covered with powdered lime. A handful of this thrown into one's face from a long handled dipper gives one the peculiar sensation of being shot. The amusements are varied by horse races—a troop of unbridled horses let loose and dashing through the street between the crowds on either side; and finally, on the last night, by the rudest attempts on the part of every body to put out each other's lighted candles. What would be the occasion in any American city of incessant fights is there only the most innocent and enjoyable fun.

THE HUSSITES BEFORE NAUMBURG, 1431.

By NECHUTREY, of Vienna, the most noted of the pupils of Kaulbach. John Huss, the great Hungarian Reformer, was burned at the stake in 1415. His followers took up arms, and for many years were victorious over all opposition, burning and destroying innumerable towns throughout Germany. It happened in this time that Procopius, the Hussite general, halted his army before the stronghold of Naumburg, and proclaimed his intention to burn the city and every one in it. The citizens, in the greatest consternation, as a forlorn hope, got together all their children and sent them with the key of the citadel to the stern old warrior, imploring his mercy. Procopius was touched by this tender appeal, and stayed his avenging hand. This celebrated painting vividly portrays the scene, which to this day is commemorated in the city of Naumburg by a yearly children's festival.

THE FESTIVAL OF THE MADONNA DELL' ARCO AT NAPLES.

By Louis Leopold Robert — (born 1794, died 1835). On the day after Whitsunday, usually in the latter part of May, all Naples puts on its holiday clothes and gayest ornaments, and repairs to the church of the Madonna dell' Arco, seven miles to the eastward at the foot of Mt. Somma. The whole intervening distance is one continuous scene of dancing and merry-making — men and women crowned with wreaths of flowers or fruits, and carrying garlands or poles surmounted with branches of fruit or flowers. It is a perfect Bacchanalian procession; and it is pointed to as indicating unmistakably the Greek origin of this festival loving people.

THE FALCONER.

In the early times of Old England, and down to the reign of the Georges, hawking was the great national sport. Persons of rank scarcely appeared outside of their castles without a hawk on their hands or carried in their train. Great sums of money were spent on the amusement. As high a sum as $5,000 has been paid for a cast of hawks. They were trained to fly high in in the air, and then swoop down on either flying or running game, striking the object dead with their strong beaks. The whistle of the falconer recalled them to the perch on his finger. Hawks of the larger kinds imported from Tartary, were trained for antelopes, bustards and cranes; those of the smaller kinds, natives of Norway, were trained for hares, partridges and pigeons.

THE GIPSIES' HOME.

By C. Laren, an English artist. If there is a people in the world that has no home, it is the strolling, vagabond Gipsy race. Sprung from the degraded caste of pariahs in India, the Gipsies have now been among civilized people four hundred and fifty years; yet they are still precisely the same in race and nature as when they first intruded themselves into Europe. They are most numerous in the south of Spain; and are there compelled by force of numbers to conform themselves somewhat to civilized modes of living.

LE MOIS D'OCTOBRE. (La Recolte des pommes de terre.)
OCTOBER. (THE GATHERING OF THE POTATOES.)

By AUGUSTE HAGBORG (born in Gothenburg, Sweden.) Pupil of the Academy of Fine Arts of Stockholm, and of Palmarole. This young and rising artist has given us here a most suggestive picture of old country peasant life. A wide view of field and sky serves as relief and contrast to two central life-size figures which for strong portraiture and perfection of detail are not excelled in modern painting.

The picture, a study and an ever-growing conception in itself, derives a further attraction from the fact that it is a representative painting, the first one brought to this country, of that peculiar school in France of which Jean Millet was the originator and master. It seeks to portray and perpetuate all there is of a nobler life and a higher humanity in the classes that have come down through centuries of serfdom. Peasant life in Europe is a sad picture at best; and there is little promise of a brighter one in the future. But we on this side of the world know that from such earnest and self-reliant toilers as stand forth in this picture, the inheritors of the reserve force of twenty generations, are born the illustrious men and the fairest women of our rising republic.

THE PROPHECY OF THE SIBYL.

By ANDREA DAL FRISO — (1551–1611). The early Christian Fathers relate that the Emperor Augustus Cæsar, when the Roman Senate passed the decree according to him divine honors, went to the Tiburtine Sibyl at Tivoli, near Rome, and consulted her whether he ought to receive them. She replied that it better befitted him whose power was declining to go away and hold his peace—that a Hebrew child would soon be born who would reign over all the gods. And she pointed to the heavens where appeared the Holy Virgin with her child, seated on an altar in the clouds. The Emperor bowed down and worshiped the miraculous vision; and on his return he erected on the Capitoline Hill an altar to the "First born of God." The church of Santa Maria in Capitolino now consecrates the ground where this first Christian altar is said to have been raised.

THE QUEEN OF SHEBA AND HER TRAIN.

By VENEZIANO BONIFACIO — (born 1494, died 1563). A thousand years before Christ, when Solomon was building his rich and costly temple, and his trade and his fame had extended through all the "Land of Ophir," there came up from the farthest coast of the Red Sea a wealthy Arabian princess, to see for herself the wisest man in the world. She questioned him and "found that the half had not been told her." Costly gifts were passed between them, and she led her princely train back to her southern home. This is the only record of the Queen of Sheba, who, but for this impulse of woman's curiosity, would have left no mark on the ages or inspired no painter's fancy.

AUCTION SALE.

By A. LUBEN, of Munich. It is acknowledged in art circles that this painting is Luben's master piece. To take an inventory of a deceased naturalist's collections, and to find customers for such odds and ends, are no slight test of an artist's ability. Yet Luben has given us here a most complete picture of the old books, the specimens, and the queer things that such an enthusiast would prize, and of the motley group that has gathered to bid them down. The moral of it all is that the treasured collections we often seek so eagerly in life are very apt to come sooner or later to point the joke of an auctioneer.

CLEOPATRA DRINKING THE DISSOLVED PEARL.

By G. B. TIEPOLO — (born 1697, died 1770). The last of Cleopatra's lovers was Marc Antony, the celebrated Roman Triumvir, who for her sake became recreant to his country, his family and his honor. But their attachment to each other seems to have been extreme and worthy of a better relation. At one time when Antony was in the east conquering kingdoms to add to her empire, he sent, by one of the almost daily messengers that passed between them, a magnificent oriental pearl which he said he presented warm with his kisses to the queen of his heart and of his ambition. The romantic woman had it dissolved in acids, and drank it as a precious love philter.

THE IMMACULATE CONCEPTION.

By MURILLO,—(born 1618, died 1682). Original in the Royal Gallery of Madrid. This is the celebrated painting that gained for Murillo his proudest distinction. He was called "The painter of the Conception." It was so superior to everything else of the kind, that it was scarcely remembered that Guido Reni and others had painted the same thing, and very beautifully too.

The doctrine that Mary the Mother of Christ was also like him born without original sin, was for many centuries a point of sharp controversy in the Catholic church. It was virtually settled in favor of the immaculate conception, about the year 1620, though not formally promulgated until 1854. From that earlier time the beautiful ideal of this painting was adopted to express the sinless origin and divine nature of the Virgin. She was represented as young—not more than fourteen—robed in white, with a blue flowing mantle, and beautiful as painting could make her. The model was taken from the vision in Revelations (12-1), "And there appeared a great wonder in the heavens; a woman clothed with the sun, and the moon under her feet, and upon her head a crown of twelve stars."

MARCO POLO.

Was the son of a Venetian merchant, and born about 1250. He traveled in Asia, chiefly in Chinese Tartary, for 24 years, and on his return was so besieged to tell his wonderful adventures and descriptions of strange peoples, that he resolved to tell them once for all in a book, which has not ceased to be read and to give interest, even six hundred years after the events.

CERES AND IASION.

UNKNOWN. As ancient fable relates, the goddess Ceres had a rustic lover named Iasion whom she met in a "thrice-plowed field" in Crete; and of the twain was born Plutus, the god of wealth. It is a rather clumsy allegory of the production of wealth from rustic toil in the grain fields.

CORIOLANUS BEFORE ROME.

By VENEZIANO BONIFACIO — (1494-1563). In the younger days of Rome, when she was first experimenting in republicanism, one of her chieftains, Caius Marcius, called Coriolanus from one of his daring exploits, set himself obstinately against the enfranchisement of the common people. It was of course the unpopular side, and he at last became so obnoxious to the plebian element that, to save his life, he had to escape from the country. He joined its enemies and led them in their wars against the Romans. He was so successful that eventually Rome itself was besieged and brought to the last extremity. Deputations of Senators and of Priests were sent out to him for terms, but all to no purpose. At last the happy thought struck the besieged to send their noble women, headed by his own mother, his wife and his children. Coriolanus could not withstand their entreaties. He yielded to his mother; but he told her that in saving her country she had lost her son. And he went off into voluntary banishment and there died like an obstinate old Roman, as he was.

ST. SEBASTIAN.

By AMERIGHI DA CARAVAGGIO — (1569-1609). The subject of this painting, and of so many other similar ones, was of noble family, and one of the guards of the Emperor Dioclesian (A. D. 300). Like many Romans in that dangerous time he was secretly a Christian. Two of his converts were accused of belonging to this proscribed sect and were condemned to the torture. As they wavered in their courage at the last moment, Sebastian, regardless of himself, boldly exhorted them to faith and constancy. Thus self-exposed, he too was condemned to death, and was left for dead, pierced with innumerable arrows. Irene, the the widow of one of his martyred friends, in going for the body found him still alive and took him to her house, where, with the aid of her daughters, she extracted the arrows and restored him to life. But the spirit of the martyr was still in the Christian hero, and he shortly paid the penalty of his faithfulness under the clubs of the heathen executioners.

THE TEMPTATATION OF ST. ANTHONY.

By ALEXANDER L. LELOIR, French, recently died. About 300 years after Christ there came out of the Egyptian deserts an old Hermit of 50 years or more, who told the most marvelous stories of his conflicts with Satan in the wilderness; how the old arch enemy had taken him on every weak side of humanity, and tempted and tortured him with perfectly diabolical ingenuity. On reading the story, one would say that the Devil must have spent pretty much all his time for 30 odd years in devising and practicing torments on this poor recluse. But St. Anthony lived 50 years longer, and paid the "old fellow" back, in good solid preaching, for all the fleshly vexations that had been practiced on him.

THE BIRTH OF LOUIS XIV, in 1638.

By JAQUES LEMAN. "A few days after the birth of the dauphin, the great dignitaries and gentlemen of the King's household were admitted to the Queen's room, to pay homage to the new-born heir of the crown of France."

It is a great undertaking to go back 240 years in the annals of a country and reproduce a court scene, with all the costumes and splendor of the times and with accurate portraits of the distinguished actors. Yet this is the work here presented, and as such it is a splendid and wonderful success. The central and most important figure, though a small one, is the infant son of Louis XIII and Anne of Austria, born in 1638, and twenty-three years after the marriage of his parents. He was made King of France when only five years old, and for the greater part of the seventy-two years of his reign he filled the role of the grandest monarch of Europe. The precocious babe in the picture seems already to realize that he is a late comer, and cannot waste any of his precious time in babyhood.

The beautiful mother and the happy king will be at once recognized. On the right, and attended by Cardinal de Retz—or Father Joseph as he preferred to be called—is the great Cardinal Duke de Richelieu, Grand Chancellor of the Empire, and at this time, without doubt, the foremost man in Europe.

THE TRANSFIGURATION.

By RAPHAEL — (born 1483, died 1520). The original is in the Vatican at Rome. This is the best work of the greatest master of Italian painting. It was unfinished at the time of his death; still it was thought worthy to be placed beside his body as it was laid out for public view. There is here represented the mystery of Christ's transfiguration on Mount Tabor.

"And after six days Jesus taketh Peter, and James, and John, his brother, and bringeth them up into an high mountain apart.

And was transfigured before them; and his face did shine as the sun, and his raiment was white as the light.

And, behold, there appeared unto them Moses and Elias, talking with him."—Matthew, 17: 1–3.

As a most striking contrast to this glorious manifestation of the divinity of the "Son of Man," the artist has introduced beneath it the scene of the pitiful attempt and failure of the disciples to cast out the evil spirit from the demoniac boy. When Christ was informed of this on coming down from the mountain he could not resist that bitter cry, "O faithless and perverse generation, how long shall I be with you? how long shall I suffer you? bring him hither to me."

BATHSHEBA AT HER TOILET.

By ANDREA DAL FRISO — (born 1551, died 1611). One evening as King David was walking on the roof of his palace, he saw at a neighboring window "a woman washing herself, and she was very beautiful to look upon." Now the good king was old enough to know better than to be disturbed by such a trifling circumstance. But he really did go and misbehave himself—so much so that he found her husband, Uriah the Hittite, very much in his way; and he had the poor man exposed in the most dangerous place at the very next battle. The consequence was that there was another widow in Israel, whom David took as one of his wives. This was the mother of Solomon—the same Bathsheba whom David first saw as in the lovely and luxurious picture drawn by the nephew and pupil of the great Paul Veronese.

JUDITH WITH THE HEAD OF HOLOFERNES.

By AUGUST RIEDEL — (born at Bayreuth in 1800; now living at Rome. Original is No. 156 in the New Royal Pinakothek, at Munich. In one of the Old Testament Apocryphal Books there is related the story of Judith, the rich and beautiful Jewish widow. Her native city, Bethulia, was once besieged by an Assyrian army and reduced to the last extremity. When there seemed no longer a chance of relief, this brave woman offered herself for its deliverance. She dressed herself in her richest attire and jewels, and with her waiting woman, presented herself before the tent of Holofernes, the chief captain of the Assyrians. Her beauty captivated him, and her simple story quieted his suspicions. He made a feast and was allured into drinking inordinate quantities of wine. In the drunken sleep which followed, Judith, shut up alone with him in his tent, cut off his head with his own sword, and bore it to her countrymen. In the early morning the Israelites fell upon their enemies while they were panic-stricken at the slaughter of their leader and totally routed them. Judith lived to receive the grateful love of her people till she was one hundred and five years old. And long afterward an annual feast commemorated the heroic deed of the Hebrew widow.

GARIBALDI ESCAPING FROM CAPRERA.

UNKNOWN. This famous Italian patriot was born at Nice in 1807. His life has been filled with perilous adventures and unceasing revolutionary projects. In 1860, the small island of Caprera, lying off the northern coast of Sardinia, was given him for a residence. It was however impossible for him to keep quiet, and he was constantly engaged in schemes for Italian unity, mainly directed against the Papal rule in Rome. In one of these attempts the Roman government, assisted by the French, thought to keep him confined to his island by a guard of ships of war; but he escaped, and was soon at the head of the insurgents on the Roman frontier. It was reserved however for a stronger man than Garibaldi to unite and renovate Italy (Victor Emanuel, in 1870).

BRENNUS IN ROME.

By G. B. TIEPOLO — (born in Venice in 1697, died 1770). The first of those incursions of northern barbarians, which eventually destroyed the Roman Empire and culture, occurred in the year 390, B. C., when Brennus came down upon Italy with an army of 70,000 Gauls. His success was uninterrupted until he had driven the Romans into their citadel on the Capitoline Hill and besieged it. Here he remained more than half a year, baffled and chafing with barbaric impatience. He finally agreed to withdraw and go back to his northern wilds upon the payment to him of one thousand pounds weight of gold. As it was being weighed out, his dishonesty caused a remonstrance on the part of the Romans, whereupon the savage king threw his sword into the scale and bade them balance that too. Never was there a subject better fitted or better employed to bring out the fierce and untamed passions of barbarism.

THE WATER GIRL OF VENICE.

By S. DELLA VALLENTINA. As there is no fresh water in Venice, except what is brought from the mainland in boats or caught from the rains, great care is taken to collect and filter, under government inspection, all the water that falls on the roofs. In the center of the courts of all the large public buildings are cisterns or wells for this purpose, which are open and free to all during certain hours of the day. To these great numbers of girls resort, each provided with her two pails and cord and hook; and for each carrying, if it is for hire, she gets one sou, equal to one cent.

THE BLUE GROTTO.

This is a spacious cave under the steep and mountainous shore of the island of Capri, on the south side of the bay of Naples. It is on a level with the water and the entrance is only large enough to admit a small boat. The light coming in through the blue water gives everything inside a tinge of blue, while objects in the water have a beautiful silvery appearance.

MARTYRDOM OF ANGELUS MERULA, in 1557.

By BAREND WYNVELD, Professor in the Academy of Fine Arts, at Amsterdam. Philip II of Spain, a cruel and bigoted supporter of the Inquisition, attempted to force this institution upon the free-spirited Hollanders, who were at this time the subjects of Spain. He seems to have had the idea that he could crush out the now rising reform of Calvinism, by hanging or burning all heretics. But a policy which might be effectual with the Latin race would not and did not succeed with the Germanic. There resulted from it only the famous Revolt of the Netherlands, which established their independence, and religious liberty in the north of Europe.

One of the first victims of King Philip's fanaticism was Angelus Merula, who was condemned to be tortured and then burnt alive. When brought, lacerated and bleeding, from the rack to the stake, the old man said his last prayer and died. They could then only burn the lifeless body—which was done at Mons, in Belgium, on the 26th of July, 1557.

GALILEO BEFORE THE INQUISITION.

By T. BANTI, of Florence. Galileo is before the Tribunal of Three called the "Inquisition," in Rome, on the 22d of June, 1633. He is seventy years old, and has been summoned from Florence to answer to the charge of heresy, and is here compelled to retract and renounce the theory of the revolutions of the earth on its axis and about the sun. He is made to repeat the odious words, "I abjure, curse and detest the error and heresy of the motion of the earth." But, rising from his knees, the indignant old man could not help saying, though in an undertone, "*E' pur si muovi,*" 'yet it does move.'

MARRIAGE OF THE SEA, AT VENICE.

After the Canaletto school (about 1750). From the earliest times of the Venetian Republic, it was the custom to celebrate the espousal of Venice to the Adriatic, on ascension day of each year. With the greatest possible display the ruling Doge was taken to the mouth of the harbor where he threw a ring into the sea. Various and costly state galleys, called Bucentaurs, had been built for this magnificent ceremony. The last, which is represented in this painting, was constructed in 1725, the gilding alone costing more than $40,000. It was destroyed when the French took possession of Venice in 1797; and the custom ceased with the loss of its two hundred oared galley and at the same time of its naval power and independence.

JOSEPH AND POTIPHAR'S WIFE.

By Gio. Biliverti — (1576–1644). It is called the Joseph of Biliverti, and is one of the most observed paintings of the Uffizi Gallery in Florence. This scene reminds us that there are two sides to every story. Joseph said: "As he went into the house, she caught him by his garment, and he left the garment in her hand and fled and got him out." She said: "The Hebrew servant came in unto me to mock me. And it came to pass as I lifted up my voice and cried, that he left his garment with me and fled out." The woman's story, as is generally the case, was believed; and Joseph was cast into prison. It would be more orthodox and no more than fair that the next Bible illustration should represent Madame's side of the question.

UNE REPETITION DE LA TRAGEDIE DE MIRIAME CHEZ LE CARDINAL DE RICHELIEU.

By Adrien Moreau, of Paris. Cardinal Richelieu was the greatest statesman of his age, perhaps of any age. He aspired to be thought equally great in literature. In his younger days he had written two dramas, really quite indifferent productions, one of which was this tragi-comedy of Miriam, the sister of Moses. It was the great desire of the Cardinal to make this piece a public success. He had put it on the stage at his own expense, but success did not come. The private rehearsal of it before the aged author and the courtiers and princesses who formed his court is one of the most suggestive and best executed subjects of modern painting.

Plate XVII.—HOUSE AND GROUP OF MAORIS, NATIVE NEW ZEALANDERS. See Page xx.

THE FATHER OF PETRARCH THROWING HIS BOOKS INTO THE FIRE.

By ACHILLE LEONARDI, of Rome. When Petrarch, the Italian poet, was a young man of twenty (in the year 1324), all his attention and study were absorbed in classical literature. His father, who wanted to make a lawyer of him, and had kept him at much expense in law schools for five years, became disgusted at his little progress in law studies. Going to his room one day, he wound up his complaints by throwing into the fire Petrarch's precious manuscripts of Cicero, Virgil, and the others. But the despair and the tears of the young student at this martyrdom of his authors, were so touching that the father relented and snatched the books from the flames, telling his son to go on reading his Latin. So a genius was saved to the world, and there was one less poor lawyer in it.

SAPPHO.

By EDWARD RICHTER, of Paris. The fair subject of this painting is the loveliest character in classic history. Six hundred years before Christ, in the very earliest dawn of literature, a young Greek girl, from the Island of Lesbos, presented herself before the rude warrior clans of Greece, overflowing with song and sweetest poetry. She captivated all hearts with her minstrelsy and her modest virtues. She was revered as a goddess. Her lovely face was stamped on the ancient coins, with the inscription, "The violet-crowned, the pure, and sweetly smiling Sappho."

SPECKBACHER AND HIS SON.

This is a reproduction of the great masterpiece of FRANZ DEFREGGER in the National Museum of Innspruck. The story of the scene is this: In the year 1809 happened the famous uprising of the Tyrolese under Andreas Hofer against the French and Bavarians whom Napoleon had quartered upon them. The women fought by the side of the men, and there was not a hand that held back. They drove out their oppressors, successively routed all the armies that the great invader could send against them, and were only beaten in the end by national treaties. It was at the very commencement of this patriotic outburst that the young son of Speckbacher, one of the prominent leaders, joined a company of sharpshooters against his father's will. He seems very soon to have had the rare fortune to shoot an eagle on the wing, which, by an old custom of these mountaineers, made him the "king of the shooters," and gave him a right to promotion which even his father could not gainsay. With the eagle's plumes as the trophies of the exploit, he is conducted by his company into the presence of his father and the other leaders, at the Boar's Inn of St. Johann. We know that the brave pleading face of that boy obtained the pardon he sought, for his name is on many pages of the stirring history of the great uprising of the Tyrol.

PROCESS OF PORCELAIN PAINTING.

The plates of Porcelain are made of the finest and purest clays and materials of stoneware, and are burned for one or two days in the highest white heat. To fill the pores and to form a glaze on the surface, a paste made chiefly of powdered quartz and feldspar is fused or melted on them by a heat a little less than that originally used. The paints are made of a paste of powdered glass, variously colored by metallic oxides, which fuses at a still lower heat. The picture is then painted on the plates (if a large one, in successive parts), and subjected to a heat sufficient to melt the glass of the paints. If a porcelain plate passes all these ordeals without fracture or imperfection, it is the most valuable and enduring, as well as the most beautiful of paintings.

A TRIP TO MEXICO.*

It was my mischance to reach Vera Cruz during one of the "northers," which are the great storm winds of the western coast of the Gulf of Mexico. They are the north-east trade winds, deflected into north winds, and increased in their violence by the lofty chain of the Cordilleras, which rises but a short distance inland, and presents an effectual barrier to the further western course of air-currents seeking the equator from the north-east. The northers are prevalent only during the winter half of the year; but while they are blowing there is no communication with any of the ports on this side of Mexico; for there are no harbors nor any artificial protections against their violence.

Our steamer came to anchor under the lee of the island and fortress of San Juan d'Uloa; and there we lay, within full view of all that was passing on the shore, and of the breakers dashing over the piers, for twenty-four hours, before the small boats could venture to come out to take us to land. This gave us ample time and occasion to meditate on the inefficiency of this people who could submit to such a great drawback and danger to an important commerce during four hundred years. When we did eventually land the next day, there were few who did not get a good wetting in the breakers as their welcome to the land of the tropics.

As there is but little of interest in Vera Cruz, the most of our passengers took the cars late the same night for the City of Mexico, 250 miles back in the interior. For a few miles the

---

* Written in 1876, and read before several Literary Societies.

railway passes through the sandy regions that line the coast. Then for a hundred miles, gradually rising, we pass through regions of the most luxuriant tropical vegetation—palm and cocoa-nut trees, mangoes and mamey, guava and aguacate, orange and coffee plantations, banana and pine-apple fields, fruits and flowers in bewildering profusion and rankness of growth. Arrived at Orizaba, one of the great fruit centers and delightful stopping places of this route, we are 3,000 feet above the sea. The snow-capped extinct volcano of the same name rises up on our right to a height of over 17,000 feet. After leaving Orizaba and skirting around the grand old peak that blocks our way, we commence to ascend the valley of Maltrata. The ascent is here so steep that the railway is laid in a zigzag course, continually passing from one side to the other of the valley, which it follows up to the very closing in of its mountainous walls. Then the track doubles on itself, turns short about and comes back, climbing the precipitous side of the very valley we have been ascending. There is here one of the most remarkable instances of railway engineering in the world. To lay a railroad track, with a uniform ascent of four feet in the hundred, against the steep craggy sides of a mountain range, to tunnel its projecting cliffs, to span its gorges with curving iron bridges, to go in and out of all its defiles, winding and coiling in that slow course to the dizzy height of 9,000 feet above the level of the sea, is one of those astounding feats of skill and enterprise which only the Anglo-Saxon race can accomplish. England built this road, commenced in 1852, and finished in 1872.

After climbing up the mountain side as we have described, through a distance of ten miles or more, we can still see from the car window, 3,000 feet beneath us, the serpentine track of the road up the valley over which we came two hours before. But in mounting thus ever upward we have passed out of the tropical climate and vegetation, into the regions of cloud and wind, of the pine and the birch tree. We are in another world. They call it "tierra fria"—the cold land.

The grade of this road up the mountain, four per cent, is the steepest of any other simple traction road, except a short one in

Peru up the Andes, which is in some places five per cent. It is very near the limit practicable for the passage of ordinary trains by simple traction. And even for this, it is necessary to make use of a specially constructed engine, known as the Fairleigh locomotive. It is a long boiler, more than double the usual length, with a smoke stack at each end, and the fire in the middle. There are eight drive wheels, and the weight of the huge machine is seventy tons. For such heavy rolling gear the track and the bridges must necessarily be of the strongest and most substantial kind. One is not surprised then to learn that this 250 miles of railway cost over thirty million dollars, and that it paid the English stockholders no dividend whatever. This, with the millions of dollars sunk in Mexican bonds and in silver mines, must make some sorrowful pages in the ledgers of our thrifty cousins.

But we must come back to our journey. At Boca del Monte, and about half way over the whole distance, we suddenly emerge from the mountains and come out on the great Mexican plateau, about 9,000 feet above the sea. From this point down into the valley of Mexico, which has an elevation of 7,500 feet, is a long dusty and rather uninteresting ride. It is the dry season. There have been no rains for four or five months; and the whole country is parched and dried up. The climate of these uplands is only divided by wet and dry portions of the year. The temperature does not materially vary. Wherever there is water for irrigation, fruits, vegetables and harvests can be had in any season that may be desired.

The last sixty miles of the road is through almost continuous haciendas, or plantations, of maguey. This is the plant from which the Mexicans obtain their intoxicating drink, called pulque. The southern races of America, as well as of Europe, devote I think half of their lands and labor to the production of what they drink. The maguey is a species of aloes. The exotic century-plant is very similar if not identical with it. But in its native habitat, and in favorable locations, it has an enormous and magnificent growth. It throws out its thick and spike tipped leaves ten and twelve feet long. When allowed to do so, it shoots up, after ten or fifteen years of growth, a straight central stem forty to fifty feet high, forming a perfect tree of magnificent flowers. But when cultivated for pulque, the bud of this stem must be cut off just at the time of its starting. The cut is hollowed out in dish-shape, and all the sap, containing the accumulated nutriment and life of the plant, flows into this receptacle, from which it is drawn out and put into goat or hog skins. One thrifty plant will furnish three or four hundred gallons of this juice, which in a few days after being gathered ferments and becomes, without further care or process, the great drink of the country. To uneducated tastes it is a bad smelling, bad tasting, sour-milky, and miserable apology for a beverage. But it is consumed in immense quantities by the Indians and lower classes. There is a daily train of cars especially for its transportation to the city called the pulque train. The Iturbe family of Mexico have one hacienda of maguey, for the rent of which they are paid $150 a day, over $50,000 a year. It is to me almost inconceivable where all the money and demand for this intoxicating product come from.

Before arriving at our journey's end, the road skirts around the northern edge of lake Tezcuco, in which the city of Mexico was said originally to have been built, but from which it is now distant at least two miles. It is a salt lake, as are all seas and lakes from which there are no outlets. Evaporation carries off all the surplus of water, leaving always the minute traces of mineral matter brought down by the inlet streams; and the accumulations of ages make the briny solutions of all undrained bodies of water. The shallow margins of this lake are divided off into beds by low embankments, and in the rainy season the salt water flows into them. When the lake falls in the dry season, there remain in them enclosed bodies of salt water, which drying leave a crust of salt on the surface. This is carefully scraped up, taken away, and cleaned or re-evaporated. From thence comes the salt supply of this country, both for domestic purposes and for a certain process in the refining of silver ore.

We are now entering the great Capitol of the Republic, a city of 250,000 inhabitants, the oldest and most interesting city on the American continent. It was first seen by white men twenty-seven years after the discovery of the New World by Columbus. A band of Spanish adventurers, scarcely numbering five hundred, with a daring and prowess unequaled in the world's history, had fought its way over the mountains to the causeways of this lake city, then two hundred years old, peopled by half a million Aztecs, and governed by the richest and most powerful monarch of the Indian Hemisphere. Cortez entered and took up his residence in this hostile city without the slightest hesitation. He shortly after seized the person of Montezuma, threw down the heathen idols and elevated the Catholic, and commenced a most desperate struggle against the overwhelming numbers of the natives, determined to defend their homes and their religion. Once he was driven out with fearful loss, on that memorable "noche triste," the gloomy night; and he gathered the remnants of his little band, about one hundred and fifty battered and beaten soldiers, under a huge cypress tree, which still stands, protected and venerated, on the northern outskirts of the city. But after a few months, Cortez returned again to the charge; and then he destroyed and leveled the city as fast as he conquered it. Three-fourths of it were thus pulled down and thrown into the canals, before the remnant submitted and the Spaniards were the acknowledged masters of Mexico.

On this site was laid out and built the present city, with its rectangular streets and its solid stone buildings. The houses, as in many cities of Europe, are constructed with courts, which are entered from the street through wide passage ways, protected by strong and massive doors. The home life is almost entirely in these open courts, which are surrounded by balconies and corridors.

The city of Mexico is so nearly on the level of lake Tezcuco that it can have no efficient drainage. In fact most of the streets have only surface drains, and none have them more than from one to two feet below the surface. Mexico would be an exceedingly unhealthy city if it were not for the rarity and excessive dryness of the atmosphere. There can be no malarious decay, for nothing remains moist. As it is, the main diseases are those which arise from imperfect oxygenation of the blood, bilious and dropsical diseases. From the great altitude of this country, a mile and a half above the sea-level, the air is very light, the mercury in the barometer standing at about 23 inches, and for those unaccustomed to the situation, it is difficult to breathe, or at least to get air enough into the lungs. One draws many a long breath; and mounting the long flights to the "first floor," one has often hard work to get the breathing function into comfortable working order again. This is no climate for consumptives. Whoever has not a full and free expansion of the lungs will very soon get out of Mexico. I heard men say there was no satisfaction up there in a good "whisky straight," or any other of the strong Americanisms. The animal functions cannot keep up to the tune of such lively stimulants.

But what seemed strangest about this city, was its inhabitants. It seemed as if we had been landed in a great overgrown Indian village. Squaws with their pappooses, and half-naked, black-maned urchins filled all the streets and every opening out of them. There was every shade of color, from the copper through all the bronzes to the dirty lead color. But all was Indian, thoroughly Indian. If we did not know what toned down the color, we should certainly think that these mongrel and parti-colored swarms were the genuine aborigines. This people are much smaller than our northern Indians, but they have the same features and motions and habits. They carry their burdens on their backs with a band around their foreheads. They have the regular Indian lope when they travel. When at rest they squat on the ground, and can sit there an indefinite time. The females carry the unfailing baby slung in a shawl on their backs; or if there are two of them, or a burden and a baby, the little one is in front and the other behind, but both in the folds of the same long shawl.

The Indians are the traders in cheap and fancy things. The markets, the street corners, and the portalis are crowded with their little stands, exposing for sale their fruits or their confections, their tasteful handiwork or their fanciful wares. Every morning, on the shady side of some of the principal streets, many native girls who have brought in their flowers from the country, sit on the curb stones, making up bouquets. They learned the art from the French who came over with Maximilian, and now there is not in any capitol of the world such a display and profusion of flowers as are offered by these Indian girls in the streets of Mexico. In a bouquet as large as one's two hands, that I have bought for a shilling, I have counted over fifty white roses, with mixture of orange blossoms, camelias, and I do not know what not.

At almost every turn some dirty half-breed will hold out to you a handful of lottery tickets for sale. There are about a thousand licensed venders of these chance schemes, mostly gotten up for the benefit of the churches. The continual cry of "quartro mil pesos," "vente mil pesos"—four, twenty, thousand dollars—becomes tiresome and annoying in the extreme. They come to your room, to your eating table, everywhere, and cannot understand that you are not tempted by such splendid chances.

In the central portion of the city, notably between the Plaza and the Alameda, the two places of resort and of promenade, are found a few pure whites. The Spanish Creoles—that is, those of Spanish descent and born in the country—some Germans, with a few English and French, compose the white population, which I do not think would amount all told to 10,000. There are no American residents except missionaries and diplomatic officers.

Of the few large fortunes remaining in Mexico, a small number took their origin from the silver mines in times past; though these are hardly paying expenses now. But the greater number of fortunes have come from the large haciendas scattered here and there over the country. The agricultural resources of the Republic are in reality far greater than the mineral, but have never been turned to any account beyond supplying home necessities. Corn and wheat can be raised there more cheaply than in any country I know of. Yet when I was there corn was worth a dollar and a half, and wheat two dollars and a quarter, a bushel. Cotton is imported from the United States, in part to supply a few factories that have started up near some of the cities. Even potatoes have been brought from the States to the country which has the credit of first furnishing to the world this most important food staple.

There is nothing in all the line of vegetables, fruits, grains, luxuries or staples, that cannot be raised somewhere in the Mexican States in the greatest abundance and cheapness. And I have often asked myself if, in view of all these natural advantages, this country would be any benefit to the United States, should the opportunity ever be offered of acquiring it. I have always decided that it would not be. There is not a land, however rich and prolific it may be, that is worth the having, if it is encumbered with a Spanish speaking people. It is the same with Cuba as with Mexico. Either one of these would prove to be the source of never-ending jealousies, intolerance, and insubordination, until the native element was exterminated, or merged into something better. And these, as we know, are long and trying ordeals to go through.

Old travelers say, if you want to travel for comfort or pleasure, never go where they speak the Spanish language. There are many reasons for this, and one of them is that you cannot trust that "Si, Siñor" as you can the "Yes, Sir." There is always in these countries a feeling of insecurity of person and of property, an uneasy doubt as to just how long you will be able to hold your own. Quiet and order are maintained within the city limits of Mexico, but it is at the cost of a large and military police. Every night, from sundown to sunrise, at every street crossing, there is a policeman fully armed with a musket and cutlass. But whenever our party made excursions into the country we took with us nothing more valuable than a few silver mounted pistols. And we should probably have given these up to any strangers we had met in a lonely part of the way.

It was my misfortune to visit Mexico during the prevalence of one of its periodic revolutions.* This word sounds terrible, and has a pretty serious meaning to us. But there it is only the usual process of a change of administration. It is the party of the outs trying to get in, and doing it in the only way it can be done in Mexico, that is by fighting. Popular suffrage is there

---

* In the Spring of 1876.

the merest farce. In most places no one goes to the polls to vote; but whichever party has military control of a district, makes a list, or a pretended list, of the voters in it, and reports them as having voted to a man for its candidates. So an administration, if unopposed by armed force, has it in its power to perpetuate itself indefinitely. I do not think there were any principles involved in the contest that was then waging. Both leaders were Catholics, and neither professed or promulgated any ideas of reform or economy or schemes of public welfare. Porfirio Diaz, the instigator of the revolt, is an Indian, and perhaps carried the sympathies of the lower classes. While Lerdo, the President of the Republic, being of Spanish descent and a man of wealth, had a greater insight and interest in government affairs.

The Mexican Congress assembled while I was there, and was opened by a speech from President Lerdo. He had been solicited by all the members to declare in his opening that he would not be a candidate for re-election. It was regarded that this would put an end to the revolution and pacify the country. But Lerdo disappointed any such expectations. He claimed to be able to put down all opposition, that the revolters were nothing but the old bands of robbers and offenders against the peace and order of the country, and that he should not yield to them. I heard it said on that occasion that his obstinacy had made him a doomed man. Mexico has already had, since her independence in 1821, thirty-six successful revolutions. And now we may count the number increased by one more; for to-day the proud and wealthy Lerdo is an exile; and Diaz, the soldier of fortune, is exacting the tribute of his success on tax ridden Mexico.

Our nearest neighbor, the Mexican Republic, is notoriously the poorest of nations. With all her wealth of mines and silver veins, with her untold capacity for the production of every commodity of commerce, she could not to-day sell her bonds for ten cents on the dollar. She has no gold, no exchange, no credit. Her wealthy men can no longer get their wealth out of the country. There is absolutely nothing into which they can turn it, to make it available in London or New York. A few words on the causes which have led to this anomalous state of things may not be uninteresting.

In the first place, no European settlers ever went to Mexico with the intention of making a permanent home and living there. Spaniard, German, French and English, all went there to make a fortune and then return to Europe to enjoy it. For three hundred years the country was ruled by Viceroys from Spain, who succeeded each other on an average every four years, that time being considered long enough for each to reap an ill-gotten harvest and to get back to his home land again. Thus from the very outset this ill-fated country has been reaped and raked and gleaned to make the wealth and fortunes of foreigners. What was left by grasping tradesmen and rapacious rulers, was gathered up by swarms of priests, and either sent back to the order at home in payment for their appointment, or expended in the erection and costly adornment of myriads of monasteries and cathedrals. But these add nothing to the wealth of nations, and the gains that go abroad make no home improvements. Thus it has come that a soil once rich and fertile, that easily sustained the swarming workers of ancient times, is now waste, without pretense of cultivation on three-fourths of it. The richest mineral veins and surface leads have been worked and wasted out, till now, under crude and slovenly processes of refining, the silver mines do not pay expenses.

The native Indians, who have had among them in times past some men of remarkable sense and judgment, saw this desolation coming upon their country, over half a century ago. They attributed it to the rule of the Spaniards; and in 1821 they succeeded, as we had done, after a long and trying struggle, in throwing off the foreign yoke. But prosperity did not come. It was not sought from the only source whence it can come—from mother Earth. Within three or four years after their independence, they had borrowed in London about forty million dollars. This kept them afloat some twelve years, when the mania for mining speculations broke out in England. Again the infatuated English invested perhaps another forty millions in Mexican silver mines, the money from which investments kept things moving there till our southern aristocracy wanted more slave territory, and we had to go over and fight Mexico for it. This caused us to expend in that country, in various ways, some thirty millions; all of which was a perfect god-send to this impoverished people. Then France wanted a hand in the great poor-house, and sent Maximilian there, and with him a score or more of millions. All this had been gleaned up and sent away, when the English took it in their heads to build that splendid railway up the mountains, and poured thirty million dollars into the needy country that seems no longer to give back anything. If here are not lessons enough for us to let this border land of ours alone, I do not know what lessons are.

I happened to take with me as a kind of guide book, Robert A. Wilson's Travels in Mexico. Now the late Judge Wilson of California was the pioneer and authority of those who in late years have been attempting to throw discredit on the Spanish accounts of the numbers and power of the ancient Aztecs, and the story of their conquest which our own Prescott has woven into such a delightful romance of history. The natural mind however revolts from having its cherished beliefs attacked. The confirmed skeptic in history is the same unlovely being with the open-mouthed skeptic in religion. Who has any sympathy with the man who tried to make out that Shakspeare never existed, or that old Homer was a myth? The very thrill of joy that went through the land when it was announced that the devoted and intrepid Schliemann had found at Mycena an Aladin's cave of Homeric heroes and treasures and evidences, ought to be a significant warning to all misbelievers and belittlers of history. So was I predisposed, both by the instincts of a faithful mind and the love of the cherished idols of popular belief, to find all the fault I could with these latter day pessimists.

And first, in regard to the reported numbers of the ancient Aztecs, which Wilson says must be taken at about one-tenth of those stated, because the country could not have sustained them all, I really could see no occasion to divide them at all. It may well be that in those days of the unexhausted fertility of a volcanic soil, and the easy abundance of an unvarying semi-tropical climate, it may be, I say, that every Indian soul was there that was numbered. It takes almost nothing to keep alive those diminutive and lowly organized beings. They live now almost altogether on black beans, which can be produced in unlimited quantities. And one may see these natives any day in Mexico, that have come in from long distances to sell a few cents worth of produce or of wares, making their dinner on a joint of sugar cane which they have brought with them. The females are marriageable at an exceedingly early age—I was told at a dozen years—and they certainly multiply beyond any of the ratios of Malthus or of mathematics. From the large proportion of old and shriveled women that are met with there, one might almost believe what is said of them, that they never die, but dry up and blow away. I certainly never saw anyone who had ever seen an Indian's grave. Unquestionably then, a few score good successive bean seasons might easily have brought out Aztecs enough to fill the roll of the most extravagant historian.

Wilson says, because he could not find heaps of ruins and building materials on the sites of the populous Indian cities spoken of by Cortez, he does not believe they ever existed, nor the stone built palaces and teocallis. Now nothing is more certain than that the Aztecs were skillful and extensive workers in stone. The relics of their quaint and massive stone carvings lie neglected everywhere in city and in country. They have been so abundant in times past that the Mexicans of to-day do not begin to realize the riches they have in the unique remains of Aztec culture. I have seen a sphinx-head carving used for a hitching block on a country road. And in a court-yard of the Government House they feed a peacock on the top of the sacrificial altar of the great god Mexitli. But go into the undisturbed wildernesses of southern Mexico, to Uxmal, Palenque, and Mitlan, and there you will find the most remarkable ruins in the world, immense structures, palaces and temples, built of hewn stone, cemented with mortar, covering acres, and scattered over miles of territory, with columns, façades and frontings, sculptured and ornamented as no other ancient remains have ever been found— and all this the work of Mexican Indians before the use and knowledge of iron tools. Is it at all probable then that the Aztecs, alone of those semi-civilized races, lived in mud houses, and served their proud Montezumas in palaces of adobe?

Cortez, in his final capture of the city of Mexico, was obliged to take it as it were by inches, and to destroy and level everything as far and as fast as he went, until almost the entire city had disappeared. Then in the rebuilding, which was immediately commenced and carried on in the most substantial manner, it may well be that all the building materials accumulated by the Indians were used up in the new structures. I do not myself think it at all strange that the visible vestiges of the Aztec sites and structures have long since vanished from the thickly peopled and ever changing valley of the Anahuac.

But these industrious natives have left works which could not be destroyed, and which fully attest the busy swarms of workers that must once have filled this hive of aboriginal races. These are enormous mounds, almost mountains of earth material, piled up in regular pyramids, by the slow and tedious work of human hands. I have climbed them to the height of hundreds of feet; and I have dug up pockets full of arrow heads and idol heads in the fields about them, wondering all the time how Wilson and his train would account for these evidences, in their abridgment of Indian histories.

But I cannot follow further this labyrinth of mazy conjecture. Suffice it to say that where such careful students and searchers as Prescott, Robertson, and Humboldt have not found reason to hesitate, it is ill-timed and mistaken effort now to raise the dicta of doubts.

But I must leave this land of delightful scenes and of thrilling reminiscences; and I leave it, as I leave these rambling sketches, with regret. Yet once more before I go I must take a last look at the lovely valley and its rampart of mountains, from the heights of Chapultepec. Here, on the fortress which our brave boys stormed and took in '47, on a standpoint 1,500 feet higher than the storm beaten summit of Mount Washington, one looks out on every side upon lakes and groves and hills and vales—the pleasantest panorama the sun ever shone upon. While, at a distance of fifty to a hundred miles, there rise on all the horizon, crests and ridges and mountains, and snow-capped cones of volcanoes two miles higher even than this lofty table land. Truly nature has prodigaled here her richest scenes, her most startling contrasts of heights and depths, of soaring peaks and yawning chasms. The eternal snows of the arctics look down on the yellowing grain fields of temperate climes, while these in their turn overhang deep barancas, in which the luscious fruits of the tropics are ripening.

But over all this scene of wildness and of beauty is cast the shadow of man's lawlessness. Danger lurks where nature revels. It is the story of the tropics the world around—lands rich in nature's gifts, but poor in humanity—

> "Where the flowers ever blossom, the beams ever shine,
> And all save the spirit of man is divine."

SIGHT-SEEING IN NEW ZEALAND.*

Whoever would see countries very much different from his own must make up his mind to cross the oceans. He who says: "I will see my own country first before I go out exploring foreign lands," will never know much by personal observation of the strange varieties of people and culture, or of the wonderful differences in the vegetable and animal developments that make this world of ours so diversified and interesting. The oceans are the great barriers to all interchanges, whether of races or manners or productions. Even cultivated and commercial nations, on opposite sides of the Atlantic, are widely dissimilar, as every one knows who has ever traveled in Europe. But in respect of natural growths and native species, which are more restricted in their spheres, there is always a far wider difference.

Countries divided off from all others by a great expanse of waters, will most likely bear no close relation to them in their stages of advancement. They will probably resemble some by-gone period in the growth of those more connected. And the more isolated a region is, the more backward seems to be its state of development. Thus eastern Australia, separated from all the rest of the world not more by its oceans than by the parched and barren wastes of its interior, had developed, when first visited by white men, only types of animals and plants that were prevalent in the northern continents during the earlier Tertiary times; such as reptiles and mursupials, the wingless emus and sluggish parrots, the great tree-ferns, the cycad palms, the araucarian pines and monstrous gum-trees.

---

*A Lecture written in 1884, and delivered before the Central Church Society of Rochester, and other Societies.

But New Zealand, separated from Australia, the nearest land, by twelve hundred miles of stormy ocean, was still more backward in the race of life. Fern brakes and lycopod mosses covered the whole country that was not forest. Grass palms, tall tree-ferns, and impenetrable jungles of evergreen trees, loaded down with orchids, climbing ferns, lianas, and every kind of parasitic growths, silent and gloomy from the almost total absence of animal life, formed its forest scenery. A few species of the apteryx (the kiwis) and the giant moas, birds without a trace of wings, constituted the land fauna of this desolate country. There were absolutely no quadrupeds, no mammalia, and no reptiles except a few lizards, that were indigenous to the islands.

A race of Malay Indians, nearest akin to the Sandwich Islanders, had in quite recent years found its way to these shores, bringing with them some dogs and rats, the sweet potato and the taro, the root from which the Sandwich Islanders make their "poi." Here was a race of men, a product of the most recent of the geological eras, stranded on a half developed relic of the old Carboniferous period, that did not produce a spear of grain, or an herb, or a tuber, or a fruit, or any vegetable that was really fit for a man to eat. I suppose it was about the hardest conditions in the way of getting a living that a colony of emigrants ever found itself in. Until the dogs and rats and roots which they brought had increased sufficiently to be levied upon, they found almost their sole food in the roots of the common fern-brake, the Pteris esculenta, and in what they could catch of the great running birds which they found there in large abundance.

At the time when they were first brought to the notice of Europeans by Capt. Cook, a little over a hundred years ago, they had eaten up all the moas on the islands, and had begun to eat up each other, in sheer necessity for fresh meat, as they always claimed. The Maoris (pronounced Mouries) were unquestionably a race of cannibals; and until about forty years ago, no white man who set any value on a decent funeral cared much to go among them. I have seen many an old tattooed chief who, they said, had eaten his man. I saw at Ohinemutu a still lingering relic of an aged chieftain. He had been a powerful warrior in his day; thought nothing of picking up a man and heaving him over the palisades. They claimed that he recollected Capt. Cook, which would make him considerably over a hundred years old. It was said that when they talked about missionaries to him, the old cannibal would waken up and move his withered lips, as if in dim recollection of some far away feast. But Capt. Cook, of blessed memory, at least on the south side of the equator, had left among them some civilized pigs; and these had increased and multiplied, and finally took the place of missionaries at the fire side.

If there is in all the world a country more rugged and mountainous than another it is New Zealand. Ranges, growing higher and wilder toward the south, run through the islands from end to end. And one sailing all around the coast, as I have done, finds only rock bound shores and cliffs and peaks rising inland as far as the eye can reach. Of course there are some exceedingly rich and some wide valleys. But the country is like California, so nearly all mountain side that valley land from its very scarcity is almost beyond price.

How this mountainous region ever came to be named after the low-lying Zealand in Holland, where they have to build walls and dykes to keep the sea out, is one of the mysteries. The good old Dutch navigator, Tasman, discovered these islands 240 years ago. He sent a boat on shore to establish friendly relations with the natives; and these took such a liking to the fat Hollanders that they immediately roasted half a dozen of them. Old Tasman was so disgusted that he at once set sail, and hove back at them the first name he could think of. It is lucky it was not a worse one. It might have been Rotterdam Spuyten Duyvils, or some other hard name, for he was awful mad. For more than a century the Cannibal Islands had a fearful letting alone, until they were rediscovered and taken possession of by Captain Cook, in 1769.

New Zealand bears evident marks of having been elevated out of the ocean in recent geological times. Not only its flora and fauna, but its physical structure shows it to be, in very great part at least, one of the newest made lands of our globe. Volcanoes, mostly extinct, but many still smoking, are found all over the North Island, while basaltic and other igneous rocks are found as abundantly in the South Island. Enormous quantities and depths of diluvium are overlying the whole country, hills, ridges, and even mountains, in positions where it is impossible to account for them except as having been deposited on the sea bottom and then recently elevated. In cuts through the hills, at various elevations inland, I often saw layers of marine shells, sometimes a foot thick, clear and clean as they had been laid up on the sea shore. In fact the evidence is so plain that even the natives have thought it necessary to account for it. So they will gravely tell you that once on a time their great god Maui went fishing in the waters that were then overlying the North Island. He had a hook made out of the jaw bone of one of his ancestors. After varying luck, he at last caught his hook under a rock, and in trying to pull it out, he lifted the bottom of the ocean right up into the hills and mountains of New Zealand.

It seems to me that I would interest you more in this lovely tourists' land, if I told you of my travels, and what I saw and thought of the people and scenes. It will necessarily bring in a good many capital "I's". But you will in reality, I imagine, find me but a small factor in the incidents and descriptions that I will be able to give you so much better in this way. I will therefore run along through my diary, catching at what I think will interest you most.

One bright summer morning in January, after a three weeks steamer voyage, I landed in Auckland, a lovely English built city of 30,000 inhabitants, as far in the southern hemisphere as Richmond, Virginia, is in the northern. With a company of our passengers I started off at once up Queen Street for the Prince Albert Hotel, to get our first breakfast on shore. But what a disappointment, when we came to see the little cramped and insignificant hotel! Why, there is not in any of the large cities of the southern colonies, a hotel that begins to equal those which we rank as second class. Our breakfast consisted of splendid meats, the best you can imagine, with bread and coffee. That was all. You get magnificent cuts of beef and mutton where

Englishmen live; but you do not get much of anything else worth speaking of.

But out of doors the summer foliage and flowers were at their best; and it was as good as a feast to the hungry, to wander through the beautiful parks and gardens of this luxuriant country. The broad-leaved, fat-armed, India-rubber trees, the Norfolk Island pines, the most symmetrical trees that grow, the Morton Bay figs, a species of Banyan with aerial roots, the Nikau palm, the strange and only palm growth of these islands, and numerous other tropical productions adorn and diversify the walks and drives in the vicinity of Auckland.

A favorite excursion is to the top of Mount Eden, an extinct volcano, some six or eight hundred feet high. There are over sixty similar cones within ten miles of this city. From this nearest one the visitor gets a grand panoramic view of a beautiful city built on hills, of a romantic country dotted with crater peaks, and of the islands and headlands of two magnificent harbors situated on either side of the narrow neck of land on which Auckland is located. One of them opens into the western ocean, and the other, the one by which we came, opens by various and distant outlets into the eastern ocean.

In a few days we had gathered together a party of six for the grand excursion to the Hot Springs and Lakes. One afternoon we took the little steamer "Glenelg," of about one hundred tons, and started out for Tauranga, a port on the south-eastern coast. Our steamer seemed to me rather a cockle shell concern to face the billows of the great Pacific Ocean. However, with some considerable tumbling as we rounded the capes, it carried us through quite comfortably, and we arrived the next morning in time for breakfast.

Crowds of Maoris, in their gay-colored blankets and paints and tattoos, were in the streets and all through the hotel, not begging nor putting themselves in our way, but pleased if they could shake hands with us, and say: "Me big chief; me fight pakeha;" that is the foreigner. For you must know that this is the center of the fiercest wars between the natives and the English. The Maoris are savage fighters, perfect devils to stick and hang, and never know when they ought to call themselves whipped. The precise and orderly British troops, who must always have everything "in good form," and who never have learned to fight behind a tree or in Indian fashion, have been beaten in nearly every encounter with the natives. And they are to-day absolutely afraid to arouse the war spirit or to even to execute the laws as against the Maoris. The very day we arrived, there was great excitement—and they said this was the cause of so many natives being in town—about a Maori named Tutu, who was out in the neighboring country somewhere, scouting about with two hundred natives. He had recently with a gang murdered five or six English families, and the authorities were trying to catch him, if they could do it in some safe and amicable way. As we were going right up the country where he was supposed to be, we made up our minds unanimously to follow the example of the authorities, and not to see him unless he was out of sight.

After breakfast we took the stage, a three-seated covered spring wagon with four horses, for Ohinemutu, 54 miles in the interior. About three miles out we pass the Gate Pah. A Pah is one of the intrenched villages or strongholds of the natives. This one in its time was fortified by three ditches or rifle-pits, with palisades and strong hurdle fences on the embankments. Here one morning, twenty years ago, "General Sir Duncan Cameron," I quote from history, "with three regiments of infantry, with sappers and miners and marines, numbering over 4,000 men, with Armstrong guns and all the appliances of modern warfare, took up his position before this mysterious fortification." Well, 500 natives, armed with rifles, dodging around in the trenches, and keeping up sham maneuvers in the rear, made this pompous army believe that there were thousands of them, and kept it cannonading, and throwing shells at red flags away in the rear till nearly nightfall. And when at last the English attempted three times to storm the breaches, the native marksmen picked off with their rifles nearly all the officers, and sent the troops flying back to the harbor miserably beaten. I read of their virtues and heroism on granite monuments in the cemetery of Tauranga—not of the brave Maoris who were defending their homes—but of the gallant officers of Her Majesty's 43rd and 68th Regiments.

For ten miles after leaving the Gate Pah, we rode through a rough and rolling country, covered all over with fern-brakes. The soil of these lands seems to be good and deep, but it is a fearful job to get rid of this fern. It seeds back and comes up again and again as fast as the land is plowed and cultivated.

After this we came to the Oropi forest, or "bush" as it is called in this land of misnomers, eighteen miles of a thick impenetrable tangle of fern trees, creepers, climbing vines, and giant forest trees. These were to me of surpassing interest; and I would not have tired studying them if the time had been three days instead of three hours. The lower forest consists of ferns of innumerable varieties and growths, from the minute filmy ferns on the surface, to the tall and splendid tree-ferns 30 to 40 feet high. Through these tower up the majestic pines and birches, the Rimu, Totara, and Matai, the Rata, Pukatea, and Kowai, many of them 12 to 15 feet in diameter and two or three hundred feet high. All these are profusely garlanded with orchids and parasitic ferns, and festooned with lianas and creepers away up in their branches as far as the eye can penetrate. But all the trees and plants are strange and unnatural. The pines you would not imagine could belong to the Pinus family. They have no cones nor needle-shaped leaves. Their fruiting is like berries, and their leaves are flat, from oval to lanceolate, and some hanging down like the willow. The birches, the laurels, and the myrtles are these only in name. They have no like species in all the world besides.

The Rata tree is the great feature of the New Zealand bush. It is the most unique and intelligent tree that ever—breathed, I was going to say—for it seems to know as much as some animals. When it first shoots up from the ground, it appears to look all around for a Rimu pine. It will not turn out of its way for any other tree; but if there is a Rimu pine within reach, it starts for it and climbs straight up the body, without a leaf or branch until its head is among the upper limbs. Then the Rata sends out branches like other trees, and at the same time the stalk from the ground up begins to push out on each side a line of aerial roots, which gradually creep around the body of the pine until they meet on the opposite side. There they grow together, and all the network of rootlets grows together, forming a complete case around the doomed pine, which the Rata in time entirely absorbs and destroys. But if the Rata sprout does not find the Rimu in its vicinity, it grows up an independent respectable forest tree, which is greatly sought for as a ship timber.

Now if this story of the performance of a tree had been told me without my having seen anything of it, I most likely should not have believed it. But I can assure you that I have seen the Rata tree in every stage of its growth, as a slender vine, as a stalk with a set of comb-like teeth on each side, then with the rootlets half way around, then all around and growing together at all points, and finally as a great hollow tree eight to ten feet in diameter.

In the middle of the bush is a hostelry, where we stop for a change of horses and our invariable roast mutton. I took the opportunity to hunt the jungle for ferns and mosses. It is perfectly safe in New Zealand to ramble anywhere, if only one does not lose his way; for there is not a snake nor a reptile nor a harmful animal there, nor a poisonous plant except the Toot berry, and the natives make their strong drink out of that.

But you will think this is a long journey, as long in telling as in doing. However we did finally get out of the woods, and come in sight of the first of the beautiful and romantic lakes that are scattered through this whole region. The first is Rotoiti; then soon after we came upon Rotorua, and saw, away around on the other side, the little native village of Ohinemutu, to which we were bound. We arrived about five o'clock, and stopped at a very comfortable hotel called the Lake House. There is another and intensely rival establishment there. Two white men, a Scotchman by the name of Graham, and an Irishman of the name of Kelly, who hadn't room in all the world to fight it out elsewhere, have come up here and built two rival hotels, on lands leased from semi-savages, and on a crust overhanging an active volcano. The bitterest competition prevails between them. They run independent stages, have runners on all the route, and get pamphlets published to put each other down. It is really the most home-like thing in all this aboriginal country.

After supper we went down among the native huts and hot springs. Everywhere there were ponds and pools of hot water, streams and brooks of hot water, springs innumerable that were bubbling and boiling with hot water. From every crevice and upturned stone the steam was issuing. Some women were putting little bags of potatoes in the steam fumeroles for cooking. One was covering up a pannikin of bread-dough in an underground oven. A lot of men were chattering away, seated on flat stones that were warmed by subterranean steam. One woman was taking a late bath in a hot pool, and some boys and girls were jumping and splashing in a pond that we could hardly bear a hand in. One had to be very careful to follow the paths, or the first he knew he would be in hot water himself. One feels that he is walking on a slender crust that overarches gulfs of seething and boiling waters; while the "putrid stench of sulphur," as Anthony Trollope called it, reminds one that he is a little nearer Tartarus than sinful mortals care to be.

The next morning I took a walk in another direction, down by the carved house, meeting house, or Runanga as they call it. Here was a lively settlement of the natives. As I passed along the old women and the boys and girls continually asked me for matches. The matches of the colonies are little cotton wicks, coated with hard tallow. Well, I gave them all the matches I had; and when I had no more to give, I handed them out small money to buy them with; all the time wondering what they could possibly want of matches, where they never thought of lighting a fire. But down in front of the carved house I saw a bevy of little girls throwing a kind of home-made dice, and wax matches were what the little gamblers lost or won. Here was another little feature of foreign society that carried me back to my own loved home, where other people's fortunes are taken and played with, as these little tawny skins played my wax matches.

A little beyond this settlement, on a point of land extending out into lake Rotorua, is where the natives bury their dead. No sooner are the bodies put under the ground, than they are acted upon and rapidly eaten up by the alkaline impregnations of the subsoil. Where this point now is, there was, a few years ago, the extended site of a regular fortified Pah or village. But one day the greater part of it sank bodily into the lake; and now only the tops of the carved posts that were in the palisades are visible above the waters. I did think when I sat down to contemplate in this tombless corpseless graveyard, that earthly things were transitory and unstable.

In the afternoon we again took the stage for Wairoa, twelve miles further on. This is another Maori village, with only one hotel and one white man. Here the natives fairly swarmed. They came and sat on the ground in front of the hotel, and straggled through it as if they owned it. The women brought out their pappooses strapped to boards; the men brought out their best blankets or old coats. We seemed to be in the midst of a regular Indian pow-wow. In fact these Maoris reminded me continually of the North American Indians—as we used to see them here in New York, before the spirit of manhood was all crushed out of them.

These tribes, the Arawas, own all this geyser country, and they will not give it up, nor sell it, nor submit to any interference from the English government. They have been so jealous of their possessions that it is only within a very few years that they have allowed any strangers to come in except by special permission from the chiefs.

In the evening we engaged a select party of the natives to give us the great national dance, the Haka, in the meeting house. In the middle, a row of sticks driven into the ground answered the purpose of candle-sticks. On one side was a crowd of natives, of every age, condition and sex, seated or sprawling over the ground, all smoking dirty pipes, with half a dozen disgusted whites wedged in among them. While on the other side was a row of twenty girls in front, with as many young fellows behind them, all in the scantiest apparel, and all attempting to go through the same contortions and howlings as a leader, who strode up and down before them, shouting and gesticulating with all his might. It was a wild and savage orgy. The horrid hissings and ejaculations, the uncouth gestures and distorted faces, the barbarous antics and unnatural contortions of the body, were fit only for a pandemonium. They kept it up for two hours, at one time the women in front, at another the men; during which time we had to furnish two pails of beer, and sundry bottles of a stronger beverage. These liquors and their little fee of half a dollar a head were the *sine qua non* of the performance. But they gave us the worth of our money in good, honest diabolism. They worked like mad, and gave us such an idea of heathen rage as never could be got elsewhere. The thing as we witnessed it was in a measure orderly and decent; but when the tribes have their great meetings, and the excitement becomes contagious, the Haka degenerates into the wildest debauch and saturnalia.

The next morning early we were off for the terraces, the grand object of all these excursions. Kate, an interesting and very fair looking native, or rather half-caste, was our guide. When the Arawas finally made up their minds to make some money out of their unique possessions, they found that they had no one who could speak English. A real full-blooded native never could learn a foreign language. All business and teaching and books, with both the Maoris and Kanakas (Sandwich Islanders), have to be in their own language. So Kate, and another one, Sophie, both half whites, who had partly mastered the hard language, were imported from another tribe. They both claimed to be of chieftain blood, and were stout enough to make good their pretentions to rank and respect from both whites and browns.

We first had a walk from Wairoa of about a mile through the bush and down a steep hill to the foot of lake Tarawera. There we took a large whale-boat with six native oarsmen, and were rowed eight miles to the head of the lake. The country about lake Tarawera is the most beautiful example of romantic and varying scenery that I have ever seen. The blending of barren volcanic peaks and verdure covered hills, the dark green forest ranges, the isolated clumps of giant Totara pines, the Pohutukawa trees, one part of a tree bright green, and the other part all scarlet blossoms, the rocky shores drooping with immense fern clusters, and the lifeless and gloomy silence that brooded over the whole scene, made this lake-ride one ever to be remembered by each one of us.

The boatmen sang or rather chanted their wild and rhythmical songs in unison with their rowing; sometimes gently, and again with a savage impulse that would send the boat aflying. This is one of the refrains that came in most frequently:

"Waka tana, Kea wheta, Haka *tu—u*."

And the boat would fairly leap under the emphasis of the last word. Our boatmen, like many of the Maoris, were great improvisers. Some one of them would give each of us in turn some native name; and then you would hear that name come out in his song with some other lingo that made them all roar with laughter. It was very evident their remarks were personal, and probably not very complimentary. It is rather a ticklish sensation, I assure you, to hear one's self described in an unknown tongue, by a parcel of savages who knew, or had often heard their fathers tell, of the different flavors of the different breeds of Englishmen.

At the head of lake Tarawera we land at the mouth of the outlet creek that connects lake Rotomahana with this lake. A canoe is paddled up this creek with the luggage, but most of us prefer to walk about a mile through the bush to lake Rotomahana. This celebrated lake with its surroundings is undoubtedly the greatest natural curiosity in the world. Here is a body of water a mile long, set in among mountains, out of the sides of which on every hand are continually pouring innumerable mineral and boiling springs of every variety and shade of impregnation—silica, sulphur, iron, lime, magnesia, soda, potash, everything but pure water. In some places the springs are building up immense deposits and incrustations; in others they are dissolving and crumbling down the solid mountains. No living thing exists in the lake, and but a scanty vegetation in its vicinity. Its waters are hot in all parts, and in places, over sunken springs, very nearly boiling. As we were paddled over these heated and fetid waters in a rolling log canoe, we called to mind the fabled Stygian lake, and wondered if Rotomahana would not have made a more impassable barrier on the borders of Erebus.

We came upon this remarkable region just at the foot of the White Terraces, "Te Tarata," "The Tattooed" as the natives call them. They are composed of a series of huge semi-circular steps, rising one back of another until they have reached up the mountain side to a height of nearly one hundred feet. The material is a silicious sinter, deposited from surcharged hot waters, and forming the purest white and most beautiful incrustations. As these chemical solutions are destructive to shoes, we climb the steps in stocking-feet. The water that trickles over them grows hotter and hotter as we ascend until we can no longer bear it, and have to hasten out to the sides. Arrived at the top, if the wind is blowing the steam away from us, we can stand on the brink of the huge caldron of boiling and spouting waters. The chasm is a hundred feet across, and in the midst of the clouds of steam we can occasionally see great columns of water thrown up fifteen to twenty feet high. The color of the water that we can see is an intense brilliant blue, even tinging the steam clouds above it the same blue color.

The fountain of the White Terraces is a true intermittent geyser. The basin is often completely emptied by an explosive effort that throws the contents to a height of forty feet, inundating everything about it with scalding waters. It however ordinarily rapidly fills up again. But the natives say that when the winds blow strong in a certain direction, the water recedes entirely from the fountain, and they can look down into it as into a deep crater. This is certainly a very singular and inexplicable phenomenon. I would hardly have believed it if I had not the evidence of a photograph of the terraces with the water nearly all drained out of the step-basins.

Very hot water will take up and hold considerable quantities of silica in solution; but as it cools it loses that power, and consequently must leave it deposited. It is owing to this fact that these remarkable terraces have been built up on this grand scale and after the thousands of years that this silicated spring has been pouring out its volumes of water. The pools of hot water that are found in most of the steps, being continually fed with hotter water from above, will not of course grow colder, and consequently will not deposit silicious matter on the bottom or sides. Therefore the basins never decrease in depth or size. But the little outlet streams that trickle over the edge of each basin are constantly cooling and depositing silicates. Thus they are all the time slowly building up the edges, and adding to the exquisitely beautiful structure of the frontal portions or walls. These are like cave formations, and have the appearance of the clearest alabaster, worked into cornices upheld by fretted stalactites. If these terraces had been carved out of the purest chalcedony, they could not have been whiter or more graceful. It is as if an immense and foaming cataract, in tumbling down the mountain side, had suddenly been transformed into Parian marble.

When we came down from the terraces to the lake, we found our canoe there, with the provisions, and we sat down by some hot springs to have our lunch. Besides some things from the hotel, we had raw potatoes and a bag of cray-fish, which had been bought of some natives on our way up. The cray-fish, as you know, is a small fresh water lobster about as large as one's thumb. These with the potatoes were cooked in the steam crevices, and proved to be exceedingly nice eating. All took a fancy that day to native dishes.

After lunch we climbed by a ravine up to the Devil's Hole, a steam vent roaring with the noise of twenty engines. Then we were taken to a wide flat basin among the hills, where apparently some considerable mountain had been dissolved away by the chemical waters, leaving a crust which, by the care that Kate took of us, seemed to be rather dangerous footing. Here were great numbers of mud springs, or little cones of viscous clay, through which hot gases were sputtering. From one of these every native that passes will eat a good round handful. I tried it and found it rather tasteless, but still very clean and eatable for mud.

In the same depression are sundry little lakes and pools of most disgusting and fetid waters—thick, green, greasy, and of execrable taste. We made up our minds that if the Devil lived about here, as Kate said he did, this must be one of his summer watering places—his Saratoga, or his Wiesbaden.

After this we visited, one after another in almost tiresome succession, geysers, foaming wells, and intermitting springs; some throwing great columns of water 30 and 40 feet high, others dashing their boiling waters about their basins as if possessed by a demon. It was frightful to witness the play of such mighty forces, and then to think that all this was only the last expiring manifestation of the tremendous volcanic agencies which once tossed and tilted this rugged island.

Leaving this side of the lake, we all got into the log canoe, twelve of us dark and white, and were paddled across to the Pink Terraces. Some think these are even more beautiful than the White Terraces. There is the same enormous fountain of silicated waters, and at about the same elevation above the lake. The overflow has not spread over as much territory, or pushed its marble pavement as far into the lake. But there is in the Pink Terraces more regularity in the great semi-circular steps, while the embossed sculpture of the frontal walls is tinged with a delicate and variegated pink. They are both, the White and the Pink, among the most exquisite creations in nature. But to decide between them is like the award of beauty among the goddesses; no mortal man could give it and have any more peace in life.

Our guide, Kate, had reserved for the last halting place of our trip, the unsurpassed luxury of a bath in a perfectly extravagant supply of deliciously warm and medicated waters. The basins of the higher steps of the Pink Terraces are spacious swimming pools having a depth of four or five feet. The water is delightfully soft, and of course can be chosen of any desired temperature. It is of an indescribable blue tint, making objects immersed in it glisten like burnished silver. The basins appear as if they had been sculptured out of gorgeously tinted carnelian, and overarched by cornices of mingled rubies and chalcedony. No such baths ever existed elsewhere, outside of oriental pictures. Here we all undressed and scrambled into the water, light and dark together; such a salt and pepper group as would have seasoned the richest painting that ever yet was put on canvas.

There is no place in any country where the thermal baths are quite as enjoyable as in New Zealand. The great abundance of the hot waters, and their exceeding softness as well as variety of mineral constituents, make them a constant delight and invigoration. They are the attractions of hotels and health resorts throughout a large extent of the country; and they are assiduously advertised for this and that ailment of suffering humanity. I however knew of them only as luxuries.

This is the end of our excursion in one direction, and I will not trouble you to return with me, nor to follow me later in circumnavigating the islands. After giving short accounts of a few noteworthy things that attract a stranger's curiosity in these distant lands, I will ask you to stop with me at a few of the prominent cities and scenery resorts. But my descriptions will be brief, and I hope your patience will bear with me to the end.

A very singular native bird was one day pointed out to me, the kea, of the parrot tribe. It has a large head with a muscular neck and a very strong beak, which it formerly used only in digging up roots for a livelihood. But after sheep were introduced on the islands, it got a taste, probably at the offal yards, of the kidney fat of this much slaughtered animal. Then apparently, as the supply was not quite regular enough to suit his parrotship, he commenced to take sly observations of the way in which the regular butchers opened up this delicious morsel; and he soon made up his mind that he could carve mutton as well as another. So now he alights on the back of a sheep, tangles his claws in the wool, and during a tearing ride to which he is then treated, he digs into the flesh with his powerful beak, until the poor bleeding victim falls exhausted and dying. But the cruel bird reaches his dainty delicacy, and the crows get the benefit of the rest of the feast. The kea has become an intolerable nuisance to sheep-raisers, and very considerable rewards are offered for his little kit of tools.

It is perfectly surprising to see how foreign weeds and brambles, that have been introduced into this country, have multiplied and overrun everything. The English gorse, or furze-bush, that in its native islands is a very well behaved bramble, when taken to New Zealand for a hedge-plant, soon overleaped all bounds, and now has to be fought with fire and sword. I saw whole fields given up to it, perfectly impenetrable tangles. The little

Plate XIX. HOT BATH BASINS IN PINK TERRACES, NEW ZEALAND. See Page xx.

water-cress of our streams was taken there and planted in the colonial streams. It forthwith grew into such luxuriant masses that it actually choked up the water courses, and some streams that I saw had been obliged to leave their native beds and seek other outlets. The dandelion and the dock, so innocuous with us, are there rampaging weeds, that take everything to themselves. The Scotch thistle, a national emblem at home, is there a national curse. The outlook in many cultivated districts reminded me of the disheartening prospect which must have opened out before our unfortunate ancestor, late of the Garden of Eden, when he saw the ground that had been cursed for his sake. "In sorrow shalt thou eat of it all the days of thy life. Thorns and thistles shall it bring forth unto thee."

Of the national bearing of the rabbit plague I will have somewhat to say later. But in climbing Ben Lomond from Queenstown on lake Wakatipu, I saw such astonishing numbers of these little brown pests, that I cannot resist telling something more about them here. The people informed me that four years before, there was not a rabbit there; yet now they overrun the whole country. They were scampering away before me all the way up that climb of 6,000 feet; and I left some figures on the rocks up there in geometrical progression and the laws of Malthus. Great quantities of these animals are dressed and canned in the colonies. Rabbit pie was one of the tiresome dishes on the long home voyage. At some of the sheep ranches the would-be scientists of another hemisphere have repeated the German Professor Koch's experiments on rabbits. They have caught some, inoculated them with tubercular consumption, and then let them go. In the close underground life they lead, this disease is communicated from one to another until they die off by thousands. Since returning home I have seen an account of the shipment of some hundreds of weasels to New Zealand as an antidote for rabbits. This is nature's means of killing off a too prolific race; and whether it is or not, it seems to me infinitely more merciful than dosing them with tuberculosis, and making them die off in such an inhumanly human manner.

I shall never forget the long watchings I have devoted to the great "wandering albatrosses" off the southern coast of New Zealand. They are the largest birds that fly, and live only on the stormy extremes of the Pacific. Their wings are extended in flight from twelve to fifteen feet. There is one preserved in the British Museum with eighteen feet of outstretched wings. I have watched them for hours when the wind was high, without once observing a motion of the wings that appeared to be made to aid them in flight. They seemed to ride on their expanded wings as if it were their simple will alone that buoyed them up; now sailing down the wind with a magnificent sweep, then turning with increased momentum and mounting in the face of the gale.

Ever since the time of Solomon, "the ways of a bird in the air" have been one of the things that have seemed to be past understanding. But after observing how often these master navigators were obliged to trim their sails and scud off on a side wind, as the sailors would say, I began to think I had some little insight to their tactics. It is well known that an ice yacht, sailing with the wind nearly abeam, can be made to go many times faster than the wind is blowing. So a sail boat can always make better speed with a side wind than with a stern wind. The reason is that with a side wind the full force of it is pressing against the sails all the time, no matter how fast the boat goes; whereas, with an aft wind, the boat is going along with it, and by just so much the force of the wind against the sails is lessened. Like the sail-crowded ice boat then, these great birds spread their enormous wings to as much of a side wind as their steering gear can hold them to, and when they have attained a speed that is faster than the wind, they turn to face the blast, and rise to it as if they mocked its fury. They are the most perfect of sailors, the most storm-daring of sea-birds, and to me the most absorbing study of the ocean.

In the museum of Dunedin, among the specimens of the great albatrosses, there is an unfledged young one, said to be ten months old. It is absolutely larger than the old birds, and looks like a huge mass of unsorted down. It is a fact that the young of both the albatross and the penguin are fed so long and kept so fat by the parent birds that they grow to an enormous size, and will not attempt to shift for themselves until they are deserted by the old ones and actually starved into flight and seeking their own food.

At Wellington, a city of 20,000 inhabitants, situated on Cook's Strait which divides New Zealand about in the middle, are located the Parliament and Government House, said to be the largest wooden building in the world. In this city resides the Governor, who is usually some titled Englishman; and the finest mansion in the land is built and provided for his use.

But that which interested me most in Wellington was its well kept and most entertaining museum. Its specialties are Maori curiosities; and chief among them is a Carved House, or Runanga, the most perfect one ever constructed by the natives. It was bought for $500, and has been removed and set up here entire. Its carvings, which literally cover all parts, ceilings, sides and front, are exceedingly elaborate, and a marvel of skill and perseverance, considering that they were all executed with stone implements. Each plank took a tree to make it, and the flint axes are shown that hewed and carved it out. The figures of the carving are elegant traceries and embossings, interspersed with hideous images, like Japanese idols, with wide open mouths and three cleft tongues protruding, which the Maoris will tell you represent their ancestors. Of their and our Darwinian theories, I think I prefer the monkey forefathers.

Within the Carved House are innumerable trophies of the art and workmanship of the natives; the *meré*, or killing weapon, a double-edged cleaver worked out of greenstone, the toughest of all rare minerals; ear pendants and other ornaments, made of this same hard stone; elaborately carved prows of their great war canoes; mats and robes of feathers; cloths and blankets made from the native flax-plant; and a thousand other things showing the great ingenuity of this remarkable people.

Christ Church, half way down the east coast of South Island, is an interesting city of 30,000 inhabitants. It is called the City of the Plains, and is the only one in the islands built on level lands. Here are magnificent parks; Hagley Park on the Avon, containing 400 acres, and the Government Domain, of 80 acres, laid out in walks and in drives and as a botanic garden, with every variety of tree and shrub and plant and flower that will grow in a semi-tropical climate. It is really a delightful spot. What astonishes the American visitor in these far off cities, is the great amount of care and cost and labor that have been expended on public and scientific resorts. In every city that he may visit he finds delightful parks, instructive botanic gardens, and well furnished museums. This little city of Christ Church, away on the outer borders of the world, in these respects would put to shame any city of our own land of ten times its population.

The museum here is the finest and best kept of any in the colonies. What interested me particularly in this splendid collection was the group of moa skeletons. The moas were wingless birds that stood twelve feet high, and probably weighed as much as a horse. There are fifteen perfect skeletons here, belonging to half a dozen different species.

Two or three centuries ago these giant birds were numerous all over New Zealand. They lived on the roots of the fern-brake, the *Pteris esculenta*, which they dug up with their powerful feet and claws. The natives captured them by driving them down to some large water course or lake, where, as the birds could not swim and were afraid of the water, they were mercilessly destroyed with the stone pointed lances. No wonder the clumsy and defenseless moas did not last long under such easy and destructive pursuit. And no wonder, when this the only game of the islands was wasted and gone, the hungry savages began to raid upon each other, and to devour the bodies of their captives. Hunger has made wild beasts of far better men than these poor castaways.

I am sorry that I do not have time to stop with you at the interesting Scotch city of Dunedin, a lesser Edinburgh, and the largest city in the islands; nor to take you with me into the grand and stupendous mountain scenery of the southern interior, where are ranges and peaks and mountain lakes that outvie anything seen in Switzerland or in any other scenery resort.

On the south-western coast are numerous sounds or inlets of the sea, like the fiords of Norway, only that they are on a far grander scale than their northern competitors. We entered them from the ocean through narrow gateways between almost perpendicular ledges that towered to six and seven thousand feet. Within are broad and deep basins, without an anchorage or a shelving shore, and in which we see only snow-capped peaks, and water falls that leap out into the air and end in clouds of spray. For wildness and grandeur there is no scenery like this in the known world.

One day on my travels by the slow and tedious colonial railways, I was left over night at Invercargill, the extremest southern city of South Island, as far in the southern latitudes as St. Johns in Newfoundland is in the northern. I will ask you for the last time to listen to a short description from my diary during this visit.

Last evening I sat at my window admiring the southern constellations. The most conspicuous object was the Cross, composed of four brilliant stars set in the brightest part of the Milky Way. At this hour it was lying flat, away up in the heavens, only half risen and pointing horizontally to the South Pole, about as far from it as the Dipper is from the North Pole. Two first magnitude stars a little below, alpha and beta Centauri, and called the pointers of the Cross, are interesting as being, one the nearest, and the other the third nearest stars to us in all the heavens, respectively twenty and forty million million miles away. Overhead was the "false cross," and still another cross in Argo. In the dark vacancy where the South Pole is located, for there are absolutely no stars in the vicinity of this Pole, are two little white clouds, like small patches of the Milky Way that had strayed off and got lost, called the Clouds of Magellan. Just under the Southern Cross and near the foot star, is a black space where the telescope reveals not a star nor a nebular haze. The sailors call it the "Devil's tar pot."

I was up in the night and sat again at my window, the bright stars and clear night-air keeping me from sleep. The Southern Cross had climbed to its zenith, almost directly overhead, and was now pointing down, or rather was standing in the natural position of a cross. The stars are not so numerous in the southern heavens as elsewhere, but they are certainly more conspicuous and interesting, perhaps from the striking contrasts that are found in the vicinity of the South Pole. The Milky Way is here the brightest, and the dark vacancies are in deeper shadow and contrast than in any other portion of the heavens.

This morning when I waked, the wind was blowing a gale from the south, with a cold and miserable rain. I was told by some persons, who however did not live about here and perhaps were prejudiced, that this was just a sample of the summer weather of southern New Zealand. And I thought that none but Scotchmen, who never knew what a decent climate was, would ever have found and settled up such a mountainous bleak and unpromising country as this.

And now what shall I say of New Zealand as one of the nations of the earth? It is a country that tourists delight in and always will. It has the most remarkable natural wonders and the finest scenery in the world. Its cities furnish unending attractions to visitors. It has many noble and generous citizens, as I know, who have experienced their kindness. But I am obliged to say, though reluctantly, that it is not the prosperous and promising country that I hoped to find. Agriculture is not a success; for although the yield of wheat, their only commercial cereal, is often immense, sometimes eighty bushels to the acre, yet the uncertainties of the weather in a moist and insular climate, in both seed time and harvest, makes as many bad years as good; and the distance from the markets of the world makes sad inroads in the final returns. Sheep-raising is not a success; for the rabbits that in an unlucky day were imported there without their natural enemies, have so multiplied and overrun the whole country, that grazing animals can no longer find a living when running at large. I passed over ranches on which they told me, one sheep could not now live, where formerly ten found abundant pasture. The gold and silver mines are exhausted. No coal of any value has been found. The government has spent all the money it could raise on splendid public buildings and improvements, and on rail roads that do not pay expenses. Complaint is loud in the land that taxes are high,—have nearly passed the point of endurance. And still the government is borrowing, and spending the money on profitless enterprises. A loan was placed in London at four per cent while I was in the Colony, and great was the rejoicing because it was taken at a small premium above par. The banks are loaning money at twelve to fifteen per cent on all kinds of real and chattel securities, are declaring large dividends, and building magnificent banking houses in all the cities. But outside of these, both city and country are already dotted with dead and non-paying enterprises.

Now it does not take much of a business eye to see in all this the elements of a collapse. Sooner or later the time will come when the government will be able to borrow no more—when the banks will be called to account for the money they have borrowed and scattered, and then will find themselves loaded down with depreciated and unsalable properties. It is the fate of men and nations that live by borrowing to end in disaster. I am fearful and sorry to think that hard times are in the future for this lovely and interesting land. But however unfortunate it may be in national affairs, it will always be rich in natural scenery and abounding in all that delights the tourist and the lover of nature.

THE SCIENCE OF RELIGION.

The latest born of all the sciences is that of Religion. It is a peculiar outgrowth of modern thought. It has arisen because of the prevalence of free opinions and unrestricted inquiry, and not in any manner from a spirit of irreverence or atheism. The time has now fully come when every man must be able to give a reason for the faith that is in him. If the religion which we profess is better and truer than those which have gone before it, we must be able to tell how and wherein it is so.

There has arisen in these latter days a Comparative Theology, corresponding to the old science of Comparative Anatomy. This last has brought out the points of excellence and adaptation which the human form has developed out of that of its old time progenitors. The other will bring to light the excellence of the Christian system as compared with the lowlier religions which preceded it. In no other way than by the searching criticism and comparison of this new science can the true Faith be made to stand out prominent among the similar beliefs which anteceded and heralded its coming. The published volume of the lectures of Max Müller on the Science of Religion is a work which redounds more to the credit of the Christian Faith than all the labored treatises on Evidence, Church History and Exigesis.

The late Wm. Whewell, a distinguished historian of science, has demonstrated that all scientific discoveries and great advances have had their preludes, their antecedent periods, in which the thoughts of philosophers were concentrating on those subjects and the lights of knowledge were gathering to the focus of those final disclosures. If I am not mistaken there was the same prelude to that which was new and peculiar in the Christian Religion, antecedent periods when the vain philosophy of the old world was struggling to the formulation of that grand truth of the immortality of the soul, and when other nations outside of Judea began to perceive the necessity of interposing a Mediator, a Divine Redeemer, between man and the Infinite God.

It has always been a subject of wonder and astonishment, and often a weapon of attack with unbelievers, that the Christian system was brought out at so late a period of the world's progress. If this scheme was devised for, and was the only means of, the salvation of men from the most awful penalty that could possibly be imagined, then surely there were peoples and races of the older times who at least equally merited and could have appreciated its provisions and benefits. It would be sad, even humiliating to think that all the refined and cultivated nations of antiquity had no part nor lot in the great plan of salvation merely because they happened to antedate the Christian era. Rather than entertain so injurious and narrow-minded a conclusion, it would be far better, so it seems to me, to enlarge the bounds, to throw down the bars, that restrict the efficacy of Faith, and to hold that a devout and earnest belief in whatever of the eternal truths of God and of nature had been in any manner made known to a people, would relieve them from the "Condemnation of the Law."

The Christian very appropriately cherishes the expectation of meeting the Hebrew Patriarchs in the Heaven to which he aspires. Yet certainly these worthies knew not Christ, either symbolically or prophetically; for the symbols or prophecies which are claimed to indicate a coming Saviour for Israel did not happen and were not written until many hundred years after their time. Besides they had no hope nor knowledge of a future life; for this tenet had no place in the Jewish theology. The rewards and punishments of the Mosaic Dispensation were wholly temporal.* The New Testament expressly claims that

---

* The learned and pious Bishop Whately writes in his Dissertation on Christianity (Enc. Brit., vol. I, p. 473, 8th Ed.): "The nation of Israel was, as we have said, placed under an extraordinary providence, which allotted to them victory or defeat,—plenty or famine,—and other temporal blessings and punishments, according to their conduct. And these were the rewards and punishments that formed the sanction of the Mosaic Law. As for a future state of retribution in another world, Moses said nothing to the Israelites about that. * * This was reserved for a *greater* than Moses, and for a more glorious dispensation than his Law."

"Christ came to bring Life and Immortality to light." But it also most beautifully and touchingly says, "And Abraham believed God, and it was counted unto him for Righteousness." The simple faith of these righteous men in the one God who ruled over the House of Israel is justly held to be their passport to glories they did not anticipate or dream of in their day.

A thousand years before the time of Abraham the Hindoos worshiped the one god Brahma as "Him who had existed from all eternity, infinitely wise, infinitely benign, and infinitely powerful." Shall this highest and purest faith of all the ancient systems be accounted to them for nothing in the great and final reckoning? All the cultivated nations of antiquity except the Jews recognized the doctrine of the immortality of the soul. And very many upright men among them, as we know from the classical studies of our school days, sought the reward of an everlasting life of happiness in the worship of the gods they believed in and in the practice of virtue and good works. Shall their faith and efforts, feeble it may be, but corresponding to the light that was in them, go for naught in the great and final Day of the Lord?

I think we may proceed to search out the antecedents of Christianity and to gather together whatever there was of good and Scripture-like in the religions of the olden times, not only without fear of injuring the cause of the true Faith, but with the conviction that the more the similitudes and the clearer the foreshadowings that we may find, the more will the Christian Religion be relieved from the great and radical objection so often urged against it, that it came only within the last one-third of the world's historic age, and has not been made known to one in thousands of those who have lived.

Scattered here and there among the crudities and abstruse speculations which the ancient philosophers, such as Pythagoras, Aristotle and Socrates, have sent down to us, there are to be found a great many precepts and doctrines that read very much like many things we have been accustomed to think were first written in the manuscript of the New Testament. In order to show this I will make a few selections from the writings and the accounts we have of the Greek philosopher Plato, who was born 429 years before Christ. He lived 80 years a life of celibacy and of such pure and exemplary conduct that his memory was held in saintly regard. He received divine honors after his death, and there was accorded to him the somewhat common ascription of hero-worship, that of having been born of a virgin, (authority of Plutarch and Hieronimus). His writings that have come down to us are very numerous and almost altogether in Dialogue, so that it is difficult to ascertain just what Plato believed; but we are not so much concerned with his belief as with the great principles and ideas which he originated or first promulgated. It is sufficient for us to know that in writings, the finish and fascination of which have made them a cherished study in all ages, he has set forth the clearest and grandest conceptions of the one supreme and omniscient God that have ever been incorporated in any uninspired religion.

According to Plato, "God is the Supreme Intelligence, incorporeal, without beginning, end or change, and capable of being perceived only by the mind." But as a being of such exalted state and majesty as he conceived the great First Cause to be, could not consistently be himself a worker in the affairs of the world and of men, Plato inculcated the belief in two other gods, emanations from and parts of the great Supreme God, a Trinity, three gods in one. The second person was the Divine Reason, the acting principle which established the order of the world. He called this the Logos, the word of God, the second person in the Godhead. The third emanation was the soul of the universe, a subordinate nature compounded of intelligence and matter. In the language of Plato, "The universe being animated by a soul that proceeds from God, is the Son of God."

Plato was so unorthodox as to believe in the eternity of matter. In common with all other ancient philosophers he held to the axiom that from nothing nothing can proceed. Consequently he could not do otherwise than regard matter as eternally existing. But its primeval condition was "without form;" and creation consisted in bringing order out of this chaos. Matter he regarded as resisting the will of the Supreme Being, so that he cannot perfectly execute his designs. Hence the mixture of good and evil which is found in the material world.

Plato taught in express terms the doctrine of the immortality of the soul; that the soul of man is derived by emanation from God, but that this emanation was not immediate but through the intervention of the soul of the world, that is the Son of God; that the soul is a simple indivisible substance, and therefore incapable of dissolution or corruption; that the objects to which it naturally adheres are spiritual and incorruptible, therefore its nature is so.

Virtue Plato defined to be the imitation of God, or the effort of man to attain to a resemblance to his original. "True virtue is really and in effect a purification from all worldly passions." "Whosoever enters the other world without being initiated and purified shall be hurled headlong into the vast abyss; but whoever arrives there after due purgation and expiation shall be lodged in the apartments of the gods." "The soul of man carries nothing along with it out of this world but its good or bad actions, its virtues or its vices, which are the cause of its eternal happiness or misery." "It is said that after the death of every individual person, the spirit or genius that was partner with it and conducted it during life, leads it to a certain place where all the dead are obliged to appear in order to be judged, and from thence are conducted by a guide to the world below. When it arrives at that fatal rendezvous of all souls, if it has been guilty of any impurity, or polluted with murder, or has committed any of those atrocious crimes that desperate and lost souls are commonly guilty of, it is abhorred and avoided by all other souls, and wanders without guides in fearful solitudes and horrible deserts. Whereas the temperate and pure soul has the gods themselves for its guides and conductors, and goes to cohabit with them in the mansions of pleasure prepared for it."

Such extracts from the translations of the Dialogues of Plato might be made almost *ad infinitum*. But enough are already given to show that this old philosopher had very advanced ideas of the divine attributes and man's duty and destiny. It would be hard to condemn to everlasting punishment those of the ancients who ruled their conduct and belief on the high standard of Plato's precepts and theology.

The very old religion of Brahma in southern Asia has been studied and its sacred books translated by such eminent oriental scholars as Capt. Francis Wilford, Sir Wm. Jones and Dr. Francis Buchanan; and their accounts and discoveries have been published in the volumes of the English magazine entitled "Asiatic Researches." In my search for antecedents of Christianity in the ancient system of the Brahmans, I shall make no claims or quotations that cannot be verified in the writings of the authorities I have named.

The oldest sacred books of India, the Vedas, claim an antiquity of at least 3,000 years prior to the Christian era; and as they contain records of astronomical observations dating as far back as that, which the distinguished astronomer Bailly and mathematician Playfair say could only have been taken by actual observation at the time, it is considered that the claims of Indian sacred literature to that great age are well founded. In those oldest books that ever were written is told the story of the disobedience and fall of the first human pair under the names of Adima and Héva. In their despair at being shut out from the island paradise in which they were created, they fall down and pray to Brahma for pardon. "And as they thus spoke there came a voice from the clouds, saying: I pardon you, but you may no more return to the abode of delight which I had created for your happiness. Through your disobedience to my commands the spirit of evil has obtained possession of the earth. Your children, reduced to labor and to suffer through your fault, will become corrupt and forget me. But I will send Vishnu, who shall incarnate himself in the womb of a woman, and shall bring to all the hope and the means of recompense in another life, in praying to me to soften their ills." This Redeemer thus promised was the god Chrishna whom Brahmans and Buddhists worship as the divine messenger or mediator from the Deity to mankind. Of this god the learned and pious Sir Wm. Jones writes: *

---

* Works of Sir Wm. Jones. London, 1799. Vol. I, p. 265, et seq.

"That the name of Chrishna and the general outline of his story were long anterior to the birth of our Saviour, and probably to the time of Homer, we know very certainly." " The Buddhists (a sect established one thousand years before Christ) claim that his incarnation in the womb of a virgin was foretold several thousand years before it came to pass." " In the Sanscrit Dictionary, which was compiled more than two thousand years ago, we have the whole story of the incarnate Deity born of a virgin and miraculously escaping in his infancy from the reigning tyrant of his country." " His birth was concealed through fear of the tyrant Cansa, to whom it had been predicted that one born at that time and of the royal line of Devaci would destroy him. At the time of his birth the tyrant ordered all new born males to be slain; yet this wonderful babe was preserved by biting the breast instead of sucking the poisoned nipple of a nurse commissioned in this way to kill him." " He passed a life of a most extraordinary and incomprehensible nature. He saved multitudes partly by his arms, and partly by his miraculous powers. He raised the dead by descending for that purpose to the lowest regions. He was the meekest and best tempered of beings. He washed the feet of the Brahmans and preached very nobly and sublimely." " One sect of Hindoos hold that Chrishna was distinct from all other avatars (divine messengers) and that he was the person of Vishnu (God) himself in human form." " Chrishna is the last avatara, or manifestation of the Deity, who according to their sacred books will reappear a little before the general dissolution of the world."

Capt. Francis Wilford says (Asiatic Researches, vol. 10), "that long before Christ a renovation of the universe was expected all over the world, with a Saviour, a king of peace and justice. This expectation is frequently mentioned in the Puranas. Vishnu comforts the earth, his consort, and assures mankind that a Saviour would come to redress their grievances and put an end to the tyranny of demons, that he would be incarnated in the body of a shepherd and be born of a virgin. The Brahminical books declare that these prophecies were fulfilled in the person of Chrishna; and they relate that a miraculous star directed the holy men who were living in anxious expectation of him, where to find this heavenly child, and that the Emperor of India, uneasy at the prophecies which he conceived portended his ruin, sent emissaries to inquire whether such a child was really born, in order to destroy him."

Salivahana, another of the avatars or gods born of women, or else the same as Chrishna under a different name, is thus described in one of the Puranas: "Great and mighty, the spirit of righteousness and justice, whose words are truth itself, free from spite and envy, and whose empire will extend all over the world and the people will be gathered unto him, the conveyor of souls to places of eternal bliss. He was the son of a carpenter. His conception was miraculous and in the womb of a virgin, and he was the son of the Great Artist. His birth was equally wonderful; choirs of angels with the celestial minstrelsy attended on the occasion. The king of the country hearing of these prodigies was alarmed and sought in vain to destroy him. He soon surpassed his teachers; and when five years of age he stood before a most respectable assembly of the doctors of the land and explained several difficult cases, to their admiration and astonishment." "It was decreed that he should be wretched and persecuted all his life-time, and ultimately that he should die upon a cross, and that he would be brought to life again. He did not marry nor had he any offspring." "He proclaimed that he came for the sole purpose of relieving the distressed, and that whatever man claimed his protection he would readily grant it to him and even lay down his life for him. Very many of all descriptions came accordingly, and among them a thief who being pursued by the officers of justice claimed his protection, which he readily granted, and he was really crucified in his stead. He then ascended into heaven and took the thief along with him. Thick darkness overspread the face of the world, and the animated creation was in the utmost distress and consternation. The holy man being afterward taken down from the cross, descended into hell and there encountered and overcame death or Yama. Then a general renovation of the world took place under the inspection of Brahma." (Capt. Wilford. Asiatic Researches. Vol. 10.)

The four Vedas of the Brahmans, which without doubt were written before the Biblical date of the Flood, inculcate the tenet of a Trinity of gods, Brahma the Creator, Vishnu the Preserver, and Siva the Destroyer, worshiped as one God under the name of Trimarti. They relate that Vishnu the second person in the Godhead, in fulfillment of a prophecy, and to become the Redeemer of his people, took upon himself the nature of a man, was born of a virgin, and under the name of Chrishna led a life of good works, healing the sick, raising the dead, and performing many other miracles; and finally after an anticipated death from violence his body was carried by angels up to Heaven.

The account of the transfiguration of Chrishna before his disciples is given in the following words: "Then abandoning the mortal form he appeared to their eyes in all the eclat of his divine majesty, his brow encircled with such light that Ardjouna and his companions, unable to support it, threw themselves on their faces in the dust, and prayed the Lord to pardon their unworthy weakness." The second coming of Chrishna is thus announced in the same sacred books: "Some time before the destruction of all that exists the struggle between evil and good must recommence on earth, and the evil spirits who at their first creation rebelled in Heaven against the authority of Brahma, will present themselves for a final struggle to dispossess God of his power and recover their liberty. Then will Chrishna again come upon earth to overthrow the Prince of the demons, who under the form of a horse and aided by all evil spirits will cover the globe with ruin and with carnage."

I might extend these quotations to any length. As Sir William Jones says, "The prolix accounts of Chrishna's life are filled with narratives of the most extraordinary kind." But I think enough has been cited from the sacred books of this oldest of religions to show that it was not only the precurser and source of all other enlightened religions, but that it had in it the elements of a high political and moral culture. It is undoubtedly true that the followers of Brahma have sadly degenerated in later ages, and that the faith and precepts which once led up to a high state of enlightenment are now the heritage of a debased and servile priesthood. The same however was true only four centuries ago of those who were the inheritors of the priceless treasures of the Christian records. The state of a society does not always keep up to the standards of morality and culture which are preserved in its archives. But we must concede, I think, that the early believers in the ancient Vedas of the Brahmans were the predecessors in direct line of the believers in the Holy Bible of the Christians, and that there descended from the one system to the other many remarkable theological tenets and almost identical scripture recitals. Shall we then condemn the Brahmans merely because they preceded the founding of our Holy Religion? Shall we say there was no good nor reward in their faith in a God and a Redeemer so closely outlining those we worship?

Shortly before the time of the Christian era Alexandrea in Egypt was the seat of all the learning and culture in the world. Here was the largest if not the only library of ancient times— 700,000 volumes, all of course in manuscript. It was unfortunately burned or destroyed in later years by Christian or Saracen fanaticism. A peculiar dialect of the Greek language was in use here called Hellenistic Greek. The Hebrew Bible was here translated into it, 270 years B. C.; and there is no doubt that the sacred books of other nations were translated into it as well. All the Books of the New Testament were first brought out here, as is proved by the fact that they were written in Hellenistic Greek, which was a language little used elsewhere and not at all in Judea. Here was the seat of innumerable sects of all manner of philosophies and followings, the home of religion-makers, kept, boarded, and paid by the Ptolemies to add volumes to their libraries. It is a matter of history that there were at this time in Alexandrea well organized societies of men who made it their life business to select what seemed to them best from all known systems of philosophy and religion, and to publish their writings as gospels according to such and such a saint. In the year 325 of our era, three hundred Bishops in Council at Nice selected the present Books of the New Testament from at least 120 different gospels, epistles, acts, and revelations that had become inextricably mixed and confounded with the true Scriptures.

Philo, "the Jew," a native of Alexandrea, known to have been in active public life at the date of the crucifixion, was a voluminous writer on all the scriptures and religions of his day. He was sent as an emissary to the Emperor Caligula at Rome on behalf of the Hellenistic Jews at Alexandrea about seven years after the death of Christ, yet very strangely he appears to have been wholly ignorant of the great event that gave rise to the Christian era. Philo has left a number of works on Neo-Platonism and the Jewish Scriptures. He also wrote one on the great religious school of his day, known as the Essenic or Ascetic philosophy. This last book has not come down to us entire, but is fully reported by Eusebius (A. D. 324), the great historian and authority of the first three centuries of Christianity.

The society of the Essenes to which Philo belonged, and which was already an old and flourishing association throughout Egypt in the time of Christ, was known under all the following names: Essenes or Therapeuts, signifying healers or doctors; Ascetics, from their austere discipline and self-mortifications; Monks, from their retirement from the world; Ecclesiastics, from their being called out, elected, set apart; and Eclectics, from their selecting from all systems. The following is the description of them as given by Eusebius on the authority of Philo, and condensed from "Ecclesiastical History," Book 2nd, ch. 16: They had in every parish their churches and monasteries in which monks performed the mysteries of the sublime life, also their bishops, priests and deacons; they renounced all property and divided up every thing equally among themselves; they observed the self same fastings and grand festivals that the Christians afterwards observed; pretended to have had apostolic founders who had handed down to them holy scriptures; practiced the very manners that distinguished the apostles of Christ, "abjuring the pleasures of the body," "nor would they eat anything that had blood in it;" they used scriptures which they believed to be divinely inspired, and which Eusebius himself believed to be none other than the substance of our Gospels; had the same allegorical method of interpreting those scriptures, the same order and manner of performing public worship which afterwards were practiced by the Christians. Eusebius says their psalms and hymns were the very same that were used in the church in his day. They had missionary stations or churches in precisely the same places as were those addressed by St. Paul, as Rome, Corinth, Ephesus, &c. Eusebius ends his account of them as follows: "That Philo wrote these things with reference to those who were the first preachers of the discipline which is according to the Gospel and to the manners first handed down from the apostles, must be manifest to every man." But Philo wrote this history, and all the things he described existed, long before there was a word of the New Testament written. Philo does not in any of his works mention the name or refer in the remotest manner to Christ or to Christians. Mosheim the great ecclesiastical historian says, "It was here (in Egypt) that the Essenes dwelt principally, long before the coming of Christ;" "that the Ascetic philosophy was in a flourishing state in Alexandrea when our Saviour was upon earth." Evidently then these societies were the forerunners, the antecedents of Christianity. And if their votaries could not be distinguished from real and true Christians by an eminent church historian of the fourth century, shall we of the nineteenth presume to say they had no part in the promises of the new religion to which they contributed so large a share of principles and observances?

If it might be permitted to predicate for religions, as it is for civilizations and governments, an element of evolution,—that is of the more perfect following and developing out of the cruder and less advanced,—then many difficulties might be removed that now are stumbling blocks. I think we have shown quite conclusively that the Christian religion was not only a great reform of the Jewish, but that it adopted in an improved form many of the tenets, observances and traditions of the classical and oriental religions that preceded it. Again in the great Reformation of the 16th century, Knox, Calvin and Luther introduced doctrines and elements of advance that had never been previously promulgated. The Christian religion of to-day is as much superior to the Christianity of the early centuries as the Republicanism of America is in advance of that of old Rome.

Theologians may say what they will about the modern churches adhering to the strict and rigid doctrines of primitive Christianity, it is nevertheless true that the whole course of Christian ideas and interpretation of dogmas has greatly changed from what it was fifteen to eighteen centuries ago. The following are instances in point: The material Heaven, the mansions in the skies, with angels ascending and descending, the excessive and inconceivable torments reserved for unbelievers, all so vividly pictured in every part of the New Testament without the least implication of an allegorical meaning; the scriptural evidences of conversion, "and these signs shall follow them that believe; in my name shall they cast out devils, they shall speak with new tongues, they shall take up serpents, and if they drink any deadly thing it shall not hurt them, they shall lay hands on the sick and they shall recover," (Mark 16 : 17, 18). The working of miracles through faith, "If ye have faith and doubt not ye shall say unto this mountain, Be thou removed and be thou cast into the sea, and it shall be done" (Math. 21 : 21); the expected second coming of the Messiah, declared in Luke 21 : 27–31, and then in verse 32, "verily I say unto you, this generation shall not pass away till all be fulfilled;" the authority of the ministers of Christ to forgive sins, " whose soever sins ye remit they are remitted unto them; and whose soever sins ye retain they are retained" (John 20 : 23); the resurrection of the natural bodies of all mankind on the last great day. All these and many other doctrines peculiar to the earlier and materialistic stages of the Christian religion are now either given up or ignored or passed over to metaphors.

If then religions have been successively and in a measure evolved out of each other, and have grown with the advancing ages, there is no point in that growth where it can be said that previous votaries were condemned by the law, while those subsequent to it were relieved from its condemnation. St. Paul, the great apostle of the Gentiles, says to the Romans (Rom. 2: 14), "For when the Gentiles which have not the law, do by nature the things contained in the law, these having not the law are a law unto themselves"; the context showing that they would not fail of their reward "in the day when God shall judge the secrets of men by Jesus Christ" (id. verse 16); and again (Rom. 4: 15), "for where no law is, there is no transgression."

The liberal minded and logical St. Paul saw at once that a man could not be condemned for disobedience who had never had an intimation of what or whom he was to obey. The sweeping and effective text, "He that believeth and is baptized shall be saved; but he that believeth not shall be damned," could not by any possibility apply to those who had never been told what to believe, nor to those who had never been informed as to the process and necessity of baptism. And even with all the light we have at the present time on this all important rite of baptism, it is not yet determined what form of it is the proper one, and whether a certain form of it is not really a saving ordinance. Just think for a moment how many good and devout men would be most wofully disappointed if there should happen to be any mistake about this simple matter of baptism. I submit therefore whether it would not be a safer and a better policy for all denominations to give up all restrictions on future rewards dependent on baptism, sectarianism, regeneration, or any peculiar religious beliefs, and to hold with St. Peter, the great preacher to the Gentiles, "That God is no respecter of persons: But in every nation he that feareth him and worketh righteousness is accepted with him" (Acts 10: 34).

SKETCHES OF SEA-LIFE.*

"Tumble out here, men, and make sail. Be lively—be lively there." And forth from the "top-gallant forecastle" came reeling and rollicking a score of drunken tars. "Come, bestir yourselves, you old rum-soakers. Lay aloft, some of ye, and turn out that canvas." "Mr. Beattie, overhaul their chests, and bring aft every drop of liquor you find. I'll know what cargo is aboard there for'ard." A stirring tune this, captain, you first strike up. But glad it sounds notwithstanding, for it tells us we soon will be alone on our broad, free home. Already, from the steamboat by our side, has been given the order, "Shoremen aboard." And on her deck are seen many countenances saddened by recent partings. The word comes to "cast off the lines," and now the noble "St. Denis," for the first time let loose on an untried element, rears its proud head on the waves, and haughtily turns from its puffing, toiling companion, as in mockery of man's power. There is a conscious pride in the power to subdue the wild sport of winds, in which the very ship seems to participate. And it has a lordly bearing, as it boldly careers through the mingled battles of air and sea. Man may bolt in the pent-up forces of steam to speed him on a joyless journey; may outride, if he please, old Boreas himself; but give to me the craft that, of its own kingly will, can peer into the "wind's eye," or before a gale can fly untiring and majestic as the eagle.

As the steamer paddled off on its return to port, we were greeted from it by three long, loud cheers. Immediately work was suspended, orders unheeded, and many a rope "went by the

---

* Written in 1847, and published in the Yale College Literary Magazine. A description of the author's first voyage (to Havre in France) as a sailor "before the mast," during the summer of that year.

run," while amid the toss of sea-caps and tarpaulins there went up three as hearty responses as ever were echoed over New York harbor. Long after, till the boat was lost to view in the forest of masts which encircles the Empire City, we could see, waving over many a sylph-like form, the white flag of woman's love. Heaven smile on the fair who thus bid "God speed" to the lone mariner, wrestling ever with the perils of the main.

It is hard to sever the last link that binds one to land and to home; and the heart sinks low with sadness, in even the bosom that has buffeted a thousand gales, as the last adieu is waved to objects of most tender associations. There was one at least among that rough, hardy crew whose thoughts were cheerless and heavy. He was a "Freshman of the sea." He was to traverse the three thousand miles of landless, boisterous ocean, in a narrow tenement, where a single false step or missing grasp might cause to close over him forever, Nature's vast sepulchre. His vessel too had never yet tested its sea-powers, or tried its arm with the fickle twins that rule the deep, and in a luckless hour it might spring a gaping leak in its uncoppered hull, or under press of sail careen beyond its balance. Yet it was not fear that weighed on his spirits, for little did he reck or know of the danger. But he thought of the changes of the few past weeks; of the strange situation into which a restless, roving disposition had led him. He thought of the strong ties—now probably severed for ever—which had bound to him as brothers, his generous classmates, who, as they pealed again their hearty welcomes, after a joyous spring vacation, would wonder at the freak which had sent so retiring a student to try the noisy, Jack-tar life of a forecastle. He thought too of loved friends at home, who soon would read, with startled, sorrowing eyes, the first intelligence of the errant course of a son and brother; and a tear of penitent regret rolled unbidden down his cheek.

But, heigh-ho! What a savage gust that was! How that huge swell tumbled us about! The arms of the bay have suddenly opened, revealing to us a shoreless expanse of waters. While I had been absorbed in revery, our "Ocean bird" had spread its broad wings to the breezes, and had lightly flitted through the

Plate **XX**. SAILOR BOY "CHARLIE." See Page xx.

Narrows. Now with beak pointing toward its destination, the far-off "Land of the Gaul," it was fast speeding on to the bosom of the Atlantic. But look! Ah, woe is me! The captain's stern eye is fastened on me. "What are you figuring at there, boy? Come! wake up, and shake the kinks out of your land legs, you young sodger!" Startled by these uncivil remarks, it was not long before I was moving. Now stumbling over a surly tar, and again rolling with another into the "lee rigging," running here to help "let go a rope," and there tugging on when the word was "belay," I managed to clear myself at least from the imputation of inactivity. Yes, Captain Howe, savage master though you were, it was the last time you ever called me "sodger," that most opprobrious epithet in the sailor's vocabulary.

The afternoon on which we left New York was occupied in setting sails and getting every thing into "ship-shape" for sea. Toward evening all hands were called on the quarter deck, to be divided into watches. Against the "lee bulwarks" twenty rugged, stalwart men ranged themselves; their broad, sinewy forms bearing powerful testimony to the healthiness and hardihood of the mariner's life; their countenances portraying the hard marks of many a winter's blast, and the swarthy hue from many a scorching calm in the tropics. Come up here, all ye Blue Devils and Doleful Dumps, ye Phantoms of Hypochondria, and Ghosts of Consumption. Look on a sight that should shame ye for so fouling the fair face of earth, and well-nigh blotting from man the impress of his God. Many a time, when admiring the brawny, symmetrical proportions, and the noble-hearted nature of the sailor, have I vowed never again to make my home amid the wasting ills and the niggard-souled multitude on land. Even now, as I recall the familiar scenes of the few months of which I am writing, there is stirring a restless spirit within me, a longing once more for the wild life of the sea; and I cannot all repress a regret for the accident which deterred me from following longer my inclinations.

Around the capstan stood four who were the "boys" of the crew. The eldest of them, a "boy" of over twenty-one years of age, was a relative of the captain, and son of a New York merchant, and had already been on a voyage to Canton before the mast. His real name was Lee; but from the fact of his having adopted every habit and quality which make up a sailor except seamanship, the mate gave him the significant title of "Chawtobacco Jack." Another was poor "Jimmy Ducks," of a wealthy family, but of the utmost personal inefficiency and arrogance. He had been another Havre voyage before with the same captain, and of all on board our ship was his only favorite. On him, by a little art, especially by feigning great ignorance in the calling of the "prodigal son," I very speedily shifted the name and duties which an almost universal usage had otherwise fixed on me. I refer to the care of the pigs and cows that were on board ship. The third who made out the trio of those whom the men called "gentlemen's sons," was that same truant from college and home, already introduced to the reader; and in default of an easier name, he went by the self-appropriated one of "Charlie." But now for "boy Harry," decidedly the most important personage aboard ship, at once the life and butt of the crew, and an everlasting plague to the officers—an absolute essential everywhere, and yet for ever in the way. I have him now in my mind's eye—his short, chubbed form, and fat, Dutch visage, in which sparkled as keen and roguish a pair of black eyes as ever a youngster sported; and then that lisping, Hollandish tongue of his—how its least movement would set the men laughing and cursing! yet it never rested. And well I may remember him, for many is the time we have raced up the rigging together in strife for the "weather yard arm;" and many is the long watch hour we have whiled away together with schemes of mischief or in kindly spats. I recollect well when I first saw him. It was on board, just before we left New York. The captain chancing to pass him, asked what he was doing there; he said, the mate had hired him for "or'nary theaman;" he had been to sea two years. The mate soon after coming up, asked him the same question; he answered promptly, that the captain had engaged him for an "or'nary theaman." And so we had "boy Harry" in our crew, though he unfortunately failed of getting ordinary seaman's wages.

Well, "old skipper," we are ready for you now to take your watch. And with apparent impartiality he made a division, numerically equal. But it did most unaccountably happen that certain of the smartest, most able-bodied seamen fell into the starboard watch, which chanced to be his own. Lee and Jimmy were apportioned to the mate's or larboard watch, and Harry and myself to the other. Then came the captain's customary address, and I wonder that each word did not perish on the false tongue that uttered it. "My hearties, I like your looks first rate. You are a hale set of fellows as I have seen in a crew for a long time, and its my opinion we're going to have a pleasant voyage, and a pleasant season for it. Now if you'll do your duty and be faithful, you'll find me a right clever master, and you shall have the best of usage and the best of fare; but if you don't, you'll find I can make this ship a perfect hell for you. Go below, the starboard watch." And down into the forecastle we bounced in a trice; when, after hearing many a hearty curse on the skipper for abducting sundry well-filled demijohns and bottles, all were soon rolling about in the hug of Morpheus.

Now that forecas'le was a queer pen at best; and ours was probably as good a specimen as any on the waters, being what was scientifically called a "Top-gallant forecastle," or "House on deck." It was as large, except in height, as a common sized room; and around its sides were ranged about twenty-four berths, upper and lower, single and double, from under which twenty-four huge chests stuck out half their lengths. In the middle of the floor was stacked up a promiscuous heap of boots, caps, oil-cloth jackets, and every sort of sea-accoutrement. Such was the bedlam confusion in which ate, slept, and lived, by turns or all together as occasion required, twenty-four persons. Yet in all this—and I took my full share of discomfort as well as labor—I was contented, ay, and happy; and who, with any conformity of disposition, would not be? Thrown together, as sailors are, with common interests and common fare, obliged to participate in common toil and dangers, they speedily lose every vestige of selfishness—that bane of ordinary society. There is nothing a sailor will not do for his shipmate—nothing he will not share to the last with him. Thus can a rough but hearty generosity, with an unvarying round of pleasantry, make of the most dismal quarters an agreeable home.

At midnight we were all roused from a deep sleep by a thundering rattle against the door, followed immediately by the deafening call, "Sta—r-b'rd wa—tch, a—h—o—y! Eight bells there! Hear the news?" We were soon up and out, giving place to the sleepy deckers; and our men in turn, wrapping around them their pea-jackets, disposed themselves for a little napping on whatever came convenient—some on a spar, some on water casks, others in the coil of a rope, and others still on the "soft side of a board." I tried all these devices, and many others equally inviting, but not the least rest could I get, much less sleep. And moreover feeling a little queer—not sea-sick, for I never was sea-sick—but a sort of indescribable all-over-ness, as some poet has written, "All was not right, yet where the wrong?" I came to the conclusion that there was no use torturing one's self so, especially as there was nothing in creation to do outside, that I could see. So in I stole, and crept into bed, where I was forthwith dreaming as sweetly as ever in my life before. How long after it was, I do not know, but I was soon brought to consciousness by a severe punching at my sides. Turning over, I saw boy Harry standing by my bunk. "Vot you thleep for? They hunt for you all over the thyip. The thecond mate, he be hell on you." In an instant I was out on the floor, but in the utmost fright and uncertainty what next to do. "Tell him," says he, "you be thick—you no can vork." I told Harry to go up slily where the men were, and not say a word about me. So as soon as I saw the mate's head turned, I followed up and "tailed onto" the rope, on which they were pulling, as if nothing had happened. Now our "second Dickey" was a gruff, but noble-hearted sailor, and was liked by the crew in proportion as he was hated by the captain, which was no small amount. But he was not to be deceived so easily by a novice in his trade. He had seen "boys" before. So singling me out shortly after, he asked me "why I did not obey the call." I answered that "I was sick and couldn't get out." But that excuse, which had so often before served me as a talisman on similar emergencies at school, he heeded not in the least. "If I ever catch you," said he, "stowing yourself away again, I'll haul you out by the ears. Now remember it." And I did remember it, Mr. White, not only to preserve those tender organs from the rough tug you threatened, but also to give no occasion for them to hear more such kind remarks. "And you, young Dutch chunk," he continued, "if you ever stay away again half the night, looking him up, I'll lash you by the ears to the main-mast." "Yeth thir," coolly replied Harry.

At eight bells again, four o'clock—for the bell was struck every half hour—we had the extreme felicity of yelling at the forecastle door, "Larbowlines a-hoy." Thus through the twenty-four hours, except six in the afternoon, we had an alternation of watches at each "eight bells;" the "dog watch," of two hours in the evening, serving to alternate the succession of watches every other night. On Sundays and stormy days we usually had "watch and watch"—that is, an alternation of watches throughout the entire day. A storm never comes amiss to poor Jack; for as well as the excitement which he longs for, it brings him more resting spells.

Let me now present to you, kind reader, our crew at meals. Around the forecastle sit, each on his own chest, one or both watches, as may be. Out from among the dirty clothes in his bunk, each one pulls a basin, quart cup, and spoon. The boys bring in from the galley and set down in the middle of the floor, two or three kids of food, out of which all help themselves. At eight o'clock comes breakfast; but such a breakfast! That eternal "scouse!"—a mushy mess of sea-biscuit or potatoes boiled up with bits of salt meat. Then each had his "pot" of the black extract of burnt peas, with a little molasses in it, vulgarly called coffee. These, without butter, salt, or seasoning of any kind, for we never had those luxuries, constituted our unvarying morning repast. At noon we fared a little better, for variety at least. Twice a week we had molasses with "duff"—a bag of flour boiled solid in salt water; twice, vinegar with beans—i. e. water-gruel with a sprinkling of beans in it; twice, corn meal mush; and for the odd time, boiled potatoes, which relished remarkably seeing that we could get nothing but rock-salt to eat them with. Supper is easily told. Salt horse-flesh, barley-meal and saw-dust sea-biscuit, and each man a quart of a decoction of some villainous herbs, a little "bewitched" with molasses. This, Captain Howe, was the good living you promised us! Yet in New York you were thought to be decently honest; some even thought you to be temperate and gentlemanly; but, alas! how speedily does the salt sea wash off a scaly virtue! Your portly, manly figure very much belied your moral qualities.

But I must pass over several days, during which we had steady, fair winds, and were constantly bowling along under all our canvas, and with every stu'n-sail set. We were now on the "Banks," groping on through that everlasting fog, which settles like night on those dark shoals. Oh! that driving, drizzling, drenching air! How many shivering, wretched hours have I spent in it, so cold and damp! Nothing is impervious to it. Often have I cast off three and four dripping duplicates of ordinary garments, and wrapped myself in as many wet blankets, to enjoy a short oblivion of trouble and discomfort. It was on one of these dismal nights, while we were on the Banks, just as our watch, which had gone below wearied with hauling in studding sails for several hours together, had fallen comfortably to sleep, that we were suddenly startled by a loud cry at the door—"all hands! shorten sail!" As soon as possible we were out of our bunks and hastening half dressed to the quarter deck. The wind, which had risen during the night, was now blowing a gale, driving fiercely against us mingled sleet and spray. The sea was capped with foam, and on its whitened surface our ship was wildly plunging, careening her bulwarks almost to the water's edge. "Hurry up here! Hurry up here!" roared the captain, who was clinging to the mizzen shrouds to windward. "Clew up the royals and top-gall'nt-s'ls! Haul up the courses! Lay up and furl!" And command followed fast on command, answered ever by the hurried "Ay, ay, sir," till all sound was lost in the din of flapping canvas and clattering ropes. I had been aloft several times before; and was now only awaiting an opportunity to learn that first and hardest duty on ship-board, to furl a royal.

So, heedless of storm and darkness, I soon found myself following Lee up the weather main rigging. Over the ratlins we clambered lustily; now into the "top," and now upon the "cross-trees." Here clapping hands and feet to the large "stays," we "shinned" up to the royal yard. Making up and fastening the "bunt" in the middle, we each ran out on the "foot-ropes," with the end of a "gasket" between our teeth, which we wound taut around both yard and sail, and bringing it in fastened it to the "tye," when our royal was furled. Thence slipping down again we were soon on deck.

Often since then have I recalled the peril of that first adventure, when scarce a week at sea, and in a midnight gale, I found myself swaying and quivering with the blast, in the highest part of the ship—now forced to cling with all my might to the yard-arm, and now, in a lull of the wind, passing another turn of the gasket—at one moment bending with the mast far down towards the water, and at the next rebounding with feet flying in mid-air. And I have wondered that I could so carelessly have gazed into the dark scowling sea beneath, and so recklessly laughed at the howling storm. Yet such were but common occurrences. To the sailor, these scenes are the romance of life, the theme of "yarns," in the leisure hours. As such I too, though young, enjoyed them; and nothing ever pleased me more than a frowning sky, and a cresting sea along the distant horizon. When I reached the deck, I was bare-headed, my oil-jacket as near wrong side out as possible, my inner raiment flying at loose ends, and every part of me soaking wet. Finding the sails, except the topsails, already stowed, I hastened down to the forecastle; whither boy Harry came soon after, in even worse plight than myself. He was swearing away "how he'd be down on that dam Dimmy Duckth. The thkippy, he thend him up to the miththen r'yal mit me. And he don't can do a dam thing. He hide in the 'top.'" And so indeed it was. Poor Jimmy had not the heart to make his first essay on such a night; and accordingly had stopped at the "lubber's hole," leaving Harry to furl his sail alone.

During the next day we set all sail again, and passing off the Banks, suddenly emerged into pleasant weather. But we were rolled about most wantonly by a tremendous sea, the relics of the last night's gale. Thus speedily every thing settled again into the usual round of day duties, "wash decks" in the morning, "pump ship, the watch," and "hold the reel, boys," every eight bells, and "braid sennet," or "make mats for chafing gear," when there was nothing else to be done.

It was one afternoon, not many days later than this, as there was a sly inkling among the younger and lighter portion of the crew that the remaining part of the day would be devoted to the peculiarly unpleasant duty of "slushing" the upper masts, when, lo! and behold! boy Harry was nowhere to be found. Immediately every nook and cranny of the ship rang to the loud cry— "Boy Harry!" "Boy Harry!" It happened to fall to my lot to rummage the forecastle for him; when hunting for some time all alone, I at last heard a low whisper, issuing out from a heap of rubbish in the back side of a bunk—"Charley! Charley! The mate he find me, he athk me vere I thick, vot I tell him?" "Tell him," said I, "you are sick to the stomach." "Vere be the thtomich?" Pointing out its locality, I hove another blanket over him, and was forthwith busily engaged again tumbling chests about, when the chief mate stepped in and commenced the search for himself. We must now introduce to the reader, Mr. Beattie, our first mate, a most skillful seaman, but a narrow, conceited soul; who dwelt most rigidly on the "minor points of the law," and seemed to think his reputation depended on his petty tyranny over the boys. After searching some time, he at last stumbled on Harry, buried in his dark nest. And out he hauled him to view rather roughly, asking, with many pretty adjuncts to his speech, what he was stowed away in there for? "I'th thick, thir—Oh! hard thick in my thtomich thir." "That's your case then, is it?" said the mate. "I'll soon fix you out." So aft he hurried, and in a few minutes came back with a wineglass nearly filled with castor oil. The instant Harry saw what the game was to be, he seized the glass from the mate, applied it to his lips, and quicker than thought, its contents were gone.

And the officer, turning about, stalked off in all the pride of conscious cunning. Ah, Mr. Beattie, if you had had the dilated pupils of my eyes in that dark corner, you might not have been quite so well pleased, as you saw your medicine taking rather an external route to the digestives of that mischievous lad. Of course it was several days before boy Harry could do any more work; and of course he presented a most doleful appearance, especially when any officer was in sight.

Onward and onward we ploughed through the wide waste, not once being obliged by contrary winds to turn from our course, and frequently cleaving the waters at the rapid rate of fifteen knots an hour. On the evening of the sixteenth day out from New York, the bold shores of Lizard Point, on the coast of England, loomed into view. Passing this almost within the distance of a stone's cast, we sailed on up the Channel. And when morning again broke upon us, we were standing, with shortened sail, off the blue hills of Normandy. Oh! glorious sight! For what though lovely France be now raving in a wild crazy-fit, and with bloody arm is dealing death to myriads of her sons; her soil will give us respite from the ceaseless tumble of old ocean, and we long to look on her beauty. During the morning a French pilot boarded us, and we again made sail. Ah! what a noble sight do we present, as the gallant St. Denis dashes by the lighthouse and along the pier, and a thousand delighted eyes are fastened on us from the shore. "Starboard the helm!" "Let go all halyards!" "Drop the larboard anchor there for'ard!" "What! cable chain parted?" "Let fly the other!" And here we are, safe moored in one of those beautiful basins which intersect the maritime city of "Havre de Grâce."

For want of time and space to continue, at present, these desultory sketches, I must, kind reader, leave you at this part of the narrative.

www.ingramcontent.com/pod-product-compliance
Lightning Source LLC
Chambersburg PA
CBHW030427300426
44112CB00009B/895